HANDBOOK
—— of ——
PRACTICAL
COAL GEOLOGY

LARRY THOMAS

Dargo Associates Ltd
Geological and Coal Resource Consultants

JOHN WILEY & SONS

Chichester · New York · Brisbane · Toronto · Singapore

Copyright © 1992 by John Wiley & Sons Ltd,
Baffins Lane, Chichester,
West Sussex PO19 1UD, England

Other Wiley Editorial Offices

John Wiley & Sons, Inc., 605 Third Avenue,
New York, NY 10158-0012, USA

Jacaranda Wiley Ltd, G.P.O. Box 859, Brisbane,
Queensland 4001, Australia

John Wiley & Sons (Canada) Ltd, 22 Worcester Road,
Rexdale, Ontario M9W 1L1, Canada

John Wiley & Sons (SEA) Pte Ltd, 37 Jalan Pemimpin #05-04,
Block B, Union Industrial Building, Singapore 2057

Library of Congress Cataloging-in-Publication Data

Thomas, Larry.
    Handbook of practical coal geology / Larry Thomas.
        p.   cm.
    Includes bibliographical references and index.
    ISBN 0-471-93557-3 (paper)
        1. Coal—Geology—Handbooks, manuals, etc.   I. Title.
    TN802.T49   1992
    553.2'4—dc20   92–5495
                                                         CIP

British Library Cataloguing in Publication Data

A catalogue record for this book is available from the British
Library

ISBN 0-471-93557-3

Typeset in 10/12pt Palatino by Acorn Bookwork, Salisbury, Wilts
Printed and bound in Great Britain by the Alden Press, Oxford

Contents

Preface   viii

Glossary   xi

Chapter 1   Introduction   1

1.1   Scope   1
1.2   Background   1
1.3   Coal and the geologist   2
1.4   Layout   3

Chapter 2   Coal as a substance   4

2.1   Physical description of coal   4
    2.1.1   Macroscopic description of coal   5
    2.1.2   Microscopic description of coal   8
    2.1.3   Mineral content of coal   13
2.2   Coalification (rank)   16
    2.2.1   Coalification   16
    2.2.2   Causes of coalification   20
2.3   Coal quality   23
    2.3.1   Chemical properties of coal   24
    2.3.2   Combustion properties of coal   32
    2.3.3   Physical properties of coal   37
    2.3.4   Coal oxidation   42
2.4   Classification of coals   43

Chapter 3   Origin of coal   55

3.1   Introduction   55
3.2   Sedimentation of coal and coal-bearing sequences   55
    3.2.1   Depositional models   56
    3.2.2   Modern peat analogues   63
    3.2.3   Facies correlation   66
    3.2.4   Facies maps   71
3.3   Structural effects on coals   77
    3.3.1   Syndepositional effects   78
    3.3.2   Post-depositional effects   82

Chapter 4   Age and occurrence of coal   **96**

4.1   Age of coal   96
4.2   Geographical distribution of coal   97
        4.2.1   United States of America   97
        4.2.2   Canada   99
        4.2.3   Europe   100
        4.2.4   Africa   108
        4.2.5   Indian Subcontinent   114
        4.2.6   Central and South America   116
        4.2.7   Commonwealth of Independent States
                    (formerly USSR)   121
        4.2.8   Far East   123
        4.2.9   Australasia   132

Chapter 5   World coal reserves and production   **135**

5.1   World coal reserves   135
5.2   World coal production   135
        5.2.1   Coal production statistics   135
        5.2.2   Regional production and consumption   139
        5.2.3   Reserves/production ratio   140

Chapter 6   Coal exploration and data collection   **141**

6.1   Introduction   141
6.2   Field techniques   141
        6.2.1   Outcrop mapping   144
        6.2.2   Remote sensing and aerial photographs   153
6.3   Drilling   156
        6.3.1   Openhole drilling   157
        6.3.2   Core drilling   158
        6.3.3   Portable drilling   162
        6.3.4   Core and openhole logging   163
6.4   Geotechnical properties   166
        6.4.1   Strength   168
        6.4.2   Weathering   169
        6.4.3   Texture and structure   170
        6.4.4   Colour   171
        6.4.5   Grain size   171
        6.4.6   Total core recovery   171
        6.4.7   Solid core recovery   171
        6.4.8   Rock quality designation   172
        6.4.9   Fracture spacing index   172
        6.4.10 Fracture logging   172
6.5   Computer applications   173

Chapter 7   Geophysics of coal   **178**

7.1   Introduction   178
7.2   Physical properties of coal-bearing sequences   179

	7.2.1	Density	179
	7.2.2	Seismic velocity	181
	7.2.3	Seismic reflection coefficients	181
	7.2.4	Magnetic susceptibility	181
	7.2.5	Electrical conductivity	181
	7.2.6	Radiometric properties	182
7.3	Surface geophysical methods		182
	7.3.1	Seismic surveys	183
	7.3.2	Gravity surveys	192
	7.3.3	Magnetic surveys	194
	7.3.4	Electrical methods	197
	7.3.5	Radioactive methods	198
7.4	Underground geophysical methods		198
	7.4.1	In-seam seismic surveys	198
	7.4.2	Pulse radar techniques	200
7.5	Geophysical borehole logging		200
	7.5.1	Radiation logs	202
	7.5.2	Caliper log	206
	7.5.3	Electric logs	207
	7.5.4	Sonic log	210
	7.5.5	Temperature log	211
	7.5.6	Advanced interpretation	211

Chapter 8   Hydrogeology of coal   **216**

8.1	Introduction		216
	8.1.1	Nature of groundwater and surface flow	216
	8.1.2	Hydrogeological characteristics of coals and coal-bearing sequences	220
8.2.	Collection and handling of hydrogeological data		224
	8.2.1	Surface water	224
	8.2.2	Groundwater	225
8.3	Effects of groundwater on mining		227
	8.3.1	Opencast mining	227
	8.3.2	Underground mining	231
	8.3.3	Groundwater quality and its effect on coal	231
8.4	Environmental concerns		233
	8.4.1	Watercourse diversions	233
	8.4.2	Run-off, erosion and sedimentation	233
	8.4.3	Mine water pollution	234
	8.4.4	Other forms of water pollution	235

Chapter 9   Coal sampling and analysis   **236**

9.1	Introduction		236
9.2	*In situ* coal sampling		236
	9.2.1	Grab sampling	237
	9.2.2	Channel sampling	237
	9.2.3	Pillar sampling	240

	9.2.4	Core sampling	241
	9.2.5	Cuttings sampling	242
	9.2.6	Bulk sampling	242
	9.2.7	Sample storage	243
9.3	Non *in situ* sampling		243
9.4	Coal analysis		246
	9.4.1	Outcrop/core samples	246
	9.4.2	Bulk samples	248
	9.4.3	Non *in situ* samples	249

Chapter 10   Gas in coal — **252**

10.1	Introduction	252
10.2	Gas detection	254
10.3	Methane gas extraction	256
10.4	Radon	258

Chapter 11   Coal resources and reserves — **260**

11.1	Introduction		260
11.2	Coal resources and reserves assessment		261
	11.2.1	United States of America	261
	11.2.2	Australia	265
	11.2.3	United Kingdom	267
	11.2.4	Germany	268
	11.2.5	United Nations	269
11.3	Reporting of resources/reserves		270
	11.3.1	Coal resources and reserves	270
	11.3.2	Mineable *in situ* reserves	271
	11.3.3	Coal resources and reserves maps	274
11.4	Calculation of coal resources		274
	11.4.1	*In situ* tonnage calculations	274
	11.4.2	Geological losses	279

Chapter 12   Report preparation — **282**

12.1	Introduction		
12.2	The geological report		282
	12.2.1	Geology	282
	12.2.2	Coal quality	284
	12.2.3	Resource/reserve calculations	293
12.3	Report finalisation		298

Chapter 13   Geological practice — **299**

13.1	Introduction	299
13.2	Geological conduct and standards	299
13.3	Technical relationships	300
13.4	The coal geologist and the environment	302

Bibliography   305

**Appendix 1 List of international and national standards
used in coal analysis and evaluation**   310
British Standards Institution (BSI)   310
International Organisation for Standardisation
(ISO)   311
Standards Association of Australia   313
American Society for Testing and Materials
(ASTM)   315

**Appendix 2 Tables of true and apparent dip; slope angles,
gradients and percentage slope**   317

Appendix 3 Calorific values expressed in different units   319

Appendix 4 Useful information   323

Index   325

Preface

This book is intended as a basic guide for coal geologists to use in their everyday duties, whether on site, in the office or instructing others. It is not intended as a definitive work on all or any particular aspect of coal geology, rather it is a handbook to use as a precursor to, or in conjunction with, more specific and detailed works.

The book is designed to give the coal geologist background information regarding the chemical and physical properties of coal, its likely origins, its classification and the terminology used. In addition, an attempt is made to highlight its currently known geographical distribution together with recent estimates of world resources and production.

The remainder of the book is devoted to the practical side of coal geology, outlining the role of the geologist in data collection, sampling, the calculation of resources/reserves and geotechnical studies. The geophysics and hydrogeology of coal are also described as modern coal exploration and development is a combination of all these activities. Mention is also made of the preparation of geological reports, together with a brief comment on standards of geological practice.

Many sources of information have been consulted, most of which are listed in the reference section, and there are appendices containing relevant information to which the coal geologist may wish to refer from time to time.

The author thanks all those colleagues and friends who have helped and encouraged the book to completion. In particular, special thanks are due to Steve Frankland of Frankland Consultants Ltd, Rob Evans of the British Geological Survey, Professor Gilbert Kelling of the University of Keele, and to Mike Coultas and Ros Todhunter for their helpful suggestions, in particular to Mike for preparing the bulk of the photographic material used in the book.

I also thank those authors and organisations who gave permission to reproduce their work; this is gratefully acknowledged.

Larry Thomas
February, 1992

Glossary

Air-dried basis: the data are expressed as percentages of the air-dried coal; this includes the air-dried moisture but not the surface moisture of the coal.

Anthracite: anthracite is the highest rank coal and is characterised by low volatile matter (<10%) and high carbon content. Semi-anthracite is coal midway between low volatile bituminous and anthracite.

Ash: the inorganic residue remaining after the combustion of coal. It is less than the mineral matter content because of the chemical changes occurring during combustion, i.e. the loss of water of hydration, loss of carbon dioxide and loss of sulphurous gases from sulphides.

Assigned reserves: coal which can be mined on the basis of current mining practices and techniques through the use of mines currently in existence or under construction.

As received basis: the data are expressed as percentages of the coal including the total moisture content, i.e. including both the surface and the air-dried moisture content of the coal.

As received moisture: the total moisture of a coal sample when delivered to the laboratory.

Billion: 1×10^{9}.

Bituminous coal: bituminous coal lies between subbituminous coal and semi-anthracite in terms of rank. Usually divided into three subgroups—low volatile, medium volatile and high volatile.

Brown coal: see **lignite**.

Calorific value: also known as specific energy. This is the amount of heat per unit mass of coal when combusted. See **Gross** and **Net calorific value**.

Channel sample: a channel of uniform cross section is cut into the coal seam and all the coal within the cut section is collected (for the whole seam or for a series of plies, i.e. divisions of the coal seam).

Coal preparation: physical and mechanical processes applied to coal to make it suitable for a particular use.

Coalification: the alteration of vegetation to form peat, succeeded by the transformation of peat through lignite, subbituminous, bituminous, semi-anthracite, to anthracite and meta-anthracite coal.

Coking coal: a coal suitable for carbonisation in coke ovens. It must have good coking and caking properties and rank should be high to medium volatile bituminous coal.

Dry ash-free basis: the coal is considered to consist of volatile matter and fixed carbon on the basis of recalculation with moisture and ash removed.

Dry basis: the data are expressed as percentages of the coal after all the moisture has been removed.

Dry, mineral matter free basis: the data are expressed as percentages of the coal on the basis of recalculation with moisture and mineral matter removed.

Exploration: the examination of an area by means of surface geological mapping, geophysical techniques, the drilling of boreholes and sampling of coals.

Extractable reserves: see **Recoverable reserves.**

Fines: very small coal with a maximum size which is usually less than 4 mm.

Float–sink tests: the separation of coal and mineral matter particles by immersion in a series of liquids of known relative density. The process is designed to reduce the ash level of the coal and so improve the product to be sold.

Gross calorific value: the amount of heat liberated during the combustion of a coal in the laboratory under standardised conditions at constant volume, so that all of the water in the products remains in liquid form.

Higher heating value: see **Gross calorific value**.

Indicated reserves: includes all coal conforming to the thickness and depth limits defined in the reserve base, bounded by similar distance limits as for indicated resources.

Indicated resources: those resources for which the density and quality of the points of measurement are not more than 2.0 km apart.

Inferred reserves: includes all coal conforming to the thickness and depth limits defined in the reserve base, bounded by similar distance limits as for **Inferred resources**.

Inferred resources: resources for which the points of measurement are widely spaced, usually not more than 4.0 km, so that only an uncertain estimate of the resource can be made.

In situ **reserves**: the amount of coal in the ground within geological and economic limits. This can include both mineable and unmineable reserves for which the term resources may be used.

Lignite: a low rank coal characterised by a high moisture content. A coal is considered a lignite if it contains >20% *in situ* moisture. Lignite is generally referred to as **Brown coal**.

Long ton: 2240 lb. Deadweight tons are expressed as long tons.

Macerals: the microscopically recognisable organic constituents of coal. A given maceral may differ significantly in composition and properties from one coal to another; this variation may depend on the rank of the coal.

Marketable reserves: those tonnages of coal available for sale. If the coal is marketed raw, the marketable reserves will equal the raw coal tonnnage. If the coal is beneficiated, the marketable reserves are calculated by applying the predicted yield to the run-of-mine or raw coal tonnage.

Measured reserves: includes all coal conforming to thickness and depth limits defined in the reserve base bounded by same distance limits as measured resources.

Measured resources: those resources for which points of measurement are not more than 1.0 km apart and allow the projection of the thickness of coal, rank and quality data for a radius of 0.4 km from a point of measurement.

Metallurgical coal: see also **Coking coal**. Coal suitable for metallurgical use because of its coking qualities and chemical characteristics.

Methane: a gas produced by the decomposition of organic material. Methane consists of carbon and hydrogen and when mixed with air it forms a highly combustible gas. Also known as 'firedamp'.

Middlings: the result of cleaning coal to produce two products, a prime product and a lower quality or 'middlings' product. The percentage yields of the two products are calculated by using an *M*-curve graph.

Mineable reserves: the tonnages of *in situ* coal contained in seams or sections of seams for which sufficient information is available to enable detailed or conceptual mine planning.

Mineral matter: the inorganic components of coal. This does not equate to the ash content; mineral matter includes other components such as carbon dioxide, sulphur oxides and water of hydration lost on combustion of the coal.

Net calorific value: during combustion in furnaces, the maximum achieveable calorific value is the net calorific value at constant pressure, and is calculated and expressed in absolute joules, calories per gram, or Btu per pound.

Peat: the first stage in the coalification process. The *in situ* moisture is high, often >75%. Original plant structure is clearly visible.

Piezometer: boreholes sealed throughout their depth in such a way that they measure the head of groundwater at a particular depth in the horizon selected.

Possible reserves: see **Inferred reserves**.

Probable reserves: see **Indicated reserves**.

Rank: coals range in composition and properties according to the degree of coalification. Rank is used to indicate this level of alteration; the greater the alteration, the higher the rank. Lignites are low rank coals and anthracites are high rank coals.

Raw coal: coal which has received no preparation other than possibly screening.

Reconnaissance: preliminary examination of a defined area to determine if coal is present; includes broad-based geological mapping and coal sampling.

Recoverable reserves: the reserves that are or can be extracted from a coal seam during mining. Recoverable reserves are obtained by deducting anticipated geological and mining losses from the *in situ* reserves (also known as **Extractable reserves**).

Reserves: the amount of mineral which is calculated to lie within given boundaries. The reserves are described in a way which is dependent on certain arbitrary limits in respect of thickness, depth, quality and other geological and economic factors.

Run-of-mine coal: coal produced by mining operations before preparation.

Saleable coal: the total amount of coal output after preparation of the run-of-mine coal. It equals the total run-of-mine tonnages minus any material discarded during preparation.

Saleable reserves: see **Marketable reserves**.

Size range: indicates the largest and smallest sizes of particles in a coal sample or stream.

Slurry: particles concentrating in a portion of the circulating water and water-borne to a treatment plant of any kind. Also, fine particles <1 mm in size recovered from a coal preparation process and containing a substantial proportion of inerts.

Short ton: 2000 lb.

Steam coal: coal not suitable as a metallurgical coal because of its non-coking characteristics; primarily used for the generation of electric power.

Subbituminous coal: lies in rank between lignite and bituminous coal. Typical *in situ* moisture levels are 10–20%.

Sulphur: may be a component of the organic or mineral, or both, fractions of a coal. Forms sulphur dioxide during coal combustion; a serious pollutant. It is also undesirable in coking coals because it contaminates the hot metal.

Thermal coal: see **Steam coal**.

Tonne: or metric tonne: 1000 kg or 2204.6 lb.

Unassigned reserves: coal which would require additional mine facilities for extraction. The extent to which unassigned reserves will actually be mined depends on future economic and environmental conditions.

Volatile matter: represents that component of the coal, except for moisture, that is liberated at high temperatures in the absence of air.

Washability curves: the results of **Float–sink tests**, plotted graphically as a series of curves. Used to calculate the amount of coal which can be obtained at a particular quality, the density required to effect such a separation and the quality of the discard left behind.

Washed coal: coal that has been beneficiated by passing through a coal preparation wash plant.

Chapter 1
Introduction

1.1 SCOPE

The object of this book is to provide geologists working in the
coal exploration and development industry, and also teachers of
courses on applied geology and other graduate and under-
graduate geologists, with a background of the nature of coal
and its various properties, together with the practice and techniques required to compile geological data that will allow a coal
sequence under investigation to be ultimately evaluated in
terms of mineability and saleability. The book is intended for
use both in the field and in the office and library.

   The assumption is made that the reader already possesses a
general knowledge of geology, together with some familiarity
with geophysics and hydrogeology. Attention is drawn to the
other handbooks in this series and the references listed at the
end of this book.

1.2 BACKGROUND

In most industrial countries, coal has historically been a key
source of energy and a major contributor to economic growth. In
today's choice of alternative sources of energy, industrialised
economies have seen a change in the part played by coal.

   Originally coal was used as a source of heat and power in
homes and industry. During the 1950s and 1960s cheap oil
curtailed the growth of coal use, but the uncertainties of oil
supply in the 1970s led to a resumption in coal consumption and
a rapid growth in the international coal trade.

   Many economies depend on coal for a significant portion of
their energy needs. Coal currently accounts for 30% of the
world's consumption of primary energy. More significantly,
coal provides fuel for the generation of around 40% of the
world's electricity, which is responsible for the utilisation of

Chapter 2
Coal as a substance

2.1 PHYSICAL DESCRIPTION OF COAL

Coal has been defined by numerous authors. Essentially, it is a sediment, organoclastic in nature, composed of lithified plant remains, which has the important distinction of being a combustible material.

The composition and character of each coal will be determined firstly by the nature of the makeup of the original organic and inorganic accumulation, and secondly by the degree of diagenesis it has undergone.

The inherent constituents of any coal can be divided into 'macerals', the organic equivalent of minerals, and 'mineral matter', the inorganic fraction made up of a variety of primary and secondary minerals. The latter is sometimes erroneously referred to as 'ash' when in fact 'ash' is the mineral residue remaining after combustion of the coal. The composition and ratio of the two fractions reflects the makeup of the original material, and indicates the coal **type**.

The degree of diagenesis or coalification that a coal has undergone by burial and tectonic effects determines the coal **rank**.

The term **brown coal** is used for low rank coals such as lignite and subbituminous coal, and **black** or **hard** coal is used for coals of higher rank, the bituminous, semi-anthracite and anthracite coals.

When confronted with a coal outcrop, an excavation or borehole core, the geologist is immediately faced with the problem of physically describing the coal. Most coals are composed of discrete layers of organic material. Such layers may possess different physical and chemical properties. It is the relative proportions and petrological characteristics of these layers that determines the character of the coal as a whole, and its usefulness as a mined product.

Coals are divisible into two main groups, the **humic** coals and the **sapropelic** coals. **Humic** coals are composed of a diversified mixture of macroscopic plant debris; the coals typically have a banded appearance. **Sapropelic** coals are composed of a restricted variety of microscopic plant debris; such coals have a homogeneous appearance.

2.1.1 Macroscopic description of coal

2.1.1.1 Humic coals

The use of a simple but distinctive system of description is fundamental to the field examination of coals. Several systems to describe the physical character of coal have been proposed and are briefly outlined in the following.

Stopes (1919) proposed four lithological types (lithotypes) for describing humic coals.

(i)   **Vitrain**: black, brittle, glassy, vitreous material, occurring as thin bands
(ii) **Clarain**: bright with a silky lustre in fine laminations
(iii) **Durain**: grey to black with a dull lustre, fractures into rough surfaced fragments
(iv) **Fusain**: black, soft, friable, easily disintegrates into a black fibrous powder

However, difficulties have arisen in using these terms to describe coals in borehole cores and in exposures. The four lithotypes often occur as thin layers or lenses, often only millimetres in thickness. Strict usage of Stopes's terms would lead to extremely detailed lithological descriptions, whereas in practice only a limited amount of lithologically distinct units are required. For practical purposes, alternative terminology has been proposed by various sources which, while essentially retaining the basic classification of Stopes, has a more descriptive lithological bias. The principal types of humic and sapropelic coals are summarised in Table 2.1.

In the USA, Schopf (1960) introduced the term **attrital** coal to include all coal not precisely defined as vitrain or fusain and which can be subdivided into five levels of lustre ranging from bright to dull. The Australian system is broadly similar in approach, but more descriptive in terminology (Table 2.2). The Australian coal industry defines vitrain and fusain as bright and dull coal, respectively, and the five categories of attrital coal are graded according to the major and minor constituents of each end member. This is very much a physical description and is eminently more suitable for the field recording of coals.

Coals with a high mineral content contained in discrete bands or as nodules or veins can best be described as **impure** coals. Such mineral matter is commonly in the form of pyrite, calcite, siderite, ankerite, or as clay coatings and infillings. In the USA,

Table 2.1 Lithotypes of humic and sapropelic coals. From McCabe (1984), by permission of Blackwell Scientific Publications

Lithotype	Description	Composition
Vitrain	Black, very bright lustre; thin layers break cubically; thick layers have conchoidal fracture	Vitrinite macerals with <20% exinite macerals
Clarain	Finely stratified layers of vitrain, durain and, in some instances, fusain, medium lustre	Variable
Durain	Black or grey, dull, rough fracture surfaces	Mainly inertinite and exinite macerals
Fusain	Black, silky lustre, friable and soft	Mainly fusinite
Cannel coal	Black, dull, lustre 'greasy', breaks with conchoidal fracture	Fine maceral particles usually dominated by sporinite
Boghead coal	Black or brown, dull, homogeneous, breaks with conchoidal fracture, lustre may be 'greasy'	Dominated by alginite

coals which contain clay disseminated throughout the coal rather than in layers are termed **bone** coals, and are of dull appearance.

In coals of lower rank, i.e. **brown** coals, these lithological descriptions are difficult to apply. Brown coals range from **lignite**, which may be anything from dull brown to black in colour, to **subbituminous** coal which is black, hard and banded. Brown coals are usually described in terms of colour and texture, e.g. they crack and disintegrate when dried out.

An internationally acceptable system of lithotypes for low rank coals does not yet exist. Hagemann (1978; 1980) proposed such a method and applied it to Saskatchewan lignites and lignite–subbituminous coals. The important criteria in Hagemann's classification are the relative proportions of groundmass and woody (xylitic) remains plus the relative abundance of mineral impurities, and the texture or banded characteristics. The groundmass consists of the more finely comminuted particles of various origins which are too small to be indentified macroscopically. In addition, intensity and hue of colour, degree of gelification and the presence or absence of inclusions are all incorporated into the system shown in Table 2.3.

Table 2.2 Macroscopic description of coals in sections and boreholes.
From Ward (1984), by permission of Blackwell Scientific Publications

Stopes (1919)	Schopf (1960); ASTM standard (1978)		Australian Standard K183 (1970)
Banded (humic) coals			
Vitrain	Vitrain		Coal, bright
Clarain	Attrital coal	Bright	Coal, bright, dull bands
		Moderately bright	Coal, dull and bright
Durain		Mid. lustre	Coal, mainly dull with numerous bright bands
		Moderately dull	
		Dull	Coal, dull minor bright bands
Fusain	Fusain		Coal, dull
Non-banded (sapropelic) coals			
Cannel coal	Cannel coal		Coal, dull conchoidal (canneloid)
Boghead coal	Boghead coal		
Impure coals	Bone coal		Coal, stoney (or shaley)
	Mineralised coal		Coal, heat altered Coal, weathered

Table 2.3 Macroscopic description of lignites. From Bustin *et al.* (1983), based on Hagemann (1980), by permission of Geological Association of Canada

Field observations		Laboratory observations			Additional features
Structure	Texture	Colour	Gelification	Inclusions	
1. Pure coal (non-xylitic)	Unbanded coal	Pale yellow	Gelified ground-mass	Resin bodies	Cracking to non-cracking
2. Pure coal (xylitic); fibrous/brittle; tree stumps; trunks, etc.	Moderately banded coal	Medium light yellow	Gelified tissues	Cuticles	Fracture even
3. Impure coal (non-xylitic) clayey/sandy/ calcareous coal, iron sulphides, etc.	Banded coal	Pale brown	Microgranular humic gel particles	Charcoal	Size breakup coarse to fine
4. Impure coal (xylitic)	Highly banded coal	Medium brown/dark brown/black	—	—	

The International Committee for Coal Petrology (ICCP) is preparing a classification of brown coal lithotypes on the basis of colour and texture rather than chemical composition, i.e. xylitic, attritic, fusitic and mineralised coals.

2.1.1.2   *Sapropelic coals*

Sapropelic coals are formed from the biological and physical degradation products of coal and peat-forming environments, with the addition of other materials such as plant spores and algae. The resulting sediment is an accumulation of colloidal organic mud in which concentrations of spore remains or algae, or both, are present. Sapropelic coals are characteristically fine grained, homogeneous, dark in colour and display a marked conchoidal fracture. They may occur in association with humic coals or as individual coal layers.

Cannel coal is composed largely of miospores and organic mud laid down under water, such as in a shallow lake.

Boghead coal is algal coal, and the criteria for the assignment of a coal as a boghead is that the whole mass of that coal originated from algal material without consideration of the state of preservation of the algal colonies, i.e. whether they are well preserved or completely decomposed. Boghead coals may grade laterally or vertically into true oil shales.

Between these two major types of sapropelic coals, transitional or intermediate forms such as cannel–boghead or boghead–cannel are recognised.

To the field geologist essentially all sapropelic coals look similar in hand specimens and can only be readily distinguished microscopically.

Coal descriptions using these terms result in a considerable amount of data that can be used in conjunction with the laboratory analysis of the coal. Such lithological logs can also provide information on coal quality that will influence the mining and preparation of the coal.

2.1.2   Microscopic description of coal

The microscopic examination of coal is not a method readily available to the field geologist; it is in the realm of the petrographer. However, a knowledge of the component materials that make up coals is required to understand those coal quality parameters that influence the future development of a coal deposit, e.g. calorific value, volatile matter content and coking properties.

The organic units or **macerals** that make up the coal mass can be identified in all ranks of coal. Essentially macerals are divided

Table 2.4 Stopes–Heerlen classification of maceral groups, macerals and submacerals of hard coals. From Ward (1984), after Stopes (1935), by permission of Blackwell Scientific Publications

Maceral group	Maceral	Submaceral
Vitrinite	Telinite Collinite	Telocollinite Gelocollinite Desmocollinite Corpocollinite
Exinite (liptinite)	Sporinite Cutinite Suberinite Resinite Alginite Liptodetrinite Fluorinite Bituminite Exudatinite	
Inertinite	Fusinite Semifusinite Macrinite Micrinite Sclerotinite Inertodetrinite	

into three groups: (i) **huminite/vitrinite**, which consists of woody materials; (ii) **exinite (liptinite)**, which consists of spores, resins and cuticles; and (iii) **inertinite**, which consists of oxidised plant material.

The original classification of maceral groups is referred to as the Stopes–Heerlen system given in Table 2.4. Other detailed descriptions are well summarised by McCabe (1984) in Table 2.5.

The combination of the three main maceral groups when identified petrographically are known as **microlithotypes**. Their compositions are listed in Table 2.6 and their interrelationship is shown in Figure 2.1.

The relationship between maceral type and the original plant material has been well documented. The plant materials that make up coal have different chemical compositions, which in turn determine the types of group macerals. Such chemical differences are clear in lower rank coals but it becomes increasingly difficult to distinguish petrographically between the various macerals with increasing coalification. This can be illustrated by an analysis of miospore floras and the petrographic types. Certain relationships have been established based on the investigation of thin layers of coal representing a moment in time during which environmental change was minimal. To illustrate this, in a thick coal seam in a stable area, the ascending

Table 2.5 Macerals and group macerals recognised in hard coals. From McCabe (1984), by permission of Blackwell Scientific Publications

Maceral group	Maceral	Morphology	Origin
Vitrinite (huminite)	Telinite	Cellular structure	Cells walls of trunks, branches, roots, leaves
	Collinite	Structureless	Reprecipitation of dissolved organic matter in a gel form
	Vitrodetrinite	Fragments of vitrinite	Very early degradation of plant and humic peat particles
	Sporinite	Fossil form	Mega- and microspores
	Cutinite	Bands which may have appendages	Cuticles—the outer layer of leaves, shoots and thin stems
Exinite (liptinite)	Resinite	Cell filling layers or dispersed	Plant resins, waxes and other secretions
	Alginite	Fossil form	Algae
	Liptodetrinite	Fragments of exinite	Degradation residues
	Fusinite	Empty or mineral filled cellular structure; cell structure usually well preserved	Oxidised plant material—mostly charcoal due to burning of vegetation
	Semifusinite	Cellular structure	Partly oxidised plant material
	Macrinite	Amorphous 'cement'	Oxidised gel material
Inertinite	Inertodetrinite	Small patches of fusinite, semifusinite or macrinite	Redeposited inertinites
	Micrinite	Granular, rounded grains ~1 μm in diameter	Degradation of macerals during coalification
	Sclerotinite	Fossil form	Mainly fungal remains

Table 2.6 Composition of microlithotypes. From McCabe (1984), by permission of Blackwell Scientific Publications

Microlithotype	Composition
Vitrite	Vitrinite >95%
Liptite	Exinite >95%
Inertite	Inertinite >95%
Fusite	Inertite with no macronite or micrinite
Clarite	Vitrinite and exinite >95%
Durite	Exinite and inertinite >95%
Vitrinertite	Vitrinite and inertinite >95%
Trimacerite	Vitrinite, exinite, inertinite, each >5%

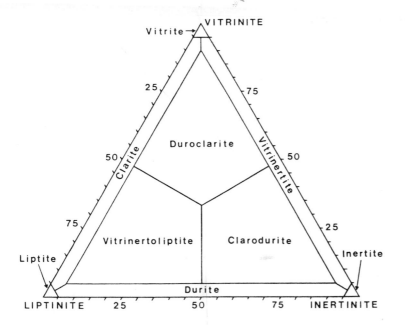

Figure 2.1 Diagrammatic representation of microlithotype classification. From Bustin *et al.* (1983), by permission of Geological Association of Canada

miospore sequence and the resultant microlithotypes are shown in Figure 2.2.

If the coal seam has splits then the sequence may revert to the early phase of seam development. Above the split the normal sequence of phases may become re-established unless the sequence is again interrupted by splitting.

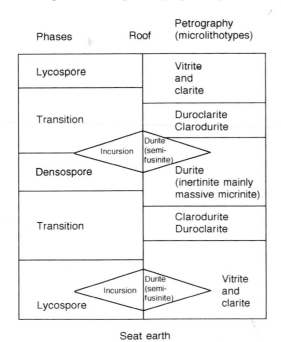

Figure 2.2 Diagrammatic profile of a coal seam showing the sequence of miospore phases and petrographic types. From Smith (1968), by permission of the author and Oliver & Boyd

Table 2.7   Huminite macerals. From Bustin *et al.* (1983), by permission of Geological Association of Canada

Maceral	Origin	Petrological features	Equivalents in hard coals
Textinite	Woody tissue	Primary cell wall structure still distinguishable; cell lumina mostly open	Telinite/ telocollinite
Ulminite	Woody tissue	Higher degree of humification; texto-ulminite = cell wall structure still visible; eu-ulminite = no visible cell wall structure, cell lumina mostly closed	Telinite/ telocollinite
Attrinite	Finely comminuted	Particle size <10 μm, product of degradation of huminite macerals	Desmocollinite
Densinite	Same as attrinite	Tighter packed than attrinite	
Gelinite	Derived from colloidal humic solutions which migrate into existing cavities and precipitate as gels	Secondary cell filling	Gelocollinite
Corpohumite	Condensation products of tannins characteristic of bark tissues	In cross section globular to tabular shape	Corpocollinite

In low rank coals, i.e. lignites and subbituminous coals, the **vitrinite** maceral group is referred to as **huminite**, and is regarded as equivalent to, and the precursor of, the vitrinite macerals found in higher rank coals. The classification of huminite macerals is summarised in Table 2.7, which gives details of their origin and their equivalents in the hard coals. An increase of coal rank leads to the homogenisation of the macerals of the huminite–vitrinite group, the term **collinite** being used to describe homogeneous structureless vitrite.

A microlithotype analysis can give an indication of the texture of a coal. If two coals have equal overall contents of vitrinite and one has a higher vitrite content than the other, this may be due to different thicknesses in the bands of vitrinite, which in turn may influence the preparation of the coal. Similarly, the size distribution of masses of inertinite may be important in the coking behaviour of the coal.

2.1.3 Mineral content of coals

The mineral content of coal is the non-combustible inorganic fraction; this is made up of minerals which are either detrital or authigenic in origin, and which are introduced into the coal in the first or second phase of coalification. The principal mineral associations are outlined in Table 2.8.

Detrital minerals are those transported into a swamp or bog by air or water. A large variety of minerals can be found in coal; these are usually dominated by quartz, carbonate, iron and clay minerals, with a diverse suite of accessory minerals which may be peculiar to the local source rock.

Water-borne mineral matter is transported into coal swamps along channels which cut through the accumulating organic debris. When such channels are in flood, detritus is laid down on top of the organic material and such events are usually preserved as mineral-rich partings in coals. Mineral-rich materials present in the floor of the peat swamp may be incorporated into the organic layer by differential compaction within the swamp and by bioturbative action.

Wind-borne mineral matter is important as this can be a significant contributor to the mineral contents of coals because of the slow accumulation rates in peat swamps. Coal swamp areas located in close proximity to active volcanic regions may receive high amounts of mineral matter. Associated lithologies with coals such as flint clays and tonsteins are indicative of such volcanic mineral deposition, and, if the volcanic event was short-lived but widespread, are extremely useful as stratigraphic marker horizons in coal sequences.

Authigenic minerals are those introduced into a peat during or after deposition, or into a coal during coalification. Precipitated minerals may be disseminated through the peat or present as aggregates, whereas mineral-rich fluids present during the later stages of coalification tend to precipitate minerals on joints and any open voids within the coal. Common products of mineralisation are the calcium–iron minerals such as calcite, ankerite, siderite and pyrite, with silica in the form of quartz. The element sulphur is present in almost all coals; it is usually present in the organic fraction of the coal, but inorganic or mineral sulphur is in the form of pyrite. Pyrite may be present as a primary detrital mineral or as secondary pyrite as a result of sulphur reduction in marine waters; there is now considered to be a strong correlation between high sulphur coals and marine depositional environments.

Table 2.8 Minerals in coal. After Stach *et al.* (1975), by permission of Gebrüder Borntraeger, Stuttgart

Mineral group	First stage of coalification: syngenetic formation, synsedimentary, early diagenetic (intimately intergrown)		Second stage of coalification: epigenetic formation	
	Transported by water or wind	Newly formed	Deposited in fissures, cleats and cavities (coarsely) intergrown	Transformation of syngenetic minerals (intimately) intergrown
Clay minerals	Kaolinite, illite, sericite, clay minerals with mixed-layer structure; montmorillonite, tonstein (smectite)			Illite, chlorite
Carbonates	—	Siderite–ankerite concretions; dolomite, calcite, ankerite, siderite, calcite	Ankerite, calcite, dolomite; ankerite in fusite	—
Sulphides	—	Pyrite concretions, melnikovite–pyrite, coarse pyrite, (marcasite), concretions of FeS_2–$CuFeS_2$–ZnS; pyrite in fusite	Pyrite, marcasite, zinc sulphide (sphalerite), lead sulphide (galena), copper sulphide (chalcopyrite); pyrite in fusite	Pyrite, from transformation of syngenetic concretions of $FeCO_3$
Oxides	—	Haematite	Goethite, lepidocrocite ('needle iron ore')	Goethite, lepidocrocite ('needle iron ore')
Quartz	Quartz grains	Chalcedony and quartz from the weathering of felspars and mica	Quartz	—
Phosphates	Apatite	Phosphorite, apatite	—	—
Heavy minerals	Zircon, rutile, tourmaline, orthoclase, biotite	—	Chlorides, sulphates, nitrates	Chlorides, sulphates, nitrates

Clay minerals on average make up 60–80% of the total mineral matter associated with coal. Their genesis is complex and they can have a detrital origin or be secondary, formed from aqueous solutions. Chemical conditions at the site of deposition also influence the type of clay minerals associated with coal. In particular, freshwater swamps with their low pH value tend to favour *in situ* alteration of smectites, illite and mixed-layer clays to kaolinite. Generally illite is dominant in coals with marine roofs, whereas kaolinite is dominant in non-marine influenced coals. Secondary clays are produced from the alteration of primary clays, e.g. chlorite is expected to occur in coals subjected to greater pressures and temperatures.

Clay minerals occur in coal in two ways: in tonsteins or as finely dispersed inclusions in maceral lithotypes. Tonsteins have been formed by detrital and authigenic processes and, in particular, are associated with volcanic activity. They usually contain kaolinite, smectite and mixed-layer clays with accessory minerals.

Clay minerals can contaminate all microlithotypes. Those with less than 20% (by volume) clay minerals are described as being 'contaminated by clay'; for clay mineral contents of 20–60% (by volume) the term 'carbargillite' is used; if higher proportions of clay minerals are present the lithology is no longer a coal but an argillaceous shale.

Clay minerals have the property of swelling in the presence of water. Swelling is accompanied by a reduction in strength and disintegration is an end result. This is most significant in mines where coals have clay-rich roofs and floors, which can result in instability, as well as difficulties encountered in drainage and dewatering in both underground and open pit mine operations.

All of the above forms of mineral content in coals can be identified macroscopically by the field geologist in outcrop and borehole core. There are other minerals that may be present in coal which affect its future potential use; these cannot be seen in hand specimen and are detectable only by chemical analysis.

The mineral matter content of coals and the surrounding country rock will influence the properties of the coal roof and floor, and in particular their resistance and response to water. It will also influence the composition of mine dust with a diameter of less than 5 μm, particularly in underground operations. Significant amounts of quartz in dust affects the incidence of silicosis. The mineral matter in the coal will also affect the washability of the coal and consequently the yield and ash content of the clean coal.

Mineral impurities affect the suitability of a coal as a boiler fuel; the low ash fusion point causes deposition of ash and corrosion in the heating chamber and convection passes of the boiler. The presence in coal of phosphorus minerals, usually in the form of phosphorite or apatite, causes slagging in certain boilers, and steel produced from such phosphorus-rich coals tends to be brittle.

Halide minerals such as chlorides, and sulphates and nitrates are present in coal, usually as infiltration products deposited

Table 2.9   Trace elements in coal. From Stach *et al.* (1975), by permission of Gebrüder Borntraeger, Stuttgart

Element	Concentration in Ruhr coals (ppm)*		Concentration in coal ash (%wt/wt)
	Maximum	Most frequent	
Antinomy	n.d.	n.d.	0.1–0.3
Arsenic	20	9	0.8–1.0
Barium	n.d.	n.d.	0.1–5.0
Beryllium	8	3	0.1–0.4
Bismuth	n.d.	n.d.	0.2
Boron	n.d.	n.d.	0.1–0.3
Chromium	30	10	0.5
Cobalt	40	10	0.15–0.2
Copper	50	20	0.005–1.0
Gallium	10	3	0.04–0.3
Germanium	10	3	0.1–1.1
Lead	100	40	0.1–3.1
Manganese	300	10	1.0–2.2
Molybdenum	6	1	0.05–0.1
Nickel	80	20	0.3–1.6
Phosphorus	400	100	n.d.
Silver	8	3	0.001–0.006
Strontium	n.d.	n.d.	0.1
Tin	n.d.	n.d.	0.05–0.1
Titanium	n.d.	n.d.	1.2–3.0
Uranium	n.d.	0.6–0.7	n.d.
Vanadium	50	30	0.1–1.1
Zinc	120	50	0.5–0.7
Zirconium	n.d.	n.d.	0.5–0.7

*n.d. = not determined.

from brines migrating through the sedimentary sequence. They become significant in mining operations as mine waters enriched with, for example, nitrates create serious corrosion effects on pipework and other metal installations in the mine workings. In addition, chlorine causes severe corrosion in coal-fired boilers.

The more important trace elements found in coals are summarised in Table 2.9. They may originate from the original plant material or be components of other minerals in the coal. Several of them, notably boron, titanium, vanadium and zinc, can have detrimental effects in the metallurgical industry.

2.2   COALIFICATION (RANK)

2.2.1   Coalification

Coalification is the alteration of vegetation to form peat, succeeded by the transformation of peat through lignite, subbituminous, bituminous, semi-anthracite to anthracite and meta-anthracite coal.

The degree of transformation or coalification is termed the coal rank and this is of prime interest to the coal geologist. The early identification of the rank of the coal deposit being investigated will determine the future potential and interest in the deposit. To consider coal rank, a brief examination of the coalification process is given, particularly those conditions under which coals of different rank are produced.

The coalification process is essentially an initial biochemical phase followed by a geochemical or metamorphic phase. The biochemical phase includes those processes that occur in the peat swamp following deposition and burial, i.e. during diagenesis. This process is considered to be in operation until the hard brown coal stage is reached. The most intense biochemical changes occur at very shallow depths in the peat swamps. This is chiefly in the form of bacteriological activity which degrades the peat, and which may be assisted in this by the rate of burial, pH and levels of groundwater in the swamp. With increased burial, bacteriological activity ceases, and is considered absent at depths greater than 10 m. Carbon-rich components and the volatile content of the peat are little affected during the biochemical stage of coalification; however, with increased compaction of the peat, the moisture content decreases and the calorific value increases.

From the brown coal stage, the alteration of the organic material is severe and can be regarded as metamorphism. Coals react to changes in temperature and pressure much more quickly than do mineral suites in rocks; coals can therefore indicate a degree of metamorphism in sequences which show no mineralogical change.

During the geochemical or metamorphic stage, the progressive changes that occur within coals are an increase in the carbon content and a decrease in the hydrogen and oxygen content resulting in a loss of volatiles. This, together with continued water loss and compaction, results in the reduction of the coal volume. Products of such coalification are methane, carbon dioxide and water; water is quickly lost and the methane to carbon dioxide ratio increases with rank.

These changes in the physical and chemical properties of the coal are in reality the changes to the inherent coal constituents. During coalification the three maceral groups become enriched in carbon. Each maceral group, i.e. exinite, inertinite and huminite (vitrinite), follows a distinct coalification path. Figure 2.3, after van Krevelen (1961), illustrates the distinct coalification paths. The petrographic properties of vitrinite change uniformly with increasing rank.

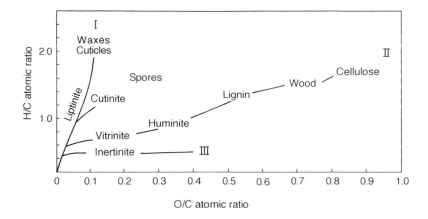

Figure 2.3 Diagram showing the coali-fication tracks of liptinite, inertite and huminite-vitrinite. From Bustin *et al.* (1983), based on van Krevelen (1961), by permission of Geological Association of Canada

In reflected light the reflectance progressively increases, whereas in transmitted light organic materials become opaque and the plant structure becomes difficult to recognise. The optical properties of vitrinite have enabled it to be used as an indicator of rank. Teichmuller and Teichmuller (1982) describe the method used in detail as applied to the medium volatile bituminous to meta-anthracite and semi-graphite range of coals, i.e. coals with less than 30% volatile matter. Reflectance is also considered the best rank parameter for anthracites; it is nearly comparable with moisture content as a rank indicator in high volatile bituminous coals. It was originally suggested that this is not so for lower rank coals; however, later studies have shown the utility of reflectance in low rank lignitic coals, provided that care is taken in the selection of the component measured. Table 2.10 suggests rank classes in terms of vitrinite reflectance. This increase in vitrinite reflectance with increase in coal rank is shown in Figure 2.4 for New Zealand coals. These have high

Table 2.10   Rank classes in terms of vitrinite reflectance. From Ward (1984), by permission of Blackwell Scientific Publications

Rank	Maximum reflectance ($\% R0_{max}$)
Subbituminous	<0.47
High volatile bituminous C	0.47–0.57
High volatile bituminous B	0.57–0.71
High volatile bituminous A	0.71–1.10
Medium volatile bituminous	1.10–1.50
Low volatile bituminous	1.50–2.05
Semi-anthracite	2.05–3.00 (approx.)
Anthracite	>3.00

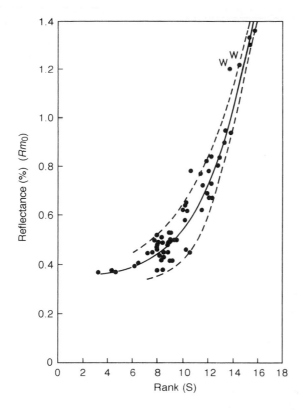

Figure 2.4 Reflectance/rank relationship. From Suggate & Lowery (1982), by
permission of *New Zealand Journal of Geology and Geophysics*. Crown copyright
W = weathered coal

proportions of vitrinite and most fall within a restricted band on
a volatile matter/calorific value plot. The mean reflectance values
given in Figure 2.4 are reported to be on the high side—
nevertheless, the reflectance–rank relationship is meaningful. It
should be noted that in high volatile South African Gondwana
coals, reflectance is a better indicator of rank than moisture due
to the presence of higher amounts of inertinite, which has a
lower moisture content.

Fluorescence microscopy of the liptinite macerals and the
coloration of the liptinite (thermal alteration index) are useful for
coals of low rank, but these methods are not as refined as
vitrinite reflectance. The applicability of the different rank parameters are summarised in Table 2.11.

During coalification, sapropelic coals undergo alteration similar to that of the liptinite component of humic coals. At the
peat stage sapropelic coals are enriched in hydrogen relative to
humic coals, but at advanced stages of coalification (90% carbon) the chemical composition of boghead, cannel and humic
coals is similar. During coalification significant amounts of bitumen may be generated from sapropelic coals.

Table 2.11 Rank parameters in humic coals. From Teichmuller & Teichmuller (1968), by permission of

Rank stages (scientific)	ASTM classification of coals (USA) (pre-1977)	Vitrite carbon (%d.a.f.)	Volatile matter (%d.a.f.)	*In situ* moisture (%)	Calorific value of vitrite (a.f.) (kcal/kg)
Peat					
		——60——		——75——	
Soft brown coal	Brown coal				
			—— c.53 ——	——35——	——4000——
Hard brown coal Dull	Lignite				
		—— c.71 ——	—— c.49 ——	——25——	——5500——
Bright	Subbituminous				
		—— c.77 ——	—— c.42 ——	——8–10——	——7000——
Bituminous hard coal Low rank	High volatile bituminous coal				
	Medium volatile bituminous coal	—87—	—29—		——8650——
High rank	Low volatile bituminous coal				
	Semi-anthracite				
		—91—	—8—		——8650——
Anthracite	Anthracite Meta-anthracite				

2.2.2 Causes of coalification

The coalification process is governed primarily by increases in temperature and the time during which this occurs.

2.2.2.1 *Temperature changes*

These can be achieved in two ways. First, by the direct contact of the coal with igneous material, either as minor intrusions or as deep seated major intrusions. The coals show a loss of volatiles, oxygen, methane and water and the surrounding sediments will show evidence of contact metamorphism, e.g. the local development of high rank coal in the Tertiary of Sumatra, Indonesia and in the Jurassic coals of South Korea. Second, by the rise in temperature associated with depth of burial. Increasing depth of burial results in a decrease in the oxygen content of the coals and an increase in the ratio of fixed carbon to volatile matter. Hilt (1873) observed these phenomena and Hilt's law states: 'In

Oliver & Boyd

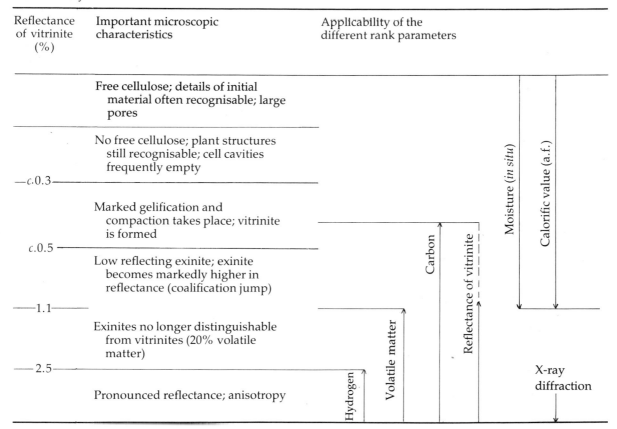

Reflectance of vitrinite (%)	Important microscopic characteristics	Applicability of the different rank parameters

a vertical sequence, at any one locality in a coalfield, the rank of the coal seams rises with increasing depth'.

The rate of rank increase, known as the rank gradient, is dependent on the geothermal gradient and the heat conductivity of the rocks. Where the geothermal gradient is high (70–80 °C/km depth), bituminous rank can be attained at depths of 1500 m (Upper Rhine graben, Germany) whereas, in the same area, the same rank is reached at depths of 2600 m when the geothermal gradient is lower (40 °C/km; Stach, 1982). Basinal studies have shown variations in the geothermal gradient in different parts of the basin. Studies of the Remus Basin in the Canadian Arctic show differing geothermal gradients of 55 °C/km in the eastern part and 20 °C/km in the western part. The Remus Basin contains 90 seams of coal with ranks ranging from lignite to high volatile bituminous with a maximum palaeothickness of 4500 m. In South Wales, it is suggested that the coalification that has produced anthracitisation is due to the proximity of

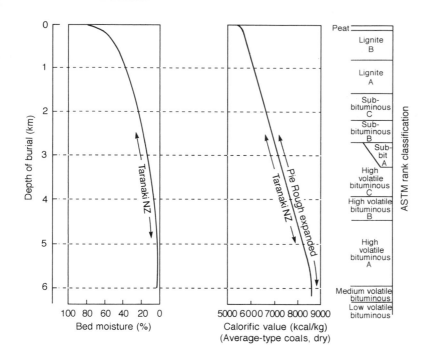

Figure 2.5 Composite sequence providing an example of the relationship between depth, calorific value and ASTM rank. The average geothermal gradient for this sequence is estimated at 26–27 °C/km. From Suggate (1982), by permission of *Journal of Petroleum Geology*

a magmatic heat source. The anthracite field has a present day geothermal gradient of 25°C/km.

Figure 2.5 illustrates the way in which ASTM rank boundaries vary in depth from the surface according to the geothermal gradient, as reflected by variations in the moisture and calorific value relationships.

2.2.2.2 *Time*

Coalification temperatures are usually lower than was once inferred from experimental coalification studies. Stach (1982) quotes temperatures of the order of 100–150°C as sufficient for bituminous coal formation according to geological observations. To attain higher ranks, higher temperatures are required with more rapid rates of heating (contact metamorphism) rather than with slower heating rates (subsidence and depth of burial). Therefore it is apparent that the degree of coalification is less where sediments have subsided rapidly and the 'cooking time' was short, and time only has a real effect when the temperature is sufficiently high to allow chemical reactions to occur. Where very low temperatures occur over a very long period, little coalification takes place, for example, the Lower Carboniferous lignites in the Moscow Basin. The influence of time therefore is all the greater the higher the temperature.

2.2.2.3 *Pressure*

The influence of pressure is at its greatest during compaction and is most evident from the peat to subbituminous coal stages, in the decrease of porosity and the reduction of moisture content with depth. Stach (1982) states that the pressure promotes 'physico-structural coalification', whereas an increase in temperature accelerates 'chemical coalification'. With the gradual subsidence of coal, both influences run parallel, but occasionally physico-structural coalification may precede chemical coalification; for example, where relatively low moisture coals have been produced by early folding. Chemical coalification will advance when additional heat is supplied, for example, from intrusive bodies. With increasing chemical coalification, pressure has less influence. Laboratory experiments suggest that the confining pressure may inhibit chemical coalification and retard the process; for example, the removal of gas is more difficult, and the alteration of macerals is postponed by pressure.

Local rises in rank can occur along shear planes. This is probably due to frictional heat.

2.2.2.4 *Radioactivity*

Increase of rank by radioactivity is rarely observed, and is likely to be only in the form of microscopic contact haloes of higher reflectivity around uranium or thorium concentrations in the coal.

2.3 COAL QUALITY

Coal quality in essence means those chemical and physical properties of a coal that influence its potential use.

The coal geologist needs to have an understanding of the chemical and physical properties of coal, especially those properties that will determine whether the coal can be used commercially. Coals need to possess particular qualities for selected usage; should they meet such requirements, then they can be mined and sold as a pure product or, if the quality could be improved, then they can be blended with other selected coals to achieve the saleable product.

The quality of a coal is determined by the makeup of the original maceral and mineral matter content of the coal and its degree of coalification (rank). For this to be understood in analytical terms, set procedures for determining the chemical and physical properties of coals have been set up [the published standards by the American Society of Testing and Materials (ASTM) and the International Organisation for Standardisation (ISO) should be consulted].

The coal geologist does not need to know the detailed laboratory methods required to analyse the coal, but the geologist should make sure that he or she is familiar with the most commonly determined properties of a coal, in particular those which are deleterious to the coal. From this the geologist must be able to use any such analyses in the evaluation of a coal deposit, i.e. to be aware of which seams or parts of seams will be unacceptable when mining commences, or, conversely, those seams or parts of seams which will yield a premium product for the pre-determined market. It is possible that after analysing a coal hitherto undetected properties may enhance the product or even suggest a different end usage for the coal, e.g. the discovery that a coal has good coking properties when it was originally considered for a steam coal product.

For the purpose of background information, and to enable the geologist to become familiar with the terms and properties determined, an outline is given of those chemical and physical properties that the geologist is most likely to encounter, and what they mean in terms of the coal's usability.

2.3.1   Chemical properties of coal

In simple terms coal can be regarded as being made up of moisture, pure coal and mineral matter. The moisture consists of surface moisture and chemically bound moisture and the pure coal is the amount of organic matter present. The mineral matter is the amount of inorganic material present which, when the coal is burnt, produces ash. Clearly the decomposition of some inorganic minerals during heating means that ash and mineral matter composition cannot be equal.

Coal analyses are often reported as proximate or ultimate analysis. Proximate analysis is a broad analysis which determines the amounts of moisture, volatile matter, fixed carbon and ash. This is the most fundamental of all coal analyses and is of great importance in the practical use of coal. The tests are highly dependent on the procedure used and different results are obtained using different times and temperatures. It is therefore important to know the procedure used and the reported basis (see Section 2.3.1.1).

Ultimate analysis is the determination of the chemical elements in the coal, i.e. carbon, hydrogen, oxygen, nitrogen and sulphur. In addition, the calculation of the amounts of those elements which have a direct bearing on the usability of the coal is necessary. These may include forms of sulphur, chlorine, phosphorus, an analysis of those elements making up the mineral matter content of the coal and selected trace elements.

2.3.1.1 *Basis of analytical data*

Before proceeding to the analysis of the coal, it is important to understand how the moisture, ash, volatile matter and fixed carbon relate to one another, and to the basis on which the analytical data are presented.

It is important in evaluating previous coal analyses that the basis on which they are presented is known. It is unfortunately a common problem that analyses are given which do not indicate on what basis they are presented. Indeed, they are often listed together on different bases which are not stated.

Coal analyses (see Table 2.12) may be reported as follows.

(i)   'As received' basis (a.r.), also 'as sampled'. The data are expressed as percentages of the coal including the total moisture content, i.e. including both the surface and the air-dried moisture content of the coal

(ii)   'Air-dried' basis (a.d.b.). The data are expressed as percentages of the air-dried coal; this includes the air-dried moisture but not the surface moisture of the coal

(iii)   'Dry basis' (dry). The data are expressed as percentages of the coal after all the moisture has been removed

(iv)   'Dry ash-free basis' (d.a.f.). The coal is considered to consist of volatile matter and fixed carbon on the basis of

Table 2.12   Components of coal reporting to different bases. From Ward (1984), by permission of Blackwell Scientific Publications

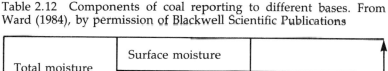
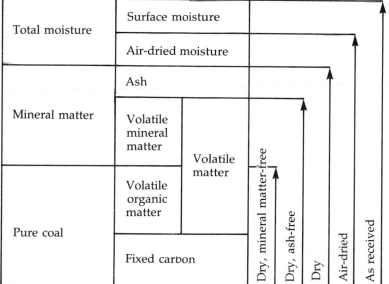

recalculation with moisture and ash removed. It should be noted that this does not allow for the volatile matter derived from minerals present in the air-dried coal. This basis is used as the easiest way to compare organic fractions of coals

(v) 'Dry, mineral matter-free' (d.m.m.f.). Here it is necessary that the total amount of mineral matter rather than ash is determined, so that the volatile matter content in the mineral matter can be removed.

Table 2.13 gives the required formulae for the calculation of results to these bases (from BS1016 part 16, 1981).

In addition, the following countries have developed equations to calculate the mineral matter content of their coals.

North America: original Parr formula

$$MM = 1.08A + 0.55S$$

Modified Parr formula

$$MM = 1.13A + 0.47Spyr + Cl$$

United Kingdom: BCURA formula

$$MM = 1.10A + 0.53S + 0.74CO_2 - 0.36$$

KMC formula (revised by British Coal)

$$MM = 1.13A + 0.5Spyr + 0.8CO_2 - 2.8SAsh + 2.8SSulph + 0.3Cl$$

Australia: Standards Association of Australia formula

$$MM = 1.1A$$

where MM = mineral matter (%), A = Ash (%), S = total sulphur (%), Spyr = pyritic sulphur (%), SSulph = sulphate sulphur (%), SAsh = sulphur in ash (%), Cl = chlorine (%), CO_2 = carbon dioxide (%). All values are expressed on an air-dried basis.

2.3.1.2 Proximate analysis

Moisture. The terminology used in describing the moisture content of coals can be confusing and needs to be clarified.

The most confusing term is inherent moisture, which has

Table 2.13 Formulae for calculation of results to different bases. From BS 1016 Part 16 (1981), by permission of the British Standards Institution

Given result	As sampled (as received; as despatched; as fired)	Result wanted			
		Air dry	Dry	Dry, ash-free	Dry, mineral matter-free
As sampled (as received; as despatched; as fired)	—	$\dfrac{100 - M_{ad}}{100 - M_{ar}}$	$\dfrac{100}{100 - M_{ar}}$	$\dfrac{100}{100 - (M_{ar} + A_{ar})}$	$\dfrac{100}{100 - (M_{ar} + MM_{ar})}$
As analysed (air dry)	$\dfrac{100 - M_{ar}}{100 - M_{ad}}$	—	$\dfrac{100}{100 - M_{ad}}$	$\dfrac{100}{100 - (M_{ad} + A_{ad})}$	$\dfrac{100}{100 - (M_{ad} + MM_{ad})}$
Dry	$\dfrac{100 - M_{ar}}{100}$	$\dfrac{100 - M_{ad}}{100}$	—	$\dfrac{100}{100 - A_d}$	$\dfrac{100}{100 - MM_d}$
Dry, ash-free	$\dfrac{100 - (M_{ar} + A_{ar})}{100}$	$\dfrac{100 - (M_{ad} + A_{ad})}{100}$	$\dfrac{100 - A_d}{100}$	—	$\dfrac{100 - A_d}{100 - MM_d}$
Dry, mineral matter-free	$\dfrac{100 - (M_{ar} + MM_{ar})}{100}$	$\dfrac{100 - (M_{ad} + MM_{ad})}{100}$	$\dfrac{100 - MM_d}{100}$	$\dfrac{100 - MM_d}{100 - A_d}$	—

Abbreviations: M = moisture (%); A = ash (%); MM = mineral matter (%); ar = as received basis; ad = air-dried basis; and d = dry basis.

many different definitions and should be avoided if at all possible. If you find it used in any tests it is necessary to ascertain the exact definition that the reference is using.

There is no exact method of determining moisture content. The coal industry has therefore developed a set of empirically determined definitions which are as follows.

(i)   Surface moisture. This is adventitious moisture, not naturally occurring with the coal and which can be removed by low temperature air drying (about 40°C). This drying step is usually the first in any analysis and the moisture remaining after this step is known as air-dried moisture

(ii) As received or as delivered moisture. This is the total moisture of the coal sample when received or delivered to the laboratory. Usually a laboratory will air dry a coal sample, thereby obtaining the 'loss on air drying'. An aggressive drying step is then carried out which determines the air-dried moisture. These results are added together to give the total/as received/as delivered moisture

(iii) Total moisture. This is all the moisture which can be removed by aggressive drying (about 150°C in vacuum or nitrogen atmosphere)

(iv) Air-dried moisture. This is the moisture remaining after drying and which can be removed by aggressive drying. In addition to this generally used term, the following terms are being increasingly used: moisture holding capacity (MHC), capacity moisture or equilibrium moisture (EQ). It is not within the scope of this book to detail the analytical procedures required, but suffice to say that they are lengthy and expensive.

These terms relate to the in-bed or *in situ* moisture of a coal. Numerically the MHC of a bituminous coal will be higher than air-dried moisture and lower than total moisture. Technically it is the MHC which increases with decreasing rank (Figure 2.6).

High moisture is undesirable in coals as it is chemically inert and absorbs heat during combustion and it creates difficulties in handling and transport. It lowers the calorific value in steam coals and lowers the amount of carbon available in coking coals.

Ash. The ash content of a coal is that inorganic residue that remains after combustion. It should be remembered that the determined ash content is not equivalent to the mineral matter content of the coal. It does, however, represent the bulk of the mineral matter in the coal after losing the volatile components such as CO_2, SO_2 and H_2O, which have been driven off from mineral compounds such as carbonates, sulphides and clays.

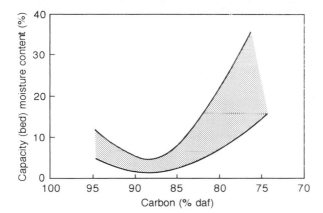

Figure 2.6 Generalised variation of capacity (or air-dried) moisture contents with rank. From Berkowitz (1979), by permission of Academic Press

In a steam coal, a high ash content will effectively reduce its calorific value. Recommended maximum ash contents for steam coals for use as pulverised fuel are around 20% (air-dried), but for some stoker-fired boilers much lower values are desirable. In coking coals, a maximum of 10–20% (air-dried) is recommended, as higher ash contents reduce the efficiency in the blast furnace.

Volatile matter. Volatile matter represents that component of the coal, except for moisture, that is liberated at high temperature in the absence of air. This material is derived chiefly from the organic fraction of the coal, but minor amounts may also be from the mineral matter present. Correction for the volatile matter derived from the latter may be made in technical works, but is not usually necessary in commercial practice.

In pulverised fuel firing for electricity generation, most boilers are designed for a minimum volatile matter of 20–25% (d.a.f.). In stoker firing for electricity generation, the volatile matter limits recommended are 25–40% (d.a.f.). There is virtually no limit for the volatile matter for coals used in the production of cement. In coke production, a high volatile matter content will give a lower coke yield so that the best quality coking coals have a volatile matter range of 20–35% (air-dried), but values of 16–36% can be used.

Fixed carbon. The fixed carbon content of coal is that carbon found in the residue remaining after the volatile matter has been liberated. Fixed carbon is not determined directly but is the difference, in an air-dried coal, between the total percentages of the other components, i.e. moisture, ash and volatile matter, and 100%.

2.3.1.3   *Ultimate analysis*

Ultimate analysis of coal consists of the determination of carbon and hydrogen as gaseous products of its complete combustion, the determination of sulphur, nitrogen and ash in the material as a whole, and the estimation of oxygen by difference.

Carbon and hydrogen. These are liberated as CO_2 and H_2O when the coal is burned and are most easily determined together. However, CO_2 may be liberated from any carbonate minerals present, and H_2O may be derived from clay minerals or from any inherent moisture in the air-dried coal, or both. Allowances have to be made for these inorganic sources of carbon and hydrogen.

Nitrogen. The nitrogen content of coal is significant particularly in relation to atmospheric pollution. Upon combustion of the coal, nitrogen helps to form oxides which may be released as flue gases and thereby pollute the atmosphere; as a result, coals which are low in nitrogen are preferred in industry.

Coals should not as a rule have nitrogen contents of more than 1.5–2.0% (d.a.f.) because of these NO_x emissions.

Sulphur. As for nitrogen, the sulphur content of coals presents problems with utilisation and resultant pollution. Sulphur causes corrosion and fouling of boiler tubes and atmospheric pollution when released in flue gases.

Sulphur can be present in coal in three forms: (i) organic sulphur, present in the organic compounds of the coal; (ii) pyritic sulphur, present as sulphide minerals in the coal, principally iron pyrite; and (iii) sulphate minerals, usually hydrous iron or calcium sulphates, produced by oxidation of the sulphide fraction of the coal.

In the ultimate analysis of the coal, only the total sulphur content is determined; however, in many instances, the relative amount of sulphur in each form is required. This is carried out as a separate analysis.

The total sulphur content in steam coals used for electricity generation should not exceed 0.8–1.0% (air-dried); the maximum value will depend on local emission regulations. In the cement industry, a total sulphur content of up to 2.0% (air-dried) is acceptable, but a maximum of 0.8% (air-dried) is required in coking coals because higher values affect the quality of steel.

Oxygen. Oxygen is a component of many of the organic and inorganic compounds in coal as well as the moisture content.

When the coal is oxidised, oxygen may be present in oxides, hydroxides and sulphate minerals, as well as oxidised organic material. It should be remembered that oxygen is an important indicator of rank in coal.

Oxygen is traditionally determined by subtracting the amount of the other elements (carbon, hydrogen, nitrogen and sulphur) from 100%.

2.3.1.4 Other analyses

Forms of sulphur. The proportions of organic, inorganic and sulphate forms of sulphur are important when considering the commercial usefulness of a coal. Coal preparation can reduce the inorganic (pyritic) and sulphate fractions, but will not reduce the organic sulphur content. Therefore if a coal has a high sulphur content, it is essential to know if this can be reduced by coal preparation methods; if not, then it may mean that the coal is unusable, or at best used in a blend with a low sulphur product. Also, pyritic sulphur can be linked to liability to spontaneous combustion.

Carbon dioxide. Carbon dioxide in coal occurs in the carbonate mineral matter fraction. The carbonates liberate CO_2 on combustion and contribute to the total carbon content of the coal. This reaction, however, reduces the amount of energy available from the coal.

Chlorine. The chlorine content of coal is low, usually occurring as the inorganic salts of sodium, potassium and calcium chloride. The presence of relatively high amounts of chlorine in coal is detrimental to its use. In boilers chlorine causes corrosion and fouling, and when present in flue gas it contributes to atmospheric pollution.

Steam coals should have a maximum chloride content of 0.2–0.3% (air-dried) and for coals used in the production of cement, a maximum of 0.1% (air-dried) is recommended.

Phosphorus. Phosphorus may be present in coal, usually concentrated in the mineral apatite. It is undesirable for large amounts of phosphorus to be present in coking coals to be used in the metallurgical industry as it contributes to producing brittle steel. It is also undesirable in stoker firing coal as it causes fouling in the boiler.

Coking coals should have a maximum phosphorus content of 0.1% (air-dried).

Ash analysis. The ash in coal represents the residue of the combusted mineral matter and it can be broken down and expressed as the series of metal oxides which make up the lithosphere. These are SiO_2, Al_2O_3, TiO_2, CaO, MgO, K_2O, Na_2O, P_2O_5, Fe_2O_3 and SO_3. These data are important in determining how a coal will behave, such as steam coal in boilers where slagging and fouling can result, because the presence of large amounts of the oxides of iron, calcium, sodium, or potassium can result in ashes with low ash fusion temperatures. In coking coals, the sodium and potassium oxide content should be a maximum of 3% in ash, as high contents of alkalis cause high coke reactivity.

Trace element analysis. Coals contain diverse amounts of trace elements in their overall composition. Those predominantly associated with the organic fraction are boron, beryllium and germanium; those predominantly associated with the inorganic fraction include arsenic, cadmium, mercury, manganese, molybdenum, lead, zinc and zirconium. Other trace elements have various associations with the organic and inorganic fractions. Those usually associated with the organic fraction are gallium, phosphorus, antimony, titanium and vanadium; those with the inorganic fraction are cobalt, chromium, nickel and selenium.

Boron can be a useful index in indicating the palaeosalinity of the coal's depositional conditions.

Certain trace elements such as lead, arsenic, cadmium, chromium and mercury, if present in high amounts, could preclude the coal from being used in environmentally sensitive situations. Others have detrimental effects on the metallurgical industry; these include boron, titanium, vanadium and zinc.

As a result of the high tonnages of coal used in industry, significant amounts of trace elements may be concentrated in residues after combustion. Therefore, trace element determinations are carried out before the coal is accepted for industrial use.

2.3.2   Combustion properties of coal

The determination of the effects of combustion on coal will influence the selection of coals for particular industrial uses.

Tests are carried out to determine a coal's performance in a furnace, i.e. its calorific value and its ash fusion temperatures. In addition, the caking and coking properties of coals need to be determined if the coal is intended for use in the metallurgical industry.

These parameters are particularly significant as they form the basis for the classification of coals (see Section 2.4).

2.3.2.1 *Calorific value*

The calorific value (CV) of a coal is the amount of heat produced per unit mass of coal when combusted. Calorific value is often referred to as specific energy (SE), particularly in Australia. The CV of a coal is expressed in two ways.

First, the gross calorific or higher heating value. This is the amount of heat liberated during testing in a laboratory when a coal is combusted under standardised conditions at constant volume, so that all of the water in the products remains in the liquid form.

Second, the net calorific or lower heating value. During actual combustion in furnaces, the gross calorific value is never achieved because some products, especially water, are lost with their associated latent heat of vaporisation. The maximum achievable calorific value under these conditions is the net calorific value at constant pressure. This can be calculated and expressed in absolute joules, calories per gram, or Btu per pound. The simplified equations for these are as follows:

In MJ/kg

$$\text{Net CV} = \text{gross CV} - 0.212H - 0.024M$$

In kcal/kg

$$\text{Net CV} = \text{gross CV} - 50.7H - 5.83M$$

In Btu/lb

$$\text{Net CV} = \text{gross CV} - 91.2H - 10.5M$$

where H = hydrogen (%) and M = moisture (%).

As an approximate value, in bituminous coals, the gross as received calorific value can be converted to net as received calorific value by subtracting the following values; 1.09 MJ/kg; 260 kcal/kg; or 470 Btu/lb. It should be noted that, in practice, the USA uses Btu/lb, the UK has used Btu/lb, although British Coal now use GJ/tonne (this is not used elsewhere). South Africa and Australia use MJ/kg, while the rest of the world usually uses kcal/kg. A conversion chart is given in Appendix 3.

2.3.2.2 *Ash fusion temperatures*

How the coal's ash residue reacts at high temperatures can be critical in selecting coals for combustion, i.e. how it will behave in a furnace or boiler.

A laboratory prepared and moulded ash sample (either in the shape of a cone, cube or cylinder) is heated in a mildly reducing or oxidising atmosphere, usually to about 1000–1600 °C.

Four critical temperature points are recognised:

(i)   Initial deformation temperature (IT): the temperature at which the first rounding of the apex or corners of the sample occurs

(ii) Softening (sphere) temperature (ST): the temperature at which the moulded sample has fused down to a lump, the width of which equals its height

(iii) Hemisphere temperature (HT): the temperature at which the mould sample has fused down to a lump the height of which is half of its width

(iv) Fluid temperature (FT): the temperature at which the mould has collapsed as a flattened layer.

Temperatures recorded under a reducing atmosphere are lower or equal to those recorded under an oxidising atmosphere. The IT and FT are the most difficult to reproduce.

The behaviour of ash at high temperatures is a direct response to its chemical composition. Oxides of iron, calcium and potassium act as fluxes and reduce the temperature at which fusion occurs; high aluminium is the most refractory. In stoker boilers a minimum IT of 1200 °C is recommended as lower values lead to excessive clinker formation. In pulverised fuel combustion in dry bottom boilers a minimum IT of 1200 °C and in wet bottom boilers a maximum of 1300 °C are recommended.

2.3.2.3   *Caking tests*

Free swelling index. The free swelling index (FSI) in BSI nomenclature [the crucible swelling number (CSN) in ISO nomenclature] is a measure of the increase in the volume of coal when heated, without the restriction of the exclusion of air. The test is useful in evaluating coals for coking and combustion.

The coal sample is heated for a specific time. When all the volatiles have been liberated, a small coke 'button' remains. The cross section of the button is then compared with a series of standard profiles (Figure 2.7).

Coals with a low swelling index (0–2) are not suitable for coke manufacture. Coals with high swelling numbers (8+) cannot be used by themselves to produce coke as the resultant coke is usually weak and will not support the loads imposed within the blast furnace. However, they are often blended to produce strong coke.

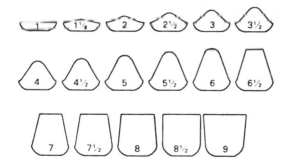

Figure 2.7 Characteristic profiles of coke buttons for different values of the crucible swelling number (free swelling index). From BS 1016, Part 12, 1980 (1989), by permission of the British Standards Institution (see Appendix 1.

Roga index test. The Roga index test again indicates the caking properties of coals. A sample of coal is combined with a standard measure of anthracite and then heated. The resultant button is then tested for mechanical strength, rather than the change in dimensions, by being rotated in a drum for a specific time.

There is a correlation between the Roga index values and the free swelling index values. For example, the Roga index values 0–5 are equivalent to the free swelling index 0–½, Roga index 5–20 to FSI 1–2, 20–45 to 2½–4 and >45 to >4.

2.3.2.4 Coking tests

Gray–King coke type. Finely crushed coal is heated slowly in a sealed tube and the appearance and texture of the coke residue is compared with standards and assigned a letter, the Gray–King coal type. Values range from A, no coking properties at all, to G, where the coal has retained its volume and forms a well fused product. If it swells beyond its volume, it is said to have superior coking properties and is further tested and designated coke type G1–8. Table 2.14 outlines the characteristics of the Gray–King coke types.

Gray–King coke types approximate to free swelling indexes as follows: Gray–King coke type A–B is equivalent to FSI 0–½; C–G2 to 1–4; F–G4 to 4½–6; G3–G9–6½–8; and G7 or above to 8½–9.

Fischer assay. This test is most widely used for testing low rank coals to low temperature carbonisation. The percentages of coke, tar and water driven off by the dry coal are determined, and gas is calculated by subtraction.

Gieseler plastometer. To form coke, coal passes from a solid form through a fluid or plastic state to become a fused porous solid. The temperature range of the fluid phase and the viscosity

Table 2.14   Characteristics for classification of Gray–King coke type. From BS to 1016 Part 12 (1980), by permission of the British Standards Institution

A, B and C: Retains initial cross section Examine for strength			D, E and F Shrunken Examine for strength		
Non-coherent	Badly coherent	Coherent	Moderately hard and shrunken	Hard and very shrunken	Hard, strong and shrunken
Usually in powder form but may contain some pieces which cannot be handled without breaking	In several pieces and some loose powder. Pieces can be picked up but break into powder on handling	Usually in one piece but easily broken; may be in two or three pieces with practically no loose powder; very friable and dull	May be fissured but can be scratched with fingernail and stains the fingers on rubbing the curved surface vigorously; usually dull and black and appearing fritted rather than fused	Usually very fissured, moderate metallic ring when tapped on a hard wooden surface; does not stain the fingers on rubbing; grey or black with slight lustre	May be fissured; moderate metallic ring when tapped on a hard wooden surface; does not stain the fingers on rubbing; cross section well fused and greyish
A	B	C	D	E	F

G Retains initial volume Examine for strength			G₁ to Gₓ Swollen Examine for degree of swelling		
Hard and strong			Slightly swollen	Moderately swollen	Highly swollen
Well fused with a good metallic ring when tapped on a hard wooden surface					G₃ and higher. Guided by swelling number, blend with minimum number of parts of electrode carbon to give a standard G-type coke
G			G₁	G₂	Gₓ

of the fluid are important features when blending coals for coke manufacture.

These parameters are measured by the Gieseler plastometer, in which a coal sample is pressed around a spindle under torque; as the coal reaches its fluid state, the spindle begins to revolve and the rate at which it turns is measured in 'dial divisions per minute' (d.d.m.), which are then plotted against temperature.

Coals with high and low fluidity may be blended to obtain improved coking properties.

Audibert–Arnu dilatometer. Coals shrink during carbonisation and such volume changes that accompany the heating of a coking coal are measured with a dilatometer. Several have been developed for this purpose and the most widely used are the Audibert–Arnu and the Ruhr dilatometers.

Dimensional changes in a coal can be measured as functions of time. While the temperature of the coal is being increased at a constant rate, curves record the length of a coal sample to define the extent of contraction and dilatation, and the temperatures at which these changes begin or end. The properties are significant in determining the volume of coal that can be fed into a coke oven, and also in blending different coals for coke production.

The resultant coke is itself subjected to rigorous testing to confirm its strength and quality for use in commercial operations.

2.3.3 Physical properties of coal

In addition to the chemical and combustion properties of a coal, its evaluation for commercial use requires the determination of several physical properties. These are the coal's density, hardness, grindability, abrasiveness, size distribution and float–sink tests.

2.3.3.1 *Density*

The density of a coal will depend on its rank and mineral matter content. It is an essential factor in converting coal units of volume into units of mass for coal reserves calculation.

Density is determined by the loss of weight incurred when immersed in water. The testing of field samples and core samples in this way gives 'apparent density', because air remains trapped within the coal. True density is determined by crushing the coal and using a standard density bottle or pycnometer. The ease with which apparent densities can be determined in the field is an important facility available to the geologist when describing coal types whose mineral matter contents may fluctuate up to levels where the coal could become uneconomic on quality grounds.

It should be noted that density is not synonymous with specific gravity or relative density; the former is defined as the weight per unit volume given as g/cm^3, whereas specific gravity or relative density is its density with reference to water at 4 °C.

2.3.3.2   Hardness and grindability

In modern commercial operations, coals are required to be crushed to a fine powder (pulverised) before being fed into a boiler. The relative ease with which a coal can be pulverised depends on the strength of the coal and is measured by the Hardgrove grindability index (HGI). This is an index of how easily a coal can be pulverised compared with coals chosen as standards.

Coals with a high HGI are relatively soft and easy to grind. Coals with low HGI values (<50) are hard and difficult to grind into a pulverised product. The HGI varies with coal rank as shown in Figure 2.8.

2.3.3.3   Abrasion index

Coarse mineral matter in coal, particularly quartz, can cause serious abrasion of machinery used to pulverise coal. Coal samples are tested in a mill equipped with four metal blades. The loss in mass of these blades determines the 'abrasion index', and is expressed as mg of metal per kg of coal used.

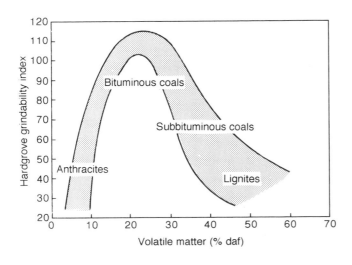

Figure 2.8   Generalised variation of the Hardgrove grindability index with rank. From Berkowitz (1979), by permission of Academic Press

2.3.3.4   *Particle size distribution*

Size distribution in a coal depends on the mining and handling it undergoes, together with its hardness, strength and its inherent degree of fracturing.

The size of coal particles affects coal preparation plant design, which in turn is related to the sized product to be sold. Tests are based on sieve analysis as for other geological materials and the results are expressed in various size-distribution parameters, such as mean particle size and cumulative size percentages.

2.3.3.5   *Float–sink tests*

The particles in coal are of different relative densities and the densities represent the various amounts of mineral matter present. Consequently, the coal preparation process is designed to remove these so that the ash level of the coal is reduced, and so to improve the product to be used or sold.

Coal particles are separated into density fractions by immersion in a series of liquids of known relative density, usually ranging from 1.30 to 2.00. Commencing with the lowest relative density, the sinking fraction is transferred to the next liquid in the series and so on. An example of float–sink analysis is shown in Table 2.15. These results may be plotted graphically as a series of 'washability curves'. These are used to calculate the amount of coal which can be obtained at a particular quality, the density required to effect such a separation and the quality of the discard left behind.

The curves shown in Figure 2.9 are the classic washability curves, i.e. the cumulative floats curve which plots column H values against column G (see Table 2.15), the densimetric curve which plots column G against column C, the cumulative sinks curve which plots column K against column J and the elementary ash curve which plots column G against column E.

Quantitatively, an examination of the cumulative floats curve will give yield values for a given quality, and the densimetric curve will indicate the density at which to wash (i.e. the washing density) to obtain that yield and quality. This can also be calculated in reverse.

The curves can also be used on a more qualitative basis, e.g. if the density value that is required is on the steep part of the densimetric curve, then it will be more difficult to maintain a consistent quality.

The significance of this is that the amounts of coal and mineral matter or discard can be determined for a specific relative density, so enabling a product of specified ash content to be produced using liquids of known relative density. For example,

Table 2.15 Washability data. Reproduced by courtesy of S. Frankland (personal communication, 1991)

Specific gravity			Fractional			Cumulative floats			Cumulative sinks		
A: sink	B: float	C: mid sg [(A + B)/2]	D: wt%	E: ash%	F: ash pts (D*E/100)	G: wt% (sum D)	H: ash% (F/G*100)	I: ash pts (sum F)	J: wt% (sum D)	K: ash% (F/J*100)	L: ash pts (sum F)
—	1.30	—	43.32	3.10	1.34	43.32	3.10	1.34	100.00	27.65	27.65
1.30	1.35	1.325	18.47	6.61	1.22	61.79	4.15	2.56	56.68	46.41	26.31
1.35	1.40	1.375	4.91	11.11	0.55	66.70	4.66	3.11	38.21	65.65	25.09
1.40	1.45	1.425	1.41	15.26	0.22	68.11	4.88	3.32	33.30	73.69	24.54
1.45	1.50	1.475	1.45	19.04	0.28	69.56	5.18	3.60	31.89	76.28	24.32
1.50	1.55	1.525	1.04	21.69	0.23	70.60	5.42	3.83	30.44	79.00	24.05
1.55	1.60	1.575	0.77	28.08	0.22	71.37	5.66	4.04	29.40	81.03	23.82
1.60	1.70	1.650	1.07	34.70	0.37	72.44	6.09	4.41	28.63	82.45	23.61
1.70	1.80	1.750	0.68	45.85	0.31	73.12	6.46	4.73	27.56	84.31	23.24
1.80	2.00	1.900	1.02	55.38	0.56	74.14	7.14	5.29	26.88	85.28	22.92
2.00	—	—	25.86	86.46	22.36	100.00	27.65	27.65	25.86	86.46	22.36

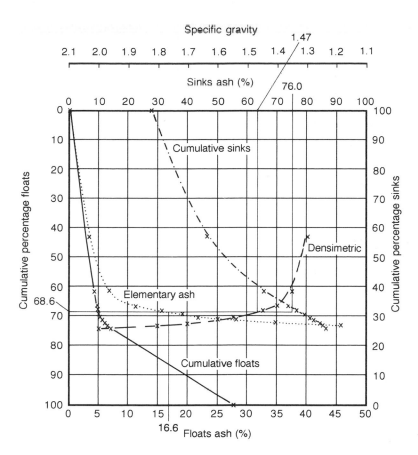

Figure 2.9 Washability curves based on data given in Table 2.15. Reproduced by courtesy of S. Frankland

in Figure 2.9, a coal with an ash content of 5% will give a yield of 68.6%, and a density of 1.47 will be needed to achieve this. The ash of the sinks (reject) will be 76% and the percentage of those ash particles in the floats will be 16.6%. The latter figure is useful to the coal preparation engineer for coal blending calculations.

Sometimes the coal is cleaned to produce two products, a prime product and a lower quality product (the so-called 'middlings'), plus a discard. Classic washability curves cannot be used to calculate the yield or quality of middlings; to determine these values, an M-curve is used (M = Mayer, middlings or mean value curve), as shown in Figure 2.10. The M-curve is produced by plotting column G against column I (Table 2.15). The angle of lines drawn from point A to intersect the abscissa represent the ash value, and the value of the ordinate represents the yield.

For example, in Figure 2.10, to calculate the yield of a prime product of 4.5% ash, a line is drawn from A to intersect the ash axis at 4.5% (F); where this line crosses the M-curve at B, a yield

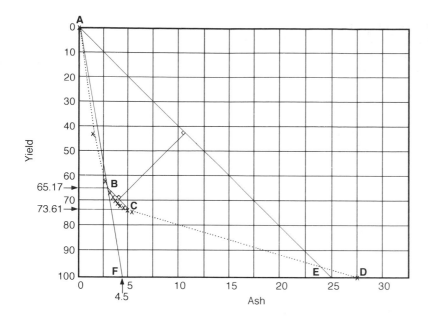

Figure 2.10 Middlings or M curve. Reproduced by courtesy of S. Frankland

of 65.17% can be read off from the yield axis. To calculate the yield of a 25% ash middling, a line is drawn from A to intersect the ash axis at 25% (E). A line is drawn from B parallel to the 25% ash line A–E to intersect the M-curve at C. This gives a total yield of 4.5% ash prime product and 25% ash middlings of 73.61%. Therefore, the yield of 25% ash middlings is 73.61 − 65.17% = 8.44%.

The densimetric curve may also be drawn on the M-curve and used in an identical way to the classical washability curves. Intersects of the densimetric curve with all lines drawn from the yield axis give the densities of separation.

2.3.4   Coal oxidation

Exposure of coals to weathering in the atmosphere, or by oxygenated groundwaters, results in the oxidation of the organic and inorganic constituents of the coal. Oxidation reduces the coal quality by altering the chemical and physical properties of coal. In particular, the calorific value is lowered and caking is eliminated. There is also a loss of floatability during washing of the coal.

The weathering of coal results in its physical breakdown to fine particles, which enhances hydration and hydrolysis. If the coal is structurally fractured, the extent of oxidation will be greater.

The degree of oxidation is determined by the maceral and mineral matter content. Vitrinite is considered by some to be the most readily oxidised maceral; however, Gondwana coals high in inertinite have a high propensity for spontaneous combustion, which indicates a rapid oxidation of the inertinite. In addition, pyrite and other sulphides readily oxidise to sulphates.

All ranks of coal are affected by oxidation and the degree to which this may occur is influenced by the coal rank, pyrite content, climate, hydrology and by the surface area within the coal accessible to oxidation. It is extremely important to establish how much of a coal deposit has been oxidised. The oxidised coal may well be excluded from the tonnage produced.

One direct side effect of oxidation is that of spontaneous combustion. This occurs when the rate of heat generation by oxidation exceeds the rate of heat dissipation. All coals have the propensity to heat spontaneously, but lower rank coals have a greater tendency to self heat. When the temperature of the coal is increased, the rate of oxidation is also increased; it is suggested that the oxidation rate doubles for every 10 °C rise in temperature at least up to 100 °C. It has also been demonstrated that low rank coal produces heat when wetted, and that if dispersed pyrite is present the reactivity is increased tenfold.

Where coals possessing some or all of these properties are stockpiled or loaded into vessels, tests and monitoring are rigorously carried out. Procedures carried out to lessen the heating effects include compaction of the coal, which reduces the oxidation rate, and protection of the coal from heat sources such as solar radiation.

Spontaneous combustion is also a hazard to underground mining. Oxidation of *in situ* coals and coal dust particles produces a potential danger. The following factors contribute to the possibility of combustion: if the coal is thicker than its mined section; steep dips; faulting; and coal outbursts. Where workings are deep, the natural strata temperature is higher and so therefore will be the base temperature of the *in situ* coal. Care in mine design and careful monitoring is needed in these circumstances to minimise heating effects. Potential fires or explosions are costly in terms of labour, materials and time, with a corresponding loss in production. This is particularly true if an area of mine has to be abandoned and sealed off through spontaneous combustion, so losing the potential reserves of coal in that area.

2.4   CLASSIFICATION OF COALS

The field geologist is most concerned with the physical appearance of coals, but nevertheless he or she must be aware that

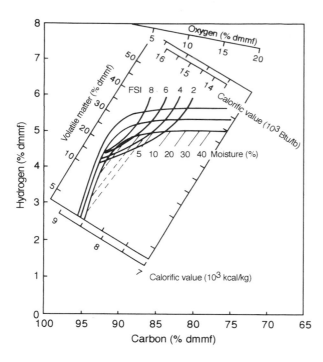

Figure 2.11 Seyler's coal chart. This version shows relationships between elemental composition, volatile matter contents, moisture contents, and caking properties. From Berkowitz (1979), based on Seyler (1899, 1931), by permission of Academic Press

coals have usually been classified according to the coal's chemical properties in relation to their industrial use.

Several classification schemes are in common use; all of these classify humic coals only and refer to particular parameters. These range from the percentage of fixed carbon and volatile matter (on a dry mineral matter free basis), calorific value (on a moist, mineral matter free basis), the caking properties of coal (free swelling index and Roga index) and the coking properties of coal (dilatometer and Gray–King tests).

Coals have been classified either for 'scientific' purposes or for coal use. The scientific classifications use carbon/oxygen or carbon/hydrogen correlations; of these, the best known is that of Seyler (1899, 1931) (Figure 2.11). This classification is applicable, however, only to British Carboniferous coals and takes little account of lower rank coals. It uses the terms 'perhydrous' for hydrogen-rich material and 'subhydrous' for hydrogen-poor samples. These prefixes plus terms for each rank are given in Table 2.16.

The principal commercial classifications of coal in current use include that of the ASTM 1977 classification, which is used on a worldwide basis (see Appendix 1). This is based on two coal properties, the fixed carbon values and the calorific values (on a d.m.m.f. basis). Further classification is given for those coals with agglomerating or coking properties (Table 2.17). Coals with atypical properties are not allowed for in this classification.

Table 2.16 Parameters used in Seyler's coal classification. From Ward (1984), by permission of Blackwell Scientific Publications. Based on Seyler (1899, 1931)

Genus	Hydrogen (%)	Anthracite (>93.3)	Carbonaceous (93.3–91.2)	Bituminous Meta- (91.2–89.0)	Bituminous Ortho- (89.0–87.0)	Bituminous Para- (87.0–84.0)	Lignitous Meta- (84–85)	Lignitous Ortho- (80–75)
Per-bituminous	>5.8	—	—	Per-bituminous (per-meta-bituminous)	Per-bituminous (per-ortho-bituminous)	Per-bituminous (per-para bituminous)	Per-lignitous	
Bituminous	5–5.8	—	Pseudo-bituminous species	Meta-bituminous	Ortho-bituminous	Para-bituminous	Lignitous (meta, ortho)	
Semi-bituminous	4.5–5.0	—	Semi-bituminous species (ortho-semi-bituminous)	Subbituminous (sub-meta-bituminous)	Subbituminous sub-ortho-bituminous)	Subbituminous	Sub-lignitous (meta, ortho)	
Carbonaceous	4.0–4.5	Semi-anthracitic species Dry steam coal	Carbonaceous species (ortho-carbonaceous)	Pseudo-carbonaceous (sub-meta-bituminous)	Pseudo-carbonaceous (sub-ortho-bituminous)	Pseudo-carbonaceous (sub-para-bituminous)		
Anthracitic	<4	Ortho-anthracite True anthracite	Pseudo-anthracite (sub-carbonaceous)	Pseudo-anthracite (sub-meta-bituminous)	Pseudo-anthracite (sub-ortho-bituminous)	Pseudo-anthracite (sub-para-bituminous)		

Class (% carbon)

Table 2.17   ASTM classification of coals by rank. Copyright ASTM. Reprinted with permission from ASTM D388-1977 (see Appendix 1). This classification does not include a few coals, principally non-banded varieties, which have unusual physical and chemical properties and which come within the limits of fixed carbon or calorific value of the high-volatile bituminous and subbituminous ranks. All of these coals either contain less than 48% d.m.m.f. fixed carbon or have more than 15 000 Btu/lb⁻¹ m.m.m.f.*

Class	Group	Abbreviation	Fixed carbon limits (%d.m.m.f.)		Volatile matter limits (%d.m.m.f.)		Calorific value limits Btu/lb⁻¹ m.m.m.f.		Agglomerating character
			Equal to or greater than	Less than	Greater than	Equal to or less than	Equal to or greater than	Less than	
I. Anthracite	1. Meta-anthracite	ma	98	—	—	2	—	—	Non-agglomerating
	2. Anthracite	an	92	98	2	8	—	—	
	3. Semi-anthracite†	sa	86	92	8	14	—	—	
II. Bituminous	1. Low volatile bituminous coal	lvb	78	86	14	22	—	—	
	2. Medium volatile bituminous coal	mvb	69	78	22	31	—	—	
	3. High volatile A bituminous coal	hvAb	—	69	31	—	14 000‡	—	Commonly agglomerating§
	4. High volatile B bituminous coal	hvBb	—	—	—	—	13 000‡	14 000	
	5. High volatile C bituminous coal	hvCb	—	—	—	—	11 500 / 10 500	13 000 / 11 500	Agglomerating
III. Subbituminous	1. Subbituminous A coal	subA	—	—	—	—	10 500	11 500	Non-agglomerating
	2. Subbituminous B coal	subB	—	—	—	—	9 500	10 500	
	3. Subbituminous C coal	subC	—	—	—	—	8 300	9 500	
IV. Lignitic	1. Lignite A	ligA	—	—	—	—	6 300	8 300	
	2. Lignite B	ligB	—	—	—	—	—	6 300	

*Moist, mineral-matter-free; moist refers to coal containing its natural inherent moisture but not including visible water on the surface of the coal.
†If agglomerating, classify in low volatile group of the bituminous class.
‡Coals having 69% or more fixed carbon on the d.m.m.f. basis are classified according to fixed carbon, regardless of calorific value.
§It is recognised that there may be non-agglomerating varieties in these groups of the bituminous class, and there are notable exceptions in high volatile C bituminous group.

The British classification system has been devised by British Coal (1964) and is shown in Table 2.18. It uses a three-figure numeral code to classify bituminous and anthracite coals. The first two digits are based on the amount of volatile matter in the coal (on a d.m.m.f. basis) and the third digit is based on the Grey–King assay value. Coals with less than 19.6% volatile matter (d.m.m.f.) are classified by this property alone. It should be noted that coals with ash contents greater than 10% must be cleaned before analysis. Coals that have been thermally altered by igneous intrusions have the suffix H added to the coal code, and coals that have been oxidised by weathering may be distinguished by adding the suffix W to the coal code.

In Europe, the International Hard Coal Classification, published by the United Nations Economic Commission for Europe (1956) and approved by the ISO, uses a series of numbers to illustrate the chemical and physical characteristics which determine the use of the coal. This classification is widely used for industrial purposes. Each coal is described by a three-figure number. The primary classification parameters are volatile matter (up to 33% d.a.f.) and calorific value (for coals above 33% volatile matter d.a.f.). These create a series of coal classes (first digit), each of which is divided into a group (second digit) on the basis of caking characteristics (defined in terms of the FSI or the Roga index). Each group is further divided into subgroups (third digit) characterised by their coking properties (as measured by the Gray–King assay or a standard dilatometer). This classification is shown in Table 2.19.

The Australian standard coal classification (SAA, 1987) for hard coals again assigns a multi-digit number to determine coal type (see Appendix 1). The first digit represents the volatile matter for coals with less than 33% volatile matter (d.m.m.f.) and the gross calorific value (d.a.f.) for other coals. The second digit is the FSI of the coal, the third digit is the Gray–King assay value and the fourth digit (given in parentheses) is based on the ash content (dry basis) of the coal (Table 2.20).

In South Africa, coals are divided for commercial purposes into three broad classes on the basis of volatile matter (d.a.f.). These are South African anthracite, semi-anthracite and steam coal. Coals of each class are graded on the basis of calorific value (a.d.), ash (a.d.) and ash fusibility.

The United Nations Economic Commission for Europe (1956) has developed an international classification for brown coals and lignites. Such coals are defined as containing less than 5700 kcal/kg (10 250 Btu/lb) on a moist, ash-free basis, and correspond to the lignites and subbituminous B and C coals of the ASTM classification. The classification parameters used are classes of bed moisture content (first and second digits) and groups of low

Table 2.18 Coal classification system used by British Coal (revision of 1964). Coals with ash of over 10% must be cleaned before analysis for classification to give a maximum yield of coal with ash of 10% or less. Reproduced from British Coal (1964) by permission

Coal Rank Code			Volatile Matter (d.m.m.f.) (per cent.)	Gray–King Coke Type*	General description
Main Class(es)	Class	Subclass			
100	101†		Under 9.1	A	Anthracites
	102†		Under 6.1	A	
			6.1–9.0		
200	201		9.1–19.5	A–G8	Low volatile steam coals
			9.1–13.5	A–C	Dry steam coals
		201a	9.1–11.5	A–B	
		201b	11.6–13.5	B–C	
	202		13.6–15.0	B–G	Coking steam coals
	203		15.1–17.0	E–G4	
	204		17.1–19.5	G1–G8	
300	301		19.6–32.0	A–G9 and over	Medium volatile coals
			19.6–32.0	G4 and over	Prime coking coals
		301a	19.6–27.5	G4 and over	
		301b	27.6–32.0	G4 and over	
	302		19.6–32.0	G–G3	Medium volatile, medium caking or weakly caking coals
	303		19.6–32.0	A–F	Medium volatile, weakly caking to non-caking coals

		Volatile matter	A–G9 and over	High volatile coals
400–900		Over 32.0	A–G9 and over	High volatile coals
400	401	Over 32.0	G9 and over	High volatile, very strongly caking coals
	402	32.1–36.0 / Over 36.0	G9 and over	
500	501	Over 32.0	G5–G8	High volatile, strongly caking coals
	502	32.1–36.0 / Over 36.0	G5–G8	
600	601	Over 32.0	G1–G4	High volatile, medium caking coals
	602	32.1–36.0 / Over 36.0	G1–G4	
700	701	Over 32.0	E–G	High volatile, weakly caking coals
	702	32.1–36.0 / Over 36.0	E–G	
800	801	Over 32.0	C–D	High volatile, very weakly caking coals
	802	32.1–36.0 / Over 36.0	C–D	
900	901	Over 32.0	A–B	High volatile, non-caking coals
	902	32.1–36.0 / Over 36.0	A–B	

*Coals with volatile matter of less than 19.6% are classified by using the parameter of volatile matter alone; the Gray–King coke types quoted for these coals indicate the general ranges found in practice and are not criteria for classification.

†To divide anthracites into two classes, it is sometimes convenient to use a hydrogen content of 3.35% (d.m.m.f.) instead of a volatile matter of 6.0% as the limiting criterion. In the original Coal Survey rank coding system the anthracites were divided into four classes then designated 101, 102, 103 and 104. Although the present division into two classes satisfies most requirements it may sometimes be necessary to recognise more than two classes.

Notes:
(1) Coals that have been affected by igneous intrusions ('heat-altered' coals) occur mainly in classes 100, 200 and 300, and when recognised should be distinguished by adding the suffix H to the coal rank code, e.g. 102H, 201bH.
(2) Coals that have been oxidised by weathering may occur in any class and when recognised should be distinguished by adding the suffix W to the coal rank code, e.g. 801W.

Table 2.19 International Classification of hard coals. UNECE (1956). Reproduced by permission of the United Nations Economic Commission for Europe

Code numbers

First figure of the code number indicates the class of the coal, determined by volatile matter content up to 33% VM and by calorific parameter above 33% VM
Second figure indicates the group of coal, determined by caking properties
Third figure indicates the subgroup, determined by coking properties

Group no.	Free swelling index	Roga index	Subgroup no.	0	1	2	3	4	5	6	7	8	9	Dilatometer	Gray-King
3	>4	>45	5	—	—	—	—	435	535	635	—	—	—	>140	>G8
			4	—	—	—	334	434	534	634	734	—	—	>50–140	G5–G8
			3	—	—	—	333	433	533	633	733	—	—	>0–50	G1–G4
			2	—	—	—	332 a / 332 b	432	532	632	732	832	—	≤0	E–G
2	2½–4	>20–45	3	—	—	—	323	423	523	623	723	823	—	>0–50	G1–G4
			2	—	—	—	322	422	522	622	722	822	—	≤0	E–G
			1	—	—	—	321	421	521	621	721	821	—	Contraction only	B–D
1	1–2	>5–20	2	—	—	212	312	412	512	612	712	812	—	≤0	E–G
			1	—	—	211	311	411	511	611	711	811	—	Contraction only	B–D
0	0–½	0–5	0	000	100 (A | B)	200	300	400	500	600	700	800	900	Non-softening	A

Class number† →	0	1	2	3	4	5	6	7	8	9
Volatile matter (dry, ash-free) →	0–3	>3–10 (>3–6.5 / >6.5–10)	>10–14	>14–20	>20–28	>28–33	>33	>33	>33	>33
Calorific parameters* →	—	—	—	—	—	—	>13 950	>12 960– 13 950	>10 980– 12 960	>10 260– 10 980

Groups (determined by caking properties); Alternative group parameters

Subgroups (determined by coking properties); Subgroup no.; Alternative subgroup parameters

As an indication the following classes have an approximate volatile matter content of:
Class 6 33–41%
Class 7 33–44%
Class 8 35–50%
Class 9 42–50%

*Gross calorific value on moist, ash-free basis (30 °C, 96% relative humidity) Btu/lb.
†Classes determined by volatile matter (VM) up to 33% VM and by calorific parameter above 33% VM.
Notes:
(1) Where the ash content of coal is too high to allow classification according to the present system, it must be reduced by the laboratory float and sink method (or any other appropriate means). The specific gravity selected for flotation should allow a maximum yield of coal with 5–10% ash.
(2) 332(a) >14–16% volatile matter; 332(b) >16–20% volatile matter.

Table 2.20 Australian Classification of Hard Coal. From Ward (1984), by permission of Blackwell Scientific Publications. Based on Australian Standard 2096–1987 (see Appendix 1)

	Value	Volatile matter (%d.m.m.f.)	Gross calorific value (d.a.f.) (MJ/kg^{-1})
1st digit (coal class)	1	<10.0	
	2	10.1–14.0	
	3	14.1–20.0	
	4A	20.1–24.0	
	4B	24.1–28.0	
	5	28.1–33.0	
	6	33–41*	>33.82
	7	33–44*	32.02–33.82
	8	35–50*	28.43–32.02
	9	42–50*	27.08–28.42

	Value	Crucible swelling no.
2nd digit (coal group)	0	0–½
	1	1–2
	2	2½–4
	3	4½–6
	4	6½–9

	Value	Gray–King coke type
3rd digit (coal subgroup)	0	A
	1	B–D
	2	E–G
	3	G1–G4
	4	G5–G8
	5	G9–

	Value	Ash [dry basis (%)]
4th digit (ash number)	(0)	<4.0
	(1)	4.1–8.0
	(2)	8.1–12.0
	(3)	12.1–16.0
	(4)	16.1–20.0
	(5)	20.1–24.0
	(6)	24.1–28.0
	(7)	28.1–32.0
	(8)	>32.0

*Values for information only.

Table 2.21   International classification of brown coals and lignite. UNECE (1957). Reproduced by permission of the United Nations Economic Commission for Europe

	Classes		Groups
Class	Total moisture ash-free (%)	Group	Tar yield ash-free (%)
10	<20	00	<10
11	20–30	10	10–15
12	30–40	20	15–20
13	40–50	30	20–25
14	50–60	40	>25
15	60–70		

temperature tar yields on a dry, ash-free basis (third and fourth digits) as outlined in Table 2.21. The moisture parameter indicates its value as a fuel and the tar yield its value in chemical processing.

The brown coals and lignites are divided into six classes according to moisture content calculated to the ash-free basis. The classes are numbered 10–15, following numerically the hard coal classification shown in Table 2.19. These six classes are further subdivided into five groups according to tar yield on the dry ash-free basis. This classification is then expressed as a code number consisting of four digits.

A variation on this classification is the ISO 2960 (1974) classification by type for brown coals and lignites (see Appendix 1 for list of ISO Standards). Again this classification is based on total

Table 2.22   ISO 2950: (1974) classification of brown coals and lignites by types based on total moisture content and tar yield (see Appendix 1)

	Classes		Groups
Class	Total moisture content of run-of-mine coal ash-free basis (%)	Group	Tar yield dry, ash-free basis (%)
1	<20	0	<10
2	20–30	1	10–15
3	30–40	2	15–20
4	40–50	3	20–25
5	50–60	4	>25
6	60–70		

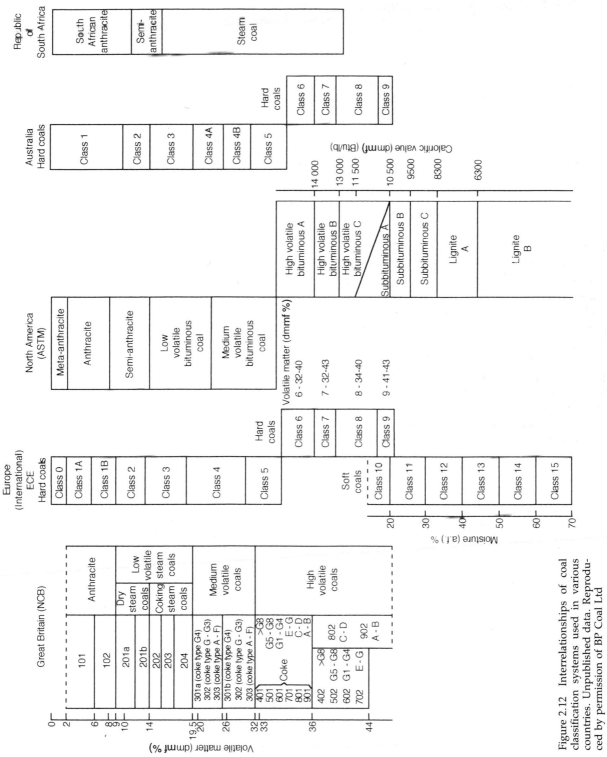

Figure 2.12 Interrelationships of coal classification systems used in various countries. Unpublished data. Reproduced by permission of BP Coal Ltd

moisture content and tar yield. In this system, total moisture is
determined by the standard ISO 1015 for brown coals and
lignites (determination of moisture content, direct volumetric
method). Classes 1–6 correspond to classes 10–15. Tar yield is
determined by ISO 647 for brown coals and lignites (determination of yields of tar, water, gas and coke residue by low temperature distillation). Group numbers 0–4 correspond to groups 00–
40. Table 2.22 gives the classes and groups used in this classification.

The interrelationships of the various coal classification systems outlined here are shown in Figure 2.12.

Chapter 3
Origin of coal

3.1 INTRODUCTION

Sedimentary sequences containing coal or peat beds are found throughout the world and range in age from Upper Palaeozoic to Recent. Coals are the result of the accumulation of vegetable debris in a specialised environment of deposition. Such accumulations have been affected by synsedimentary and post-sedimentary influences to produce coals of various ranks and various degrees of structural complexity, the two being closely interlinked.

Remarkable similarities exist in coal-bearing sequences, due for the most part to the particular sedimentary associations required to generate and preserve coals. Sequences of vastly different ages from areas geographically separate have a similar lithological framework, and can react in similar manners structurally.

3.2 SEDIMENTATION OF COAL AND COAL-BEARING SEQUENCES

During the last 25 years, interest has grown rapidly in the study of sedimentological processes, particularly those characteristic of fluviatile and deltaic environments. It is these in particular that have been closely identified with coal-bearing sequences.

Today the geologist is faced with an enormous amount of published work covering the physical processes of sedimentation and with numerous case histories to illustrate these. In the light of this a complete survey of the sedimentation of coal-bearing sequences is considered inappropriate to this book.

The coal geologist does need to give consideration to the recognition of the principal environments of deposition, and to the recent changes in emphasis regarding those physical processes required to produce coals of economic value. In addition, an understanding of the shape, morphology and quality of coal seams is of fundamental significance for the future planning and mining of coals.

3.2.1   Depositional models

The recognition of depositional models to explain the origin of coal-bearing sequences and their relationship to surrounding sediments has been achieved by a comparison of the environ-

Table 3.1   Sedimentary features used to identify depositional environments. From Horne *et al.* (1979) by permission of the University of South Carolina

Recognition characteristics	Fluvial and upper delta plain*	Transitional lower delta plain*	Lower delta plain*	Back-barrier*	Barrier*
I Coarsening upwards					
A Shale and siltstone sequences	2–3	2	1	2–1	3–2
1 Greater than 50 ft	4	3–4	2–1	2–1	3–2
2 5–25 ft	2–3	2–1	2–1	2–1	3–2
B Sandstone sequences	3–4	3–2	2–1	2	2–1
1 Greater than 50 ft	4	4	2–1	3	2–1
2 5–25 ft	3	3–2	2–1	2	2
II Channel deposits					
A Fine grained abandoned fill	3	2–3	1–2	2	3–2
1 Clay and silt	3	2–3	1–2	2	3–2
2 Organic debris	3	2–3	1–2	2–3	3
B Active sandstone fill	1	2	2–3	2–3	2
1 Fine grained	2	2	2–3	2–3	2
2 Medium and coarse grained	1	2–3	3	3	2–3
3 Pebble lags	1	1	2	2–3	3–2
4 Coal spars	1	1	2	2–3	3–2
III Contacts					
A Abrupt (scour)	1	1	2	2	2–1
B Gradational	2–3	2	2–1	2	2
IV Bedding					
A Cross beds	1	1	1	1–2	1–2
1 Ripples	2	2–1	1	1	1
2 Ripple drift	2–1	2	2–3	3–2	3–2
3 Trough crossbeds	1	1–2	2–1	2	2–1
4 Graded beds	3	3	2–1	3–2	3–2
5 Point bar accretion	1	2	3–4	3–4	3–4
6 Irregular bedding	1	2	3–2	3–2	3–2
V Levee deposits					
A Irregularly interbedded sandstones and shales, rooted	1	1–2	3–2	3	4
VI Mineralogy of sandstones					
A Lithic graywacke	1	1	1–2	3	3
B Orthoquartzites	4	4	4–3	1–2	1
VII Fossils					
A Marine	4	3–2	2–1	1–2	1–2
B Brackish	3	2	2	2–3	2–3
C Fresh	2–3	3–2	3–4	4	4
D Burrow	3	2	1	1	1

*(1)Abundant; (2) common; (3) rare; and (4) not present.

ments under which modern peats are formed and ancient sequences containing coals.

There is no model available that can act as a panacea for all coal deposits. However, a large number of coal deposits have been identified with particular depositional regimes. The terminology used to describe sedimentary environments and structures is that in use in modern published work, a selection of which is listed in the bibliography.

The traditional depositional model used by numerous workers is based on the 'cyclothem', a series of lithotypes occurring in repeated 'cycles'. More recently this concept has been modified to a model that relates lateral and vertical sequential changes to depositional settings that have been recognised in modern fluvial, deltaic and coastal barrier systems.

This model is based on the work carried out in the USA by Horne, Ferm, Caruccio and Baganz in a series of studies in the 1970s. The sequences or lithofacies are characterised by the sedimentary features listed in Table 3.1.

3.2.1.1 Coastal barrier and back-barrier facies

The coastal end of the depositional model is characterised by clean barrier sandstones, which, in a seaward direction, become finer grained and intercalate with red and green calcareous shales and carbonate rocks, the latter containing marine faunas. Landwards they grade into dark grey lagoonal shales with brackish water faunas, and into marginal swamp areas on which vegetation was established. The barrier sandstones have been constantly reworked and are therefore more quartzose than those sandstones in surrounding environments with the same source area.

They exhibit a variety of bedding styles: firstly, extensive sheets of plane-bedded sandstones with rippled and burrowed upper surfaces, interpreted as storm washover sands; secondly, wedge-shaped bodies that extend landward, can attain thicknesses of up to 6 m, and contain landward dipping planar and trough cross beds, interpreted as flood-tide delta deposits; and thirdly, channel-fill sandstones which may scour to depths of over 10 m into the underlying sediments, interpreted as tidal channel deposits.

A depositional reconstruction is shown in Figure 3.1 based on studies carried out in the USA. The lagoonal back-barrier environment is characterised by upwards coarsening, organic-rich grey shales and siltstones overlain by thin and discontinuous coals. This sequence exhibits extensive bioturbation zones, together with bands and concretions of chemically precipitated iron carbonate (sideritic ironstone). The extent of such

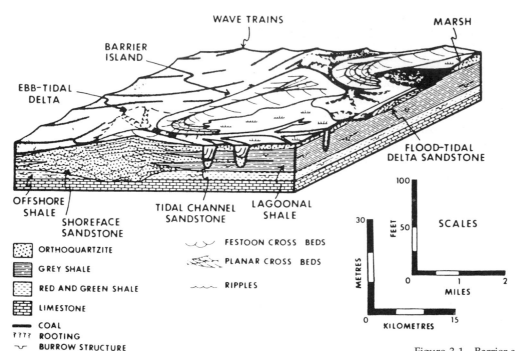

Figure 3.1   Barrier and back-barrier environments including tidal channels and flood-tidal deltas, based on exposures in Kentucky, USA. From Horne *et al.* (1979), by permission of the University of South Carolina

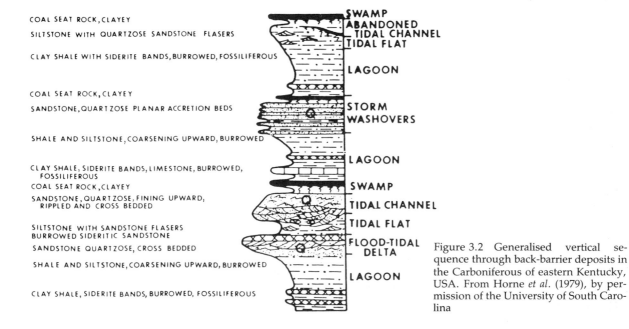

Figure 3.2   Generalised vertical sequence through back-barrier deposits in the Carboniferous of eastern Kentucky, USA. From Horne *et al.* (1979), by permission of the University of South Carolina

sequences is considered to be of the order of 20–30 m in thickness and 5–25 km in width. A typical vertical sequence of back-barrier deposition is shown in Figure 3.2.

3.2.1.2 *Lower delta plain facies*

Lower delta plain deposites are dominated by coarsening upwards sequences of mudstone and siltstone, ranging from 15 to 55 m in thickness and 8 to 110 km in lateral extent. The lower part of these sequences are characterised by dark grey to black mudstones with irregularly distributed limestones and siderite [Figure 3.3(A)].

Sandstones are common in the upper part, reflecting the increasing energy of the shallow water as the bay fills with sediment. Where the bays have filled sufficiently to allow plant growth, coals have formed. Where the bays did not fill completely, bioturbated, siderite-cemented sandstones and siltstones have formed. This upwards coarsening pattern is interrupted in many areas by crevasse-splays [Figure 3.3(B)]. In the Carboniferous of the USA, crevasse-splay deposits can be more than 10 m in thickness and 30 m to 8 km wide.

In many instances, a transitional lower delta plain sequence is characteristic, featuring alternations of channel, interdistributary bay and crevasse-splay deposits. A depositional reconstruction is shown in Figure 3.4(A) and a generalised vertical sequence in Figure 3.4(B).

Overlying and laterally equivalent to the bay-fill sequences are thick lithic sandstones up to 25 m in thickness and up to 5 km in width. These are interpreted as distributary mouth bar deposits; they are widest at the base and have gradational contacts. They coarsen upwards and towards the middle of the sand body. In some places, fining-upwards sequences are developed on the top of the distributary mouth bar and bay-fill deposits. These distributary channel-fill deposits have an irregular sharp basal contact, produced by scouring of the underlying sediments. At the base, pebble and coal-fragment lag deposits are common.

As a result of the rapid abandonment of distributaries, fine grained mudstone fills are common in lower delta plain deposits. They represent silt and organic debris which has settled from suspension in the abandoned distributary. In some areas, thick organic accumulations filled these channels, resulting in the formation of lenticular coals. Apart from those formed in the abandoned channels, coals are generally relatively thin and widespread. Such coals are oriented parallel to the distributary patterns.

Coal
Seat rock, clayey
Sandstone, fine to medium grained multi-
   directional planar and festoon cross beds
Sandstone, fine grained, rippled
Sandstone, fine grained, graded beds
Sandstone, flow rolls
Sandstone, fine grained, flaser bedded
   and siltstone

Silty Shale and Siltstone with calcareous
   concretions thin-bedded, burrowed,
   occasional fossil

Clay Shale with siderite bands, burrowed,
   fossiliferous

(A)

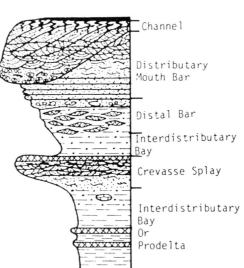

Distributary
Mouth Bar

Distal Bar

Interdistributary
Bay
Or
Prodelta

SAND ┊ SILT ┊ CLAY

Coal
Rooted Sandstone
Sandstone, fine grained, climbing ripples
Sandstone, fine to medium grained
Sandstone, medium grained, festoon cross beds
Conglomerate Lag, siderite pebble, coal spar
Sandstone, Siltstone, graded beds

Sandstone, flow rolls
Sandstone, Siltstone, flaser bedded
Siltstone and Silty Shale thin bedded,
   burrowed
Burrowed sideritic Sandstone
Sandstone, fine grained
Sandstone, fine grained, rippled

Silty Shale and Siltstone with calcareous
   concretions, thin-bedded, burrowed

Clay Shale with siderite bands burrowed,
   fossiliferous

(B)

Channel

Distributary
Mouth Bar

Distal Bar
Interdistributary
Bay
Crevasse Splay

Interdistributary
Bay
Or
Prodelta

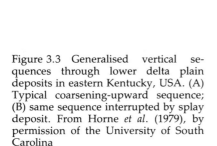

Figure 3.3 Generalised vertical sequences through lower delta plain
deposits in eastern Kentucky, USA. (A)
Typical coarsening-upward sequence;
(B) same sequence interrupted by splay
deposit. From Horne *et al.* (1979), by
permission of the University of South
Carolina

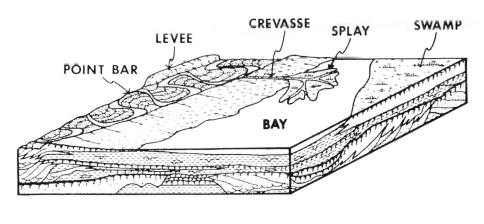

SANDSTONE

SANDSTONE AND SILTSTONE

SHALE

COAL

ROOTING

BURROW STRUCTURE

MARINE FOSSIL

BEDDING PLANES

TROUGH CROSS BEDS

SCALES

(A)

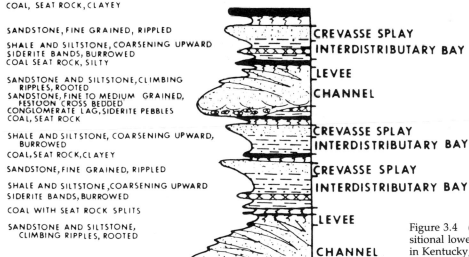

COAL, SEAT ROCK, CLAYEY

SANDSTONE, FINE GRAINED, RIPPLED

SHALE AND SILTSTONE, COARSENING UPWARD
SIDERITE BANDS, BURROWED
COAL SEAT ROCK, SILTY

SANDSTONE AND SILTSTONE, CLIMBING
   RIPPLES, ROOTED
SANDSTONE, FINE TO MEDIUM GRAINED,
   FESTOON CROSS BEDDED
CONGLOMERATE LAG, SIDERITE PEBBLES
COAL, SEAT ROCK

SHALE AND SILTSTONE, COARSENING UPWARD,
   BURROWED
COAL, SEAT ROCK, CLAYEY

SANDSTONE, FINE GRAINED, RIPPLED

SHALE AND SILTSTONE, COARSENING UPWARD
SIDERITE BANDS, BURROWED

COAL WITH SEAT ROCK SPLITS

SANDSTONE AND SILTSTONE,
   CLIMBING RIPPLES, ROOTED

SANDSTONE, FINE TO MEDIUM GRAINED,
   FESTOON CROSS BEDDED
CLAY SHALE, BURROWED

COAL

CREVASSE SPLAY
INTERDISTRIBUTARY BAY

LEVEE

CHANNEL

CREVASSE SPLAY
INTERDISTRIBUTARY BAY

CREVASSE SPLAY
INTERDISTRIBUTARY BAY

LEVEE

CHANNEL

Figure 3.4   (A) Reconstruction of transitional lower delta plain environments in Kentucky, USA. (B) Generalised vertical sequence through transitional lower delta plain deposits of eastern Kentucky and southern West Virginia, USA. From Horne *et al.* (1979), by permission of the University of South Carolina

(B)

3.2.1.3 *Upper delta and alluvial plain facies*

In contrast to the thick fine grained sequences of the lower delta plain facies, upper delta plain deposits are dominated by linear, lenticular sandstone bodies up to 25 m thick and 11 km wide. These sandstones have scoured bases and pass laterally in the upper part into grey shales, siltstones and coals. The sandstones fine upwards with abundant pebble conglomerates, and coal clasts in the lower part. The sandstones are characterised by massive bedding and are overlain by siltstones.

These sandstone bodies widen upwards in cross section and are considered to have been deposited in the channels and on the flanks of streams that migrated across the upper delta plain [Figure 3.5(A)].

Coal seams in the upper delta plain facies may be more than 10 m in thickness, but are of limited lateral extent. Figure 3.5(B) illustrates a vertical sequence of upper delta plain facies from eastern Kentucky and southern West Virginia, USA.

Between the upper and lower delta plains, a transition zone exhibits characteristics of the two sequences. This zone consists of a widespread platform on which peat mires were formed. This platform was cut by numerous channels and the sequence

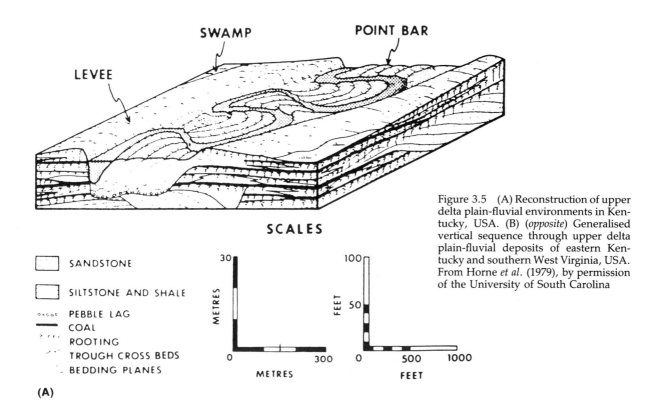

SWAMP   POINT BAR   LEVEE

SCALES

SANDSTONE

SILTSTONE AND SHALE

PEBBLE LAG

COAL

ROOTING

TROUGH CROSS BEDS

BEDDING PLANES

METRES   30   0   300   METRES

FEET   100   50   0   500   1000   FEET

(A)

Figure 3.5   (A) Reconstruction of upper delta plain-fluvial environments in Kentucky, USA. (B) (*opposite*) Generalised vertical sequence through upper delta plain-fluvial deposits of eastern Kentucky and southern West Virginia, USA. From Horne *et al.* (1979), by permission of the University of South Carolina

disrupted by crevasse-splay deposits. The coals formed on the platform are thicker and more widespread than the coals of the lower delta plain; such a sequence is shown in Figure 3.4(B).

3.2.2 Modern peat analogues

Most facies studies used to construct depositional models have simply interpreted coals as the product of deposition in 'swamps'. Conversely, detailed studies of coal itself have concentrated on petrology and maceral analysis with little consideration for the surrounding sediment. Depositional models for peat/coal facies are now receiving much closer attention, particularly as the resultant coal quality is of prime importance for economic exploitation.

About 3% of the earth's surface is covered by peat. A great variety of peats form when waterlogging of vegetation is caused by groundwater. However, of greater extent but less varied are peats dependent on precipitation, which are known as ombrotrophic peats. Workers now use the term 'mire' to cover all non-saline wetlands in which peat accumulation may occur.

For a mire to build up and for peat to accumulate, the following equation must balance:

Inflow + precipitation = outflow + evapotranspiration + retention

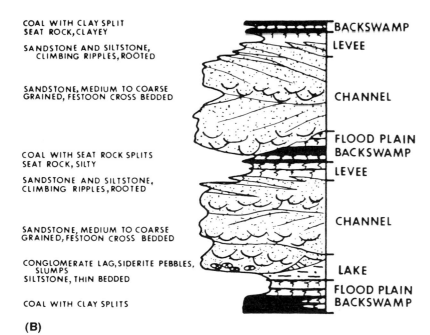

COAL WITH CLAY SPLIT
SEAT ROCK, CLAYEY — BACKSWAMP

SANDSTONE AND SILTSTONE,
CLIMBING RIPPLES, ROOTED — LEVEE

SANDSTONE, MEDIUM TO COARSE
GRAINED, FESTOON CROSS BEDDED — CHANNEL

FLOOD PLAIN
BACKSWAMP

COAL WITH SEAT ROCK SPLITS
SEAT ROCK, SILTY

SANDSTONE AND SILTSTONE,
CLIMBING RIPPLES, ROOTED — LEVEE

SANDSTONE, MEDIUM TO COARSE
GRAINED, FESTOON CROSS BEDDED — CHANNEL

CONGLOMERATE LAG, SIDERITE PEBBLES,
SLUMPS — LAKE
SILTSTONE, THIN BEDDED

FLOOD PLAIN
BACKSWAMP

COAL WITH CLAY SPLITS

(B)

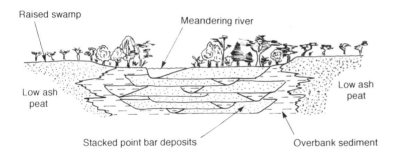

Figure 3.7   Theoretical model of fluvial architecture in area of raised swamps. The elevated swamp restricts overbank flooding and prevents avulsion, leading to the development of stacked channel sandstones. From McCabe (1984), by permission of Blackwell Scientific Publications

3.2.3   Facies correlation

The recognition of the variety of facies types described in the facies model is only of real value to the coal geologist if their lateral and vertical relationships can be determined and correlated to produce the geometry of lithotypes within a study area.

To achieve this, examination of surface exposures, both natural and man-made, and borehole data is required to establish the particular lithological sequence present at each data point. It is the correlation between data points that is critical to the understanding of the patterns of coal development and preservation in any given area of interest.

It is an unfortunate fact that for a great number of coal-bearing sequences, good recognisable and widespread marker horizons are rare. In part this stems from the very localised patterns of deposition within many coal-forming environments. However, some distinctive deposits may be present; for example, marine mudstones, usually overlying a coal seam, may contain marine or brackish-marine fauna and may also have a particular geochemical or geophysical profile. In areas where contemporary volcanic activity took place during coal deposition, deposits of fine grained volcanic ash intercalated with coal-bearing sediments produce widespread 'tonstein' horizons, which also have a distinctive geochemical or geophysical signature, or both.

Other less reliable lithotypes can be used, certainly on a local scale (for example, within a mine lease area), such as sandstone complexes, freshwater limestones with their associated fauna, and the coal seams themselves.

Lithotype correlation from boreholes and surface exposures from an area in South Wales, UK, is shown in Figure 3.8. The marine horizon is used as the principal means of correlation, and the sequence can be seen to correlate reasonably well both above and below this, although there are variations in the presence or absence of erosive sandstone members below the marine horizon. Similar lithotype correlations are shown in

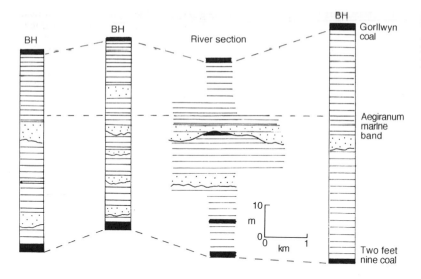

Figure 3.8 Lithotype correlation in the Upper Carboniferous in the northern part of the South Wales Coalfield, UK using boreholes and surface exposures. From Thomas (1967), unpublished

Figure 3.9 from the USA and Figure 3.10 from India, the latter illustrated by the much used 'fence' diagram presentation.

In modern coal sequence correlation, increasing use is being made of downhole geophysical logs of boreholes. The individual profile of each borehole can be compared with its neighbouring boreholes. An example of Canadian coal-bearing sequences showing the correlation of lithotypes with their geophysical profiles is shown in Figure 3.11. Details of the variety of geophysical logs used in coal sequence correlation are described in Chapter 7.

Once the distribution pattern of the various lithotypes present in an area has been established, it may be possible to predict the likely sequence in adjacent areas. This is particularly important for neighbouring areas with proven coal reserves, which may be concealed beneath younger deposits, or which may lack quantitative geological data. If it is likely that coal is developed at an economic thickness and depth, then a facies study of the known area may guide predictions for drill sites in adjacent areas. In the early stages of exploration this can be an important tool for the coal geologist to deploy.

In the example shown in Figure 3.12, Area 1 has a known distribution pattern of coal and non-coal deposits, determined from the correlation of the boreholes present. Area 2 is as yet unexplored, but from the data available in Area 1, together with an appraisal of the topography in Area 2, it is likely that coal A will be present at a similar depth and thickness, at least in that part closest to the nearest known data points in Area 1, i.e. at points 2a, 2b, 2c and 2d. If Area 2 is considered for

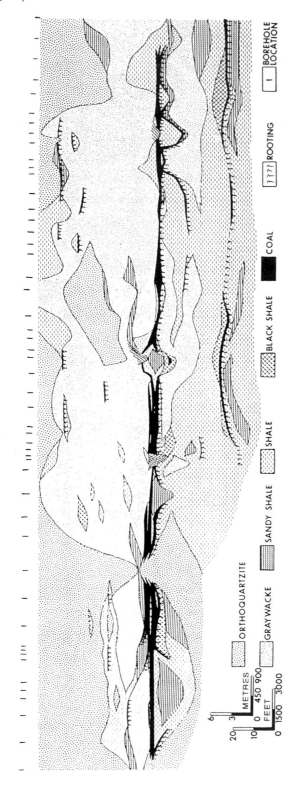

Figure 3.9   Cross section showing correlation of lithofacies and associated coals above and below the Beckley Seam, West Virginia, USA based on borehole data. From Ferm *et al.* (1979), by permission of the University of South Carolina

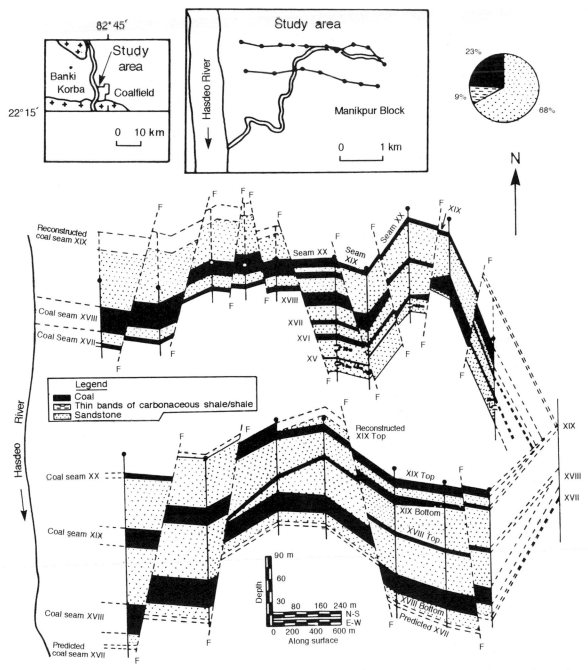

Figure 3.10 Fence correlation diagram showing the geometry of a coal and sandstone sequence in the Lower Permian Barakar Formation, Korba Coalfield, India. From Casshyap and Tewari (1984), by permission of the author and Blackwell Scientific Publications

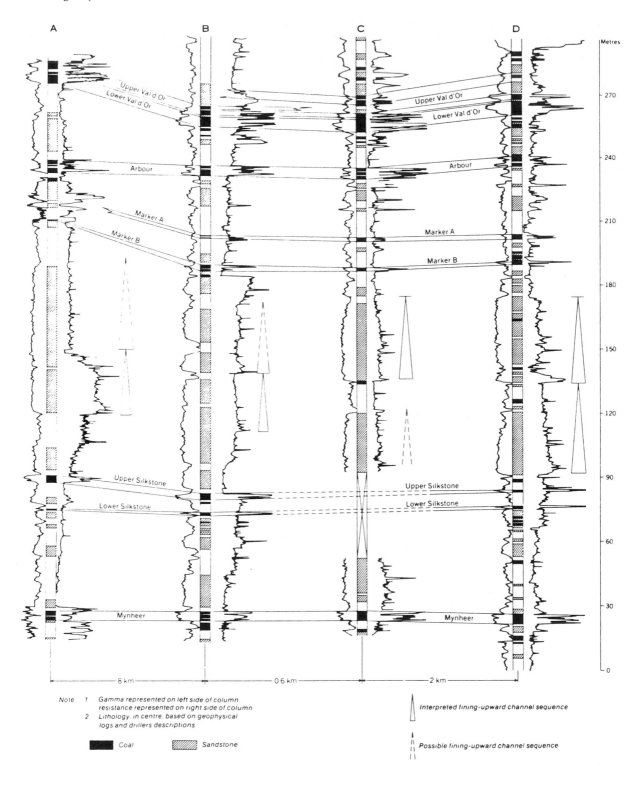

Note   1   Gamma represented on left side of column.
          resistance represented on right side of column
       2   Lithology, in centre, based on geophysical
          logs and drillers descriptions

■ Coal   ▨ Sandstone

▲ Interpreted fining-upward channel sequence

╷╷ Possible fining-upward channel sequence

development, exploratory drill sites would be located at sites 2a to 2u before any closely spaced drilling would be sanctioned. Similarly, the areas of split coal and channel sandstone in Area 1 would need to be identified in Area 2 to determine how much coal loss is likely to occur here.

Figure 3.11 *(opposite)* Correlation based on geophysical logs, Coalspur Beds Upper Cretaceous/Lower Tertiary, Alberta, Canada. From Jerzykiewicz and McLean (1980), Geological Survey of Canada, Department of Energy, Mines and Resources paper 79–12, reproduced by permission of the Minister of Supply and Services Canada, 1992

Figure 3.12 Lithofacies map illustrating how such mapping can be extended to an adjoining area to locate an additional area of thick coal and an area of coal split

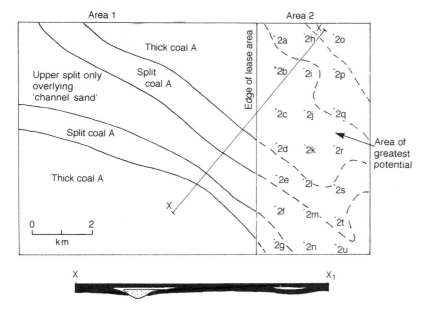

3.2.4 Facies maps

In close association with the correlation of facies, the most significant sedimentological features for the coal geologist are those of seam splitting, washouts and floor rolls, as well as the more obvious variations in seam thickness, seam quality, interburden and overburden nature and thickness, together with the identification of igneous intrusions in the coal-bearing sequence. From borehole and surface data, all of these features can be quantified and portrayed in plan or map form. In the normal course of his or her duties the coal geologist would be expected to compile such plans.

Facies maps are usually compiled for the area of immediate interest, i.e. the mine lease area, but plans covering larger areas can be produced which give a useful regional picture of coal development. Such a large scale study is shown in Figure 3.13, which illustrates a palaeogeographical reconstruction of the depositional setting of the Beckley Coal of southern West Virginia. The reconstruction is based on 1000 cored boreholes in an

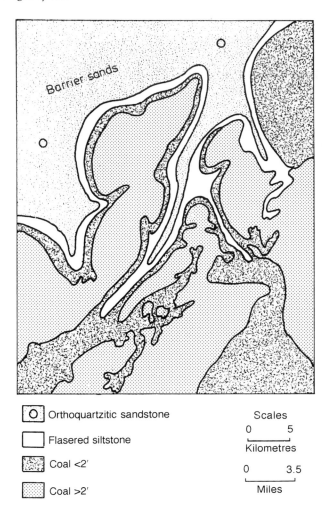

Figure 3.13 Mapped lithotypes compiled from 1000 boreholes over an area of 1000 km², illustrating the regional depositional setting of the Beckley Coal, West Virginia, USA. From Horne *et al.* (1979), by permission of the University of South Carolina

Orthoquartzitic sandstone

Flasered siltstone

Coal <2'

Coal >2'

Scales

0   5
Kilometres

0   3.5
Miles

area of 1000 km². In this example, coal thickness variations are closely related to the pre-existing topography, produced by depositional environments that existed before coal formation. The shape of the coal body has also been modified by contemporaneous and post-depositional environments, such as channels. Consideration of these features during mine planning can maximise the recovery of the thicker areas of coal while avoiding the areas of 'want', i.e. those areas depleted in coal.

3.2.4.1 *Seam splitting*

This common phenomenon occurs when a coal seam, traced laterally, is seen to 'split' into a minimum of two individual coals or 'leafs' separated by a significant thickness of non-coal strata. Such non-coal materials within a seam are referred to as 'part-

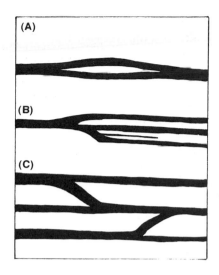

Figure 3.14 Common types of coal seam split. (A) Simple splitting; (B) multiple splitting; and (C) 'Z' or 'S' shaped splitting

ings' or 'bands', and may be composed of a variety of lithotypes. Such partings and bands are the result of clastic deposition replacing organic accumulation. They may represent crevasse-splay overbank deposits, or, if the partings are well developed laterally, represent either widespread flooding of the mire from adjacent river courses or periodic marine flooding into those mires close to the coast.

Seam splitting can be simple or form a complex series of layered organic and clastic materials (Figure 3.14). Simple splits occur when organic accumulation is interrupted and replaced for a short period by clastic deposition. Once the influx of detrital material ceases, vegetation is re-established and organic accumulation thus continues. This may occur once or many times during the deposition of a coal seam. When traced laterally splits may coalesce or further divide. This has the detrimental effect of reducing good sections of coal that can be mined, particularly if the partings are quartz-rich, thus creating mining difficulties, particularly in underground workings. Figure 3.15 illustrates differential splitting of a coal seam across a mine working; such variations are significant to the economics of coal mining, more particularly in underground operations.

Figure 3.15 Development of coal seam splitting in the Beckley Coal across a mine working. From Ferm *et al.* (1979), by permission of the University of South Carolina

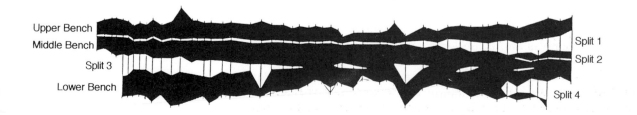

Upper Bench
Middle Bench
Split 3
Lower Bench

Split 1
Split 2

Split 4

Other types of seam splitting are known as 'S' or 'Z' splits (Figure 3.14). This feature is characterised by two seams, usually separated by 20–30 m of sediment. The upper seam splits and the bottom leaf apparently descends through the clastic interval to unite with the lower seam. Such features, which are well documented in the UK and Australia, are considered to be produced by accelerated subsidence induced by differential compaction of peat, clay and sand-rich lithotypes which have been deposited in two adjacent 'basin' areas on the delta plain. The features require continuous peat formation and accumulation on the abandoned 'basin' surfaces and in interbasin areas. Coal seam splits are also formed by the influence of growth faulting as described in Section 3.3.1.2 and illustrated in Figure 3.21.

Splits are of considerable significance to the coal geologist. Coals that have been identified as being of workable thickness may in one or more areas split into two or more thinner seams that are uneconomic to exploit. Such splitting effectively limits those areas of economically recoverable coal reserves.

High angle splitting can produce instability, particularly in opencast workings, where mudstones or fractured sandstones overlying such an inclined split may readily allow the passage of groundwater or produce slope failure, or both.

3.2.4.2   Washouts

Washouts occur where a coal seam has been eroded away by wave or river current action and the resultant channel is filled with sediment. The coal may be wholly or partly removed by this process. Washouts are usually elongate in plan, and infilled with clastic material such as mudstone, siltstone or sandstone, depending on whether the erosive phase was followed by a reduction in current energy, so reducing the grain size of the sediment transported to infill the channel (Figure 3.16). Initially the edges of the washout tend to be sharp, but then they may become diffused by differential compaction of the coal and non-coal materials.

Washouts are a major problem in mining operations, particularly in underground workings. Washouts can seriously reduce the area of workable coal, and therefore the delineation of such features is an essential prerequisite to mine planning. Detailed interpretation of the sedimentary sequences exposed in outcrops, boreholes and in underground workings allows a facies model to be constructed, and this in turn may help to predict the orientation of washouts. Contemporaneous fault and fold influences during sedimentation can result in clastic wedges pinching out against these positive elements, with coal seams

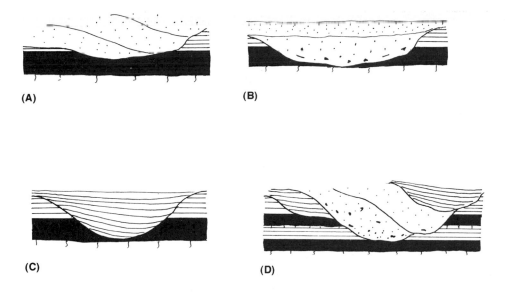

(A)

(B)

(C)

(D)

tending to merge over the structural highs. Another feature is the 'stacking' or localisation of channelling along the flanks of such flexures, producing elongate sandstone bodies which can influence mine planning operations.

3.2.4.3 Floor rolls

These are the opposite phenomenon to washouts, and are characterised by ridges of rock material protruding upwards into the coal seam. Like washouts they reduce the mineable thickness of the coal seam. If they have to be mined with the seam, as is commonly the case, the dilution of the coal quality will result in an increase in the ash content. Floor rolls are often the result of differential compaction of peat around clastic deposits in the lower part of the seam as the upper part of the seam accumulates.

3.2.4.4 Coal seam thickness variations

The importance of these is self evident as, depending on the economics of the mine site, coal less than a predetermined thickness will not be mined. This means that an area containing significant reserves may not be exploitable due to the thinness of a good mining section, particularly if the coal becomes inferior above and below the good coal section, i.e. it makes a poor floor and roof to the seam. Conversely, there can be problems with an excessively thick coal in underground conditions producing poor roof or floor conditions. In opencast mines, thick coals are desirable, and the geotechnical nature of the overlying and

Figure 3.16 Channelling in coal seams. (A) Sand filled channel producing a sandstone roof to the coal seam; (B) sand and coal detritus filled channel with coal seam eroded; (C) mudstone filled channel with coal seam eroded; and (D) multiple channel sequence with sandstone and mudstone fills. The channel has removed the upper leaf of the coal seam

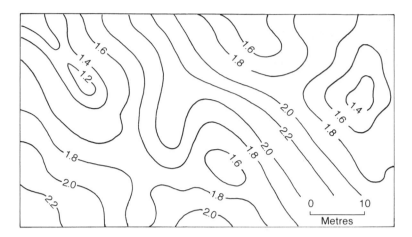

Figure 3.17 Coal seam thickness iso-pach map, hypothetical example (thickness values are in metres)

underlying strata is important, particularly with regard to water movement and collection, as well as ground and slope instability. Thickness isopachyte maps of individual coal seams are essential to mine planning. Figure 3.17 shows an example of the variations in thickness of a coal seam in which the areas of thick and thin coal are clearly defined. The areas of coal thinning may indicate the attenuation of the seam, or that the seam is splitting, producing a thinner upper leaf. Such occurrences are influential on the siting of mining panels in underground workings, and also affect the coal to overburden ratios in opencast operations.

3.2.4.5   *Interburden/overburden thickness*

The amount and nature of the lithotypes present between coal seams and between the uppermost coal seam and the present land surface all have particular relevance to opencast mining operations. If the ratio of the thickness of such sediments to the thickness of workable coal is excessive, then the deposit will be deemed uneconomic. Such ratios are variable and may be dependent on other costs such as labour and transport. Usual maximum coal to interburden/overburden ratios are of the order of 15:1 and 10:1, and although they may be higher in certain circumstances it is preferable if they are much lower than these figures. In addition, if the lithotypes include hard indurated sandstone which will require blasting, then this is an added cost which has to be allowed for in the economic appraisal of the coal deposit.

3.2.4.6   *Coal seam quality variations*

Variations in the environments of deposition strongly influence the resultant quality of coals. As described in Section 3.2.2, peat mires can intermittently receive influxes of detritus by marine invasion, overbank flooding or from airborne sources such as contemporaneous volcanism. Such occurrences will cause all or part of the coal seam to contain a higher ash level; this may be local or widespread. If the peat mire has been invaded by marine waters for a long period of time, the precipitation of minerals into the uppermost part of the peat is likely. In particular, the sulphur content in those parts of a coal seam so affected may be greatly increased.

The plotting of coal seam quality parameters will not only give an indication of their distribution, but also indicate the palaeoenvironmental influences that existed during the depositional and post-depositional phases of coal formation. Conversely, the interpretation of the palaeoenvironment will help to predict coal quality in selected areas. That is, those areas considered to be distant from marine influence should have lower sulphur contents, and coals deposited away from the main distributary channels and only subjected to low energy currents can be expected to have lower ash contents.

These relationships have been summarised as follows: rapid subsidence during sedimentation generally results in abrupt variations in coal seams, but is accompanied by low sulphur and trace element contents, whereas slower subsidence favours greater lateral continuity but a higher content of chemically precipitated material.

The examination of the coal quality analyses, particularly from cored boreholes, allows the coal geologist to plot coal quality variations across the study area. The parameters that are particularly relevant are volatile matter, ash and sulphur content. Deficiencies in the volatile matter content (notably in proximity to igneous intrusions), and too high amounts of ash and sulphur can lead to the coal under consideration being discarded as uneconomic due to increased costs of preparation or by simply just not having those properties required for the market that the coal is targeted for.

Figure 12.9 shows ash and sulphur percentages (for a hypothetical coal seam) generated by computer. Similar maps can be produced for the other important parameters and allow a graphic overview of the properties of any seam within a lease area.

3.3 STRUCTURAL EFFECTS ON COAL

Any significant lateral or vertical structural change in a coal seam has a direct bearing on its thickness, quality and mineability. Such changes can be on a small or large scale, affect the internal character of the coal, or simply displace the coal spatially, replacing it with non-coal sediment, or, in certain circumstances, with igneous intrusives.

An understanding of the structural character of a coal deposit is essential to perform stratigraphic correlation, to calculate coal resources/reserves, and to determine the distribution of coal quality before mine planning. This account is only intended to highlight some of the structural effects encountered in coal-bearing sequences and their influence on the economics of coal deposits.

3.3.1   Syndepositional effects

Most coal-bearing sediments are deposited in or on the margins of tectonic basins. Such a structural environment has a profound influence on the accumulating sediments both in terms of the nature and the amount of supply of detrital material required to form such sequences, and on the distribution and character of the environments of sedimentation. In addition, diagenetic effects within the accumulating sediments produce structural deformation. This may be due to downward pressure from the overlying strata and may be combined with water loss from the sediments while still in a non-indurated or plastic state.

3.3.1.1   *Microstructural effects*

The combination of thick sediment accumulation and rapid basin subsidence can produce instability, particularly along the basin margins. The effects on coal-bearing sediments are frequently seen in the form of slumping and loading structures and liquefaction effects, the latter characterised by the disruption of bedding laminae and the injection of sediment into the layers above and below. Under such loading effects, coal may be squeezed into overlying strata and the original seam structure may be completely disrupted. In addition, coals may be injected by surrounding sediment in the form of sedimentary dykes. Interbedded sequences of mudstone, sandstone and coal that have undergone loading deformation exhibit a variety of structures such as accentuated loading on the bases of erosive sandstones, flame structures, distorted and dislocated ripples, and folded and contorted bedding (Figure 3.18).

Instability within environments of deposition, whether induced by fault activity or simply by the overloading of accumulated sediment, can produce movement of sediments in the form of gravity flows. Figure 3.19 illustrates such a phenomenon. If a coal is transported in this manner, the result can be an admixture of coal material and other sediment with no obvious

Figure 3.18 Deformed bedding in Tertiary coal-bearing sediments, East Kalimantan, Indonesia. Photograph by LPT

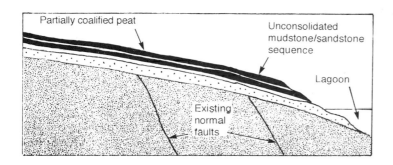

Figure 3.19 Normal fault reactivation causing instability in a partially coalified peat sequence, with downslope slumping to produce a 'melange' of coal and intermixed sediment

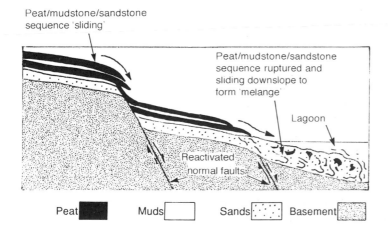

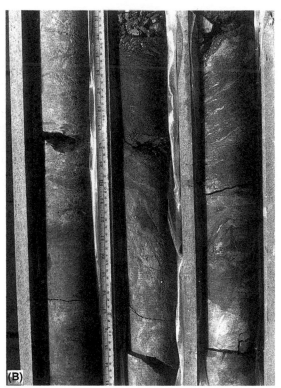

bedding characteristics. Figure 3.20 shows a coal which has become intermixed with the surrounding sediment; it is now in an unworkable state as the ash content is too high and the geometry of the coal seam is irregular.

3.3.1.2   Macro structural effects

Within sedimentary basins, existing faults in the underlying basement may continue to be active and influence the location, thickness and character of the sedimentary sequence. Many coal-bearing basinal sediments display evidence of growth faulting. In West Virginia and Pennsylvania, USA broad scale tectonic features have caused local thickening of the sequence in response to an increased rate of subsidence, as distinct from more stable platform areas (i.e. less rapidly subsiding), where sedimentation prograded rapidly over the shelf. In South Wales, UK growth faults have again influenced sedimentation. Here, in addition to active basement elements, faults are developed that owe their origin to gravity sliding within the sedimentary pile. Overpressured, non-compacted argillaceous sediments initiate faults on gentle gradients. Such faults tend to have a curved

Figure 3.20   Cores exhibiting 'melange' or mixing of lithotypes due to gravity sliding. Tertiary coal-bearing sediments, East Kalimantan, Indonesia. Photographs by LPT. (A) Left core: mixing of sandstone and siltstone with subordinate coal. Centre core: coal mixed with mudstone and siltstone. Right core: coal and mudstone mixing. (B) All cores: sandstone, siltstone and coal mixing

cross sectional profile, steep at the top and flattening progressively into bedding plane faults, often along the roof of a coal. In many instances such faults are partially eroded before the succeeding sediments are laid down.

Seam splitting can also, in certain circumstances, be attributed to growth faulting. Reactivation of faults with changes in the sense of movement can result in the downwarping of sections of peat beds; this is then followed by non-peat deposition on the downwarped section, and then peat deposition resumes at the original level of the first peat. Figure 3.21 shows the possible mechanism for the formation of such a coal seam split.

Periodic changes in the base level in deltaic areas through fault activation will result in changes in the development and character of coals. With emergence, coals may become more extensive and, where the influx of detritus is curtailed, have a lower ash content. If submergence occurs, coals may be restricted areally, or receive increased amounts of detritus which may increase the ash content, or even cease to develop at all. Furthermore, submerged coals may be contaminated with marine waters, which could result in a higher sulphur content in the uppermost parts of the seam. .

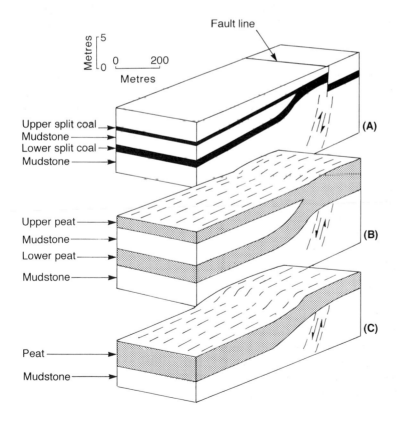

Figure 3.21 Seam splitting caused by differential movement of faults during peat deposition. (A) Fault downthrow results in downwarping of the peat; (B) downwarp filled in with mudstone, peat development resumed at original level; and (C) fault throw sense reversed, uplifting split coal and downthrowing unsplit section of the coal seam. From Broadhurst and Simpson (1983) by permission of the authors and *Journal of Geology*

Growth folds also influence the deposition patterns in coal basins; local upwarping can accelerate the rates of erosion and deposition in some parts of a basin, but can also have the effect of cutting off sediment supply by uplift or by producing a barrier to the influx of detritus.

In very thick sedimentary sequences, the continued growth of such folds can result in the production of oversteepened fold axes. Where this occurs, overpressured mudstone at depth may be forced upwards and actually breach the anticlinal axial areas; this can be seen by the breaking up of the surface strata and the intrusion of material from below. Such diapiric intrusion breccia can be found in East Kalimantan, Indonesia, and these are often accompanied by the development of mud volcanoes along the axial region of the anticlines.

In the Kutei Basin in East Kalimantan, Indonesia, the established structural pattern continually evolved throughout the Tertiary. In this area, the anticlines are tight with steep or overturned dips accompanied by steep reverse and normal faults in the complex axial regions. The synclines are broad and wide with very low dips; the transition between the two structures can be abrupt, now represented by steep reverse faults. These growth folds are thought to have been further accentuated by gravity sliding associated with very thick accumulations of sediment (up to 9000 m) in the Kutei Basin, and rifting in the Makassar Strait to the east. The structural grain and the palaeo-strike were roughly parallel in this region, the resultant sequence characterised in its upper part by upper delta plain and alluvial plain sedimentation with numerous coals. This structural pattern is shown in the map (B) in Figure 3.31.

Penecontemporaneous volcanism can also have a profound effect on the character of coals. Large amounts of airborne ash and dust together with water-borne volcanic detritus may result in the deposition of characteristic dark lithic sandstones, possible increases in the ash content in the peat mires, and the formation of tonstein horizons.

3.3.2 Post-depositional effects

All coal-bearing sequences have undergone some structural change since diagenesis. This can range from gentle warping and jointing up to complex thrusted and folded coalfields usually containing high rank coals.

These post-depositional structural elements can be simply summarised as faults, joints (cleat), folds and igneous associations. Mineral precipitation may also produce some changes in the original form and bedding of coal-bearing sequences.

A great deal of work has been carried out on the structure of coalfields and individual coal seams, some of which the coal geologist should be familiar with; if not, he or she is recommended to consult the relevant texts. For the purposes of this account a brief summary is given of the main structural features likely to be encountered by the coal geologist in the normal course of his or her work.

3.3.2.1 *Faulting*

The development of strong joint and fault patterns in coal-bearing sequences is the most common post-depositional structural expression. The principal fault types are summarised in the following.

Normal faults are produced by dominantly vertical stress resulting in the reduction of horizontal compression, leaving gravity as the active compression; this results in the horizontal extension of the rock sequence.

This form of faulting is common and movements can be of the order of a few metres to hundreds of metres. Figure 3.22 shows a normal fault with a throw of about 2 m; such faulting does not cause too many problems in opencast workings, but in underground workings can result in cessation of the mining of automated faces.

The dip of normal faults ranges widely; in coalfields most are thought to be in the region of 60–70°. Some normal faults die out along their length by a decrease of throw towards either one or both ends of the fault. Again, a fault may pass into a monoclinal flexure, particularly in overlying softer strata. Such faulting also

Figure 3.22 Normal fault with down-throw of 2 m to the right. Tertiary coal-bearing sediments, Sumatra, Indonesia. Photograph by LPT

Figure 3.23   Large fault zone exposed in high wall in an opencast mine, South Wales, UK. Photograph by LPT

produces drag along the fault plane, the country rock being pulled along in the direction of movement. Where large faults have moved on more than one occasion, and this applies to all kinds of faulting, a zone of crushed coal and rock may extend along the fault plane and have a width of several metres; such a crush zone can be seen in the high wall of the opencast working shown in Figure 3.23.

Large scale normal faults are produced by tensional forces pulling apart or spreading the crustal layer. Where these faults run parallel with downfaulted areas in between, they are known as graben structures. Many coalfields are preserved in such structures; the brown coalfields of northern Germany and the concealed coalfields of Bangladesh are examples.

Low angle faults with normal fault displacements are known as lag faults. They originate from retardation of the hanging wall during regional movement, as shown in Figure 3.24. Lag faults are common in the coalfield of South Wales, UK.

Reverse faults are produced by horizontal stresses with little vertical compression. This results in the shortening of the rock section in the direction of maximum compression.

Very high angle reverse faults are usually large structures,

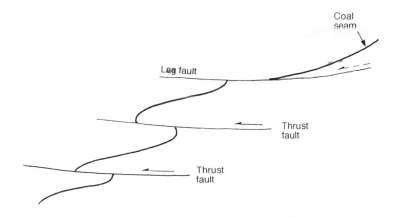

Coal
seam

Lag fault

Thrust
fault

Thrust
fault

Figure 3.24 Lag fault produced by retardation of the upper part of the sequence during the forward movement of the lower sequence by thrust faulting. From Sherborn Hills (1975) *Elements of Structural Geology*, 2nd edn, by permission of Chapman & Hall

associated with regional uplift and accompanying igneous activity. In coal geology, those reverse faults with low angles (<45°) are more significant. A typical reverse fault structure is seen in Figure 3.25, where the fault has dislocated a coal seam by several metres. When the angle is very low, and the lateral displacement is very pronounced, such faults are termed thrust faults. The shape of such low angle reverse faults is controlled by the nature of the faulted rocks, especially when a thrust plane may prefer to follow the bedding planes rather than to cut across them.

In typical sequences of coal, seat earth and mudstone with subordinate sandstone, such low angle faults often follow the roof or the floor, or both, of coal seams as these allow ease of

Figure 3.25 Coal seam dislocated by a reverse fault, throw 1.5 m, UK opencast mine. Photograph by M. C. Coultas

Figure 3.26   Highly sheared coal seam (seam thickness 1.2 m) in opencast mine, South Wales, UK. Photograph by LPT

movement, the seat earths often acting as a lubricant. One detrimental effect is the contamination of the coal seam with surrounding country rock, so reducing its quality, and in some instances its ability to be mined.

In highly tectonised coal deposits, a great number of coal seam contacts have undergone some movement and shearing. In some instances the whole seam will have been compressed and moved and this may be displayed in coals as arcuate shear planes throughout. Figure 3.26 portrays this feature.

The development of thrust zones in coal sequences can be illustrated as in Figure 3.27. Here, lateral compression has produced thrusting along preferred lithological horizons and continued compression has resulted in the upper part of the sequence being more tectonically disturbed than the lower part. This deformation is now termed progressive easy-slip thrusting. Such events are particularly common in coalfields which have suffered crustal shortening, as in South Wales, UK, coalfields in the Republic of Korea and in the Appalachians, USA. Thrusting is also accentuated where coal and mudstone sequences are sandwiched between thick sequences of coarse clastics, the upper and lower portions of the sequence reacting to compressive forces very differently to the incompetent coals and mudstones.

Strike-slip faults have maximum and minimum stress in the two horizontal planes normal to one another. This has the effect of producing a horizontal movement either in a clockwise (dextral) or anticlockwise (sinistral) sense. Strike-slip faulting is usually found on a regional scale and, although important, has a

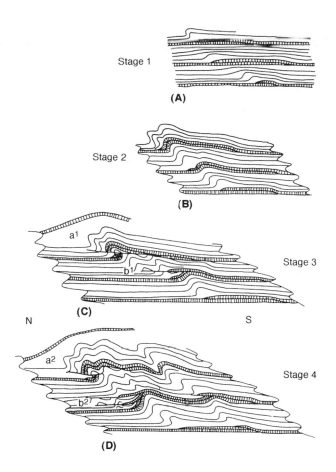

Figure 3.27 Model for four stages in progressive easy-slip thrusting. (A) Thrusts develop simultaneously as flats along the floors of overpressured coal seams, cutting up to the roof of the seams along short ramps; propagation folds grow at the thrust tips. (B) Thrusts continue to propagate with amplification of the tip folds, until a lower propagation fold locks up a higher thrust, producing downward facing cut-offs. (C) Continued out of sequence movement on higher thrusts results in break back-thrusting in the hanging wall and foot-wall areas; thrusts locally cut down stratigraphy in the transport direction. (D) Progressive out of sequence hanging wall break back produces distinctive geometry with the structure in a lower thrust slice being apparently unrelated to that in a higher thrust slice. Progressive footwall break back produces folded thrusts. From Gayer *et al.* (1991) by permission of *Proc. Ussher. Soc.*

lesser influence on the analysis of small coal deposits and mine lease areas.

Evidence of faulting on the rock surface can be seen in the form of slickensides. These are striations on the fault plane parallel to the sense of movement. Some fault planes have a polished appearance, particularly where high rank coal has been compressed along the fault plane. Conical shear surfaces are characteristically developed in coal. These are known as cone-in-cone structures and are the result of compression between the top and bottom of the coal.

3.3.2.2   *Jointing/cleat in coal*

Coal, and in particular black coal, is noted for the development of its jointing, more commonly referred to as cleat. This regular pattern of cracking in the coal may have originated during coalification; the burial, compaction and continued diagenesis of the organic constituents results in the progressive reduction of porosity and permeability. At this stage, microfracturing of the coal is thought to be generated. The surfaces and spaces thus created may be coated and filled with mineral precipitates, chiefly carbonates and sulphides. Such microfracture patterns are usually developed in two directions approximately at right angles to each other and to the bedding. Often one cleat direction is better developed than the other; the dominant direction is known as cleat or bord, and the lesser direction as the end or

(A)   mm 10   20   30   40   50   60   70   80   90   100   110   120   130   140   150   160

(B)

Figure 3.28   (A) Orthogonal cleat pattern in Meltonfleet Coal, Upper Carboniferous, Yorkshire, UK. Reproduced by permission of the Director, British Geological Survey; NERC copyright reserved. (B) Well developed joint and cleat pattern in Triassic anthracite, Republic of Vietnam. Photograph by LPT

end cleat. Figure 3.28(A) shows a well developed orthogonal cleat pattern in a coal from the Midlands, UK. It is noticeable that cleat can be seen in all thicknesses of coal, even in the thinnest films of coal included within other lithotypes. Figure 3.28(B) shows a strong cleat pattern in an anthracite from the Republic of Vietnam.

3.3.2.3 Folding

Coals in coal-bearing sequences may be folded into any number of fold styles; for example, as shown in Figure 3.29. In coalfield evaluation, the axial planes of the folds need to be located and the dips on the limbs of the folds calculated. In poorly exposed country the problem of both true and apparent dips being seen has to be carefully examined. Also, in dissected terrain, dips taken at exposures on valley sides may not give a true reflection of the structural attitude of the beds at this locality. Many valley sides are unstable areas and mass movement of strata is common, resulting in the recording of oversteepened dips. This is characteristic of areas of thick vegetation cover where a view of the valley side is obscured and any evidence of movement may be concealed. If the field data suggests steeper dipping strata this will give less favourable stripping ratio calculations for an opencast prospect and may contribute to the cancellation of further investigations. Similarly, in underground operations, if the dip of the coal seam steepens, it can make the working of the coal difficult, and in longwall mining prevent further extraction.

Figure 3.29 Folded Jurassic coal-bearing sediments, Taechon, Republic of Korea. Photograph by LPT

Therefore it is important to be sure that all readings taken reflect the true nature of the structure in the area of investigation.

Compression of coal seams during folding can produce tight anticlinal folds with thrusting along the nose of the fold; these have been termed queue anticlines. Coal seams can be pinched out along the fold limbs and appear to have flowed into the axial areas of the anticlines. Where this occurs from two directions approximately normal to one another, coals can be concentrated

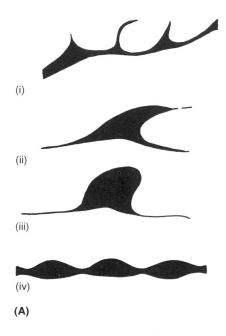

(i)

(ii)

(iii)

(iv)

(A)

Figure 3.30   (A) Tectonic deformation of coal seams due to compression. (i) Squeezing into the overlying formation; (ii) queue anticline; (iii) 'pepper-pot' structure; and (iv) 'rosary' structure. (B) Carboniferous anthracite squeezed in and around overlying sandstone, Samcheog Coalfield, Republic of Korea. Photograph by LPT

(B)

in 'pepper-pot' type structures. Such features are usually found
only in highly tectonised coalfields, and examples of such
intense deformation are illustrated in Figure 3.30(A); a coal seam
squeezed in this way is shown in Figure 3.30(B). Here the coal
has been compressed in and around the overlying sandstone. In
many instances such structural complications will render a coal
seam unminable except by the most primitive of methods, but
coal concentrations in the axial regions of folds have been mined
in the same manner as mineral 'saddle reefs'.

Detailed mapping of folded coal deposits is an essential part
of the exploration process. Examples of folded coal deposits are
illustrated in Figure 3.31. In Figure 3.31(A), a pattern of zigzag
folds characterises the Wurm Coal Basin, Germany; Figure
3.31(B) shows a series of asymmetrical folds with associated
thrusting from the Kutei Basin, Indonesia; and Figure 3.31(C) is
an example of a coalfield subjected to severe tectonic deformation, from the Republic of Korea, in which the circular pattern of
outcrops is characteristic. Such examples serve to show the
necessity of acquiring a good understanding of the structural
elements and style of the coal deposit to identify those areas
where coal is preserved in such amounts, attitude and depth as
to allow mining to develop.

3.3.2.4 Igneous associations

In many coalfields associated igneous activity has resulted in
dykes and sills being intruded into the coal-bearing sequence.

The intrusion of hot molten rock into the coals produces a
cindering of the coal and a marked loss in volatile matter content
which has been driven off by heat. This can have the effect of
locally raising the rank of lower rank coals, and can therefore, in
certain circumstances, make the coal attractive for exploitation.
Such 'amelioration' of coal seams is a common feature in areas
of igneous activity. Good examples are found in Indonesia and
the Philippines where Tertiary subbituminous coals have been
ameliorated up to low volatile bituminous and some even to
anthracite rank.

Most dykes and sills are doleritic in composition, as in the
South African coalfields, but occasionally other types are found.
In the Republic of Korea acidic dykes and sills are intruded into
the coals; Figure 3.32 shows acidic igneous material intruding a
coal seam in an underground working.

In areas where igneous intrusions are prevalent in mine
workings, plans showing the distribution and size of igneous
bodies are required to determine areas of volatile loss where the
coal has been baked, and because of the hardness of the igneous
material, tunnelling has to be planned with the position of

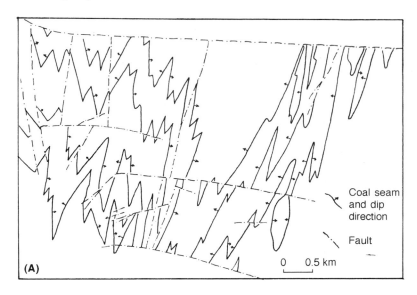

(A)

Coal seam
and dip
direction

Fault

0   0.5 km

Figure 3.31   Outcrop patterns in folded coalfields. (A) Zigzag folding of coal seams and associated faulting, Wurm Coal Basin, Germany. From Stutzer and Noe (1940), by permission of the University of Chicago Press. (B) (*opposite*) Asymmetrical folding, broad synclines and steep anticlines associated with thrusting, Samarinda, East Kalimantan, Indonesia. Reproduced by permission of the Geological Society of London, from Land, D. H. and Jones, C. M. (1987) 'Coal geology and exploration of part of the Tertiary Kutei Basin in East Kalimantan, Indonesia'. In: *Coal and Coal-bearing Strata: Recent Advances* (Ed. A. C. Scott), *Geol. Soc. London Spec. Publ. No. 32.* (C) (*below*) Intensely folded and overturned Jurassic coal-bearing sequence, Chungnam Coalfield, Republic of Korea. Adapted from *Geologic Atlas of the Chungnam Coalfield*, Ministry of Commerce and Industry, Republic of Korea (1974). Reproduced by permission

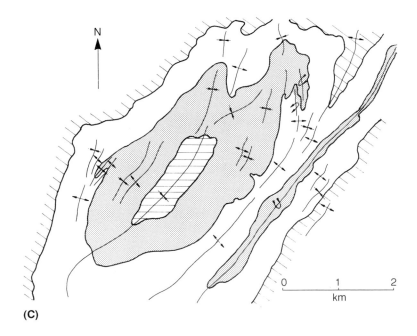

N

0   1   2
km

(C)

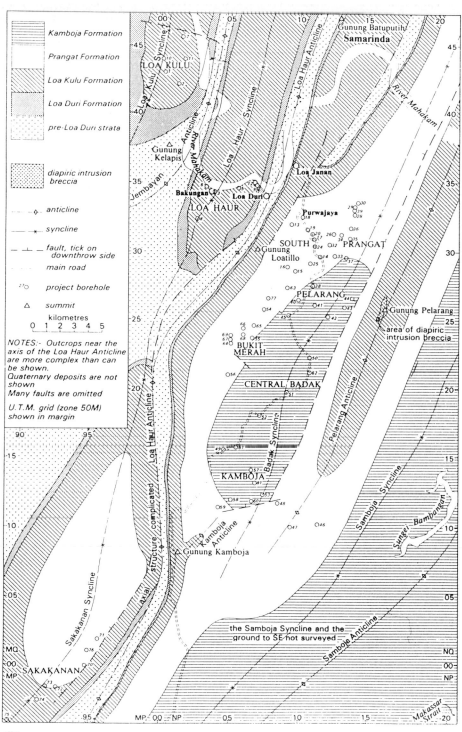

(B)

Figure 3.32 Jurassic anthracite (dark colour) intruded by granitic dykes and sills (light colour). Chungnam Coalfield, Republic of Korea. Photograph by LPT

intrusions in mind. Igneous sills have a tendency to jump from one coal seam to another so that closely spaced drilling is often required to identify precisely the nature and position of such intrusions. Igneous intrusions are found in coal sequences worldwide but in particular are a common feature of South African coal workings. Where such igneous bodies exist, the coal geologist must identify the areas occupied by igneous material within the mine area, and also those seams affected by igneous activity.

In addition, there is the possibility of methane gas driven off during the intrusion having collected in intervening or overlying porous sandstones. Mine operatives need to investigate this possibility when entering an intruded area of coal.

3.3.2.5   *Mineral precipitates*

A common feature of coal-bearing sequences is the formation of ironstone, either as bands or nodules. These bands or nodules usually consist of siderite ($FeCO_3$) and can be extremely hard. Where ironstone nucleation and development takes place either in, or in close proximity to, a coal seam, this can deform the coal, cause mining difficulties, and, because of the difficulty in separ ating the coal and ironstone while mining, will have an effect on the quality of the run-of-mine product.

Iron sulphide (FeS) in the form of iron pyrite may be precipitated as disseminated particles, as thin bands, or, as is more common, as coatings on cleat and bedding surfaces (the coal specimen in Figure 6.7(A) displays pyrite in this form). Inorganic sulphur held in this form in coal can be removed by crushing and passing the coal through a heavy liquid medium. Organic sulphur held elsewhere in the coal cannot be readily removed, and remains an inherent constituent of the coal.

Other mineral precipitates are usually in the form of carbonates, coating cleat surfaces, or occasionally as mineral veins. Where quartz veining occurs, this has the detrimental effects of being hard, liable to produce sparks in an underground environment where gas is a hazard, and a respiratory health hazard when crushed.

Chapter 4
Age and occurrence of coal

4.1 AGE OF COAL

Although land plants first developed in the Lower Palaeozoic
era, it was not until the Upper Palaeozoic, particularly the
Carboniferous, that sufficient plant cover was established and
preserved to produce significant coal accumulations. The oldest
coals are thought to be those of Middle and Late Devonian age
in China, and Late Devonian age in the Canadian Arctic.
Throughout the geological column, i.e. from the Carboniferous
to the Quaternary, coal deposits have been formed. Within this
time range there were two major episodes of coal accumulation.

The first took place during the Late Carboniferous–Early
Permian periods. Coals formed at this time now form the bulk of
the black coal reserves of the world, and are represented on all
of the continents. The coals are usually of high rank and may
have undergone significant structural change. Carboniferous–
Permian coal deposits stretch across the northern hemisphere
from Canada and the USA, through Europe and the CIS (formerly the USSR) to the Far East. In the southern hemisphere,
the Carboniferous–Permian coals of Gondwanaland are preserved in South America, Africa, the Indian Subcontinent,
South-east Asia, Australasia and Antarctica.

The second major episode occurred during the Tertiary. Coals
formed during this period range from lignite to anthracite.
Tertiary coals form the bulk of the world's brown coal reserves,
but also make up a significant percentage of black coals currently mined. They are characterised by thick seams and have
often undergone minimal structural change. Tertiary coals are
also found worldwide, and are the focus of current exploration
and production as the traditional Carboniferous coalfields
become depleted or geologically too difficult to mine.

Coals of the intervening Triassic, Jurassic and Cretaceous

periods make up significant reserves worldwide, but are not as widespread as those of the Carboniferous and Tertiary.

For precise age determinations of a particular coal-bearing sequence, the coal geologist is referred to the detailed stratigraphical works that may cover his or her area of interest, or, if no such information exists, to apply the standard field procedures of collecting flora and fauna or microfaunas to ascertain the age of the sequence.

4.2 GEOGRAPHICAL DISTRIBUTION OF COAL

A brief summary is given of the geographical distribution of the known coal deposits of the world. It is not intended to be anything like comprehensive, but rather is designed to give the coal geologist an overview of the location of the principal coalfields throughout the world. The precise ages of the deposits are not given, only the period in which they were formed. The distribution of coal deposits throughout the world are dealt with in nine geographical regions, as shown in Figures 4.1 to 4.9. Many information sources have been used, including the *Concise Guide to World Coalfields* (IEA Coal Research, 1983).

4.2.1 United States of America

The coal deposits of the USA have been divided into six separate areas or provinces, based on the findings of the US Geological Survey (Figure 4.1).

The Eastern or Appalachian Province is the oldest and most extensively developed coal province in the USA. The coal is of Carboniferous age, and the Eastern Province contains two-fifths of the nation's bituminous coal plus almost all the anthracite. Coal rank increases from west to east in this province, such that high volatile bituminous coal gives way to low volatile bituminous and anthracite. Most reserves are in high and medium volatile bituminous coal, used chiefly as steam coal. The largest reserves of coking coal in the USA are low volatile, low sulphur coals situated in central Pennsylvania and West Virginia.

Seams are usually between 0.5 and 3.6 m in thickness, with various degrees of structural intensity. Deep mines characterise the older workings; more recently, opencast mining in the form of contour mining and mountain top removal has been established.

The Interior Province consists of a number of separate basins containing Carboniferous bituminous coal. With one exception all of the coal in the Interior Province is high volatile bituminous

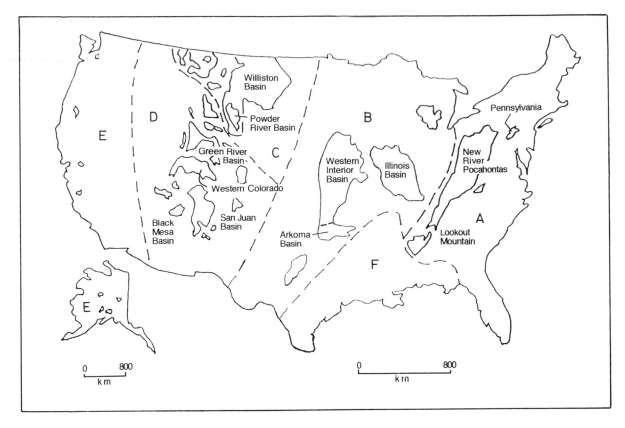

Figure 4.1 Coal deposits of the USA. (A) Eastern or Appalachian Province; (B) Interior Province; (C) Northern Great Plains Province; (D) Rocky Mountains Province; (E) Pacific Coast Province; and (F) Gulf Coastal Plain Province

with a high sulphur content (3–5%). The Arkoma basin has coals of higher rank, including semi-anthracites with low sulphur contents. Some of the low sulphur coal has coking properties.

In the eastern part of the Interior Province, coal seams range from 0.5 to 2.5 m in thickness, and two seams, the Springfield and Herrin Coals are more than 1.5 m thick and cover thousands of square kilometres. These seams have accounted for more than 90% of production for this region. The western Interior Province is characterised by thinner (<1.5 m) but laterally extensive seams, mined exclusively by opencast stripping.

The Northern Great Plains Province contains coals of Cretaceous to Tertiary age. The area covers parts of Wyoming, Montana and North and South Dakota. Some bituminous coals are present, but the main reserves are of subbituminous coal and lignite.

The rank increases from east to west. Lignite is present in the Williston Basin, and subbituminous coals are found in the Powder River Basin and other Tertiary basins, while the Cretaceous coals of northern Montana are bituminous in rank. As a result of the low sulphur content of many of the Tertiary coals, there has been an increase in demand for these coals in the light of environmental regulations.

The Tertiary coals are characteristically thick, commonly greater than 30.0 m, and are mined by opencast methods.

The Rocky Mountain Province contains coal preserved in a series of intermontane basins. Most Cretaceous coal is bituminous and subbituminous, and Tertiary coals are subbituminous and lignite. The seams are thick, in the range 3.0–10.0 m. Some are structurally affected and some are ameliorated by igneous intrusives.

Most Rocky Mountain coal is subbituminous or high to medium volatile bituminous, with small areas of coals suitable for coking purposes. Again these coals tend to have low sulphur contents (<1%). The usual mining practices are opencast and contour stripping mining, with some drift mining.

The Pacific Coast Province covers those coal deposits found west of the Rocky Mountains, and those in Alaska. The coal is Tertiary in age, and is found in small widely scattered basins from California in the south to Washington in the north. The coal has been tectonised and metamorphosed.

In Alaska, numerous deposits of subbituminous and high volatile bituminous coal have been identified. As yet the area is not fully explored; however, indications are that the coal resources could be up to 10% of the economically recoverable coal in the world.

Finally, the Gulf Coastal Plain Province contains lignites of Tertiary age. The lignite is produced from large opencast pits, where seams range from 1.0 to 7.5 m in thickness. Production has greatly increased in the last 20 years and is primarily for electricity generation.

4.2.2   Canada

The largest coal-bearing region is located in western Canada, stretching from south Saskatchewan across Alberta into British Columbia (Figure 4.2). The coals that underlie the plains are relatively undisturbed Tertiary and Mesozoic (Late Jurassic–Early Cretaceous) lignites and subbituminous coals, while those occurring in the mountains are Mesozoic high volatile to low volatile bituminous coals. Seam thicknesses of 3.0–5.0 m have been recorded in the subsurface of Alberta. Elsewhere in British Columbia, Mesozoic bituminous coal and anthracite are found, highly tectonised, together with younger Tertiary lignites.

In eastern Canada, Carboniferous coals are mined in the Minto Coalfield, New Brunswick and in the Sydney Coalfield, Nova Scotia (Figure 4.2). All are bituminous coals, some with high sulphur contents and coking properties. The Minto

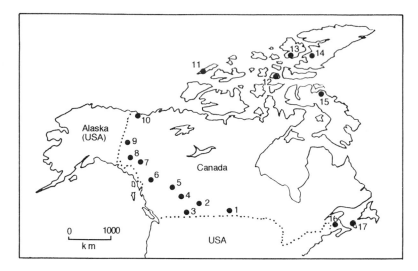

Figure 4.2 Coal deposits of Canada. (1) South Saskatchewan; (2) Central and Eastern Alberta; (3) South-east British Columbia; (4) West Central Alberta; (5) North-east Coal Block; (6) North-west British Columbia; (7) Watson Lake; (8) Whitehorse; (9) Dawson; (10) Mackenzie Bay; (11) Prince Patrick Island; (12) Cornwallis Island; (13) Axel Heiberg Island; (14) Ellesmere Island; (15) Baffin Island; (16) Minto Coalfield; and (17) Sydney Coalfield

Coalfield supplies coal for generating electricity from a single 0.5 m seam. The Sydney Coalfield is now restricted to mining offshore and again supplies power stations and some coking coal for export.

In northern Canada, coals are found in the Yukon Territory and Northwest Territories. They are of the same age as the coals described for western Canada, consisting of Mesozoic high, medium and low volatile bituminous coals, often highly tectonised, and Tertiary subbituminous coals and lignites. The Mesozoic coals are principally from the Yukon Territory, and Tertiary coals are found in both Yukon Territory and the Northwest Territories, including the Canadian Arctic islands. Older coals (Devonian) are known to occur in the Arctic islands.

4.2.3 Europe

Coal deposits of Palaeozoic (Carboniferous), Mesozoic and Cainozoic (Tertiary) age are developed in a series of basins which stretch from the United Kingdom in the west to Turkey in the east. The full range of black and brown coals are present, and all of the most accessible deposits have been extensively worked over the last 150 years.

Those European countries with recorded coal deposits are listed alphabetically and shown in Figure 4.3.

4.2.3.1 Albania

Albania has small isolated occurrences of subbituminous coal and lignite scattered throughout the country. They produce

Figure 4.3 (*opposite*) Coal deposits of Europe. (1) Tirane; (2) Tepelene; (3) Korce; (4) West Styria; (5) Kempen; (6) Dobrudza; (7) Maritsa; (8) Ostrava-Karvina; (9) North Bohemia; (10) Sokolov; (11) Herning; (12) Lorraine; (13) Nord et Pas de Calais; (14) Provence; (15) Aachen; (16) Ruhr; (17) Saar; (18) Lower Saxony; (19) Rhenish; (20) Halle Leipzig Borna; (21) Lower Lausitz; (22) Florina Amyndaeon; (23) Ptolemais; (24) Serrae; (25) Megalopolis; (26) Disko; (27) Nugssuaq; (28) Mecsek; (29) Leinster; (30) Kanturk; (31) Slieveardagh; (32) Connaught; (33) Valdarno; (34) Sulsis; (35) Upper Silesia; (36) Lower Silesia; (37) Lublin; (38) Belchatow; (39) Konin; (40) Lower Lausitz; (41) Turoscow; (42) Sao Pedro da Cova; (43) Cabo Mondego; (44) Rio Maior; (45) Jiu; (46) Almas; (47) Comanesti; (48) Banat; (49) Oltenia; (50) Leon; (51) Puertollano; (52) Teruel; (53) Garcia Rodriguez; (54) Calaf; (55) Mequinenza; (56) Arenas del Rey; (57) Longyearbyen; (58) Svea; (59) Zonguldak; (60) Elbistan; (61) Canakkale; (62) Mugla; (63) Bursa; (64) Ankara; (65) Cankiri; (66) Istra; (67) Dobra; (68) Sarajevo-Zenica; (69) Trans-Sava; (70) Kolubara; (71) Kosovo; (72) Scotland; (73) North-East England; (74) Yorkshire–Nottinghamshire; (75) Lancashire– North Wales; (76) East and West Midlands; (77) South Wales; (78) Kent; (79) North and South Staffordshire; (80) Warwickshire; (81) Leicestershire; and (82) Northern Ireland

small amounts of coal for local industrial use, chiefly from Tirane, Tepelene and Korce.

4.2.3.2 Austria

In Austria there are a number of small coal deposits; all are structurally complex. They include anthracite and bituminous coals, principally in the west of the country. Tertiary lignite and subbituminous coal is present in the West Styria area. Mining is on a small scale only.

4.2.3.3 Belgium

The Carboniferous Coalfield of Kempen in the north of the country produces all of Belgium's coal. The coal ranges from

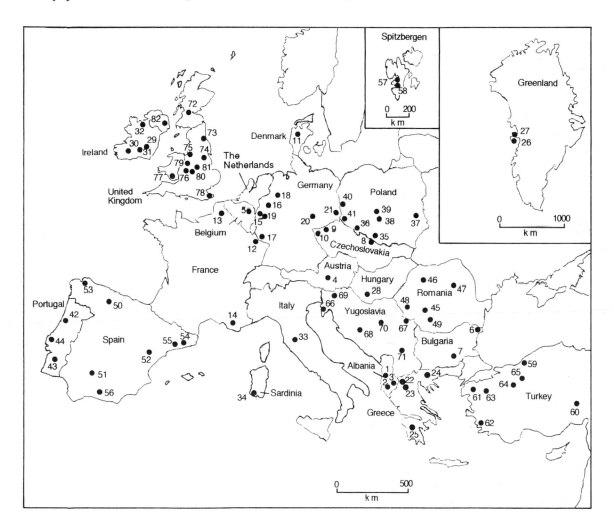

anthracite to low volatile bituminous, with low sulphur content, some of which is used as coking coal. Seams may be up to 2.0 m thick, and are worked by underground methods.

Smaller coal deposits are known to the south, but mining has long ceased because of thin seams and difficult mining conditions.

4.2.3.4 *Bulgaria*

The most extensive coal deposits in Bulgaria are subbituminous coal and lignite of Tertiary age. The seams are thick, some over 20 m, and have undergone little structural disturbance. Most of the mining areas are situated in the west of the country, with one important deposit occurring at Maritsa in the east.

High rank bituminous coals are known from the Dobrundza area on the east coast; here the coals are deep and so far have not been mined on a significant scale.

4.2.3.5 *Czechoslovakia*

Czechoslovakia has numerous deposits of black and brown coals spread widely across the country. The chief black coalfield is that of Ostrava-Karvina on the northern border. It is of Carboniferous age and represents a continuation of the Upper Silesian Coalfield in Poland. The area is structurally complex, but contains numerous seams, some of which are over 10.0 m in thickness. The coal produced is low volatile bituminous, which is strongly caking and with low sulphur contents. Other smaller bituminous coal deposits are found north and west of Prague.

Subbituminous coals of Tertiary age are located in the north-west of Czechoslovakia in the North Bohemia and the Sokolov region. Seams are up to 30.0 m in thickness, with low sulphur contents and little structural disturbance.

4.2.3.6 *Denmark*

Tertiary lignites are found at Herning, but are no longer worked as reserves are small.

4.2.3.7 *France*

Two large Carboniferous basins, those of Lorraine and Nord et Pas de Calais, contain high volatile bituminous coal, some suitable as coking coal. Seams are up to 2.0 m thick and have been highly tectonised; all are mined by underground methods.

Smaller scattered coal deposits are known from western and south-western France; all are structurally complex and mining has virtually ceased in these areas.

Lignite is mined in the Provence district. The seams are relatively undisturbed and supply the local electricity industry.

4.2.3.8 Germany

The black coals of Germany are located in the Carboniferous basins of Aachen, Ruhr and Saar, with small deposits present in the south-east of the country.

The Aachen basin produces high and low volatile bituminous coal with low ash and sulphur, some of which is coking coal, from seams up to 1.5 m in thickness.

The Ruhr basin produces high volatile bituminous coal with low ash and sulphur which is a good coking coal. Seam thicknesses range from 0.5 to 3.0 m. A northern extension of this area is the Lower Saxony Coalfield which produces low volatile anthracite.

The Saar basin is less structurally disturbed and produces bituminous coal from seams 0.5 to 2.0 m in thickness. This coal is not suitable for coking purposes.

The brown coals of Germany are of Tertiary age, and significant deposits are found in three basins, the Rhenish, the Halle Leipzig Borna and Lower Lausitz. These areas are currently the largest producers of brown coal in the world.

The Rhenish basin is situated close to the Ruhr. It contains thick seams (up to 90.0 m) of lignite with low ash and sulphur contents. The coalfield has suffered little structural disturbance, and is mined on a large scale by opencast methods for use in the electricity generation industry. The Halle Leipzig Borna and Lower Lausitz Coalfields are situated in the east of the country. Again they contain thick seams of lignite which has high volatile, low ash and low sulphur properties. Both areas are mined on a large scale by opencast methods.

4.2.3.9 Greece

Tertiary lignites are mined throughout the country. The principal deposits are situated in the north of Greece at Florina Amyndaeon and Ptolemais, where lignite seams are up to 40.0 and 28.0 m thick, respectively. The lignite is high volatile, with low ash and sulphur contents. All is surface mined chiefly for electricity generation.

Other lignite deposits are situated at Serrae in the north-east and at Megalopolis in the south.

4.2.3.10 Greenland

Although geographically separate from Europe, Greenland is included here for convenience. Coal occurrences have been reported from several areas in Greenland. The most significant are the subbituminous coals with low sulphur contents that are found on the coast at Disko and Nugssuaq.

4.2.3.11   Hungary

Black coal is mined in the south-west of Hungary, in the area around Mecsek. Here coals of Mesozoic age are present in a structurally complex area, strongly folded and faulted, with associated igneous intrusives. Seams are steeply dipping but can be thick locally (>5.0 m). The coal is weakly caking bituminous with high ash and sulphur contents. The area is a well established coalfield, with mining in difficult conditions.

Brown coal deposits of Mesozoic and Tertiary age are found in a north-east–south-west belt of country in the north of Hungary. The subbituminous coals are mined by underground and opencast methods, the lignites by opencast only.

4.2.3.12   Ireland

The coal deposits of Ireland are all of Carboniferous age. Four main coal-bearing areas have been mined, at Leinster, Kanturk and Slieveardagh in the south and at Connaught in the north-west. The coal is anthracite with variable sulphur contents in the south, and medium volatile bituminous coal in the north-west. Coal has been mined on a small scale from thin seams.

4.2.3.13   Italy

Carboniferous coals are present in the structurally complex areas of the Alps and Sardinia.

Tertiary lignites and subbituminous coals are found in the Apennines and Sardinia. The latter coalfield at Sulcis has bituminous coal as a result of volcanic amelioration. Mining is on a very small scale.

4.2.3.14   The Netherlands

Coal-bearing Carboniferous sequences are known at depth beneath younger sediments; however, seams are thought to be thin. No coal mining is presently carried out in The Netherlands.

4.2.3.15   Poland

Poland has large reserves of coal and a long established coal mining industry. Black coal in Poland is centred around three coalfields, Upper Silesia, Lower Silesia and Lublin. These areas represent large basins which have undergone various degrees of structural disturbance.

The Upper Silesian Coalfield contains numerous seams up to 4.0 m in thickness. The coal is primarily high volatile bituminous, with low ash and sulphur contents. The Lower Silesian Coalfield is a much smaller area containing thinner seams which are highly tectonised. Remaining reserves are deep, but it is an important supplier of coking coal. The Lublin Coalfield, only discovered relatively recently, is a very large area with potentially enormous reserves. The seams appear to be less structurally disturbed than in the Silesian Coalfields. Lublin has bituminous coals with low ash and sulphur contents together with strong coking properties. The Lublin Coalfield is likely to be the principal supplier in the future.

Tertiary brown coals are found in the central and south-western regions of Poland. In central Poland, the Belchatow and Konin regions contain lignite seams up to 70.0 and 20.0 m, respectively. The lignite is high volatile, with a high ash content, and is used locally for electricity generation. The brown coalfields situated in south-west Poland, in the Lower Lausitz and Turoscow regions, contain lignite seams up to 60 m in thickness, of similar quality to those in central Poland, and are also used for electricity generation.

4.2.3.16 Portugal

Anthracite of Carboniferous age is present in the north-west of the country, but is not extensively worked. At Cabo Mondego, bituminous coal, high in ash and sulphur, is produced on a small scale.

A number of basins contain lignite; in particular, that at Rio Maior is a small producer.

4.2.3.17 Romania

The bulk of coal production in Romania is of brown subbituminous coal. The coalfields of Kiu, Almas and Comanesti are free from structural disturbance, and each contains several thick seams. The Jiu Coalfield is the most important and contains seams in excess of 30.0 m.

Other areas include a small deposit of higher rank Palaeozoic coal at Banat, and lignite at Oltenia.

4.2.3.18 Spain

The principal black coal basin is that in the Leon region in the north of the country. The basin contains low volatile bituminous coals with low sulphur contents, some of which are usable as coking coal. Seam thicknesses are up to 1.5 m and the area is structurally complex. In the south of Spain, south-west of Puertollanos, low volatile bituminous coals are found.

Spanish brown coals are located at Teruel, where shallow lignites of Cretaceous age are mined for power generation. At Garcia Rodriguez in the extreme north-west of the country, high volatile, high sulphur lignite is used for local electricity needs. Other lignite deposits are present at Calaf and Mequinenza in the north-east, and Arenas del Rey in the extreme south of Spain. These are also used for local electricity requirements.

4.2.3.19 Spitzbergen

Carboniferous and Tertiary coals are present on the western side of the island. At Longyearbyen and Svea, high volatile bituminous coal with low sulphur is present in seams up to 5.0 m in thickness. Current mining is on a small scale.

4.2.3.20 Turkey

Turkey has considerable reserves of Carboniferous black coal and Tertiary brown coal. The principal black coal deposit is the Zonguldak Coalfield on the northern coast, where numerous seams ranging from 0.7 to 10.0 m are present. The coal is bituminous with low ash and sulphur contents, and is suitable for use as a coking coal.

Tertiary brown coals are widespread across Turkey. The most important deposit is that of Elbistan, where a single seam of lignite is up to 84.0 m in thickness. The lignite is high volatile, high ash and sulphur, and it is planned to opencast this seam for electricity generation.

Other lignite occurrences are worked on a small scale at Canakkale, Mugla, Bursa, Ankara, Cankiri and Bingol.

4.2.3.21 United Kingdom

In the United Kingdom, a series of coal-bearing basins are distributed throughout the country. The coals are of Carboniferous age and are principally bituminous with some anthracite, notably in South Wales. The principal areas are those of Scotland, north-east England, the Yorkshire–Nottinghamshire region, the Lancashire–North Wales region, the East and West Midlands, South Wales and Kent.

Scotland contains high volatile bituminous coals with low sulphur; this area has been extensively mined in the past. In north-east England, most of the current coal reserves are offshore, and are bituminous coals suitable for coking purposes.

The Yorkshire–Nottinghamshire region is the most important coal producing area in the United Kingdom, supplying coal for electricity generation and coking coal to industry. The region is less structurally affected than other areas and, because of this, recent coalfield developments have been in the Selby area, where several seams, notably the Barnsley Seam (3.5 m) have produced high volatile bituminous coal, some of which is strongly caking, and in the Vale of Belvoir area where it is planned to produce high volatile bituminous coals chiefly for the electricity generating industry.

The Lancashire–North Wales region has produced high volatile bituminous coal with low sulphur content. Owing to extensive working and difficult mining conditions the region is now in decline.

The East and West Midlands contain four coal mining areas, north and south Staffordshire, Warwickshire and Leicestershire. The region produces high volatile bituminous coal for electricity generation; in particular, in Warwickshire, the Warwickshire Thick Seam, which can be up to 8.0 m in thickness, is a major producer.

South Wales, once the principal coalfield in the United Kingdom, still produces bituminous coal and anthracite with low sulphur contents; seams are usually between 1.0 and 3.5 m, and underground mining conditions are difficult. In recent years opencast mining has been established in the coal outcrop areas.

Kent, a small coalfield in the south-east of the United Kingdom, contains high quality bituminous and anthracite coal, but has recently ceased to be a producer.

Tertiary lignites are found in south-west England and in Northern Ireland. In Northern Ireland, lignite deposits have been identified for future use in local power stations.

4.2.3.22 *Yugoslavia*

Yugoslavia, in common with many other European countries, has black coal of Palaeozoic (Carboniferous) and Mesozoic ages, preserved in the older structurally complex regions of the country, and Tertiary brown coals which are not affected structurally. The latter are more extensive than the older deposits.

Along the north-eastern border of Yugoslavia a series of black coal deposits occurs; most are low volatile bituminous coal with relatively high sulphur contents. Some of the coals have good coking properties but the high sulphur restricts their use. Small occurrences of anthracite are also found in the region. These coals have been mined in the Istra and Dobra areas.

The largest subbituminous coalfield is at Sarajevo-Zenica. Others are situated at Trans-Sava, together with small areas in the north-east of the country.

Lignites are mined at Kolubara and Kosovo, all providing fuel for electricity generation.

4.2.4   Africa

Black coal occurs in Africa as, firstly, those deposits of Carboniferous age found on the northern coast, in Morocco in the west and Egypt in the east, and, secondly and more importantly, the widespread Karroo deposits of Late Carboniferous–Permian age which are found throughout central and southern Africa. The Karoo sequences were deposited on the Gondwana supercontinent which split apart in the Mesozoic, hence the similarities of African Gondwana coals to those of India and South America.

Brown coals of Tertiary age are present, but in Africa it is the black coals that are of prime interest.

The geographical distribution of coal deposits in Africa is shown in Figure 4.4.

4.2.4.1 Angola

Lignites of Tertiary age have been identified in Angola, firstly in the east around the headwaters of the Lungue-Bungo river, where seams of lignite up to 2.5 m have been recorded, and secondly in the west around Luanda, where lignites are present in the Tertiary coastal sediments. None of these deposits have been worked.

4.2.4.2 Botswana

Botswana has large reserves of black coal of Karroo age. These coal deposits extend from north to south along the eastern edge of the country. The more important coalfields are those of Morupule and Mmamabula. At Morupule, seams up to 9.5, 4.5 and 2.0 m in thickness are present. At Mmamabula, the average seam thicknesses are 2.8, 5.4 and 2.0 m. In both these coalfields the coals are relatively undisturbed and contain bituminous coal with a high ash and sulphur content; these coals have no coking properties. Other smaller coalfields are present in close proximity to Morupule and Mmamabula.

Botswana has the potential to be a significant coal producer, but at the present time it is geographically disadvantaged to be a coal exporter.

4.2.4.3 Cameroun

In the Bamenda district, lignites are found interbedded with lava flows. They are of Cretaceous–Tertiary age and locally can be up to 6.0 m in thickness, but are undeveloped.

Figure 4.4 (*opposite*) Coal deposits of Africa. (1) Lungue-Bungo; (2) Luanda; (3) Morupule; (4) Mmamabula; (5) Bamenda; (6) Al Maghara; (7) Imaloto-Vohibory; (8) Sakoa; (9) Sakamena; (10) Antanifotsy; (11) Livingstonia; (12) North Rukuru; (13) Ngana; (14) Lengwe; (15) Mwabvi; (16) Jerada; (17) Ezzhiliga; (18) Tindouf-Draa; (19) Meknes Fez; (20) Moatize; (21) Mmambansavu; (22) Chiomo; (23) Itule; (24) Enugu-Ezimo; (25) Orukpa-Okaba-Ogboyoga; (26) Asaba; (27) Karroo Basin; (28) Waterberg; (29) Springbok Flats; (30) Limpopo; (31) Lebombo; (32) Mhlume; (33) Mpaka; (34) Maloma; (35) Ketewaka-Mchuchma; (36) Ngaka; (37) Songwe-Kiwira; (38) Galula; (39) Njuga; (40) Ufipa; (41) Luena; (42) Lukuga; (43) Luangwa; (44) Luano; (45) Maamba; (46) Kahare; (47) Wankie; (48) Lubimbi; (49) Sessami-Kaonga; (50) Tuli; (51) Bubye; (52) Chelga; (53) Wuchalle; (54) Dobre-Brehan; and (55) Bourem

4.2.4.4   Egypt

Carboniferous coal is present in the Sinai Peninsula. Coals are of bituminous and subbituminous rank. Coal has been produced from workings at Al Maghara, at which future development is to be considered.

4.2.4.5 *Ethiopia*

Tertiary brown coals are known from many localities on the Ethiopian Plateau; beds are up to 15.0 m thick and range from lignite to subbituminous coal. They have high ash and low sulphur contents. Principal localities are Chelga, Wuchalle and Dobre-Brehan.

4.2.4.6 *Madagascar*

Black coal is present in the Karroo sediments on the western side of the island, where they overlie the Precambrian basement. At the southern end of the Karroo outcrop, five coal-bearing areas have been identified.

The northernmost area is the Imaloto Coalfield, which contains seams averaging 1.0 m in thickness. The coal is medium volatile bituminous with high ash and some high sulphur contents. The Vohibory and Ianapera Coalfields have seams up to 2.3 and 0.6 m, respectively; both areas are structurally complex. The Sakoa Coalfield is the best known area, with seams of 3.0 and 7.0 m in thickness. The coals are high volatile bituminous with high ash and low sulphur contents; they are non-coking. The Sakamena Coalfield is similar to Sakoa except that the seams are thinner.

Lignite deposits of Tertiary age are present in the region of Antanifotsy, and are thought to cover a large area.

4.2.4.7 *Malawi*

In Malawi, a series of separate basins contains coal-bearing Karroo sediments; these are located in the extreme north and south of the country.

The main coalfields are those of Livingstonia, Ngana and North Rukuru, with small deposits at Lengwe and Mwabvi in the south. The Livingstonia coalfield contains seams 1.0–2.0 m in thickness, which are mined to supply fuel to local industry. At Ngana, one seam is up to 15.0 m in thickness, but seams usually average around 1.0 m and show rapid vertical and lateral variations in thickness. The southern coalfields have thin seams and are not well developed.

Malawian coals are subbituminous to high volatile bituminous with high ash and low sulphur contents.

4.2.4.8 *Mali*

Upper Cretaceous and Tertiary brown coals are recorded from the Mali–Niger basin in the south-eastern part of the country, around Bourem. Seams are thought to reach 2.0 m in thickness, and have moisture values of 24% and ash values of 21%.

4.2.4.9 Morocco

Carboniferous black coals are found in the north-east of Morocco, at Jerada, and have been identified at depth beneath younger sediments at Ezzhiliga and Tindouf-Draa.

At Jerada, four seams of up to 0.7 m in thickness are mined; they are structurally unaffected and the coal is low volatile anthracite with low ash and high sulphur contents.

Lignites have been identified at Meknes-Fez in northern Morocco.

4.2.4.10 Mozambique

Karroo sediments are preserved in a series of basins in the Precambrian basement. The coal-bearing Karroo outcrop is a long strip running eastward from the southern tip of Lake Malawi. Four coalfields have been identified and of these the Moatize deposit is the most important.

At Moatize, seams range from 0.4 to 4.0 m in thickness. Structurally, the coalfield is heavily faulted. Coal is low volatile bituminous, with high ash and low sulphur contents. The coal deposits at Mmambansavu, Chiomo and Itule are as yet little known.

4.2.4.11 Namibia

The eastern half of Namibia is covered by post-Karroo sediments of the Kalahari Group. It is possible that Karroo sediments underlie a portion of this area and may contain coals of similar aspect to those found in Botswana.

4.2.4.12 Niger

The Mali–Niger basin contains coals of Upper Cretaceous to Tertiary age. Little information is available but these coals may be worked locally.

4.2.4.13 Nigeria

Coal-bearing sediments of Cretaceous and Tertiary age overlie Precambrian basement in the south-eastern part of Nigeria. These sediments dip to the west where they are overlain by floodplain deposits of the Niger river.

The Nigerian Coalfield is divided into several mining areas, the Enugu, Ezimo, Orukpa, Okaba and Ogboyoga Coalfields. Seams range from less than 1.0 to 3.0 m, and all the coalfields are affected by faulting and gentle folding. Coals from these coalfields are high volatile subbituminous with high ash and low sulphur contents. Similar coal is reported from the Lafia area situated to the north of the Enugu coalfields. Here the coal is similar but has a higher sulphur content.

Tertiary lignites are found in the Asaba region close to the Niger river; seams are 3.0–7.0 m in thickness. They are high volatile, high ash lignite with low sulphur content.

4.2.4.14   South Africa

The coal deposits of South Africa are found in a series of basins situated in the north and east of the country. The main Karroo basin is commercially very important. Coals are up to 5.0 m in thickness and have suffered little tectonic disturbance. The coal is high volatile bituminous, with high ash and low sulphur contents; some of the coal is weakly caking.

Within the Karroo basin are numerous coalfields, including the Eastern Transvaal, Highveld, Springs Witbank, South Rand, Utrecht, Vierfontein and Vereeniging, most of the mines being underground operations. The basin as a whole produces large tonnages for electricity generation and to produce liquid fuel. The region is also a major exporter of steam coals.

Other coalfield basins in the north-east of the country are less developed. Of these, the Waterberg Coalfield on the Botswana border and the Springbok Flats area appear to have future potential. The Limpopo and Lebombo Coalfields have bituminous coals with high ash contents; these are not worked at this time.

4.2.4.15   Swaziland

Coal-bearing Karroo sediments are located on the eastern side of the country. The seams are thicker in the north and are flat lying; some have been ameliorated by dolerite intrusions. The Mhlume Coalfield in central Swaziland produces anthracite on a small scale. Coal is also known from the Maloma area in the south of the country.

4.2.4.16   Tanzania

There are eight coalfields in Tanzania. The Karroo sediments are preserved in depressions in the Precambrian basement; all are located in the south-west of the country. The Ruhuhu Coalfields have been known for a century but have never been fully developed. Of these, the Ketewaka-Mchuchma and Ngaka Coalfields are the most important. In these coalfields coals occur in two zones, the lower containing the better coals. Seams can be as thick as 7.0 m but this is exceptional. Coals are high to low volatile bituminous with high ash and low sulphur contents.

Other coalfields with similar characteristics are those of Songwe-Kiwira, Galula, Njuga and Ufipa.

4.2.4.17   Zaire

Small separate basins of coal-bearing Karroo sediments occur in the south-east of the country at Luena and Lukuga. Seams are up to 2.0 m in thickness and are disrupted by faulting. The coals are bituminous with high ash contents and are used locally for electricity generation.

4.2.4.18   Zambia

Karroo sediments are preserved in depressions in the Precambrian basement. A series of such basins is present in the east and south-east of the country, namely the Luangwa, Luano and Maamba areas, and also in the west-central district around Kahare.

The Luangwa coals are up to 1.6 m thick and are high volatile bituminous high ash coals. The Luano area has fairly thin seams which are high volatile bituminous, with high ash content; some coal has coking properties. The Maamba area in the south-east has seams 2.0–3.0 m in thickness, and is high volatile bituminous with high ash content. The Maamba area produces most of Zambia's coal.

At Kahare, coals are preserved beneath younger sediments. Coal quality is similar to other Zambian coals, but this area has not yet been fully investigated.

4.2.4.19   Zimbabwe

The Karroo sequence in Zimbabwe is preserved in the Zambezi basin in the northwest, and the Limpopo basin in the southeast. The northwest includes the coalfield districts of Wankie and Lubimbi, with Sessami-Kaonga to the east of these. In these coalfields, the coal is the Wankie Main seam, a medium to high volatile bituminous coal, comprising a lower coking coal up to 4.0 m in thickness, and an upper steam coal up to 8.0 m, all generally with low sulphur contents.

In the southern coalfields of Bubye and Tuli, the coals have variable qualities. Some low sulphur coking coal has been identified in the Tuli Coalfield.

4.2.5   Indian Subcontinent

The area referred to as the Indian Subcontinent extends from Iran in the west to Bangladesh in the east. Black coals are of Palaeozoic (Carboniferous–Permian), Mesozoic and Cainozoic age. Brown coals are of Cainozoic age.

Palaeozoic Gondwana coals are found in India, Pakistan and Bangladesh; Mesozoic coals are present in Afghanistan, India, Pakistan and Iran; and Cainozoic coals are found in all the countries listed in this region (see Figure 4.5).

4.2.5.1   Afghanistan

Mesozoic (Jurassic) black coals are present in the northern mountainous region of Afghanistan. The coal is relatively undisturbed with seams up to 1.5 m in thickness. The coal is bituminous with low ash and sulphur contents, with little or no coking properties. Coal is mined at Herat in the north-west and at several other sites in the north. All are small operations and produce for the local market only.

4.2.5.2   Bangladesh

Gondwana coals are found at depth, concealed beneath Tertiary sediments in north-western and eastern Bangladesh. The Gondwana sediments represent the infilling of depressions in the

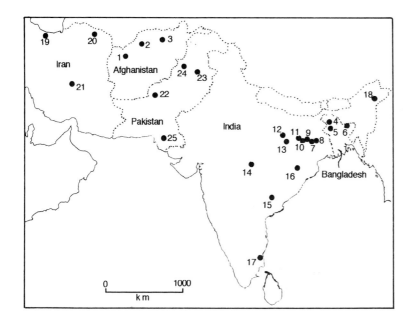

Figure 4.5   Coal deposits of the Indian Subcontinent. (1) Herat; (2) Sari-i-Pul; (3) Dara-i-Suf; (4) Barapukuria-Khalaspir; (5) Jamalganj; (6) Sylhet; (7) Raniganj; (8) Jharia; (9) Bokaro; (10) Ramgarh; (11) Karanpura; (12) Singrauli; (13) Bisrampur; (14) Pench-Kanhan–Tawa; (15) Godavari; (16) Talchir; (17) Neyveli; (18) Makum; (19) Elburz; (20) Khorasan; (21) Kerman; (22) Quetta-Kalat; (23) Salt Range; (24) Makerwal; and (25) Hyderabad

underlying crystalline basement. These basins have been faulted at the margins, resulting in gently dipping coal seams being preserved in graben structures.

In the north-west, the concealed coal basins of Barapukuria, Khalaspir and Jamalganj contain numerous seams ranging in thickness from less than 1.0 to 20.0 and 30.0 m. The coals are medium to high volatile bituminous, with high ash and low sulphur contents. In the east of Bangladesh, lower rank coal is located at Sylhet; the coal is subbituminous and lignite.

Coals in Bangladesh have yet to be developed.

4.2.5.3 *India*

In India, coal resources are of Palaeozoic (Gondwana) and Cainozoic (Tertiary) age.

About 98% of India's coal reserves are of Gondwana coal, which also accounts for 95% of production, chiefly for electricity generation and the metallurgical industries. The Gondwana coals are present in over 14 separate basins centred in the north-eastern and central eastern parts of peninsular India.

Tertiary brown coals are present in the north-eastern and north-western parts of the country, together with an important lignite deposit in the south at Neyveli.

Gondwana coals are well developed in the eastern states of Bihar, West Bengal and Orissa, the principal coalfields being Jharia, Raniganj, Bokaro, Ramgarh, Karanpura, Singrauli and Bisrampur. In addition, numerous other fields in the same region are producing coal. Seams in these coalfields range in thickness from 1.0 to 30.0 m, with an exceptionally thick seam of 134.0 m discovered in the Singrauli Coalfield. The coalfields have been faulted but otherwise are not highly tectonised. Coals range from high to low volatile bituminous with high ash and variable sulphur contents. In the Jharia and Raniganj Coalfields, good quality coking coals are produced.

In central eastern India, the Pench-Kanhan-Tawa, the Godavari and Talchir coalfields contain Gondwana coals, 1.0–4.0 m in thickness and free from structural disturbance. The coal is high volatile bituminous non-coking coal.

The Tertiary coals are highly disturbed tectonically and are located in the mountainous regions of north India. In the Makum coalfield in Assam, seams are lens-shaped, in places reaching thicknesses of 33.0 m. Coals are subbituminous to high volatile bituminous with high sulphur contents.

In southern India, Tertiary lignites are found in Neyveli, the thickest seam being up to 20.0 m in thickness. Here the lignite has a high sulphur content and is used locally for electricity generation.

4.2.5.4 *Iran*

The black coal deposits of Iran are Mesozoic (Jurassic) in age, with some lignites of Tertiary age. The Jurassic coals are bituminous with high ash and sulphur contents, and have coking properties. All are strongly tectonised with seam thicknesses ranging from 1.0 to 4.0 m. The coal supplies local needs and the metallurgical industry. Principal coalfields are located at Elburz and Khorasan in the north and at Kerman in central Iran. Lignites are found in north-west Iran but are not worked.

4.2.5.5 *Pakistan*

All the principal coalfields in Pakistan are of Tertiary age, although Palaeozoic and Mesozoic coals are present. The coalfields of economic importance are situated in the Indus basin in three distinct coal regions, Hyderabad, Quetta-Kalat and Salt Range–Makerwal. Most of these coalfields have been structurally disturbed.

The Hyderabad province contains the coalfields of Lakhra, Sonda-Thatta and Meting-Shimpir. Seams are up to 2.0 m in thickness, and the coal is subbituminous, non-coking with high sulphur content. The Quetta-Kalat province contains the coalfields of Sor Range-Daghari, Khost Sharig-Harnai and Duki-Chamalang. Again the coal is subbituminous with high ash and sulphur contents. The Salt Range–Makerwal province consists of the coalfields of eastern, central and western Salt Range, together with the Makerwal coalfield to the west of these. Coals are subbituminous, with high ash and sulphur contents. Overall production is small, the coal being used chiefly for electricity generation.

4.2.6 Central and South America

Coal deposits are distributed throughout Central and South America and make up a significant proportion of world reserves of black coal. Most of the coals are of Cainozoic (Tertiary) age, with coals of Palaeozoic (Gondwana) age present chiefly in eastern South America, in Brazil and Uruguay; in addition, Mesozoic coals are found in discrete deposits throughout the region.

The geographical distribution of coal deposits in Central and South America is shown in Figure 4.6.

4.2.6.1 *Argentina*

The coal deposits of Argentina are preserved in a series of basins in the Andean Cordillera and pre-Cordillera and in Austral

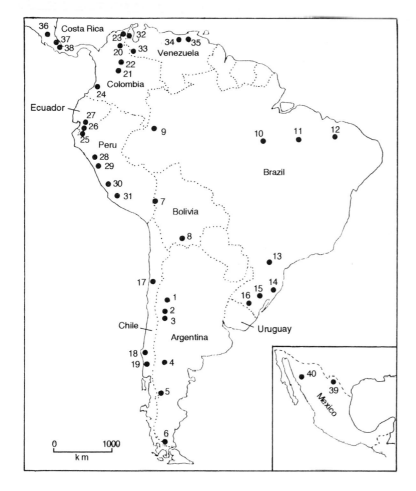

Figure 4.6 Coal deposits of Central and South America. (1) La Rioja; (2) San Juan; (3) Neuquen; (4) Mendoza; (5) Pico Quemado; (6) Rio Turbio; (7) Copacabana Peninsula; (8) Tarija Basin; (9) Amazon; (10) Rio Fresco; (11) Tocantins-Araguaia; (12) Western Piaui; (13) Parana; (14) Santa Catarina; (15) Rio Grande do Sul; (16) Candiota; (17) Copiapo; (18) Arauco; (19) Valdivia; (20) Magallanes; (21) Cundinamarca; (22) Santander; (23) El Cerrejon; (24) Valle del Cauca; (25) Malacatus; (26) Loja; (27) Canar-Azuay; (28) Alto Chicama; (29) Santa; (30) Oyon; (31) Jatunhuasi; (32) Zulia; (33) Lobatera; (34) Caracas-Barcelona; (35) Naricual; (36) Venado; (37) Zent; (38) Uatsi; (39) Coahuila; and (40) Sonora

Patagonia. Coals are of Carboniferous–Triassic, Jurassic and Tertiary ages. Of these, the Tertiary coals are the principal deposits of economic interest.

Coals of Carboniferous and Permo-Triassic age are found in the La Rioja–San Juan region. They consist of thin discontinuous seams less than 1.0 m thick and highly tectonised. Coals are low to medium volatile bituminous with some anthracites. Jurassic coals are found south of San Juan in the Neuquen region, preserved in a series of small basins. Seams are thin, normally less than 1.0 m thick and are medium volatile bituminous at Neuquen and anthracitic at Mendoza.

Tertiary coal-bearing sediments are preserved in a large basin which extends from Pico Quemado in the north to Tierra del Fuego in the south.

At Pico Quemado coal seams 1.0–2.0 m in thickness are high volatile bituminous with coking properties, their high rank possibly being due to a locally high geothermal gradient related to magmatic phenomena. In the southern part of the basin around Rio Turbio, two coal zones contain seams up to 2.0 m in thickness. They are subbituminous to bituminous with no coking properties. All the Tertiary coals have low sulphur contents and are suitable for the electricity generating industry and, in the case of the Pico Quemado coal, can be used in the metallurgical industry.

4.2.6.2   Bolivia

Two types of coal are known from Bolivia: anthracite of Permian age and lignite of Tertiary age.

Anthracite is located on the Copacabana Peninsula and on the Isla del Sol, Lake Titicaca. Seams are in the form of coal lenses or very thin beds of anthracite with low sulphur content. The Tertiary lignites are found in the Tarija Basin, where seams are thin, less than 1.0 m, and have a high sulphur content (6–8%).

4.2.6.3   Brazil

Brazil has five coal-bearing regions which may have potential: the Upper Amazon, the Rio Fresco, Tocantins-Araguaia, Western Piaui and southern Brazil. Only the southern Brazil region is currently considered prospective.

The Amazon region contains lignites of Tertiary age. Seams are thin (less than 1.5 m) with high ash and sulphur contents. The Rio Fresco region contains thin seams of anthracite with very high ash contents (40%); seams up to 1.7 m have been reported.

The Tocantins-Araguaia region has very thin coals of Carboniferous age and is not considered of economic importance. The Western Piaui region also contains Carboniferous coals, which are thin and not significant.

The principal Brazilian coal deposits are situated in the southern Brazil region. They are of Carboniferous–Permian (Gondwana) age and are exposed in a lenticular belt which runs from the states of Parana in the north through Santa Catarina to Rio Grande do Sul in the south. Rio Grande do Sul coalfield contains numerous seams up to 3.0 m in thickness; the Santa Catarina region contains ten coal seams of which the thickest is 2.2 m thick. In Parana, seams are usually less than 1.0 m thick. The coals are high volatile bituminous with high ash contents. At Candiota in Rio Grande do Sul the coal has a low sulphur content (1%), but Santa Catarina and Parana do have coals with high sulphur values (3–10%). In the Parana area the coals become low volatile bituminous–semi-anthracite due to the intrusion of dolerite dykes into the coals. Some Santa Catarina coals have some coking properties, but the bulk of south Brazilian coal is mined as a thermal coal product.

Some lignites are present in the São Paolo region but their economic potential is unknown.

4.2.6.4   Chile

There are four areas of coal-bearing sediments in Chile. These are, from north to south, the Copiapo region, the Arauco region, the Valdivia region and the Magallanes region.

The Copiapo coals are of Mesozoic (Rhaetic) age. They are strongly folded, with seams occurring as thin lenses of anthracite with high ash and variable sulphur contents.

The Arauco region lies on the Chilean coast just south of Concepcion and the coalfield extends offshore to a distance of 7 km. Dips are steep and faulting common. Seams are of Tertiary age and average 1.0–1.5 m in thickness. They are high volatile bituminous coals with low ash and variable sulphur contents, and have poor coking properties. Coals of the Valdivia region are concealed beneath younger sediments. Seams reach 3.0 m in thickness and are subbituminous with low sulphur contents. These coals are used for local purposes.

The Magallanes region forms part of a large sedimentary basin in which over 3800 m of Late Cretaceous–Tertiary sediments are preserved. Coal seams up to 7.0 m are present and upwards of 12 coal seams have been identified. All the coals are high volatile subbituminous, non-coking with low ash and sulphur contents. This large coal deposit is geographically remote but is a large resource and may be of future importance.

4.2.6.5   Costa Rica

Costa Rica contains deposits of Tertiary coals and lignites. Individual seams are up to 1.0 m in thickness. Locally the subbituminous coals and lignites have been ameliorated by igneous intrusions. Sulphur contents range from 1.0 to 4.0%. The three principal coal deposits are at Uatsi and Zent on the south-east coast, and at Venado in the north of Costa Rica.

Areally extensive peat deposits (up to 2.0 m thick) are present in the Talamanca Cordillera and may represent a large resource for future development.

4.2.6.6   Colombia

Coal deposits of Mesozoic (Cretaceous) and Tertiary age are found in numerous localities in the northern half of Colombia.

All have been highly tectonised and coals range from lignite to anthracite. Cretaceous coals are found just north of Bogota, in the Cundinamarca-Santander region. In this area the coals are bituminous with low ash and sulphur contents, strongly coking, and are suitable for coke production. Tertiary coal deposits are located north of Santander on the Venezuelan border, in the extreme north of Colombia at El Cerrejon, around Cordoba on the north coast and at Valle del Cauca in the west of Colombia. These coalfields produce non-coking bituminous coal with generally low ash and sulphur contents. It is ideally suited for use in the electricity generating industry.

The deposit at El Cerrejon is one of the most important in South America. Coals dip gently eastwards and more than 50 seams are greater than 1.0 m in thickness, locally reaching 26.0 m. Owing to the high quality of these coals, El Cerrejon is now a significant exporter of steam coal.

4.2.6.7   Ecuador

Small lignite deposits are present in the Tertiary sequences of the Amazon basin, the Pacific coast, and in intermontane basins in the Andes. Only the latter are considered to be of significance. The Malacatus basin contains seams of up to 4.0 m in thickness, disrupted by faulting. To the north the Loja basin contains seams of up to 2.0 m in thickness and the Canar-Azuay basin has seams of up to 5.0 m. All the coals are high volatile subbituminous coals with high ash and sulphur contents.

4.2.6.8   Mexico

Coals of Mesozoic (Cretaceous) age are found throughout Mexico. All are highly tectonised and are structurally complex. The principal coalfield is at Coahuila, close to the border with Texas, where shallow, gently dipping seams reach 2.0 m in thickness. The coal is low volatile and bituminous with high ash and low sulphur contents and with no coking properties. Output is used for local industry and power generation. Another location of note is in the north-west of Mexico at Sonora where anthracites averaging 1.0 m thickness are found.

Numerous other small deposits of bituminous coal are present in Mexico. Seam development is irregular and often ameliorated by volcanic activity.

4.2.6.9   Peru

Mesozoic coals are located within the Andean Cordillera, which extends throughout Peru from north to south.

The northern coalfields are highly tectonised and affected by associated igneous activity, resulting in the formation of anthracite as well as bituminous coal. The principal areas are those of Alto Chicama and Santa. Subbituminous and bituminous coals are found in the southern coalfields of Oyon and Jatunhuasi. All production is for local needs.

4.2.6.10 Uruguay

The north-east of Uruguay contains Carboniferous–Permian (Gondwana) sediments which represent the southern extension of the south Brazilian coalfields. Coals are found in this area, but no development has yet occurred.

4.2.6.11 Venezuela

All the known coal-bearing sequences in Venezuela are Tertiary in age and occur in a series of basins across the country north of the river Orinoco. The principal areas of interest are Zulia, Lobatera and the Caracas-Barcelona basin. Other coal occurrences are known in the Lara region and within the eastern Orinoco basin.

The Zulia deposit is the most important so far identified in Venezuela and is situated in the extreme north-west of the country. Between 25 and 30 seams with thicknesses of between 0.5 and 15.0 m are present. The coal is high volatile, non-coking bituminous with variable ash and low sulphur contents, suitable as a steam coal for export.

The Lobatera coalfield is in the west of Venezuela, close to the Colombian border. Here 35 seams over 0.3 m thick are present. The coal is high volatile with low ash and sulphur contents.

The Caracas-Barcelona coalfield contains the deposits of Naricual and Fila Maestra. Naricual contains 15 seams, ranging from 1.0 to 10.0 m in thickness, of high volatile bituminous coal with a low sulphur content; some of these seams have coking properties. The deposit at Fila Maestra is currently being investigated.

In the Lara region thin lenticular seams of low volatile bituminous coal occur with low sulphur content. In the eastern Orinoco basin seams of lignite occur up to 1.2 m thick, with high sulphur contents. These have not been considered significant.

4.2.7 Commonwealth of Independent States (formerly USSR)

The Commonwealth of Independent States (CIS) is the third largest coal producer in the world. It has vast reserves of all

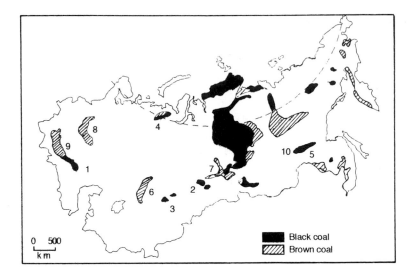

Figure 4.7 Coal deposits of the Commonwealth of Independent States (formerly USSR). (1) Donetsk Basin; (2) Kuznetsk Basin; (3) Karaganda Basin; (4) Pechora Basin; (5) South Yakutsk Basin; (6) Ekibastuz Basin; (7) Kansk-Achinsk Basin; (8) Moscow Basin; (9) Dnepr Basin; and (10) Neryungri

ranks of coal stretching across the whole of the country. Thick coal-bearing sequences range from Palaeozoic (Carboniferous–Permian), Mesozoic (Triassic, Jurassic and Cretaceous) to Cainozoic in age. These are preserved in a series of large sedimentary basins, which generally become younger from west to east (Figure 4.7). Most of the older basins are structurally disturbed, resulting in steeply dipping seams and extensive faulting.

The principal black coal areas are the basins of Donetsk, Kuznetsk, Karaganda, Pechora and South Yakutsk, and the principal brown coal basins are those of Ekibastuz, Kansk-Achinsk, Moscow and Dnepr.

The Donetsk Basin is located in western CIS. It contains numerous steeply dipping seams with thicknesses up to 2.5 m. The coals are anthracite and low volatile bituminous, with good coking properties, with variable ash and high sulphur.

The Kuznetsk Basin is situated in south-central CIS and again contains numerous seams which range from 1.0 to more than 15.0 m in thickness and range from anthracite and low volatile bituminous coal with low sulphur contents to subbituminous coal.

The Karaganda Basin lies to the south-west of the Kuznetsk area and contains various seams, some >5.0 m in thickness. Coals are high volatile bituminous with good coking properties.

The Pechora Basin is located on the Arctic Circle north-east of Moscow. Here are found high volatile semi-coking bituminous coals with high ash and low sulphur contents.

The South Yakutsk Basin in the extreme south-east of the asiatic CIS contains thin seams of high volatile bituminous coals with good coking properties together with high ash and low sulphur contents. The principal region producing coal is the Neryungri area.

The last two basins are geographically remote and are subject to deep permafrost conditions. The Ekibastuz and Kansk-Achinsk Basins are large producers of brown coal. Both produce subbituminous coals with high ash and low sulphur contents. They are relatively undisturbed structurally and have the potential to be very large producers.

The Moscow Basin produces subbituminous coal with high ash and sulphur contents. Seams are thin and mining conditions difficult. Coal from this area is used for power generation due to its proximity to Moscow. Similarly, the Dnepr Basin is close to the industrial centre of the CIS and has supplied brown coals over a long period.

The CIS has numerous other deposits of both black and brown coals; because of this its potential for production is enormous, but its geographical location and severe climatic conditions may curtail the development of many of these deposits.

4.2.8   Far East

The Far East region contains 13 countries with known coal deposits. By far the largest of these is China, which has vast resources of all ranks of coal.

The coals of the Far East range in age from Palaeozoic to Cainozoic, and all ranks of coal are present. Their distribution is shown in Figure 4.8.

4.2.8.1   Brunei

Coals in Brunei are Tertiary in age and occur in the north-east of the country close to the capital Bandar Seri Begawan, and also in the headwaters of the Belait river in the south-west of Brunei. Coal seams are 0.5 to 5.0 m in thickness and are high volatile bituminous with low ash and variable sulphur content. Those seams close to Bandar Seri Begawan have been extensively worked in the past, while those in the Belait river basin are undeveloped, but are geographically remote.

4.2.8.2   Burma

The coal deposits of Burma consist of scattered occurrences of Tertiary lignite, with some Mesozoic black coals which have been highly tectonised.

Lignites are found in the western and southern parts of the country, notably at Kalewa and Pakokku. The black coals are

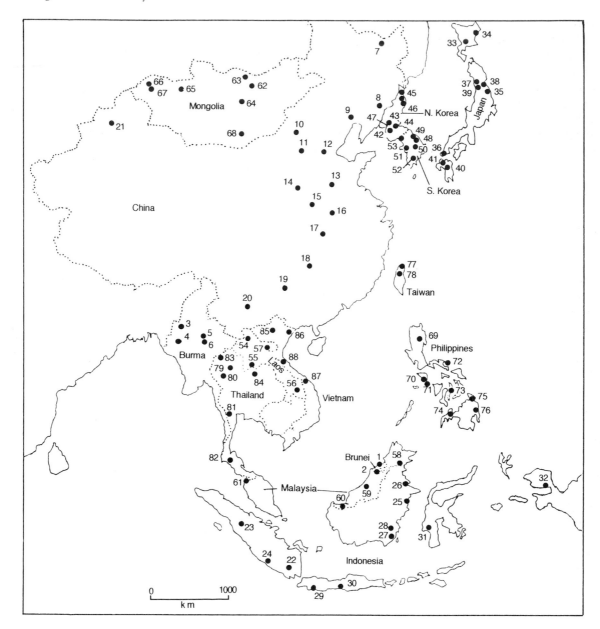

situated inland in the east-central region of Burma, in the Panlaung and Henzada districts. The coals are reported to be of poor quality and are only worked on a very small scale.

4.2.8.3   China

China possesses enormous resources of coal which cover all ages and ranks. The main producing coalfields are located in the eastern half of China stretching from the far north to the southern border. Mining is intensive, traditionally underground but with more modern opencast operations becoming established. In the north, Palaeozoic and Mesozoic sediments are preserved in a series of basins which are relatively undisturbed. The principal areas are Kirin, Heilungkiang, Liaoning, Inner Mongolia, Shansi and Hopeh. The rank of the coal is predominantly bituminous, with some anthracite and brown coals. The northernmost areas contain high volatile bituminous coal with high ash and low sulphur contents. Those coals located at Kirin have good coking properties suitable for the metallurgical industry.

The coalfields in the Liaoning region have numerous seams, some extremely thick (>100 m) and have undergone little structural disturbance. Coals are high volatile bituminous with low ash and sulphur, some having good coking properties.

The Inner Mongolia region contains seams up to 10.0 m in thickness of low volatile bituminous coal to anthracite, with low ash and sulphur. Some is suitable for coke production.

Shansi produces low volatile bituminous coal and anthracite with low ash and sulphur content, with some coals suitable for coke production. Seams are up to 10.0 m in thickness and are relatively undisturbed.

The Hopeh region includes several coalfields containing seams of which the thickest reaches 5.0 m. The coal is low volatile bituminous and anthracite with low ash and sulphur.

Eastern central China contains the coal mining districts of Shantung, Shensi, Honan, Anhwei and Hupeh. The Shantung region is an important producer of export quality coals. Seams are 1.0–10.0 m in thickness and undisturbed. They are bituminous coals, low in ash and sulphur and are some of the best coking coals in China. The Shensi region also has thick undisturbed seams of bituminous coal, but these are not coking coals as in the Shantung region. In the Honan region, coal seams are deep, up to 10.0 m in thickness, and contain high volatile bituminous coals. In the Anhwei region, steeply dipping seams reach 6.0 m in thickness. The coals are bituminous with a low sulphur content and some are suitable for coke production. The Hupeh region is close to the Yangtze river and produces low volatile bituminous coal with high ash and high sulphur.

In south-eastern China, the regions of Kweichow and Yunnan have seams up to 12.0 m in thickness and have undergone little structural disturbance. The coals are low volatile bituminous coking coals, those at Yunnan having a lower sulphur content.

There are numerous other coal deposits mostly situated close to those listed. An exception is the large deposit of Jurassic low volatile bituminous and subbituminous coal located in a broad belt in the extreme north-west of China in the Sinkiang-Uighur

Figure 4.8 (*opposite*) Coal deposits of the Far East. (1) Bandar Seri Begawan; (2) Belait Basin; (3) Kalewa; (4) Pakkoku; (5) Panlaung; (6) Henzada; (7) Heilungkiang; (8) Kirin; (9) Liaoning; (10) Inner Mongolia; (11) Shansi; (12) Hopeh; (13) Shantung; (14) Shensi; (15) Honan; (16) Anhwei; (17) Hupeh; (18) Hunan; (19) Kweichow; (20) Yunnan; (21) Sinkiang-Uighur; (22) Bukit Asam; (23) Ombilin; (24) Bengkulu; (25) Sangatta; (26) Berau; (27) Senakin/Tanah Grogot; (28) Tanjung; (29) South Java; (30) Central Java; (31) South Sulawesi; (32) Bintuni; (33) Ishikari; (34) Kushiro; (35) Joban; (36) Omine; (37) Mogami; (38) Miyagi; (39) Nishitagawa; (40) Miike; (41) Chikuho; (42) Pyongyang; (43) North Pyongyang; (44) Kowon-Muchon; (45) Kyongsang; (46) Kilchu-Myongchon; (47) Anju; (48) Samcheog; (49) Janseong-Kangnung; (50) Mungyeong; (51) Chungnam; (52) Boeun; (53) Kimpo-Yeoncheon; (54) Phongsaly; (55) Ventiane; (56) Saravan; (57) Muongphan; (58) Silimpopon; (59) Bintulu; (60) Silantek; (61) Bukit Arang; (62) Baganur; (63) Sharin Gol; (64) Nalayh; (65) Mogoyn Gol; (66) Achit Nuur; (67) Khartarbagat; (68) Taban Tologoy; (69) Cagayan; (70) Mindoro; (71) Semirara; (72) Catanduanes; (73) Cebu; (74) Zamboanga; (75) Gigaquit; (76) Bislig; (77) Chilung; (78) Hsinchu; (79) Mae Moh-Li; (80) Mae Tun; (81) Nong Ya Plong; (82) Krabi; (83) Vaeng Haeng; (84) Na Duang; (85) Nan Meo-Phan Me-Bo Ha; (86) Quang Yen; (87) Nong Son; and (88) Huong Khe autonomous region. Large reserves of coal are present in this geographically remote area; many very thick seams of steam and coking coal are present, which represent a future source of coal in China.

4.2.8.4 *Indonesia*

Indonesian coal deposits are Tertiary in age and are situated on the islands of Sumatra, Borneo, Java, Sulawesi and Irian Jaya. There is a range in rank from lignite to low volatile bituminous, the higher rank coals being affected by local igneous intrusions or, more importantly, by regional heating due to magmatic activity at relatively shallow depths.

On the island of Sumatra, three coalfield areas are currently exploited. At Bukit Asam at the south-eastern end of the island, seams up to 12.0 m in thickness are present. Coals are generally subbituminous with low ash and sulphur contents, but some bituminous coal is present in close proximity to igneous intrusions. The coals are mined by opencast methods and used primarily for electricity generation. Ombilin, located in central Sumatra, has a few thick seams of high volatile bituminous and subbituminous coal with low ash and sulphur contents. Mining is by both opencast and underground methods, and the coal is used for electricity generation and cement manufacture. In the Bengkulu region on the south-west coast of Sumatra, small occurrences of mostly subbituminous coals with low sulphur content are worked on a small scale.

On the island of Borneo, the Indonesian territory of Kalimantan has coal deposits situated along the east coast. In East Kalimantan, subbituminous and bituminous coals are found, notably in the Sangatta and Berau areas. These coals are up to 10.0 m in thickness with extremely low ash and low sulphur contents. Some of these coals are now exported as prime quality steam coals. In South Kalimantan, in the Senakin/Tanah Grogot and Tanjung areas, subbituminous and bituminous coals with similar characteristics are mined both for export and for local power generation needs. In the north-eastern part of Kalimantan, north of Berau, bituminous coals are present at Tarakan, but high sulphur contents have halted the development of these deposits.

In Java, subbituminous coals have been worked on a very small scale in central and western parts. These coals are thin and irregularly developed.

In South Sulawesi, similar subbituminous coals are present which have been mined for local needs.

In West Irian, the western half of the island of New Guinea, subbituminous coals and lignites are present in the Bintuni region at the western end of the island, but have not yet been developed.

Large deposits of recent peat are present in West Kalimantan but these have not been commercially developed.

4.2.8.5 *Japan*

Japanese coal deposits are widespread and range from Permian to Tertiary in age. The productive coals are Tertiary, while the Permian and Mesozoic coals are of minor importance except for the Omine Coalfield in western Honshu.

The principal Tertiary coalfields are located on the three Japanese islands of Hokkaido, Honshu and Kyushu.

On Hokkaido Island, the structurally complex area of the Ishikari Coalfield provides strongly caking bituminous coal with high ash and low sulphur content. The coals are produced for local use. The Kushiro Coalfield is less disturbed and produces non-coking bituminous and subbituminous coal.

On the island of Honshu, the Joban Coalfield has seams up to 3.0 m in thickness and is thought to extend eastwards offshore. The Omine Coalfield on the south-west coast is important as a source of anthracite for Japanese industry. The Mogami, Nishi-tagawa and Miyagi Coalfields are situated in the northern half of the island and are the chief lignite producers in Japan.

On Kyushu Island, the Miike Coalfield is structurally undis-turbed and is mined offshore. The coal is bituminous with good coking properties. The Chikuho Coalfield has similar coals to Miike, and is a source of coking coal for the metallurgical industry.

Numerous smaller coalfields containing bituminous coals and lignites are worked on a small scale.

4.2.8.6 *Democratic Republic of (North) Korea*

Coals of Palaeozoic, Mesozoic and Cainozoic age are present throughout the Korean peninsula.

The principal Palaeozoic coalfields are Pyongyang and North Pyongyang in the north-west, and Kowon-Muchon in the east. All have been highly tectonised, consequently seam thicknesses are variable due to intense folding. However, thicknesses of 5.0 m and 15.0 m are reached. The coals are low volatile anthra-cites with low ash and sulphur contents. All the coal is mined by underground methods and is used for local industry and domestic heating.

Mesozoic coals form small deposits of anthracite. These are also strongly folded, but to a lesser extent than the Palaeozoic coals.

The Cainozoic coalfields contain subbituminous coal and lignite and are found chiefly in the north-east of the country. The Kyongsang and Kilchu/Myongchon Coalfields contain lignites, and the Tumangang in the extreme north-east contains subbituminous coal which is used for electricity generation. The Anju Coalfield is located north of Pyongyang and is a large deposit of subbituminous coal which is being developed as an opencast operation.

4.2.8.7   *Republic of (South) Korea*

Coals in South Korea are of similar age and character to those in the north of the peninsula. Again, all of the mining operations are underground.

The principal Palaeozoic coalfields are Samcheog, Jeongseon, Kangnung, Danyang and Mungyeong. These coalfields are highly tectonised and intensely folded. Seam thicknesses vary considerably due to the squeezing of the coals; 1.0–2.0 m is usual. All the coal is anthracite with a low sulphur content and is exclusively used for local industry and domestic heating.

Mesozoic (Jurassic) coal deposits are present at Mungyeong and Chungnam. The latter is structurally complex; again all the coal is anthracite. Small anthracite deposits are found at Boeun and Honam in the south, and at Kimpo and Yeongcheon on the northern border of the country. Small workings produce anthracite for local use.

Tertiary deposits containing thin seams of lignite are found in small areas bordering the south-east coast of South Korea.

4.2.8.8   *Laos*

Palaeozoic, Mesozoic and Cainozoic coals are present in Laos. The Palaeozoic deposits are chiefly anthracite with a high ash content. There are three principal occurrences; at Phongsaly in the north, the Ventiane coal basin in west-central Laos, and the Saravan coal basin in the south of the country. In the Ventiane basin, five seams ranging from 2.6 to 6.0 m are present; in the other areas the seams are considerably thinner.

Some Mesozoic (Triassic–Jurassic) coals are found in the Phongsaly region. All are steeply dipping and seams range in thickness from 0.1 to 10.0 m. The coals are high volatile bituminous with low ash and low sulphur contents.

Cainozoic brown coals are present in several Tertiary basins located in the east of the country, chiefly at Muongphan, with other occurrences at Khang Phanieng, Hua Xieng and Bam O. These Tertiary basins are highly faulted and contain subbituminous coals and lignite. At Muongphan, lignite seams are 1.0–6.0 m in thickness and have high volatile and ash contents.

All Laotian coal produced is used for local needs.

4.2.8.9 *Malaysia*

Malaysian coals are found on the west coast of the West Malaysian peninsula, and on the East Malaysian side of the island of Borneo in the states of Sabah and Sarawak.

All the coals are of Tertiary age. Those in Sabah are subbituminous with some coking properties, but often with high sulphur contents; these have been mined at Silimpopon in east Sabah. In Sarawak, higher quality bituminous and subbituminous coals with low sulphur contents have been identified at Bintulu, Balingian and Silantek, and mined on a local scale.

In West Malaysia at Bukit Arang on the Malaysian/Thailand border, extensive lignite deposits have been identified; another occurrence of lignite is reported north of Kuala Lumpur at Batu Arang.

4.2.8.10 *Mongolia*

Coal deposits in Mongolia are concentrated in the north of the country. Highly tectonised Palaeozoic coals in the form of anthracite and low volatile bituminous coals are found in small isolated deposits.

Mesozoic (Cretaceous) coals are less deformed and consist of low volatile bituminous coal with low sulphur contents, found principally in the Baganur Coalfield, where seam thicknesses can be up to 25.0 m. In the same region occur the coalfields of Sharin Gol and Nalayh, and in the west of the country are the coalfields of Achit Nuur and Khartarbagat.

In southern Mongolia, at Taban Tologoy, is a large deposit of bituminous coal; however, its geographical location has so far prevented its development.

4.2.8.11 *Philippines*

Throughout the Philippines archipelago is situated a series of Tertiary basins containing coal-bearing sediments. The coals are predominantly of subbituminous rank although variations in rank do occur related to local structure and contemporaneous and recent igneous activity.

The northern island of Luzon contains the Cagayan basin. This area is only partially explored, but is known to contain seams up to 2.0 m in thickness and is structurally undisturbed. The coals are high volatile subbituminous with low ash and sulphur. The deposit covers a large area and is amenable to opencast mining operations. Such coals would be suitable for local electricity generation.

The island of Mindoro has coal deposits in the south. The seams are up to 2.8 m in thickness and are subbituminous with variable sulphur contents.

Semirara Island lies to the south of Mindoro and contains coals up to 6.0 and 12.0 m in thickness. The coals are subbituminous with low ash and sulphur.

Catanduanes Island contains lenticular seams up to 5.0 m in thickness. These are steeply dipping and are ameliorated by igneous intrusions. This has resulted in the formation of bituminous coals with high sulphur and moderate coking properties.

Cebu Island contains several coal deposits. Seams are up to 4.0 m in thickness, dip steeply and are high volatile subbituminous coals with low ash and variable sulphur contents.

Mindanao Island has coal deposits at Malangas and Zamboanga in the west, and at Gigaquit and Bislig in the east. The Malangas-Zamboanga area has ameliorated coals, anthracite and bituminous coking coal. At Gigaquit, low rank coals with high ash contents are characteristic, and at Bislig some bituminous coal with locally high sulphur content is mined. Numerous other small coal deposits are worked locally throughout the archipelago.

Small scale underground mining characterises the bulk of the coal exploration in the Philippines; however, those deposits at Cagayan, Semirara and Zamboanga could be developed further.

4.2.8.12 Taiwan

Coals in Taiwan are Tertiary in age, and the coalfields are grouped into a northern and a central province. Of these, only the northern province has economic significance. The Taiwan coalfields have been highly tectonised, and some have been ameliorated by igneous intrusions. The coals are high volatile bituminous and subbituminous with low ash and sulphur contents. At Chilung in the north of Taiwan, ameliorated coals (semi-anthracites) have been mined in small areas. Further south, low volatile bituminous coal, low in sulphur and with good coking properties, has been mined at Hsinchu, Nanchuang, Shuangchi and Mushan. Four seams exceed 1.0 m in thickness and because of the high level of tectonic disturbance there are only underground operations working at increasingly deeper levels. This may result in the cessation of mining in these areas.

4.2.8.13 Thailand

In Thailand virtually all the known coal deposits are of Tertiary age, together with some Mesozoic coals found in the north-east of Thailand at Na Duang. The Tertiary sediments are preserved in a series of basins; of these, the Mae Moh basin in north-west Thailand is the most extensive. Other basins in close proximity are Mae Tip, Li, Mae Tun and Vaeng Haeng. Other Tertiary coals are found east of Bangkok at Nong Ya Plong, and at Krabi in the extreme south-west.

Seams in Thailand generally range from 2.0 to 12.0 m; however, at Mae Moh and Krabi, seams up to 30.0 m are worked. Most coals are relatively undisturbed structurally. These Tertiary coals range from lignite to high volatile subbituminous, with generally low sulphur contents, as found at Mae Moh, Mae Tip, and Li, and some with higher rank, high volatile bituminous as found at Mae Tun and Nong Ya Plong.

The Mesozoic coal at Na Duang is semi-anthracite with a low sulphur content.

The bulk of Thailand's coals are mined and supplied to the electricity generating industry.

4.2.8.14 Vietnam

In Vietnam, black coals are of Mesozoic (Triassic) age, and are located firstly in a broad belt running east to west, situated north and north-east of Hanoi. This belt consists of four sedimentary basins each containing coal-bearing strata; these are the Nan Meo, Phan Me, Bo Ha and Quang Yen basins. Secondly, they are found in central Vietnam at Nong Son and Huong Khe.

The Nan Meo, Phan Me and Bo Ha basins contain low volatile bituminous coals, some with coking properties. These areas were worked on a small scale in the past.

The most important coal basin is the Quang Yen basin, the eastern part of which borders the north-east coast. Coals are preserved in a series of folds orientated parallel to the coast, and are bounded by large east–west running faults.

In the east part of the Quang Yen basin, the Hong Gai Coalfield is the chief coal producer in Vietnam; up to six seams with thicknesses of 2.0–8.0 m are worked. Coals are low volatile anthracites with low ash and sulphur contents.

In central Vietnam, in the Nong Son area, is a thick seam up to 20.0 m in thickness. This is low volatile bituminous to semi-anthracite with a variable sulphur content. The Huong Khe area is believed to contain several seams of anthracite.

4.2.9   Australasia

Australasia is one of the major coal producers in the world. The bulk of the coal resources are located in the eastern part of Australia, with smaller coal deposits in Western Australia and New Zealand, as shown in Figure 4.9.

4.2.9.1   Australia

Australia contains coals of Palaeozoic, Mesozoic and Cainozoic age. The whole of the black coal resources are of Palaeozoic age and are located on the western and eastern sides of Australia. Some Mesozoic coal is present in Queensland and an important deposit of Cainozoic coal is found in Victoria.

The Palaeozoic coals are preserved in a series of basins, the principal ones being the Collie and Fitzroy basins in Western Australia, the Bowen and Galilee basins in Queensland, and the Sydney basin in New South Wales. Other smaller areas are known from South Australia and Tasmania.

The Collie basin contains seams ranging from 1.5 to 11.2 m; these are structurally undisturbed and are mined in the Cardiff and Muja areas. The coals are subbituminous with low ash and sulphur contents. Elsewhere in Western Australia coals have been located but have yet to be developed.

In Queensland, the Bowen basin has been explored extensively. The lack of structural disturbance has resulted in the preservation of shallow flat-lying coals which reach thicknesses of up to 30.0 m. The coal is high volatile bituminous, with variable ash and low sulphur content; the coals have good

Figure 4.9   Coal deposits of Australasia. Australia: (1) Collie Basin; (2) Fitzroy Basin; (3) Bowen Basin; (4) Galilee Basin; (5) Cooper Basin; (6) Sydney Basin; (7) Brisbane Basin; (8) Gippsland Basin; (9) Ackaringa Basin; and (10) Tasmania. New Zealand: (1) Northland Coalfield; (2) Waikato Coalfields; (3) Taranaki Coalfields; (4) Otago; (5) Southland; (6) Ohai; (7) Kaitangata; (8) Reefton; (9) Collingwood; (10) Buller; and (11) Pike River–Greymouth

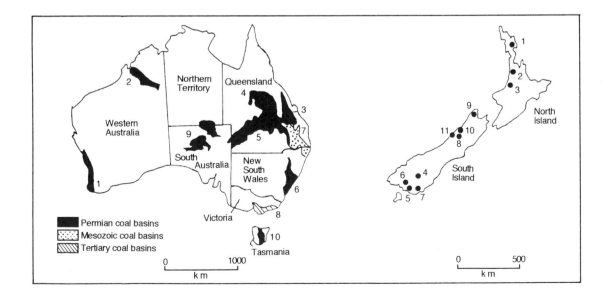

coking properties. The coal is worked by large opencast operations and large reserves have been identified. In the other coal-bearing areas of Queensland, e.g. the Galilee and Cooper basins, large reserves of coal have yet to be developed.

In New South Wales, the Sydney basin is the most important coal producing area in Australia. Again, as in the Bowen basin, there is little structural disturbance. Seam thicknesses reach 10.0 m, and the coal produced is high volatile bituminous with variable ash and low sulphur contents; some of the coals have good coking properties. Coals are mined by underground and opencast methods. The principal mining districts are the Western District, the Burragorang Valley, the Hunter Valley and the Southern District. Much of the coal is exported as steam and coking coal, as well as supplying local needs.

In South Australia, the Ackaringa basin is currently being explored, and in Tasmania some development of the coal deposits may occur in the future.

The Mesozoic coals of south-east Queensland, in the Brisbane area, are subbituminous coals and have not been extensively developed.

The Tertiary coals of the Gippsland basin in Victoria are thick developments of lignite and the principal seams reach enormous thicknesses of 300.0 m. The seams are shallow and flat-lying and are high volatile lignite with low ash and low sulphur contents. This basin is worked in a number of separate coalfields, the most important of which is the Latrobe Valley. This lignite is used exclusively for the Victorian electricity industry.

4.2.9.2 New Zealand

With the exception of a few thin uneconomic coals of Jurassic age, all significant New Zealand coals are Cretaceous–Tertiary in age. The coalfields are located in the western part of North Island, and in the north-western and south-eastern districts of South Island.

In North Island, the Waikato coal region contains New Zealand's major subbituminous coal resource. Coal seams are discontinuous but are thick locally, up to 30.0 m. They are subbituminous with low ash and low sulphur contents. To the north, the Northland area has a few seams up to 2.0 m thick and are of poorer quality.

To the south of the Waikato coal region lies the Taranaki coal area, where seams are usually less than 3.0 m in thickness and are subbituminous with higher sulphur contents.

In South Island are located the Cretaceous–Tertiary coalfields of Otago, Southland, Ohai and Kaitangata in the far south, and on the north-west coast, the Westland coal region includes the Greymouth, Pike River, Charleston, Buller, Reefton and Collingwood Coalfields.

The southern coalfields have seams up to 6.0 and 10.0 m, although they are discontinuous and lensoid. The coals vary from lignite to high volatile subbituminous with variable sulphur contents, some of which may be a high as 6%.

In the Westland coal region, the coals range from subbituminous at Charleston to high volatile bituminous at Pike River, Collingwood and Reefton. In the Buller and Greymouth Coalfields coals range from high volatile to low volatile bituminous.

Production from the New Zealand coalfields is small at the present time.

4.2.9.3   *Antarctica*

Cretaceous coals of mixed quality have been recorded from James Ross Island, on the south-east flank of the Weddell Sea. Other occurrences have been in the area of the Transantarctic Mountains. These generalised occurrences are not shown in the accompanying figures.

Present legislation will prohibit any development of these possible resources for many years to come.

Chapter 5
World coal reserves and production

5.1 WORLD COAL RESERVES

Table 5.1 gives estimates of the proved coal reserves for black coal, i.e. for anthracite and bituminous coals, and for brown coal, i.e. subbituminous coal and lignite. These proved reserves are those which can be regarded with reasonable certainty to be recoverable from known deposits under present-day conditions, and does not include those large resources of coal which are currently being, or will be in the future, fully evaluated.

The table gives an overall total of 1 085 306 million tonnes for known deposits in the world today. Such a figure in itself is meaningless, but the regional totals do give an indication as to the geographical distribution of the bulk of the world's black and brown coal resources.

In the regions containing Gondwana coal deposits, black coal reserves are greater than those for brown coal. This is true for Africa, Central and South America and the Indian Subcontinent. Australia is an exception to this in that its black and brown coal reserves are evenly divided.

In the Far East, the total black coal reserves far exceed those for brown coal; however, if the figures for China are excluded, then the reverse is true.

In Europe, the USA and the CIS (formerly the USSR), brown coal reserves are larger than those for black coal.

5.2 WORLD COAL PRODUCTION

5.2.1 Coal production statistics

Table 5.2 gives the production figures for black and brown coals for the nine world regions. The total world coal production, based on 1989–90 figures, is 5075 million tonnes.

Table 5.1   World coal reserves (million tonnes) at the end of 1989

Region	Black coal (anthracite, bituminous coal)	Brown coal (subbituminous coal, lignite)	Total
USA	130 194	131 059	261 253
Canada	3753	3071	6824
Europe			
Belgium*	127	—	127
Bulgaria*	24	2179	2203
Czechoslovakia*	2493	2322	4815
France	188	44	232
Germany	23 761	55 318	79 079
Greece	—	2908	2098
Hungary*	225	725	950
Poland	28 329	11 555	39 884
Romania*	50	363	413
Spain	341	360	701
Turkey	165	5823	5988
UK	8694	500	9194
Yugoslavia*	35	8430	8465
Others	443	13 150	13 593
Total Europe	64 875	103 677	168 552
Africa			
Botswana*	3 500	—	3500
Malawi*	500	—	500
Mozambique*	600	—	600
Nigeria*	400	200	600
Tanzania*	450	—	450
South Africa	54 977	—	54 977
Zambia*	300	—	300
Zimbabwe	726	—	726
Others	800	70	870
Total Africa	62 253	270	62 523
Indian Subcontinent			
Bangladesh*	250	—	250
India	—	1883	62 166
Pakistan*	60 283	200	200
Total Indian Subcontinent	60 533	2083	62 616
Central and South America			
Brazil	1940	2323	4263
Chile*	20	500	520
Colombia	9632	—	9632
Mexico	1232	634	1866
Venezuela	416	—	416
Others	966	903	1869
Total Central and South America	14 206	4360	18 566
CIS (formerly USSR)	102 980	136 667	239 647
Far East			
China	153 701	13 374	167 075
Indonesia	991	2000	2991
Japan	835	17	852

Table 5.1 (*cont.*)

Region	Black coal (anthracite, bituminous coal)	Brown coal (subbituminous coal, lignite)	Total
North Korea*	600	100	700
South Korea	114	—	114
Philippines*	50	180	230
Taiwan	98	100	198
Thailand*	1	690	691
Vietnam*	100	—	100
Others	400	1300	1700
Total Far East	156 890	17 761	174 651
Australasia			
Australia	45 054	45 508	90 562
New Zealand	22	90	112
Total Australasia	45 076	45 598	90 674
Total world	640 760	444 546	1 085 306

*Figures from various sources; all other figures are from *BP Statistical Review of World Energy* (1990).

Table 5.2   World production of coal (million tonnes) based on 1989–90 figures

Region	Black coal (anthracite, bituminous coal)	Brown coal (subbituminous coal, lignite)	Total
USA	933.7	283.8	1217.5
Canada	37.6	31.7	69.3
Europe			
Belgium	1.0	—	1.0
Bulgaria	0.2	31.5	31.7
Czechoslovakia	23.5	91.8	115.3
France	10.5	0.5	11.0
Germany	76.5	414.1	490.6
Greece	—	46.0	46.0
Hungary	1.7	18.2	19.9
Poland	145.0	71.5	216.5
Portugal	0.2	—	0.2
Romania	4.0	52.3	56.3
Spain	19.6	17.9	37.5
Turkey	3.9	55.0	58.9
UK	89.2	—	89.2
Yugoslavia	0.3	78.3	78.6
Others	0.9	3.8	4.7
Total Europe	376.5	880.9	1257.4
Africa			
Botswana	0.5	—	0.5
Morocco	0.8	—	0.8
Mozambique	0.1	—	0.1

Table 5.2 (*cont.*)

Region	Black coal (anthracite, bituminous coal)	Brown coal (subbituminous coal, lignite)	Total
South Africa	174.7	—	174.7
Swaziland	0.1	—	0.1
Zaire	0.1	—	0.1
Zambia	0.3	—	0.3
Zimbabwe	4.8	—	4.8
Others	0.2	—	0.2
Total Africa	183.1	—	183.1
Indian Subcontinent			
Afghanistan	0.1	—	0.1
India	185.5	8.5	194.0
Iran	1.3	—	1.3
Pakistan	2.8	—	2.8
Total Indian Subcontinent	189.7	8.5	198.2
Central and South America			
Argentina	0.5	—	0.5
Brazil	8.4	—	8.4
Chile	2.1	—	2.1
Colombia	21.0	—	21.0
Mexico	10.0	—	10.0
Peru	0.1	—	0.1
Venezuela	2.5	—	2.5
Others	1.8	—	1.8
Total Central and South America	46.4	—	46.4
CIS (formerly USSR)	537.0	164.7	701.7
Far East			
China	980.0	81.2	1061.2
Indonesia	6.0	—	6.0
Japan	8.5	—	8.5
North Korea	55.0	15.4	70.4
South Korea	19.0	—	19.0
Philippines	1.3	—	1.3
Thailand	—	2.5	2.5
Vietnam	5.6	—	5.6
Others	5.0	—	5.0
Total Far East	1080.4	99.1	1179.5
Australasia			
Australia	171.0	48.3	219.3
New Zealand	2.4	0.2	2.6
Total Australasia	173.4	48.5	221.9
Total world production	3557.8	1517.2	5075.0

Figures compiled from various sources, including BP *Statistical Review of World Energy* (1991) and International Coal Report's *Coal Year* (1991).

It can be seen that the total production figure for black coal (3557.8 million tonnes) is more than double that of brown coal (1517.2 million tonnes). This is in part due to the greater usefulness of black coal as steam and coking coal, and its widespread development in those countries that are more economically advanced. Black coals also make up all internationally traded coal in the world.

China is the largest producer of black coal and Germany produces the greatest tonnage of brown coal.

The development of the coal industry in countries such as Indonesia and Venezuela will increase production in their regions, while the political and economic reorganisation in Eastern Europe may influence future European production figures.

5.2.2.   Regional production and consumption

The bulk of all coal mined is actually consumed in the area in which it is produced. Figure 5.1 shows a comparison of coal consumed with coal produced worldwide for the period 1985–90. Those countries in which coal production is greater than its consumption and where the coal quality is marketable, are large coal exporters, e.g. the USA, Australia and South Africa. Smaller producers such as Colombia export a large percentage of their total production, while others such as China and North Korea produce large tonnages but use almost all domestically. Those developing producers such as Venezuela and Indonesia will produce more coal than they will consume; this production is intended for the export market.

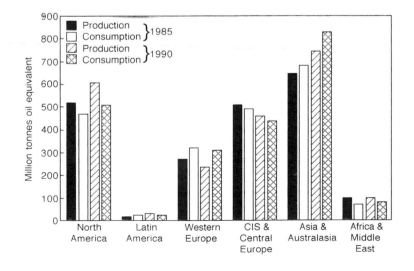

Figure 5.1   World coal production and consumption 1985–90. Reproduced by permission of The British Petroleum Company plc (1991)

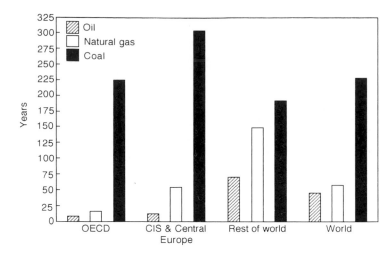

Figure 5.2   Fossil fuel R/P ratios at end of 1990. Reproduced by permission of The British Petroleum Company plc (1991)

5.2.3   Reserves/production ratio

The reserves/production (R/P) ratio is based on those reserves remaining at the end of any year divided by the production in that year. The result is the length of time that those remaining reserves would last if production were to continue at the present level.

Figure 5.2 illustrates R/P figures projected over 300 years. It can clearly be seen that at today's production rates, the world's reserves of coal will last twice as long as the combined reserves of oil and gas.

Chapter 6
Coal exploration and data collection

6.1 INTRODUCTION

The principal role of the geologist in the exploration for coal is to determine the location, extent and quality of the resources available in a particular area, and to identify those geological factors which will facilitate or constrain mine development.

Such a role encompasses the evaluation of existing data, geological mapping and sampling, the use of geophysics and drilling. Once adequate resources of coal of suitable quality have been identified, the geological input will be concentrated on supporting the engineers in the design and development of the mine; this will include additional drilling and sampling followed by geotechnical studies.

The emphasis of geological input will gradually change from exploration to development without a break in continuity. Figure 6.1 illustrates the various stages in this process from exploration mapping and sampling through to reserve calculations, coal quality results and geotechnical investigations.

6.2 FIELD TECHNIQUES

The field examination of coal-bearing sequences is an essential component of any exploration programme, particularly the identification and assessment of a new potential coal-bearing area. Field examination of surface exposures of coal is the precursor to formulating a drilling programme to identify coal in the subsurface.

The first step in carrying out a geological study of a selected area is to collate all available information on that area. This may include published geological maps, topographic and cadastral maps, scientific papers and reports, land records, aerial photographs and satellite imagery. If such information exists for the

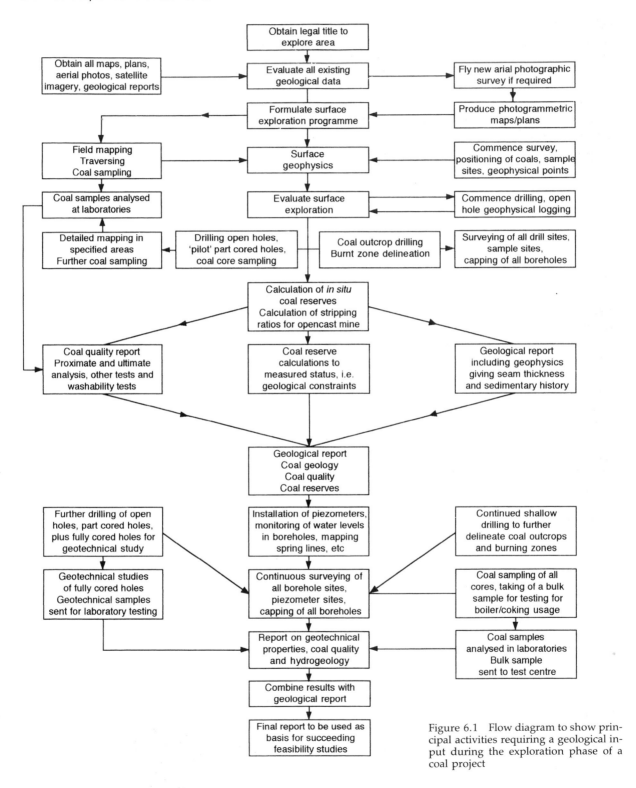

Figure 6.1 Flow diagram to show principal activities requiring a geological input during the exploration phase of a coal project

selected area, then the geological setting can be ascertained as well as topography, water supply and land access, and the availability of base maps. If no surveyed maps exist, photogrammetric maps constructed from available air photographs will be required to carry out ground surveys.

The bulk of this information is usually available from the geological survey or land survey departments of the country in question. Additional data can be obtained from universities, libraries and local government departments.

The study should make special note of any previous history of coal exploration or mining, and details of which companies were involved. In particular, attention should be given to any coal quality data, and the basis on which it is quoted, reserves calculations and production figures.

The scale of maps is important; to carry out a reconnaissance survey, base maps of 1:20 000 and 1:50 000 will be adequate. However, for further detailed mapping and sampling, and for planning drilling sites at set intervals, a scale of 1:10 000 is necessary. For mine operations, large scale plans are required; those of 1:2000 and 1:5000 are most commonly used. If the area has not previously been surveyed, aerial photographs will be used for map compilation (see Section 6.2.2).

Fieldwork will be necessary at all stages of coal mine development, with the concentration of field activities in the reconnaissance and exploration stages of the project.

The style of field surveys varies greatly. In tropical rain forests traverses are made along water courses either on foot or by using some type of boat. Alternatively, local agriculture or industry may have constructed roads or tracks with exposures of bedrock. In hill or mountain country, outcrops may be frequent but require a helicopter for access and observation, while in low relief arid or scrub country, outcrop may be almost non-existent, but there is unrestricted access by four-wheel drive vehicles and trail bikes.

Safety during fieldwork is of prime importance. Suitable clothing should be worn dependent on the climatic region, e.g. tropical jungle boots for wet jungle conditions, together with strong cotton shirts and trousers with as many pockets as possible. When working in temporary pits or sampling coal, protective headwear and footwear is essential.

The principles of working in hostile terrain are a combination of common sense and experience (or learning from an experienced colleague). The adoption of routines to check your own health and hygiene are essential at the end of a day of fieldwork. This greatly facilitates the next day of work and monitors any potential problems that might arise, e.g. the daily foot inspection is important as the feet take the brunt of fieldwork, particu-

larly in mountainous and jungle areas. Carelessness about your health can result in discomfort and an inability to carry out fieldwork and, in extreme cases, gives rise to the necessity of leaving a remote field area, which may be difficult and expensive. Although such situations are more likely to occur in geographically difficult areas, such routines are still good practice in logistically accessible countries.

In addition to health checks, at the end of each day of fieldwork all equipment should be checked for damage or losses, all notebooks and field record sheets and maps should be clearly labelled and kept as dry and secure as possible.

Temporary and permanent campsites must be kept clean, and food and equipment should not be left lying about. Kitchen, washing and toilet areas should be clearly separated and adhered to; toilet areas should never be upstream of the campsite. Campfires must be carefully controlled, ecpecially in areas in which the vegetation is likely to ignite easily. Carelessness in this respect can result in the destruction of habitat or property, or both, and even loss of life to plants and animals in the area.

Each day of work should be planned in sequence, with time allowed for travelling, sampling and data recording. It is important to remember that field mapping is the only method apart from drilling by which basic information on the geology of an area is obtained. All later studies are only as good as the original information collected.

6.2.1 Outcrop mapping

Fundamental geological field procedures are described in Barnes's *Basic Geological Mapping* in this handbook series (Barnes, 1981), and include the basic elements of geological mapping, rock identification and structural measurements. Mapping is ideally suited to areas where coal-bearing sequences are exposed due to erosion, folding and faulting. However, it is common to have to evaluate areas with a scarcity of outcrops to provide at least some basic geological data.

The geologist will need the following items of equipment to carry out fieldwork: topographical and geological maps and site plans (if any), map case, aerial photographs and pocket stereoscope, Chinagraph pencils, notebook or field record sheets, marker pens, geological hammer, chisel, trowel or fold-up spade, polythene bags, sample bags and labels, clinometer/ compass, hand lens, small and large tape measures, penknife and camera. Some of these items are shown in Figure 6.2.

The coal geologist will be required to determine the location, structural attitude and extent of coals and associated strata, together with structural features such as faults and fold axes and

Figure 6.2 Field equipment used by coal geologists

igneous intrusions, all of which, if present, influence future mining conditions. If, for the area of interest, geological information already exists, then further fieldwork may only involve verification of coal seam locations, taking fresh samples and filling in any gaps in the previous data.

In the absence of published base maps, plans have to be produced by field traverses, usually in the form of tape and compass traverses. A long plastic tape measure (30 m graduated in centimetres) is used along the traverse in conjunction with a compass bearing at the beginning of each measurement. All such traverses must be connected in closed loops and the closing errors between the surveys must be corrected before any geological information is plotted. The latter is usually carried out at base camp. The beginning and end of each traverse must be clearly marked together with all distinct physical features such as hills, river bends, waterfalls, road crossings and buildings. Geological features such as thick sandstones, coal seam outcrops, sample locations, faults and fold axes will also be put

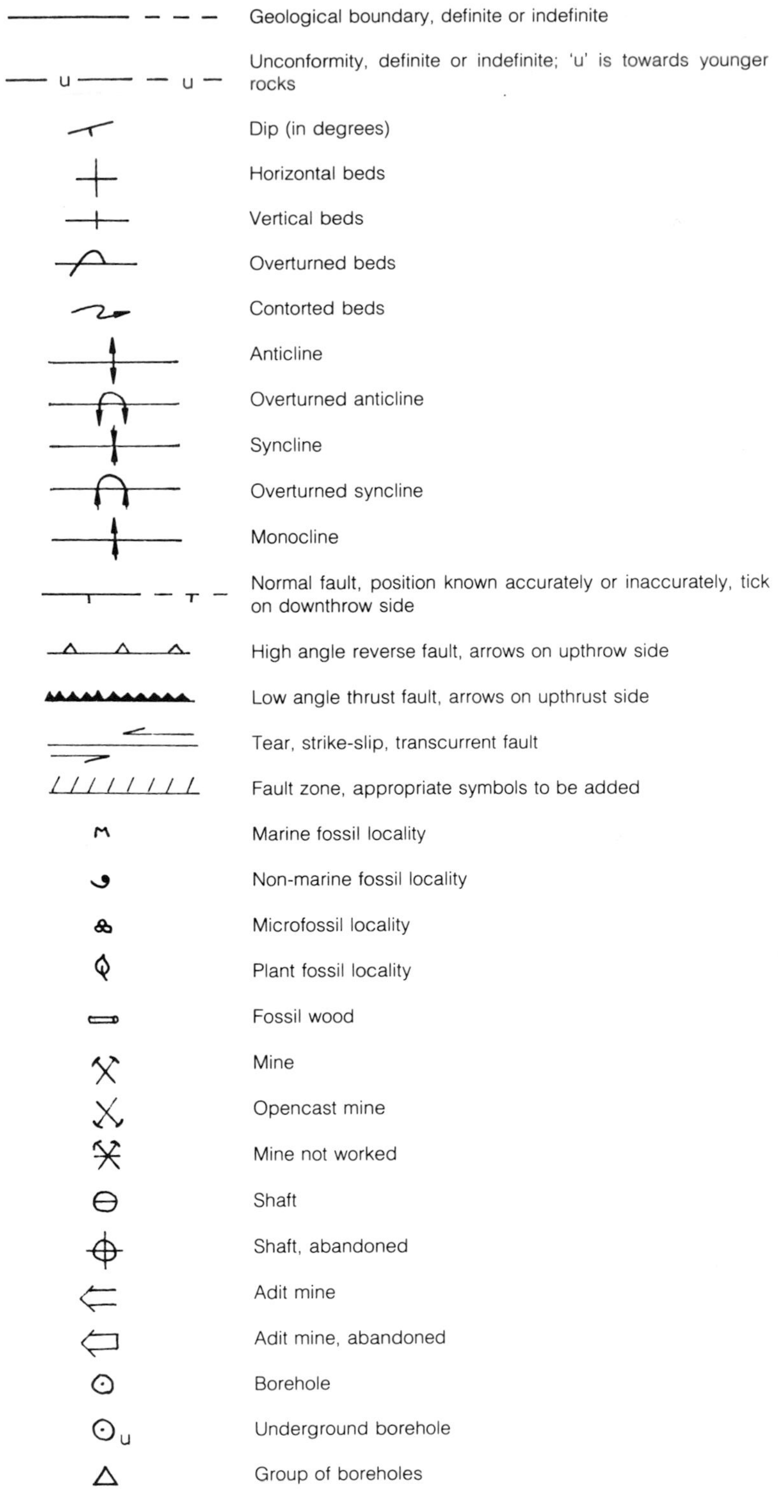

Figure 6.3   Symbols for geological maps

——— – – –	Geological boundary, definite or indefinite
—u——– u–	Unconformity, definite or indefinite; 'u' is towards younger rocks
	Dip (in degrees)
	Horizontal beds
	Vertical beds
	Overturned beds
	Contorted beds
	Anticline
	Overturned anticline
	Syncline
	Overturned syncline
	Monocline
	Normal fault, position known accurately or inaccurately, tick on downthrow side
	High angle reverse fault, arrows on upthrow side
	Low angle thrust fault, arrows on upthrust side
	Tear, strike-slip, transcurrent fault
	Fault zone, appropriate symbols to be added
M	Marine fossil locality
	Non-marine fossil locality
	Microfossil locality
	Plant fossil locality
	Fossil wood
	Mine
	Opencast mine
	Mine not worked
	Shaft
	Shaft, abandoned
	Adit mine
	Adit mine, abandoned
	Borehole
	Underground borehole
	Group of boreholes

onto the plan. Standard symbols used to portray geological elements on plans together with mining symbols are shown in Figure 6.3 and the graphic portrayal of the principal lithotypes found in coal-bearing sequences are shown in Figure 6.4. Figure 6.5 shows the results of a typical traverse survey in dissected terrain using these methods. It is important that these identified features can be revisited at a later date to survey the area and plot elevations accurately using a theodolite.

Field traverses should record all geological features seen; when lithological associations have been recognised they should be linked up wherever possible between traverses. Extrapolation across country from one traverse to another should take into account the effects of dip and topography. Where lines obviously do not tie up, then this may be the effect of faulting and should be checked on the ground and on the aerial photographs.

Significant coal-bearing outcrops and the surrounding strata should be mapped in detail and stratigraphic sections should be measured where exposure allows. Individual units such as coal beds and marker beds should be traced laterally to ascertain their lateral correlation. Where possible, the environments of deposition should be interpreted during section measuring and

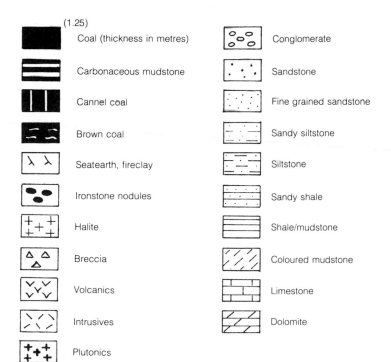

(1.25)
Coal (thickness in metres)

Carbonaceous mudstone

Cannel coal

Brown coal

Seatearth, fireclay

Ironstone nodules

Halite

Breccia

Volcanics

Intrusives

Plutonics

Conglomerate

Sandstone

Fine grained sandstone

Sandy siltstone

Siltstone

Sandy shale

Shale/mudstone

Coloured mudstone

Limestone

Dolomite

Figure 6.4 Graphic portrayal of principal lithotypes in coal-bearing sequences

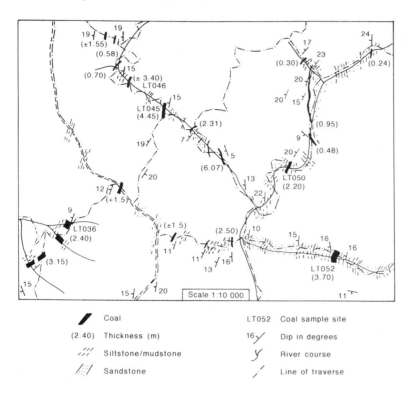

Figure 6.5 Typical traverse survey showing coal outcrops, coal sample sites and structure

coal seam correlation. Care must be taken in measuring sections of strata which may be faulted; low angle or bedding plane thrust faults can pass undetected through a coal section, which can result in exaggerated thickness or missing intervals. Gentle folding can change along strike to isoclinal and recumbent folding.

Recognition and tracing of marker horizons is important. These may be beds of distinctive lithology such as volcanic deposits or limestone, or beds containing fauna such as foraminifera, bivalves and other organisms, or beds containing floral assemblages in the form of plant remains, spores and pollen. Such distinctive horizons can serve to correlate coal seams, identify structural dislocations and establish facies patterns.

National geological surveys adopt this approach when mapping coalfield areas. Figure 6.6 shows a typical field map produced by the British Geological Survey for a coalfield area where a large amount of data has been compiled to produce the final geological map.

The coal geologist will need to be able to recognise all the lithological types associated with coal and coal-bearing sequences. The ability to do this undoubtedly improves with experience. In the USA, handbooks have been produced illustrating in colour all the lithologies found in coal-bearing

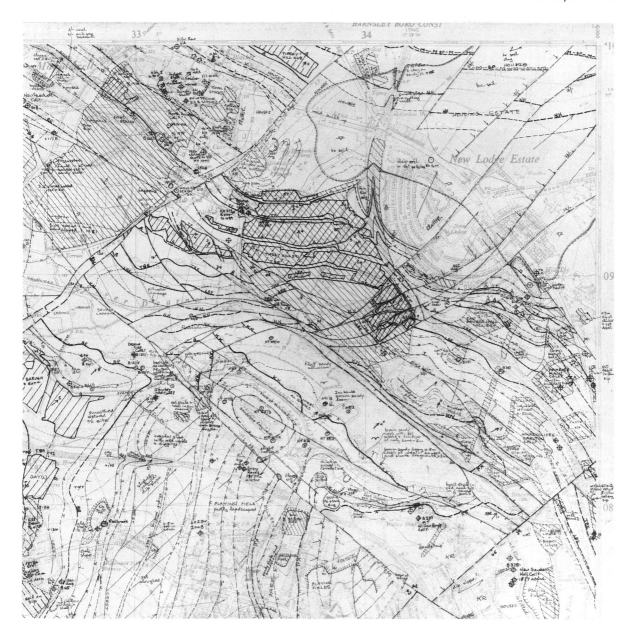

Figure 6.6   Field map of a UK coalfield area, showing geology and past and present coal mining activity, scale 1:10 000. Reproduced by permission of the Director, British Geological Survey; NERC copyright reserved

sequences in the eastern USA. These are invaluable to the inexperienced geologist and, for the most part, can be used on a global basis allowing for the occasional local lithological term. The descriptions of the varieties of sandstone, siltstone, shales, mudstones and coals and their intimate interrelationships are a fundamental part of the data recording stage of fieldwork.

The lithological description of coal itself is essential to the understanding of the physical subdivisions (plies) of the coal.

Figure 6.7   Varieties in black (hard) coal type. (A) Banded bituminous coal from Northumberland, UK with pyrite mineralisation on the cleat face; (B) high volatile, low ash bituminous coal, non-banded, from East Kalimantan, Indonesia; and (C) (*opposite*) bright, high rank anthracite, highly tectonised, from Samcheog Coalfield, Republic of Korea

(A)

(B)

(C)

Most coals have components of bright and dull coal ranging from all bright to all dull with combinations of both in between. Brightness in coal is indicative of the ash content; the brighter the coal the lower the ash content.

Figure 6.7 shows examples of bright coals, a banded bituminous coal from Northumberland, UK, a bright non-banded high volatile coal from East Kalimantan, Indonesia, and a bright high rank anthracite from the Republic of Korea.

In Australia, the Australian Standard K183-1970 gives a graphic representation of coal as shown in Figure 6.8. A shading, ruling and letter system is used, beginning with bright coal (>90% bright coal) and ranging to dull coal (<1% bright coal); also illustrated are symbols for cannel coal, weathered and heat-altered coals. The system used in South Africa closely follows the Australian Standard, and this is also used in countries influenced by these areas, e.g. Indonesia.

In the United Kingdom, British Coal have used a system of graphic representation for coals in their underground operations. These range from bright coal to banded coal to dull coal; Figure 6.9 shows the symbols used together with those for cannel and dirty coal.

In the USA, there is no standardised system for the graphic representation of coals. However, an example produced for ASTM is shown in Figure 6.10. Coals are described as ranging from bright to intermediate bright, intermediate dull and dull. Coals with a high mineral content (bone coal) are also shown.

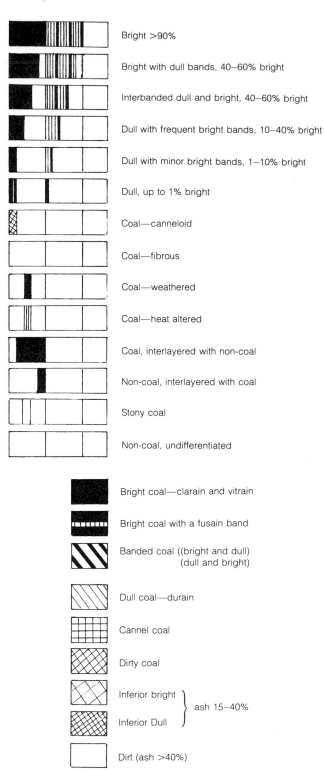

Bright >90%

Bright with dull bands, 40–60% bright

Interbanded dull and bright, 40–60% bright

Dull with frequent bright bands, 10–40% bright

Dull with minor bright bands, 1–10% bright

Dull, up to 1% bright

Coal—canneloid

Coal—fibrous

Coal—weathered

Coal—heat altered

Coal, interlayered with non-coal

Non-coal, interlayered with coal

Stony coal

Non-coal, undifferentiated

Bright coal—clarain and vitrain

Bright coal with a fusain band

Banded coal ((bright and dull)
            (dull and bright)

Dull coal—durain

Cannel coal

Dirty coal

Inferior bright
Inferior Dull   } ash 15–40%

Dirt (ash >40%)

Figure 6.8 Graphic representation of coal seams: Australian Standard K183-1970. Reproduced by permission of Standards Association of Australia

Figure 6.9 Graphic representation of coal seams as used by British Coal (UK). Reproduced by permission of British Coal Corporation

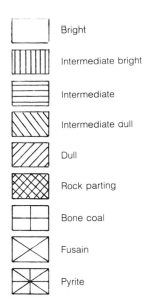

Bright

Intermediate bright

Intermediate

Intermediate dull

Dull

Rock parting

Bone coal

Fusain

Pyrite

In addition to the coal itself, a careful description of the roof and floor of the coal seam is necessary to provide a useful framework for later geotechnical and mining studies.

A description of a coal seam section should include the following.

  (i) Composition of coal seam roof and floor: siltstone, sandstone, carbonaceous shale
 (ii) Structure of coal seam and immediate roof and floor: faults, strike/dip, stratigraphic displacement
(iii) Coal cleat: face cleat, end cleat, strike
 (iv) Slickensides: frequency, continuity
  (v) Joints: strike/dip, frequency, continuity
 (vi) Chemical structures: nodules, ironstone, pyrite, concretionary structures
(vii) Soft sediment structures: slumping, folding, liquefaction structures
(viii) Degree of weathering: from fresh to completely weathered
 (ix) Roof and floor or seam structure: flat, rolling, discontinuities of bedding, splitting
  (x) Mineralisation

6.2.2 Remote sensing and aerial photographs

The use of aerial photographs, together with Landsat imagery and side-looking radar, provides invaluable information on the topography and structural style of an area. When used by experienced interpreters, these techniques, known as 'remote sensing' techniques, can provide a geographical and geological framework rapidly and cheaply. Such a framework can then be used for more detailed coalfield exploration in the form of ground surveys.

Landsat imagery illustrates regional fault patterns and the different geological 'imprint' of a variety of lithological successions within delineated areas. Modern interpretive techniques include computer enhancement of the imagery and enable data to be interpreted at scales of up to 1:1 000 000. Landsat imagery is provided in four separate bands of the visible spectrum from blue to infra-red. In tropical terrain with thick vegetation cover, the red and infra-red spectra are most useful for interpreting geological features. Landsat interpretation is usually used in conjunction with geological and geophysical maps, if available.

The use of overlapping aerial photographs to provide a stereoscopic (three dimensional) interpretation of areas will give a more detailed geological picture. The scale of the photographic coverage, usually 1:50 000 but can be 1:25 000, provides a basis for making photo-interpretation maps of prospective coal deposits by defining regional geological features such as fault lines and zones, persistent lithological horizons, major fold patterns and amounts and changes of dip and strike. The symbols used to portray such geological features on plans are shown in Figure 6.11.

When no, or inadequate, aerial photographic coverage is available, it is necessary to prepare a new set of photographs to work from. This enables a ground crew to mark out 'targets' on the ground which can later be accurately surveyed and used as permanent reference points. The scale of the photographs should be of the same order of magnitude as the scale required for the ground plans. The compilation of maps and plans from aerial photographs is discussed in Barnes (1981).

Dense vegetation cover can mask the ground surface, but can still reflect closely the underlying geology. When combined with fieldwork, subtle lithological differences become apparent. Such photographic interpretation is essential when used in reconnaissance and detailed exploration fieldwork, in identifying traverses and pinpointing physical features on those traverses, e.g. river junctions and road intersections, coal outcrops and for locating preliminary drilling sites.

One drawback with aerial photographs is that in areas of high rainfall, cloud-free conditions are infrequent, and so good photographic coverage of the area is prohibited. Should this occur, side-looking radar surveys, using synthetic aperture radar, can be used to compensate for the lack of aerial photographic cover, as it can highlight structural features not seen at

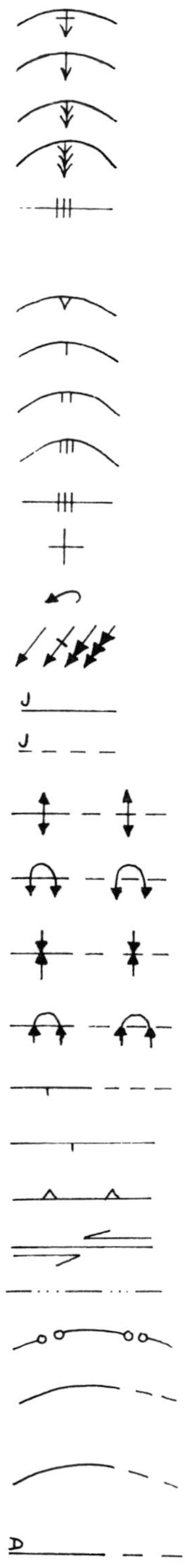

	Bedding scarps with dip slopes	Colour (if used)
	<10°	
	10–25°	
	25–45°	
	>45°<90°	
	Vertical	
	Bedding traces dip slopes absent or very short <10°	Purple
	10–25°	
	25–45°	
	>45°<90°	
	Vertical	
	Horizontal bedding	
	Overturned beds	
	Generalised dips, undefined, gentle, medium, steep	
	Joints, certain	Blue
	Joints, uncertain	Blue
	Anticlinal axis, certain, uncertain	Red
	Overturned anticline, certain, uncertain	Red
	Synclinal axis, certain, uncertain	Green
	Overturned syncline, certain, uncertain	Green
	Fault, certain, uncertain	Red
	Normal fault	Red
	Thrust fault	Red
	Tear fault	Red
	Lineament of unknown origin	Purple
	Unconformity	Red
	Lithological boundary, certain, uncertain	Purple
	Lithological boundary for superficial deposits, certain, uncertain	Brown
	Dykes, certain, uncertain	Red

Figure 6.11 Photogeological symbols for use on aerial photographs and photogrammetric plans (from various sources)

ground level, accurately locate structural elements in the field, and provide a regional structural framework that can be used for planning field traverses and exploration drilling grids.

6.3 DRILLING

Once the field survey has been completed, the position and attitude of all coal seams will be plotted on the base plan. If the dip, structure and initial quality results indicate that the coal is of economic interest, then the next stage in exploration will be the locating of drill sites to provide data in those areas between known coal outcrops and in areas where no outcrops have been located but in which coal is thought to occur.

It is important that the geologist maintains a good and close relationship with the drilling supervisor, drillers and mechanics during the drilling programme. To maintain proper records of the drilling operation, the geologist should liaise with the drilling supervisor to ensure that the driller records the following information for each shift drilled: site details; borehole number; details of openhole drilling; details of hole diameter; details of casing sizes and depths (if used); deatils of each core run; length of core recovered; details of water encountered; strata description; details of timing of each operation; details of flush losses and bit changes; details of core barrel and core bit type; and details of drilling crew.

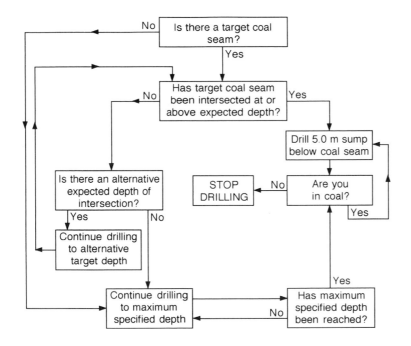

Figure 6.12 Drilling procedure to correctly complete a borehole containing one or more targeted coal seams. Reproduced by courtesy of M. C. Coultas

If the geologist is supervising junior or less experienced geological staff who may be assigned to a particular drilling rig, the procedure that should be followed is outlined in Figure 6.12. This will ensure that the borehole will be completed in the correct fashion by recording the presence or absence of all coal seams targeted, and that the borehole is drilled to at least 5.0 m below the lowest coal seam to allow geophysical logging tools to record the total coal section.

6.3.1   Openhole drilling

Exploration drilling will be carried out to determine coal seam depth, thickness and quality at any given point within an area, and details of the strata associated with the coal.

For most boreholes drilled in the main area of interest, rotary drilling rigs are used. These rigs have good penetration rates, relatively low cost and are mobile. They provide the most economical means of shallow (down to 400 m) openhole and core drilling of coal deposits. Exploration boreholes are usually vertical, but in areas of high dips inclined boreholes may be drilled, particularly in underground workings.

Rotary rigs are usually truck mounted but can be adapted to fit on a bulldozer (Figure 6.13) or on skids. The rigs can use high pressure air circulation (air flush), water or drilling fluid (mud flush), and cut with tungsten carbide bits. In principle, a string of metal rods is rotated axially, and a bit at the base of the string is forced downward under controlled pressure cutting into the sediments, therefore advancing the depth of the hole. Rock

Figure 6.13   Dando dual air–mud flush rig mounted on a bulldozer for use in difficult tropical terrain. Photograph by M. C. Coultas

cuttings are circulated away from the bit and lifted to the surface by the pumped fluid or compressed air. Several types of drill bits are available; the blade bit gives a high penetration rate, needs little maintenance and the 'blades' can be re-sharpened on site. They also have the added advantage of providing larger rock cuttings so facilitating the identification of the lithologies by the geologist logging the borehole. Blade bits are often changed for roller bits when drilling harder strata such as limestone.

Air flush drilling rigs have higher penetration rates for non-core rotary drilling, where compressed air is used in place of water to cool the drill bit and flush the cuttings out of the hole. Air flush also brings up the cuttings much faster, enabling the position of lithological changes to be located more accurately. Air flush drilling is impeded by high rates of groundwater influx; small compressors then find difficulty in maintaining enough pressure to lift the rock cuttings to the surface. However, above the water-table, air flush drilling is particularly useful although there is the drawback of producing large amounts of dust, which may be environmentally unacceptable in certain areas. Again, air flush drilling may be a better option when drilling in zones of burnt coal or broken strata where there is a likelihood of losing drilling fluids.

From the point of view of the geologist, water and mud circulation methods are messy, and do not allow rapid changes of lithology to be noted easily. The cuttings are slower reaching the surface, which allows a certain amount of mixing resulting in the less accurate positioning of lithological boundaries.

There are numerous makes and types of rotary rigs. Examples of those widely used are the Dando (Figure 6.13), the Gryphon (Figure 6.14A) dual air and fluid flush rigs and the Mayhew 1000 (Figure 6.14B), a fluid flush rig.

6.3.2   Core drilling

Cored boreholes are drilled to obtain fresh coal samples and a detailed record of the complete lithological sequence associated with the coals.

Core drilling can be accomplished by using rotary rigs such as the Dando and Mayhew 1000, or by diamond drill rigs such as Longyear 38, 44 and Edeco 40. These rigs use a tungsten carbide or diamond bit attached to a series of metal rods, the lowest of which is designated a core barrel, and rotated under downward pressure; diamond drilling requires the use of drilling fluids. A circle of rock is ground away and a cylindrical core remains in the hollow centre of the core barrel. The recovery of the rock core is facilitated by a non-rotary second metal tube within the core barrel; the core passes into this tube and is protected from

Figure 6.14 (A) Gryphon dual air–mud flush rig operating in UK; (B) Mayhew 1000 truck-mounted fluid flush rig, operating in tropical conditions. Photographs by M. C. Coultas

damage. This is called a double tube core barrel. Even better core recoveries can be obtained by placing a smooth metal tube, split longitudinally, inside the non-rotating inner segment of the double tube core barrel. This type of equipment is called a triple tube core barrel.

When the core is to be removed, the split inner tube is withdrawn with the core still inside. It can then be laid out horizontally and the upper half of the inner tube removed to expose the core for examination. It is then transferred to a segmented core box for logging at a later stage.

Removal of the core barrel can be time consuming. Some equipment allows the central part of the core barrel to be drawn up the centre of the hollow drill rods on a steel cable. This technique is known as 'wireline' drilling. The rods themselves are only removed when the drill bit needs to be changed.

The different diameters of core barrels for rotary and diamond drill rigs are given in Table 6.1. As the diameter of the core decreases, there is a tendency for the core to break up and core losses to increase. It is general practice that the core recovery through a coal or coaly horizons should be not less than 95%. Boreholes drilled in soft sediments or unconsolidated deposits often have unstable sides, particularly in the top part of the hole. For the drill rods to rotate and drill correctly, casing is inserted into the hole to support the collapsing section of the hole. The casing may be metal or PVC and is normally pulled out of the hole once logging has finished.

The core should be placed in a tube of polyethylene sheeting in the core box. This ensures that there is no loss of moisture and that no oxidation of the coal occurs before analysis. Ideally the core should be photographed before sealing in the polyethylene using a measuring tape for scale. The core should be labelled with the borehole number and depth indicators. Core boxes are usually made up of three or four one metre compartments with lids, usually of wood, as shown in Figure 6.15, but metal boxes are used in areas subject to fungal and termite damage.

Figure 6.15 Borehole core laid out in wooden boxes, with depth markers, awaiting examination by the geologist. Photograph by LPT

Table 6.1   Core sizes for wireline, conventional and air flush drilling

1. Wireline core barrels:

Q Series (Longyear)

	AQ	BQ	NQ	HQ	PQ
Hole diameter (mm)	48.0	60.0	75.8	96.0	122.6
Core diameter (mm)	27.0	36.5	47.6	63.5	85.0

Craelius Diabor series

	46	B	N	H	SK6L
Hole diameter (mm)	46.3	60.0	75.7	96.3	146.0
Core diameter (mm)	29.0	36.4	47.6	63.5	102.0

Diamand-Boart

	ADBG.AQ	BDBG.BQ	NDBG.NQ	HDBG.HQ	PDBG.PQ	SDB.G
Hole diameter (mm)	47.6	59.6	75.3	95.6	122.2	145.3
Core diameter (mm)	27.0	36.4	47.6	63.5	85.0	108.2

2. Conventional core barrels:

WF Series (Petroc)
Double tube swivel type

	HWF	PWF	SWF	WWF	ZWF
Hole diameter (mm)	98.8	120.0	145.4	174.5	199.6
Core diameter (mm)	76.2	92.1	112.8	139.8	165.2

Craelius

	E(EWM)	A(AWM)	B(BWM)	N(NWM)	H(HWM)	S(T6S)
Hole diameter (mm)	37.4	47.6	59.6	95.3	98.8	146.0
Core diameter (mm)	21.5	30.1	42.0	54.7	80.9	122.0

Air flush core barrels

	412F	HWAF
Hole diameter (mm)	105.2	99.4
Core diameter (mm)	75.0	70.9

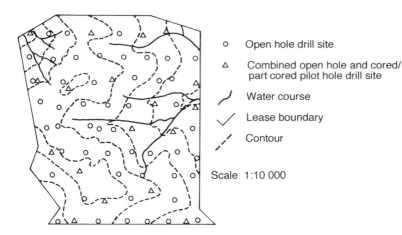

o   Open hole drill site

△   Combined open hole and cored/
     part cored pilot hole drill site

⌇   Water course

∨   Lease boundary

⸝⸍   Contour

Scale 1:10 000

Figure 6.16 Exploration drilling grid showing distribution and position of open holes and cored and part-cored pilot holes

It is essential that the core is placed in the core box in the correct stratigraphical order. Occasionally drillers put cores in boxes the wrong way up, but luckily a comparison with the geophysical log usually shows the error.

The geologist will open up the polyethylene sheeting to log the core; he or she will calculate any core losses, measure the roof and floor of the seam, and record the coal seam lithotypes in detail, together with any partings or splits. In addition he or she will record the degree of weathering, mineralisation and any structural features in the coal and associated strata.

Fully cored boreholes are rare in the exploration phase of a coal deposit. Usually boreholes are only cored for the coals and the coal roof and floor, the depths of these being pre-determined by previous openhole drilling. These part-cored boreholes are sited as 'pilot' holes next to completed open holes to accurately predict the depths and thicknesses of the coal seams. Figure 6.16 shows a typical exploration borehole grid with open holes and part-cored pilot holes.

Fully cored boreholes are usually drilled during the geotechnical investigation stage of the project to fully examine the strengths and structural character of the coals and the associated strata.

6.3.3 Portable drilling

Portable drilling, as the name suggests, involves the use of drilling equipment that can be dismantled into portable components. This is particularly useful in mountainous and jungle terrain where access with conventional drilling rigs is difficult. They normally operate by using a small motor (lawn mower or power saw type motor) which drives an axially rotating set of drill rods with a small blade or roller bit at the bottom; the holes

Figure 6.17   Portable drilling rig using manpower to exert downward pressure on the drill bit, East Kalimantan, Indonesia. Photograph by LPT

are circulated with water or drilling fluid. If the rig motor is not very powerful, to obtain greater penetration the downward pressure may be increased by adding increasing numbers of personnel to sit or stand on the top of the rig, as shown in Figure 6.17.

These small portable rigs are capable of drilling to depths of 60 m and are used to prove coal outcrops, to complete gaps in stream or road sections, and to delineate limits of underground burning zones in coal seams. There are several commercially produced rigs, e.g. Craelius Minuteman, Minogue Packsack and the hydraulic Marlow Mole DD2, as well as small drills made up by companies for specific use on their own projects.

6.3.4   Core and openhole logging

6.3.4.1   Core logging

As core drilling is an expensive part of the exploration and development programme, cores that are obtained should be logged in as much detail as possible, particularly the coal seams and their roofs and floors.

Figure 6.18 Coal geologist logging borehole core in a core shed on-site. Photograph by LPT

Core logging is usually carried out in a core shed where benching is provided on which are placed those core boxes currently being logged. Figure 6.18 shows typical conditions under which core logging takes place. The core shed also provides storage space for the cores already logged as well as for new cores awaiting examination. Core sheds are important for protecting the cores (and the geologist) from the elements; it is worth remembering that the quality of the core log can vary with the conditions under which the geologist has had to work.

The core box will be marked with the depths at which the core run began and ended. Great care should be taken in relating these markers to the depths and thicknesses of the lithologies actually cored. Core losses may occur and these should be clearly marked. Thickness and depth figures will have been reconciled to the geophysical log which will have been run after coring has been completed (see Section 7.5).

Where possible, a photograph of the cored material with way up and depths clearly marked should be taken for the record, as shown in Figure 6.15, and any special feature of the coal or its contact with the beds above and below should be photographed. Figure 6.19 shows a core exhibiting an erosive sandstone roof to a coal seam.

Figure 6.19 Borehole core photographed to show special features. In this instance the erosive sandstone contact above the coal and the siderite nodules contained in the upper part of the coal seam are seen. Photograph by LPT

The state and condition of the core should be described. A complete solid core is a solid core attached to the roof and floor; a fragmented solid core is a broken seam, although all the fragments join up so that there is no doubt of the core recovery. Part core indicates that only part of a solid length of core has been recovered, but that all the lithotypes are present. Fragments indicate that no cores fit together, and that it is not possible to accurately state what length of the core the fragments represent.

Once the measurements of seam roof and floor boundaries, major partings, core loss and any other significant features have been reconciled, and the individual ply sections have been identified, the core can then be split for detailed lithological logging. Splitting is achieved by using a wide chisel or bolster and hammer to split the core lengthwise, making sure that the split is a fresh surface and does not follow a joint.

Low rank coals such as lignite can be cut lengthwise using a saw. One half can then be examined for colour and lithological variations, while the other is left until the core has sufficiently dried out before the texture of the lignite can be described.

Core logging data can be recorded either as a written descriptive log or, as is now common practice, using printed coding sheets designed for computer use. Figure 6.20 shows a core logging sheet giving depths, lithological description, rock strength, weathering, bedding character and sample numbers.

As a general guide, the following features should be recorded.

(i)   Lithology: dominant lithotype; colour and shade; grain size and sorting; distinctive mineralogy and cementation; associated lithotypes and relative proportions

(ii) Sedimentary character: thickness and type of bedding; lamination; types and dimensions of cross bedding; bioturbation; disturbed bedding; contacts with units above and below; fossil content

(iii) Mechanical character: degree of weathering; degree and type of fracturing, orientation and frequency; strength characteristics; mineralisation

6.3.4.2   Openhole logging

The logging of open boreholes involves the identification of rock chippings collected for every metre drilled. The chippings are washed, laid out on polyethylene sheets on benches, and then examined by the geologist, as shown in Figure 6.21. The basic lithology is recorded and the depth at which the predominant lithology in the chippings changes. The accuracy of the depths of the top and bottom of important lithologies, such as coals and thick sandstones, can be reconciled when compared with the geophysical log of the borehole. The lithologies are recorded on data sheets in exactly the same fashion as cored boreholes except that there will be less geological detail for the individual lithologies encountered.

Open borehole logs are important as they give the best indication of where to site cored boreholes, and to predict the depths at which coals can be expected to occur. This is particularly important for the siting of part-cored boreholes in which only coal cores are required for analysis. The coal geologist can expect to spend the greater part of his or her time logging open boreholes in the exploration stages of a project.

6.4   GEOTECHNICAL PROPERTIES

The geotechnical logging of surface exposures in trial pits, dug sections and more particularly in fully cored boreholes is an integral part of the overall geological studies of a coal deposit before the engineering studies to determine mine design and the specification of the coal product to satisfy market requirements.

The geotechnical logging of surface excavations is similar to that of cored boreholes. Those at the surface will tend to give greater information in a lateral sense while borehole cores give better control in a vertical sense.

The fully cored boreholes drilled during the exploration and reserve proving stages of mine development provide a large amount of information useful to the geotechnical engineer. Therefore it is part of the duties of a coal geologist to record as

Figure 6.20 (*opposite*) Example of a core logging sheet used by the coal geologist in the core shed. Reproduced by permission of Antrim Coal Company Ltd. Key to core logging sheet: (CL) clay; (CT) clayey lignite; (IS) ironstone; (LG) lignite; (D) dark; (BK) black; (BF) buff; (DB) dark brown; (EB) grey-brown; (LG) light grey; (MB) medium brown; (MG) medium grey; (OB) orange- brown; (RB) red-brown; (FC) finely comminuted; (SR) sideritic; (SF) smooth; (ST) silty; (WD) woody; (FM) fine–medium; (S) slightly weathered; (R1) very weak rock; (R2) weak rock; (R3) moderately weak rock; (R4) moderately strong rock; (S5) very stiff soil; (IB) interbedded; (TN) thin interbeds; (BU) towards base of unit; (MU) towards middle of unit; (TM) towards middle and top of unit; (XN) very thin interbeds (20–60 mm); (IL) irregularly laminated; (MS) massive bedding; (XL) thinly laminated (<6 mm); (DF) diffuse base; (IN) inclined base; (F3) medium spaced (200–600 mm); (F4) closely spaced (60–200 mm); (L) low angled; (V) vertical; (W) low and medium angled; (C) common; (S) sparse; (CY) clayey; (LM) laminated; (LN) lignitic; and (WL) woody lignite

Hole No. ⊔⊔ S1
PAGE 4 OF 3
ENCODED BY (initials)

Project code / Type / Number	⊔⊔ S1			
Commenced / Completed / Geo. Contr. / Driller Contr. / Geo.	1.2.1.87 / 1.5.11.87 / 546			
Elevation	24.45	Total Depth	115.82	
Core Size (mm)	63.5			

Depth to Base of Unit	Recovered Thickness	Rock Type	Shade	Colour	Lith. Adj. / Grain Size	Weath. Tex.	Mec. Rock St. Rel. (Minor)	%	Bedding Sed. Str.	Base Dip	Disc. Cond	Spac.	Qual. Adj. A Adj. Qual.	Form-ation	Seam	Spill Occur.	Sample Number
60.98	0.61	GT		DEBDB			SR2IB		XLIL	DF10				LNK	LNK		⊔⊔S1LL52
62.01	1.03	LG		DB			SR2	71	IL	10				LNK	LNK		⊔⊔S1LL53
		LG		DEB			SS										
65.40	3.39	GT		DB			SR2TM	87						LNK	LNK		
		IS		MGBFSRGM			R4TN										
				IRONSTONES AT: 62.84 – 62.92, 63.11 – 63.21, 63.98 – 64.06, 64.84 – 64.92m													
65.55	0.15	LG		MG SF			SS			IN				LNK	LNK		⊔⊔S1LL4
65.70	0.15	GT		MG ST			SS							LNK	LNK		⊔⊔S1LL5
				ROOF LOWER LIGNITE 65.70m													
66.75	1.05	LG		DBBK			SR2		XLIL	10	F3V	SCYLM		LNKLLGC	LNK	LLGC	⊔⊔S1LL6
67.70	0.95	LG		DBRB			SR2		XL			GWLLN		LNKLLGC	LNK	LLGC	⊔⊔S1LL7
68.72	1.02	GT		DBRB			SR2	68		5	F3L			LNKLLGC	LNK	LLGC	⊔⊔S1LL8
69.80	1.08	LG		DBBK			SR2TU	81	XL	5	F3L			LNKLLGC	LNK	LLGC	⊔⊔S1LL9
		LG		DBBKWD			SR3XN										
70.90	0.90	GT		DBKB			SR2	69	XL	5	F4L			LNKLLGC	LNK	LLGC	⊔⊔S1LL10
		LG		DBMB			SR2BU										
73.19	2.29	LG		DBKB			SR2	91	XLIL	5	F3W			LNKLLGB	LNK	LLGB	⊔⊔S1LL11
		GT		DEBMB			SR2XN										
74.52	1.33	LG		DBRB			SR2	88	XL	5	F4W			LNKLLGC	LNK	LLGC	⊔⊔S1LL12
		GT		DB			SR2MU										
76.00	1.48	LG		DBRB			SR2	89	XL	5	F3W			LNKLLGB	LNK	LLGB	⊔⊔S1LL13
82.00	6.00	LG	FL	DOB			QSR1TN				F3W			LNKLLGB	LNK	LLGB	⊔⊔S1LL14
88.00	6.00	LG	FL	DB2B			QSR1XN	94	XL		F3W			LNKLLGB	LNK	LLGB	⊔⊔S1LL15
94.00	6.00	LG	FL	DBRB			QSR1XN	89	XL	5	F3W			LNKLLGB	LNK	LLGB	⊔⊔S1LL16
95.18	1.18	LG	FL	DB			SR2	70	XL		F3L			LNKLLGA	LNK	LLGA	⊔⊔S1LL17

LL2/LL1 BOUNDARY RE-ASSESSED AT 91.88m.
SAMPLE 16 THEREFORE INCLUDES SPLITS A AND B.
BOUNDARY IS TAKEN TO NEAREST SAMPLE ie 94.00 m.

END OF RECORD

Figure 6.21 Coal geologist logging borehole chip samples in an on-site core shed, Botswana. Photograph by M. C. Coultas

accurately and as detailed as possible all the relevant geological information. As well as the basic lithological data, the detailed recording of discontinuities (their type, attitude, spacing and density) will provide valuable data to ensure safe mine design and working methods.

The drilling history of each borehole may indicate where drilling difficulties, loss of circulation and core losses have occurred. These may take on a new significance as the data are evaluated. The potential for inducing fractures into the core is greatest during the extrusion and subsequent handling and transport of the core. The use of core barrel liners is recommended as this not only enhances recovery but minimises damage to the core during extrusion and transport.

The general description of the rock materials can be as follows: strength, e.g. moderately weak; weathering, e.g. fresh; texture and structure, e.g. thinly cross laminated; colour, e.g. light grey; grain size, e.g. fine to medium; name, e.g. sandstone; other properties, e.g. slightly silty with mudstone laminae.

Definitions of the various levels of strength, weathering, texture, structure and grain size vary. For the purposes of this book the definitions given in British Standard 5930 (see Appendix 1) have been adopted.

6.4.1 Strength

There are several kinds of rock strength which can only be accurately determined by testing in the laboratory. These are designed to measure both the stress needed to rupture a rock

Table 6.2   Terms used to assess material strength in the field

Description	Characteristics of rock
Strength of rock material:	
R7: Extremely strong	Great difficulty in breaking with hammer, hammer rings
R6: Very strong	Requires several hammer blows to break
R5: Strong	Requires one hammer blow on hand-held sample to break
R4: Moderately strong	Hammer pick indents *c.* 5 mm. Cannot be cut with a knife
R3: Moderately weak	Hammer pick indents deeply, difficult to cut with a knife
R2: Weak	Rock crumbles under hammer blows, cuts easily with a knife
R1: Very weak	Broken by hand with difficulty
Cohesive soil and clay:	
C4: Stiff	Can be indented by thumbnail, cannot be moulded with fingers
C3: Firm	Can be moulded by strong finger pressure
C2: Soft	Easily moulded with fingers
C1: Very soft	Exudes between fingers when squeezed
Non-cohesive soils:	
S4: Weakly cemented	Lumps can be abraded with the thumb
S3: Compact	Not cemented, but would require pick for excavation
S2: Loose	Could be excavated with a spade
S1: Very loose	Hand could penetrate 'running sand'

and the strain developed during the application of stress. It may be argued that in the absence of laboratory test results the estimates of material strength are subjective. However, they should always be made, using the guidelines provided, as it is possible to use the later laboratory results from selected samples to 'calibrate' the logger's assessment of the material strength.

Field guidelines to the assessment of material strength by minimal inspection and handling are given in Table 6.2.

6.4.2   Weathering

The degree of weathering is an important element of the full description of the rock material and should always be included. Omission of any reference to weathering should not be taken as an implication of fresh material; this is particularly true of coals.

Weathering is important because it has a direct effect on the strength of the rock. It may indicate the movement and chemical action of groundwater, either through the rock fabric or along open discontinuities. The presence of weathering in the rock

Table 6.3 Terms used to describe degree of weathering in the field

Description	Characteristics of rock
W6: Fresh	No discoloration and maximum strength
W5: Slightly weathered	Discoloration along major discontinuity surfaces, may be some discoloration of rock material
W4: Moderately weathered	Discolored, discontinuities may be open with discolored surfaces, rock material is not friable, but is noticeably weaker than fresh material
W3: Highly weathered	More than half the rock material is decomposed, discoloration penetrates deeply and the original fabric is only present as a discontinuous framework; corestones present
W2: Completely weathered	Discolored, decomposed and in a friable condition, but the original mass structure is visible
W1: Residual soil	Totally changed, original fabric destroyed

profile will indicate the likelihood of oxidation in any coal seam within this sequence. In old mine workings the degree of weathering will help to indicate the state of the rock mass around existing or closed voids.

In the examination of rock types the terms given in Table 6.3 can be used to describe the degree of weathering.

6.4.3 Texture and structure

Reference to the bedding spacing will be sufficient to describe the texture and structure of the rock mass (Table 6.4).

In rocks which are heavily fractured, sheared or faulted, mention of this could draw attention to a particularly weak mass strength. For example, a description could be: strong (intact

Table 6.4 Terms used to describe the bedding spacing in the field

Description	Spacing (m)
Very thick	>2.0
Thick	0.6–2.0
Medium	0.2–0.6
Thin	0.06–0.2
Very thin	0.02–0.06
Thickly laminated	0.006–0.02
Thinly laminated	<0.006

strength), weak (mass strength), slightly weathered, indistinctly thinly bedded, heavily sheared, light grey, fine sandstone with some soft clay associated with shears. Note that the term 'heavily sheared' is not a standard term but serves to draw attention to the weak rock mass.

6.4.4   Colour

Colour is the most subjective of any observation made during the logging of lithotypes and uniformity between geologists is difficult to achieve. There are several published rock colour charts and these can be used together with supplementary terms such as light, dark or mottled, and secondary descriptors such as reddish or greenish. Colour is important to note as it can be an aid to correlation and, during the course of an investigation, it may become apparent that a distinctive coloured horizon is of particular significance.

6.4.5   Grain size

Grain size is important in the description of rock and soil material. Its omission can only be justified when describing mudstones, claystones, shales and siltstones in hand specimen. In conglomerates and breccias the sizes of clasts should be included.

   Typical grain sizes are as follows: conglomerates, larger clasts in a finer grained matrix, 2.0–>20 mm; sandstones, 0.06–2.0 mm; siltstones, 0.002–0.06 mm; and mudstone/claystone, <0.002 mm. Grain shapes include descriptions of angularity (e.g. angular, subangular, subrounded, rounded) and of form (equidimensional, flat, elongated, flat and elongated, irregular).

6.4.6   Total core recovery

This is the length of core recovered, both solid stick and broken, expressed as a percentage of the full core run. It is a simple percentage figure entered on to the log. When core is lost this will be less than 100%, but can be greater than 100% if dropped core is overdrilled and recovered. The percentage core recovery is important as, in general, recoveries less than 95% are not accepted, and a redrill may be required.

6.4.7   Solid core recovery

This is the total length of pieces of core recovered which have a full diameter, expressed as a percentage of the full core run. Like total core recovery, this can be less or more than 100%.

6.4.8   Rock quality designation

This is the total length of core recovered with a full diameter for a length of 0.10 m or longer, expressed as a percentage of the full core run. Only core lengths terminated by natural fractures are considered. As with total core and solid core recovery, percentages can be more than 100%, but the rock quality designation (RQD) cannot be greater than solid core recovery. For a core with one large fracture along the entire length, 0% should be recorded. RQD is sometimes expressed for lithological units rather than core runs. Examples of descriptions are: RQD 0–25%, very poor; 25–50%, poor; 50–75%, fair; 75–90%, good; and 90–100%, excellent.

6.4.9   Fracture spacing index

This is the number of fractures per metre of core. It is defined for lithological units and is independent of core run or recovery. If in one lithological unit there is a marked change in the fracture spacing, then the index for subunits should be given. An upper limit to the fracture spacing index should be defined, above which the index is not calculated but is recorded as being greater than the defined limit, e.g. >25. Non-intact material should be recorded separately. This applies to sections of lost core, core badly broken and disorientated during drilling, and non-cohesive broken core from fault zones or old mine workings.

6.4.10   Fracture logging

The clearest way of presenting fracture details is to draw a graphic log alongside the lithological description. The log shows the exact position of the discontinuity which is numbered and described on the separate fracture log. It is common practice to describe each discontinuity as in Table 6.5.

In Table 6.5, the number is the reference number given on the lithology log and type is the type of discontinuity (e.g. B, bedding; J, joint; F, fault; S, shear; Fr, fracture; FrZ, fracture zone; SZ, shear zone; FZ, fault zone). The dip is the angle between the discontinuity and the plane perpendicular to the core axis and azimuth is the angle between the bedding and the

Table 6.5   Terms used to describe discontinuities in the field

No.	Depth	Type	Dip	Azimuth	Description	Aperture	Infill
1	24.82	B	20	90	Planar, smooth	T	—
2	25.31	Fr	30	90	Irregular	2.0	Clay
3	26.18	Fr	30	320	Stepped, rough	T–O(4)	Broken rock

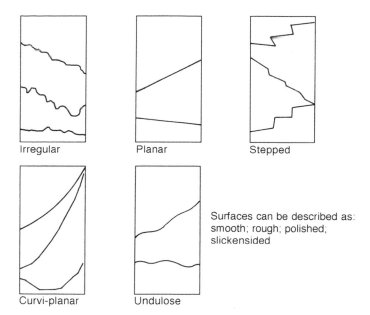

Irregular   Planar   Stepped

Curvi-planar   Undulose

Surfaces can be described as: smooth; rough; polished; slickensided

Figure 6.22 Types of discontinuities, including bedding and joints which have no displacement, and faults and shears which have a measurable or unknown displacement. Reproduced by permission of Dargo Associates Ltd

dip of the discontinuity measured clockwise, looking from the top of the borehole. Irregular, planar, stepped, undulose or curviplanar are the commonly used descriptions and, if seen, the surface can be described as smooth, rough, polished or slickensided (Figure 6.22). The aperture is usually described as tight or open (T, tight; 2.0, open, with maximum opening in millimetres; and T–O(2), tight to open, maximum opening in millimetres). The infill is a description of the material filling the aperture, usually materials such as clay, calcite and broken rock.

An example of a combined geotechnical logging sheet is shown in Figure 6.23.

6.5 COMPUTER APPLICATIONS

Modern geological investigations of coalfields and mine developments increasingly make use of computers in the handling and storage of geological data.

Large amounts of field data and borehole records can be unwieldy in hard copy form. Most field records are now coded on to forms by the coal geologist as shown in Figure 6.20 and then encoded into the data storage system. A future streamlining of this process will be when the geologist carries his or her own personal computer into the field and the core logging shed and encodes directly all the relevant lithological and structural data, together with all depths, thicknesses and locational information.

Figure 6.23 Example of a geotechnical logging sheet. Reproduced courtesy of M. C. Coultas

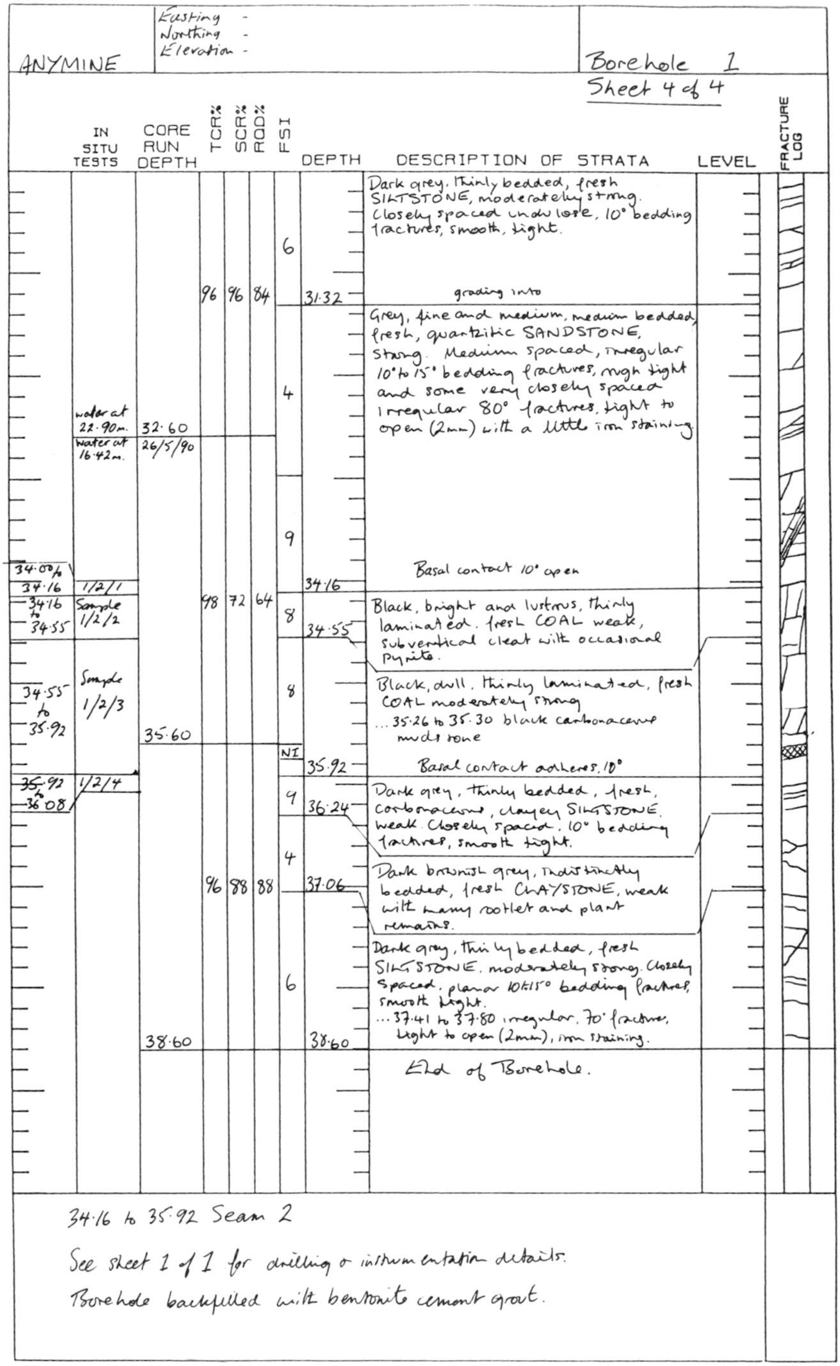

ANYMINE

Easting -
Northing -
Elevation -

Borehole 1
Sheet 4 of 4

IN SITU TESTS	CORE RUN DEPTH	TCR%	SCR%	RQD%	FSI	DEPTH	DESCRIPTION OF STRATA	LEVEL	FRACTURE LOG
					6		Dark grey. Thinly bedded, fresh SILTSTONE, moderately strong. Closely spaced undulose, 10° bedding fractures, smooth, tight.		
		96	96	84		31.32	grading into		
water at 22.90m. water at 16.42m	32.60 26/5/90				4		Grey, fine and medium, medium bedded, fresh, quartzitic SANDSTONE, strong. Medium spaced, irregular 10° to 15° bedding fractures, high tight and some very closely spaced irregular 80° fractures, tight to open (2mm) with a little iron staining		
					9				
34.00 34.16	1/2/1	98	72	64		34.16	Basal contact 10° open		
34.16 to 34.55	Sample 1/2/2				8	34.55	Black, bright and lustrous, thinly laminated. fresh COAL weak, subvertical cleat with occasional pyrite.		
34.55 to 35.92	Sample 1/2/3				8		Black, dull. thinly laminated, fresh COAL moderately strong ...35.26 to 35.30 black carbonaceous mudstone		
	35.60				NI	35.92	Basal contact adheres. 10°		
35.92 36.08	1/2/4				9	36.24	Dark grey, thinly bedded, fresh, carbonaceous, clayey SILTSTONE. weak. Closely spaced. 10° bedding fractures, smooth tight.		
		96	88	88	4	37.06	Dark brownish grey, indistinctly bedded, fresh CLAYSTONE, weak with many rootlet and plant remains.		
	38.60				6	38.60	Dark grey, thinly bedded, fresh SILTSTONE, moderately strong. Closely spaced, planar 10 to 15° bedding fractures, smooth tight. ...37.41 to 37.80 irregular, 70° fractures, tight to open (2mm), iron staining.		
							End of Borehole.		

34.16 to 35.92 Seam 2

See sheet 1 of 1 for drilling or instrumentation details.

Borehole backfilled with bentonite cement grout.

The development of computer graphics is important because of their influence on geological interpretation. In the coal industry, the contouring of two-dimensional surfaces is the most widely used technique. Modern programs offer important capabilities which allow the manipulation of large quantities of data, and allow data on many variables to be collected quickly, providing numerous data points. This ability to store and manipulate large amounts of data is extremely important for the following reasons:

(i) Speed. The computer can contour data more rapidly than can a geologist, especially when a series of maps or plans must be constructed. The creation of several maps or plans with the computer requires little extra effort than is needed to create just one

(ii) The ability to manipulate old maps or plans to create new ones, e.g. interburden thicknesses between selected seams can be determined quickly

(iii) Updates can be performed with little effort; later data can be added to the database and replots made

(iv) The greater the amounts of data fed into the computer, the better maps or plans that can be produced

The most common types of geological data that are contoured are topography, structural elevation, thickness and coal seam or interburden properties.

The bulk of the information comes from outcrops and boreholes, the spacing of which may be random (outcrops) or gridded (boreholes). Geophysical surveys are usually spatially organised. Contouring typically starts at an area of dense data points; the data points surrounding this location define the gradients and contours are drawn to suit the data and gradients. Once a number of contours has been drawn, geological reasoning and regional trends are applied to extend the contours into adjacent areas. The computer can consider the numerous combinations of groups of point data; if spatially organised data are used, the ordered data set will be easier to use and ordered information leads to the concept of the grid, a tool used by most current contouring programs.

Gridding is based on the delineation of the area and the lithologies to be mapped, the selection of the spacing desired, the calculation of values to be assigned to each grid point, and the use of these values to draw contours. To avoid the computer projecting unrealistic values in peripheral areas and areas of sparse data, null or dummy values can be inserted into the grid until actual data can be obtained for these areas.

The shape of the grids used is variable; squares, triangles and polygons are common (Figure 6.24). Restrictions on grids can be

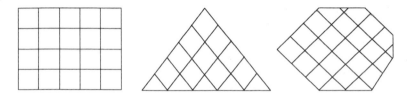

Figure 6.24   Types of gridding shape options for geological contouring programs

geographical, the imposition of maximum and minimum values to data to be used, e.g. to prevent the grid in certain circumstances from producing negative values, and the choice of contour interval, e.g. too narrow an interval may make the plan unreadable in areas where steep gradients result.

In addition, for structural plans, grids can be built for each fault block, or simply by using data from opposite sides of a fault. Similarly, coal resources or reserve calculations or coal quality parameters can be gridded in a similar manner.

Advances on the horizontal gridding technique include the production of cross section profiles by plotting the grid values along a line or connected group of lines. The latest development

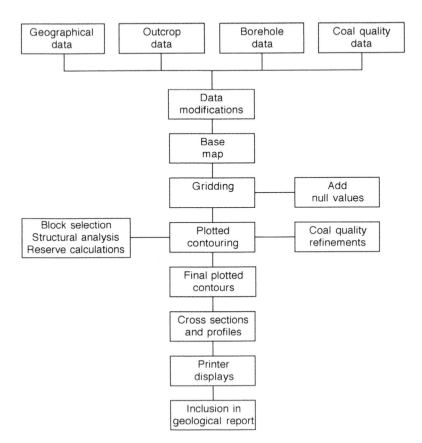

Figure 6.25   Simplified flow diagram of a geological contouring program

of the gridding system is the perspective or isometric view of the gridded surface. Such displays show the surface or variable as a block diagram which can be viewed from any selected point of origin. A simplified flow diagram of a contouring program is shown in Figure 6.25, and examples of contoured plans are illustrated in Figure 12.8.

Computers are also used in producing correlation techniques in geophysics. The graphic display of gamma and density geologs alongside a lithological interpretation of the sequence is an important tool for the coal geologist to have at his or her disposal. A series of such displays can greatly facilitate cross correlations in coal-bearing sequences. Figure 7.22 shows a typical geolog/lithological log printout used for this purpose.

Apart from geological applications, the use of computers in the coal mining industry is increasing all the time, particularly in mining simulation, scheduling, coal preparation and product quality monitoring. With the improvement of communications in the more remote areas of coal investigation, all future programmes in the coal industry will be computerised, so that the coal geologist will have to regard computer literacy as an important additional skill.

Chapter 7
Geophysics of coal

7.1 INTRODUCTION

The use of geophysics in the exploration for coal basins and in the delineation of coal seams and geological structures in particular coal deposits is now well established.

Since the oil crisis in 1973, there has been an enormous increase in the use of geophysical methods to identify coal deposits, and to futher determine their economic potential. Several of the techniques have been used initially in the exploration for oil and gas and adapted where applicable to coal exploration.

Large scale studies make use of regional gravity, deep seismic and aeromagnetic surveys to determine the sedimentary and structural framework of the area under consideration. Smaller scale, more detailed examination of the coal deposits utilises shallow seismic, ground magnetic, electrical resistivity and microgravity measurements coupled with the geophysical logging of all boreholes, which in turn involves the use of density, electrical, electromagnetic and radiometric techniques.

In established coal mining areas, the combination of geophysical logging with high resolution seismic and ground magnetic surveys contributes significantly in the delineation of economic mining areas, both for opencast and underground operations.

This combination is used on both large and small scale investigations; the drawback is that it can be an expensive exercise to carry out such investigations. When planning an exploration programme, any use of geophysics, whether as a field survey or in borehole logging, will be a high cost item on the exploration budget. The benefits of using such techniques, such as whether the amount of drilling required will be reduced, will be set against such costs.

The coal geologist does not necessarily carry out geophysical surveys by himself or herself, but he or she should be sufficiently familiar with the techniques, results and interpretations to relate such data to the overall geological framework and mine planning. For established mines, the geologist will use geophysical results to aid seam correlations and identify areas of structural complexity including igneous intrusions.

The background principles of physics governing the various geophysical techniques employed in coal exploration and development are not covered in this book as they are available in standard geophysical texts. Instead a simple outline is given of the basic physical properties of coal-bearing sequences together with an outline of the field methods used to locate and quantify coal deposits.

7.2 PHYSICAL PROPERTIES OF COAL-BEARING SEQUENCES

Coal as a lithology responds well to most geophysical methods in that its physical properties contrast with those of other lithologies commonly found in coal-bearing sequences. Coal has in general a lower density, a lower seismic velocity, a lower magnetic susceptibility, a higher electrical resistivity and low radioactivity compared with surrounding rocks in typical coal-bearing sequences.

7.2.1 Density

Density measurements of rocks are not usually made *in situ*, but in the laboratory on some small outcrop or drill core samples. Such results rarely give the true bulk density because samples may be weathered or dehydrated, consequently density is not often well known in specific field situations. Table 7.1 gives saturated density ranges and averages for coals, sediments in coal-bearing sequences, and igneous and metamorphic rocks which may be associated with coal basins either as underlying basement or as intrusives into the coal-bearing strata.

Low and high rank coals ($1.1–1.8$ g/cm^3) are less dense than the surrounding sediments ($1.6–2.9$ g/cm^3), which in turn are less dense than igneous and metamorphic rocks ($2.1–3.1$ g/cm^3). In sedimentary rocks, the wide range of density is due to variations in porosity, the nature of pore fluids, age and depth of burial and mineralogical composition. Some igneous rocks, such as volcanics, have high porosities and therefore lower density; for example, pumice can have a density less than 1.0 g/cm^3. Density also increases with the degree of metamorphism, as recrystallisation reduces the pore space to form a denser rock as well as converting some minerals to more dense forms.

Table 7.1   Physical properties of coals and associated sedimentary and igneous rocks. Based on Telford *et al.* (1990) by permission of Cambridge University Press

Lithology	Density (wet) (g/cm^3)		Seismic velocity (km/s)	Magnetic susceptibility ($\times 10$ SI units)		Electrical resistivity (Ω m)
	Range	Average		Range	Average	Range
Sandstone	1.61–2.76	2.35	3.6	0–20	0.4	1–6.4×10^8
Shale	1.77–3.20	2.40	2.8	0.01–15	0.6	20–2×10^3
Limestone	1.93–2.90	2.55	5.5	0–3	0.3	50–1×10^7
Lignite	1.10–1.25	1.19				9–200
Bituminous coal	1.20–1.80	1.32	1.8–2.8	—	0.02	0.6–1×10^5
Anthracite	1.34–1.80	1.50	4.0–5.5			1×10^{-3}–2×10^5
Acid igneous rock	2.30–3.11	2.61		0–80	8.0	4.5×10^3 (wet granite) 1.3×10^6 (dry granite)
Basic igneous rock	2.09–3.17	2.79	4.0–7.0	0.5–100	25.0	20–5×10^7 (dolerite)
Metamorphic rock	2.40–3.10	2.74	5.0–7.0	0–70	4.2	20–1×10^4 (schist)

7.2.2 Seismic velocity

The seismic velocity of a rock is the velocity at which a wave motion propagates through the rock media.

As shown in Table 7.1, the seismic velocity of coal is in the range 1.8–2.8 km/s; mudrocks such as shales have similar values. Sandstones have a higher value which increases with increasing quartz content, while dense limestones, igneous and metamorphic rocks have much higher velocities of 4.0–7.0 km/s.

7.2.3 Seismic reflection coefficients

The seismic reflection coefficient determines whether an interface gives a reflection and depends on the density as well as the seismic velocity. Coal seams with a low density and low seismic velocity often have high reflection coefficients and can be picked up well on seismic sections.

7.2.4 Magnetic susceptibility

The magnetic susceptibility of a rock depends primarily on its magnetite content. Weathering generally reduces susceptibility because of the oxidation of magnetite to haematite.

As for rock density, measurements of magnetic susceptibility in the field do not necessarily give a bulk susceptibility of the formation; however, outcrop magnetic susceptibility measurements by portable instruments have led to improved bulk susceptibility measurements. Although there is great variation in magnetic susceptibility, even for a particular lithology, and wide overlap between different types, sedimentary rocks generally have the lowest average susceptibilities, with coals having among the lowest susceptibility within the sedimentary suite (Table 7.1). Basic igneous rocks have high susceptibility values. In every instance, the susceptibility depends on the amount of ferromagnetic minerals present, mainly magnetite, titano-magnetite or pyrrhotite. It is worth noting that the sulphide minerals such as pyrite, which is a common mineral in coals and associated sediments, has a low susceptibility value; like many of the sulphide minerals it is almost non-magnetic. Table 7.1 gives the range and average values in rationalised SI units for those rocks associated with coal.

7.2.5 Electrical conductivity

Electrical prospecting involves the detection of surface effects produced by the flow of electric current in the ground. It is the enormous variation in electrical conductivity found in different rocks and minerals that requires a greater variety of techniques to be used than in the other prospecting methods.

Several electrical properties of rocks and minerals are significant in electrical prospecting; of these, by far the most important in coal prospecting is electrical conductivity or the inverse electrical resistivity, which is expressed in ohm metres (Ω m), the others being of less significance.

As most rocks are poor conductors, their resistivities would be extremely large were it not for the fact that they are usually porous, and the pores are filled with fluids, mainly water. The conductivity of a porous rock varies with the volume and arrangement of the pores, and the conductivity and amount of contained water. Water conductivity varies considerably depending on the amount and conductivity of dissolved chlorides, sulphates and other minerals present, but the principal influence is usually the sodium chloride or salt content.

7.2.6   Radiometric properties

Trace amounts of radioactive materials are found in all rocks. Small amounts of cosmic radiation passing through the atmosphere produce a continuous background reading which may vary from place to place. In general, the radioactivity in sedimentary rocks and metamorphosed sediments is higher than that in igneous and other metamorphic types, with the exception of potassium-rich granites.

In coal-bearing sequences, the contrasts in natural radioactivity in coals and surrounding sediments has led to the development of the use of nuclear well logging instruments for measuring the radioactivity of formations encountered in boreholes.

Coals have very low radioactivity, as do clean sandstones, sandstones with high contents of rock fragments and clay matrices; siltstones and non-marine shales have low to intermediate values, whereas marine shales and bentonite (tonstein) have high radioactivities due to the presence of uranium and thorium minerals in the shale and potassium in the bentonite.

7.3   SURFACE GEOPHYSICAL METHODS

The petroleum industry has used various seismic geophysical methods for a number of years as an aid in the exploration for geological structures suitable for hydrocarbon entrapment. To locate sedimentary basins, electrical, electromagnetic, gravity and magnetic surveys together with reflection and refraction seismic surveys are used. These are usually large scale operations involving a great deal of equipment, manpower and finance. Although of use in broad regional investigations, they are little used in the examination of coal-bearing sequences for small selected areas.

In the investigation of mine lease areas high resolution seismic reflection surveys are most effectively employed. Other methods used are cross borehole seismic techniques and seismic refraction, which are particularly useful in opencast mine development.

7.3.1 Seismic surveys

Exploration for mineable coal is generally concerned with the top 1.5 km of strata. As a result of the shallow nature of these investigations, high resolution seismic profiling is required to detect relatively thin coal seams. The recording system is designed to retain as much of the high frequency reflections as possible.

The efficiency of surface seismic reflection surveying has steadily improved over the last 20 years, and it is now applied to coal mining with increasing accuracy and confidence. Background information and a full discussion of equipment and techniques used in gathering and processing seismic reflection data are not given in this text but are referred to in the reference section.

7.3.1.1 *Seismic reflection surveys*

The principle of seismic reflection is that an acoustic signal or seismic wave produced by an explosion or other impulse source is introduced into the ground at selected points, and this signal radiates through the ground. The velocity at which the signal travels depends on the rock type encountered. Typical velocities are 3.6 km/s in hard, dense limestone and this ranges between 1.8 and 2.8 km/s for most types of hard coals. These and other velocities of typical lithologies encountered in coal-bearing successions are given in Table 7.1. The velocity of the seismic wave is a function of the lithology through which it passes. When the wave reaches a boundary marking a lithological change, a reflected and a refracted ray result. When the change in velocities and density at a boundary is large, there is a large reflection coefficient and a strong reflection is generated. This reflection is detected by receivers or geophones, which produce an electrical signal which is recorded, as shown in Figure 7.1.

The instant the signal is generated it is also recorded, and by recording the time it took for the signal to reach the reflection point and return, referred to as the two-way travel time (TWT),

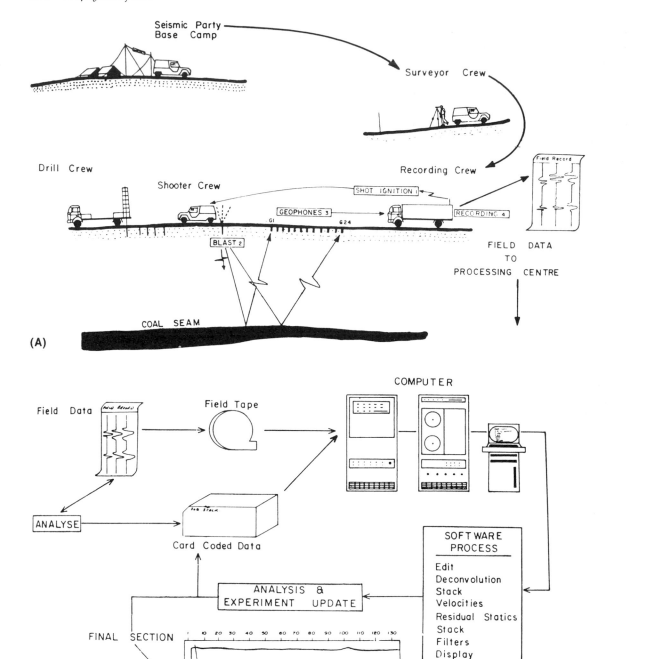

Figure 7.1 Seismic reflection survey. (A) Field data acquisition; (B) seismic data processing. From Peace (1979), by permission of Miller Freeman Publications, Inc.

the depth of the reflection point can be determined, providing the velocities of the traversed lithologies are known.

The physical property of coal and its surrounding strata which makes seismic surveys feasible is its accoustic impedance, which is defined as the product of its density and seismic velocity. Coal has a much lower density and velocity relative to other sedimentary rocks normally encountered in coal-bearing sequences; the contrast in acoustic impedance between coal and sediments may be between 35 and 50%. This produces large reflection coefficients.

In seismic surveys of coal deposits, reflections from most features of interest return to the surface during the first second after the seismic wave has been generated, i.e. the TWT is less than one second. This would give a maximum reflection depth of 1.5 km if the overlying rocks have an average seismic velocity of 3.0 km/s.

The identification of faults, folds, washouts, seam splits and thickness changes by the use of seismic reflection techniques is an effective method whereby potential geological hazards can be identified. This can then be built into mine planning and design.

The source commonly used in seismic reflection surveys for coal is either the detonation of an explosive charge such as dynamite, although this produces environmental problems in populated areas, or a lower energy impulse produced by an earth compactor known as the Mini-SOSIE. Another energy source used for shallow reflection surveys is a 'gun' firing blank ammunition into the ground, but this is only suitable for investigation to around 150 m in rocks with good transmission properties.

One of the main problems with any shallow seismic survey is the effect of the total travel time when the waves have to pass through a low velocity weathered zone near the ground surface. Variations in the thickness and velocity characteristics of the weathered zone produce variations in the arrival times of the wave reflections.

This can be partly overcome by placing the shot point and, if possible, the geophone in holes drilled to below the low velocity zone, although this is often not feasible due to the extent and depth of weathering. This can be further complicated by the presence of superficial deposits masking the rockhead. Weathering is a particular problem in subtropical and tropical countries such as Africa and Australia, whereas superficial deposits are a common problem in Europe and North America.

The ease of processing and interpreting the data from surface seismic surveys is naturally influenced by the local geology. Where coal deposits are geologically uncomplicated, i.e. thick seams with low dips, little faulting and close to the surface with

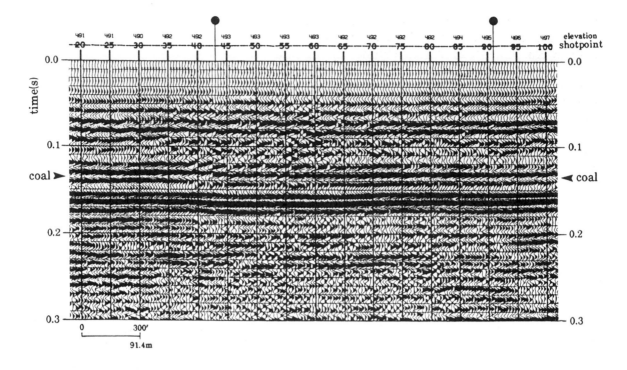

few weathering effects, interpretation will be relatively easy. Contrast this with other geological scenarios where coal seams showing complexities in splitting and variation in thickness, with a high incidence of faulting or the presence of washouts in the coal seams, and perhaps lying at depths of up to 1.0 km, then the interpretation of seismic data from surveys in such areas is a lot more difficult.

Figure 7.2 illustrates a seismic reflection profile across a coalfield in the USA. The section shows the coal seam reflection to be robust and continuous from SP20 to SP100, indicating uniform coal seam thickness across the entire section.

Figure 7.3(A) shows a seismic reflection profile across a lignite deposit in Northern Ireland, UK. This is a product of a shallow reflection seismic survey using a 'gun' energy source. In this survey, to provide depth resolution, higher frequencies of seismic waves were used. The sequence consisted predominantly of saturated Tertiary clays which have a very low attenuation for seismic energy; this suggests an expectation of good high frequency transmission. This is also dependent on the effects of the superficial deposits in which the energy source is coupled. The geology of the area consists of superficial heterogeneous glacial deposits overlying Tertiary clays and lignite; these in turn lie on a zone of weathered basalt with fresh basalt at depth. In this instance there is little seismic velocity contrast between the clays

Figure 7.2   Seismic section showing a robust and continuous coal seam reflection. This indicates uniform coal seam thickness with no detectable geological disturbance (USA). From Gochioco (1991), by permission of *Geophysics*

and lignites, but because there is a large density contrast, the acoustic impedence is sufficiently large to produce a large reflection coefficient and a detectable reflection.

The interpretation of Figure 7.3(A) is shown in Figure 7.3(B). The good reflectors at about 0.07 and 0.1 s (TWT) on the south-east margin mark the top and bottom of the lignite. The weathered–fresh basalt interface is seen on the south-east margin at about 0.13 s (TWT) and can be seen clearly to shallow towards the north-west. In addition, two faults with downthrows to the south-east can be detected. The irregularly shaped body at X on the section is considered to be a raft of lignite that has become detached from the main lignite due to frost action during the Quaternary glacial period.

In Wyoming, USA high resolution reflection profiles were recorded over a prospective underground coal gasification test site. The target seam was the Wyodak Coal about 180 m below the surface with a thickness of 30 m. Seismic reflection profiling was considered to be the most effective technique on technical and financial grounds. This survey used a dynamite energy source, and one profile line is shown in Figure 7.4. The top and bottom of the Wyodak Coal give strong reflections, as does the overlying Badger Coal (3 m thick). All the sections show a gentle anticlinal structure in the sequence, particularly in the top of the seam; this may be due to differential compaction of the coal

Figure 7.3   (A) Shallow seismic reflection survey, Northern Ireland UK; (B) interpretation of seismic section (A), clearly showing interbedded lignite and underlying basalt. Unpublished figure, reproduced by permission of Antrim Coal Company Ltd

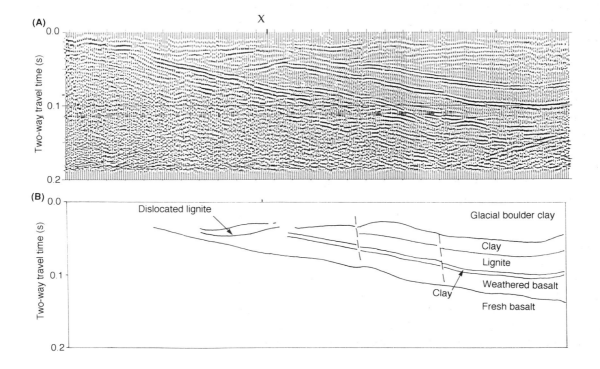

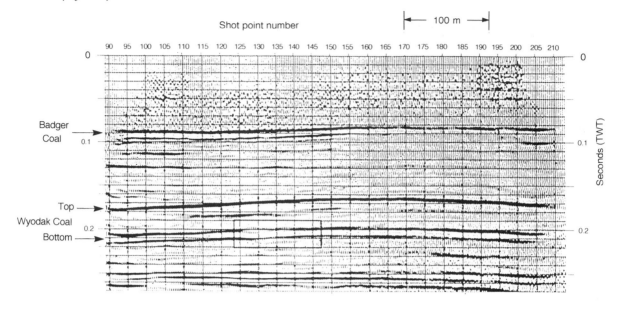

Figure 7.4 Seismic profile showing anticline structure of Wyodak Coal and the good reflection of Badger Coal. Seismic anomaly (boxed area) is interpreted as a channel cut into the base of the Wyodak Coal, Wyoming, USA. From Greaves (1985), by permission of the Society for Mining, Metallurgy, and Exploration, Inc.

seam or movement within the coal seam as a response to gravity in a down-dip direction before coalification occurred. No faulting was observed in the profile. The base of the Wyodak Coal has a zone of anomalous amplitude (Figure 7.4) interpreted as a washout in the basal section of the seam. This was later proved to be so by drilling.

Figure 7.5 shows a distinct washout structure in the roof of a lignite in the Texas Gulf Coast region. The edges of the strata surrounding the washout are very distinct; from this profile the dimensions of the channel can be measured and located within any proposed mine development. In this example, the washout is approximately 35 m (115 ft) thick, extending from 141 m (465 ft) to 176 m (580 ft) on the section.

The dynamite shot hole method has been widely used, and although it gives a higher frequency content and better resolution, such surveys are expensive and environmentally problematic. The cheaper Mini-SOSIE technique has been applied and can provide data of equal quality in the right circumstances. The method uses a similar recording spread as for dynamite, and the Mini-SOSIE wackers can put 800–1500 impulses into the ground for each record.

Mini-SOSIE has been widely used, with particular success in Australia. Difficulties have, however, been encountered in using the technique in dissected hilly terrain combined with deep weathering profiles.

In the United Kingdom, seismic reflection techniques using an energy source situated at depth in a borehole have been developed for use in investigating opencast coal operations.

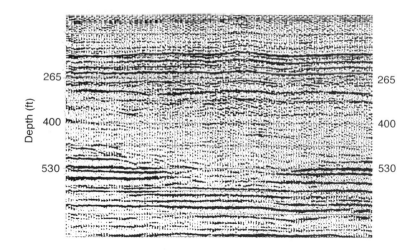

Figure 7.5 Seismic reflection profile showing a buried channel at a depth of 500 ft (152.4 m), Texas Gulf Coast, USA. From Peace (1979), by permission of Miller Freeman Publications, Inc.

The hole-to-surface reflection data are processed with standard vertical seismic profiling (VSP) techniques. Small downhole shots are fired at 2.0 m spacing below the water-table in the borehole and geophones with a spacing of around 4.0 m are deployed at the surface along a line intersecting the top of the borehole. The travel time along a seismic ray path is independent of the direction of travel. Using this method, the rays are traversed in opposite directions from conventional reflection surveys and can be processed accordingly. A seismic depth section obtained from such a survey is shown in Figure 7.6, together with the coal seam stratigraphy and velocities and the migration interval used in seismic data processing. The coal seams at 30, 54, 58, 70 and 128 m all give a good reflection, but the thin seam at 80 m is hardly seen at all. Other reflections at 100 and 110 m may be weaker reflections from differing lithotypes in the sequence.

This technique has been used to correlate between boreholes. Figure 7.7 shows the stratigraphy and combined seismic section from three hole-to-surface surveys with the migration interval velocities used in seismic data processing. In Figure 7.7, the coal seam at 20 m has a good reflection, and the worked-out seam at 50 m has a very good reflection because the air-filled void in the old workings produces a very large reflection coefficient. This worked-out seam also shows two small faults with downthrows 1–2 m to the right. The weaker reflections below 50 m are interpreted as a sandstone–mudstone interface at 70 m and a coal seam at 85 m; the fault in this seam is inferred from the borehole data.

Cross hole seismic reflection surveys are possible in certain opencast exploration sites which have closely spaced boreholes. This method involves downhole seismic sources and detectors

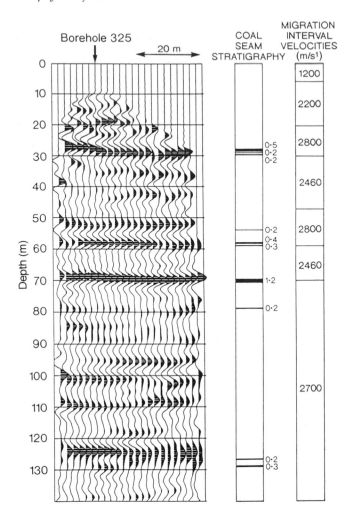

Figure 7.6 Seismic depth section obtained from the hole-to-surface survey in borehole at opencast site, UK, with the coal seam stratigraphy and velocity profile used for migration. From Kragh *et al.* (1991), by permission of the European Association of Exploration Geophysicists

sited below the water-table (hydrophones). This provides better resolution than surface seismic surveys and even vertical seismic profiling, but requires the availability of numerous boreholes.

The seismic methods described are particularly useful in identifying old mine workings and worked-out coal seams as well as illustrating the geology and structure of the area. In areas of the UK which have a long mining history, the position and extent of shallow underground workings have not always been recorded. In planning opencast operations, hole-to-surface seismic reflection surveys and cross hole seismic reflection methods can help to identify such potential problems before detailed mine planning begins.

(A)

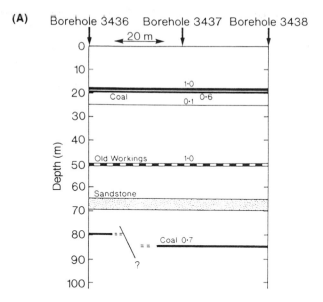

Figure 7.7 (A) Coal seam stratigraphy for three boreholes at opencast site, UK; (B) combined seismic section from the three hole-to-surface surveys conducted in these boreholes with the velocity profile used for migration. The section is true scale, zero phase, normal polarity, and an equal energy trace normalisation has been applied. From Kragh *et al.* (1991), by permission of the European Association of Exploration Geophysicists

(B)

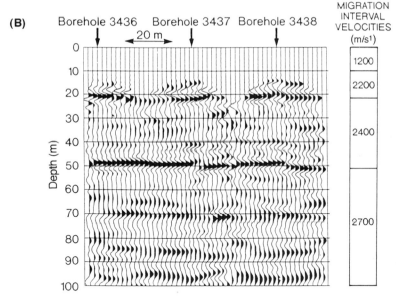

7.3.1.2 Seismic refraction surveys

The energy input to the ground must be stronger for refraction shooting. Consequently, explosives continue to be the dominant energy source, although other sources are also used, such as a falling weight for shallow studies. Refracted waves differ from reflected waves in that the principal portion of the refracted wave path is along an approximately horizontal interface between two rock layers before refraction to the detectors at the surface.

Refraction methods have been used in opencast coal exploration to locate previous workings, to determine the variation in thickness of glacial deposits overlying coal-bearing sequences and to locate faults at shallow depths. Refraction methods have limitations when applied to the location of subsurface positions of coal seams, but are successful in locating previous workings because of the contrast in seismic velocity between backfilled mine workings and unworked areas.

7.3.2   Gravity surveys

The distribution of rock masses of different densities in the earth's crust gives rise to local and regional variations in the earth's gravitational field.

Gravity measurements are made using a gravimeter, taking readings at stations whose spacing may vary from 1 m to 20 km. The station interval is usually selected on the basis of assumed depth and size of the anomalous bodies sought.

Areas with an anomalously high Bouguer gravity value (a positive anomaly) can indicate relatively dense rock such as crystalline basement. A low Bouguer gravity value (a negative anomaly) is associated with the presence of less dense material, such as a thick succession of sedimentary strata. The magnitude and form of the anomaly is related to the shape, orientation and depth of the feature, together with the contrast in density between the different rock types involved.

Gravity surveys are important, particularly on a regional scale, and are used in coalfield exploration both to detect the presence of sedimentary basins and to provide information on the overall structure of individual sedimentary basins. The results of a gravity survey are usually supported by additional geological data such as density determinations on rock samples and field mapping results. Typical densities of coal and coal-bearing sediments together with igneous and metamorphic rocks are given in Table 7.1.

The major use of gravity surveys has been in the location of sedimentary basins that could be coal-bearing and which may be concealed by younger strata.

Those areas containing Gondwana coalfields, i.e. Australia, South Africa, India and Brazil, are especially suited to the use of gravity surveys. Most Gondwana sediments are preserved in basins lying directly on crystalline basement. These produce negative Bouguer anomalies which contrast with the surrounding positive values over areas of crystalline rocks.

In Western Australia, the Collie coal measures occur in a basin

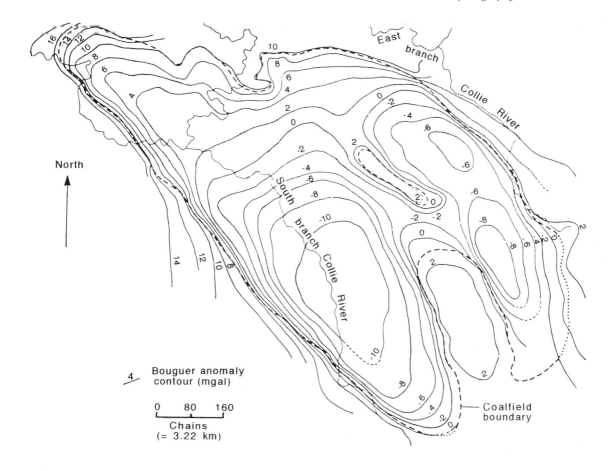

North

4 ─ Bouguer anomaly
    contour (mgal)

0   80   160
├────┴────┤
    Chains
   (= 3.22 km)

─ ─ ─ Coalfield
      boundary

Figure 7.8 Bouguer anomaly map of the Collie Coalfield, Western Australia. From Parasnis (1966), by permission of SEG and Elsevier Science Publishers

of Gondwana age, extending for about 180 km². The basin is a remnant of a once extensive deposit preserved by downfaulting or folding in the Precambrian basement. The surrounding granites and the coal measures themselves are almost wholly covered by laterite and Pleistocene or Recent lacustrine deposits. Figure 7.8 shows the negative Bouguer gravity anomaly map of the Collie coal basin. The principal feature is the Bouguer gravity anomaly low representing the less dense sedimentary coal-bearing sequence. The boundary of the coal sediments is indicated by a large Bouguer gravity anomaly gradient where anomaly values increase as they pass across from the lighter sediments to the denser granite basement. The gravity survey indicates that the Collie basin is divided into two main troughs, separated by a basement ridge extending from the south-east end, through the Bouguer gravity anomaly high to the northern boundary (Figure 7.8). A drilling programme has confirmed these results and discovered a new coal-bearing sequence covering approximately 25 km² in the eastern trough, containing a coal seam 10.0 m in thickness, which is now being mined.

In India and Bangladesh, similar coalfield basins have been identified. In north-west Bangladesh, Gondwana coal-bearing sediments are present in a series of small basins, now preserved as graben structures in the underlying crystalline basement, with the whole area concealed beneath Tertiary sediments. Gravity (and magnetic) surveying has identified these areas and subsequent drilling has confirmed the presence of thick Gondwana coals down to depths of 300 m.

7.3.3 Magnetic surveys

The magnetic properties of rocks may differ by several orders of magnitude rather than by a few tens of per cent. Typical values for coal and coal-bearing sediments together with igneous and metamorphic rocks are given in Table 7.1.

Coal-bearing sequences have relatively low magnetic susceptibilities in contrast with the higher magnetic properties of basement igneous and metamorphic rocks. Magnetic surveys are used to delineate the broad structural framework of a coal-bearing area. Such surveys do not detect coal, but help in locating sedimentary sequences likely to contain coals at accessible depths.

In north-west Bangladesh, aeromagnetic surveys have indicated in some areas that the depth to crystalline basement is less than 250 m. The aeromagnetic survey together with subsequent drilling has delineated coal-bearing sediments preserved in-graben structure in the basement. This has enabled those areas identified as accessible by mining to be targeted, and further drilling has identified sediments of Gondwana age containing a number of thick bituminous coals. Such regional aeromagnetic survey results are often combined with regional gravity data to confirm the presence of sedimentary basins.

Distinct from large scale aeromagnetic surveys, detailed ground magnetic surveys are used to locate the presence of basic igneous (dolerite) dykes in mine areas, and also to detect the limits of burnt coal seams.

To locate dolerite dykes, a series of profiles are surveyed and plotted approximately perpendicular to the strike of each dyke and magnetic readings are taken every few metres. An example of a lenticular shaped magnetic anomaly from Causey Park, north-east England shows the configuration of a dolerite dyke (Figure 7.9). The anomaly contours are expressed in 100 nanotesla (nT) intervals, a nanotesla being a unit of magnetic field strength. The location of dykes of significant size is important,

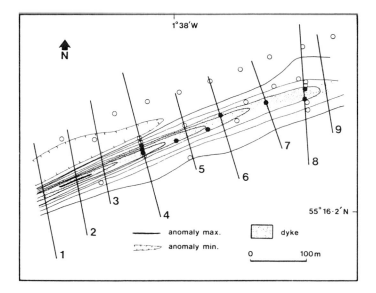

Figure 7.9 Magnetic anomaly map for part of the Causey Park dyke, UK. Contours are at 100 nT intervals. Boreholes which encountered dolerite at rockhead are shown as solid circles. From Goulty *et al.* (1984), by permission of the European Association of Exploration Geophysicists

particularly in opencast mining; coals which are in contact or close proximity to dykes will have undergone devolatilisation due to baking and therefore many have deteriorated (or in some instances improved) in rank and quality. This phenomenon is particularly important in South Africa where dyke and sill swarms are intruded into the coal-bearing Karroo sediments. Undetected dykes cause problems in underground mining by making tunnelling through them difficult and expensive and by affecting coal quality.

In the delineation of burnt zones in coal seams, the magnetic susceptibility of unbaked sedimentary rocks is fairly low, whereas the magnetic susceptibility of the baked rocks is variable. Most of the maghaematite and magnetite in the baked rocks is derived from the thermal alteration of sedimentary minerals. Some baked areas have undergone iron enrichment as iron is mobile during thermal metamorphism and can be redeposited in the baked rocks. On heating, shales and siltstones undergo a significant reduction in volume; however, shales tend to separate into small pieces so exposing a greater surface area available for iron enrichment. The sediments around the edges of a burnt seam may contain appreciably more magnetite if the coal fire is extinguished due to a lack of oxygen, which reduces more iron oxides and hydroxides to magnetite. In these instances larger magnetic anomalies may be expected along the margins of the baked zones. Figure 7.10 shows a magnetic profile over a burnt coal zone in East Kalimantan, Indonesia. The zone of burnt coal is about 160 m wide, extending in from the outcrop. The magnetic profile shows a distinct magnetic

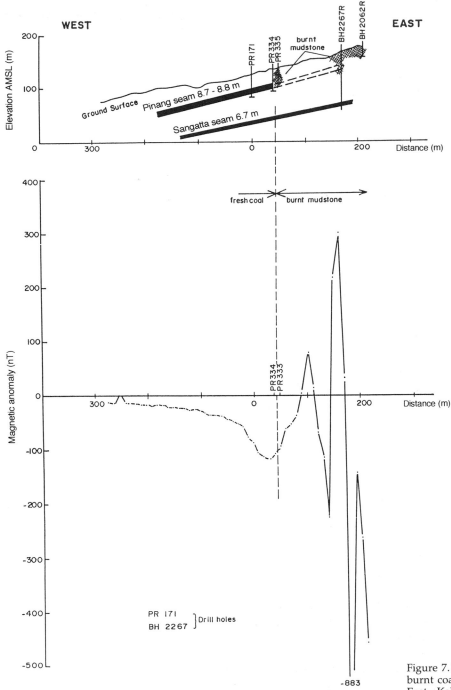

Figure 7.10 Magnetic profile over burnt coal and geological cross section, East Kalimantan, Indonesia. Reproduced by permission of P.T. Tambang Batubara Bukit Asam, Indonesia

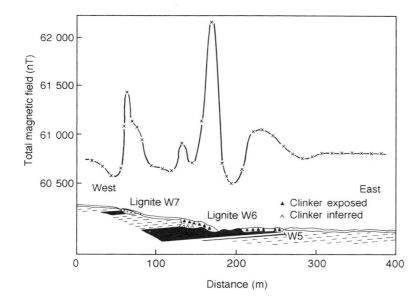

Figure 7.11 Total magnetic field profile and geological cross section, southern end of New Vale Coal Co. eastern Southland, New Zealand. From Lindqvist *et al.* (1985), by permission of *New Zealand Journal of Geology and Geophysics*

anomaly of over 1000 nT amplitude when passing across the burnt mudstones.

Similar anomalies produced by baked sediments over burnt coal seams in the Southland District of New Zealand are shown in Figure 7.11.

By carrying out a series of traverses perpendicular to the strike of the coal, a zone of burnt coal can be accurately determined and the loss of coal within the area of investigation can be calculated.

7.3.4 Electrical methods

7.3.4.1 *Electrical resistivity methods*

Resistivity values for coal and coal-bearing sediments are given in Table 7.1.

Electrical resistivity mapping is primarily used for detecting local, relatively shallow inhomogeneities, and is employed typically in delineating geological boundaries, fractures and cavities.

In the Raniganj Coalfield, India, a combination of resistivity depth sounding and surface electrical mapping has been used to identify lithological contacts and the presence of faults and dykes under tropical weathering conditions.

Electrical resistivity to locate coal seams has also been applied to the Pennsylvanian anthracite field and in Wyoming, USA, where resistivity has detected the splitting of a coal seam into two, separated by a sand body. It has also been used in

Australia. In the UK, electrical resistivity has been used to locate old concealed mine shafts and other mining cavities.

7.3.4.2   *Pulse radar methods*

Pulse radar systems have been used from the surface to locate and calculate the thickness of coal pillars in abandoned mines in the USA usually to depths of less than 20 m. The method is also being applied to the detection of cavities and abandoned workings beneath opencast operations.

7.3.5   Radioactive methods

In coalfields, radioactive surveys can be used to trace marine shales high in radioactivity. This can be useful as an indirect method of mapping coal seams when the position of the radioactive shale is known in the vertical sequence and also its position in relation to known coal seams.

Topographic irregularities, dispersion of radioactive materials due to weathering and 'background radiation' affect instrument readings.

7.4   UNDERGROUND GEOPHYSICAL METHODS

The use of geophysical techniques underground encounters difficulties. Space restrictions and safety requirements, particularly in the use of some electrical equipment, limit the use of certain geophysical methods underground. Nevertheless, in-seam seismic and pulse radar methods have been used underground.

7.4.1   In-seam seismic surveys

These surveys involve the use of channel waves propagating in the coal seam to detect discontinuities in advance of mining.

The seismic velocity in coal is only about one half of the velocity in the surrounding rocks (Table 7.1); because of this, a coal seam is a very good channel for the guiding of seismic waves. As the seismic recorder is not flameproof, it is located either on the surface or in an intake roadway in which the methane concentration is less than 0.25%. In Germany, a flameproof digital recording unit has been developed which will help to overcome this problem.

The in-seam seismic method can be used as shown in Figure 7.12, which illustrates the behaviour of channel waves reflected

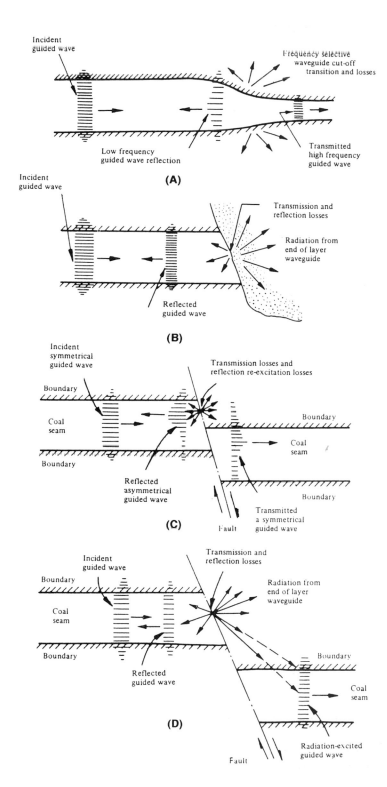

Figure 7.12 Conceptual behaviour of channel waves on encountering (A) a coal seam pinchout; (B) a channel sand cutout; (C) a fault with a throw less than the seam thickness; (D) a fault with a throw greater than the seam thickness. Reproduced by permission of IEA Coal Research (1983)

Incident guided wave

Frequency selective waveguide cut-off transition and losses

Low frequency guided wave reflection

Transmitted high frequency guided wave

(A)

Incident guided wave

Transmission and reflection losses

Radiation from end of layer waveguide

Reflected guided wave

(B)

Incident symmetrical guided wave

Transmission losses and reflection re-excitation losses

Boundary

Coal seam

Boundary

Reflected asymmetrical guided wave

Boundary

Coal seam

Boundary

Fault

Transmitted a symmetrical guided wave

(C)

Incident guided wave

Transmission and reflection losses

Boundary

Radiation from end of layer waveguide

Coal seam

Boundary

Reflected guided wave

Boundary

Coal seam

Fault

Radiation-excited guided wave

(D)

from or transmitted through a variety of discontinuities. Depending on the target structure, shot holes and receivers can be located in the same or different roadways.

The recorded seismic data are then processed to construct a map of the distribution of faults or washouts in the coal seam.

In-seam seismology is particularly useful where longwall mining techniques are employed. Where advancing longwall faces are used, it is essential to have prior knowledge of the nature of the coal seam through which the advance will be made. The high financial investment in establishing longwall faces is at risk due to loss of production if structurally affected ground is encountered. The prediction of faults in a panel of coal is important in maintaining the lifetime of existing longwall faces.

7.4.2 Pulse radar techniques

Pulse radar work in underground mine roadways is used to detect hazards in advance of mining, and to measure the thickness of the coal layer remaining in the roof of mine roadways. It is also used to detect geological discontinuities in the coal panel to be worked. This is important in longwall face operations in controlling the cutting position of the continuous coal cutting machines, and for safety reasons. Pulse radar methods have been employed in underground workings in the UK and USA to determine coal thickness; in addition, in the USA, pulse radar has been used to determine mine roof stratigraphy enabling clay and shale layers within the coal to be identified.

7.5   GEOPHYSICAL BOREHOLE LOGGING

Geophysical logging (geologs) is the measurement of the variation with depth of particular physical properties of surrounding rocks with geophysical measuring tools (sondes) located in boreholes. Measurements are made by lowering a sonde attached to the end of a cable to the bottom of the borehole, and then raising the sonde back out of the borehole at a constant rate to record the geolog. It is easier to maintain a constant rate by raising rather than lowering the sonde, which is important for data quality.

The sonde is connected by electrical conductors within the cable to recording and control instrumentation situated on the surface. This instrumentation is referred to as the logging unit, which also contains the powered winch used to lower and raise the sonde. In coal exploration, such units are small and portable. The logging unit makes a permanent record of the log data on a paper chart and on magnetic tape or disk, the latter suitable for future computer analysis.

The objective of geophysical logging is to determine *in situ* the rock type and other properties such as porosity, fluid content and ash content, which may characterise the sedimentary lithotypes and igneous rocks intersected in boreholes.

The coal geologist has to be familiar with those geologs applicable to coal identification. All exploration and development drilling programmes will have a logging unit ready to log cored and openholes within the area of interest. The coal geologist will be required to reconcile depth and thickness estimates on the drilling lithological logs with the corrected depths recorded on the geolog. He or she will also need to interpret all features of interest on the logs and use such interpretations to site additional exploratory boreholes, and to site additional boreholes alongside selected logged boreholes (pilot holes) to take coal cores for quality analysis.

In coal exploration, the geologist wishes to measure and identify one or more of the physical properties of the coal-bearing sequence. The appropriate geologs are selected to obtain the required geological information. The geological information sought includes: the identification of coal; the identification of depths to coal seam roof and floor, and the coal seam thickness; the identification of partings within the coal seams, and quality variations within the seam; the determination of geological features such as faulting, jointing, washouts and thick sandstones and igneous intrusions; and the determination of hydrogeological and geotechnical characteristics.

Once this information has been obtained, it can be built into the geological database, so that assessment of coal quality and geotechnical properties can be made, together with coal resource/reserves calculations with geological losses (see Chapter 11). This information will then be incorporated into the mine planning programme.

Geolog interpretation is essentially a three phase exercise. First, log calibration, converting the measured log units into either standardised log units or recognised physical properties. The second phase is the basic interpretation: locating and measuring the bed boundaries, the depths and thicknesses, and an average value of log units for the formation. Finally, there is log analysis, relating the standard log units or physical properties to formation characteristics.

The logs most useful and most used to identify coal and coal-bearing sequences are: gamma ray; density; neutron; caliper; sonic; and resistivity logs. Of these, the first two, gamma ray and density are usually sufficient to identify coal horizons and other common lithotypes in coal-bearing sequences.

7.5.1 Radiation logs

Gamma ray, density and neutron logs measure nuclear radiation emitted from naturally occurring sources within geological formations, or emitted from sources carried on the logging tool. Unlike electric logs, radiation will work in the absence of a borehole fluid (air filled boreholes) and through casing.

In coal exploration, where boreholes tend to be shallow (less than 350 m), narrow and often dry, with the walls in poor condition, radiation logs are often the only tools available for coal identification.

7.5.1.1 Gamma ray log

The gamma ray log measures the naturally occurring radiation in geological formations. The principal source of radioactivity in rocks is usually the potassium-40 isotope associated with clay minerals, and therefore found more abundantly in mudstones and clay-rich siltstones.

Conversely, good quality coals and clean sandstones have a very low level of natural radiation. As the amount of included clay material increases, in the form of clay partings in coal and as clay clasts and clay matrix in sandstones, so the natural radiation increases. For marine mudstones, higher levels of potassium together with other radioactive isotopes in the form of uranium and thorium may be preserved. This causes the natural radiation levels to be much higher than in the more typical non-marine mudstones.

The occurrence of horizons exhibiting high levels of radiation is extremely useful for correlation purposes. This is also so for very low radiation levels in clean coal. Figure 7.13 shows the relationship of the gamma ray log response to selected lithotypes found in coal-bearing sequences.

The use of natural radiation to determine the ash content of coals is an unreliable technique, as coals with the same ash content may emit differing amounts of natural radiation due to the make up of the mineral content of the ash fraction in the coal.

The gamma ray log is not wholly diagnostic, and in normal practice it is used in conjunction with other geophysical logs to fully distinguish formations. Gamma ray logs are calibrated according to the American Petroleum Institute (API) standards and adjusted so that the log gives values expressed in API units.

Gamma ray logs have relatively poor vertical resolution, as the gamma ray tool 'senses or sees' a fairly large area (up to 40 cm vertically). As absorption increases as the density increases, the depth of investigation becomes lower in high

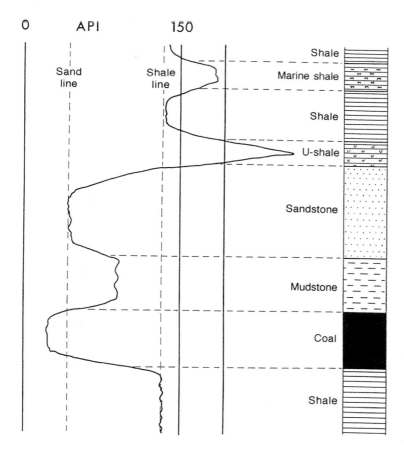

Figure 7.13 Coal-bearing sequence lithotypes and gamma ray log response. Reproduced by permission of BPB Instruments Ltd (1981)

density formations such as basic igneous rocks. As a guide, coal seam thickness can be interpreted by taking the point on the gamma ray curve one-third down from the base of a typical mudstone. Such interpretations are asymmetrical as gamma rays travel further in the less dense coal medium.

Gamma ray performance is not impaired by borehole caving or loss of borehole fluids, as air, water and mud are not high absorbers of gamma rays. In addition, gamma rays can be run through casing, as casing tends only to attenuate the radiation received, the shape of the log being preserved although the base level is altered. For accuracy, however, an adjustment to allow for casing has to be made.

As illustrated in Figure 7.13, the trace of the gamma ray log identifies a sharp geological boundary between two formations as a curve with a vertical height equal to the average vertical resolution of the gamma ray detector, and a horizontal length equal to the difference between the gamma ray count of the formations either side of the geological boundary.

7.5.1.2   Density logs

In coal exploration, the density log is used as a principal means of identifying coal, as coal has a uniquely low density compared with the rest of the coal-bearing sequence (see Table 7.1). In certain circumstances there is the additional benefit of an approximately linear relationship between ash content and density for a given coal seam in a given area.

In the density sonde, two detectors are used to measure gamma rays passed into the formation from the source and reflected to the detector by scattering. The long and short spacing logs are shielded from direct radiation from the source used, and measure the gamma rays which have been reflected, or back-scattered, from the rock.

Induced gamma rays in the energy range used for density logging are usually scattered in a forward direction. This means that density logs only respond to the formations between the source and the detector. The gamma rays can be considered to have 'diffused' through the material between the source and detector, and the density logs will equally be affected by all this material. The vertical resolution of the density logs is thus approximately equal to their spacing of the source and detector.

The density log is calibrated by measuring the sonde output in homogeneous blocks of material of known density, and plotting a calibration graph, the results of which are applied automatically by a surface logging unit.

The density log will respond not only to the formation but also to the fluid in the borehole. As the borehole diameter increases, so the effect of the borehole fluid increases. This adverse effect is removed by designing the sonde so that the measurement system is focused to give a narrow beam directed into the formation and forced against the borehole wall by a spring-loaded arm (caliper), so that it is always in contact with the formation. This removes the effects of the borehole fluid except where irregularities in the borehole diameter occur during drilling due to material being washed out (caving), or deviations in the borehole diameter. The problem of caving is significant for density logging in coal exploration, as a short spaced density log can produce a response in a caved mudstone which resembles a response from a coal seam. Usually reference to the three arm caliper log printout should highlight such anomalies.

A density log will show a sharp boundary between two formations as a curve with a vertical height approximately equal to the source to detector spacing (S) of the log and a horizontal length equal to the difference in densities between the formations either side of the boundary. Figure 7.14 shows the response of short and long spaced density logs. If the relation-

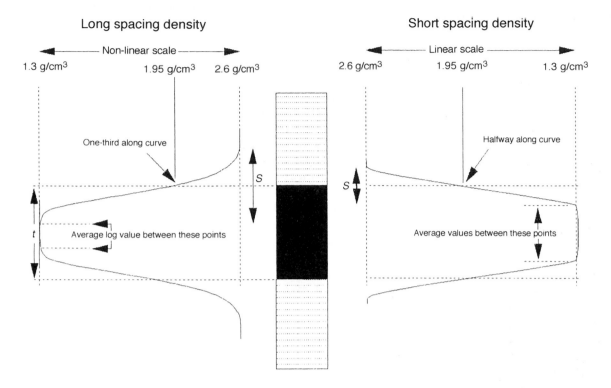

ship between the gamma ray intensity measured at the detector and the formation density is linear (short spaced density log), the boundary is taken as the halfway point along the curve. If the response is non-linear (long spaced density log), the boundary point can be read off using the log calibration scale in g/cm^3 on the log or, if only the count rate is available, it is assumed to be two-thirds along the curve from the high count rate value as shown in Figure 7.14. In coal seams with thicknesses less than S (the source to detector spacing), the full log value of the thin bed is not recorded. Accurate thickness and log values for thin beds are thus more difficult to evaluate; this is particularly so for coal horizons with multiple thin partings.

With the development of a parallel sided drill rod, it has become possible to run geophysical logs through the rod. This has resulted in gamma ray and density logs being used in this way. This has minimised the likelihood of a radioactive source being lost down a borehole, with serious financial and environmental consequences. If there are such problems, the drill rod can be removed bringing the tool up with it.

Figure 7.14 Long and short spaced density log response to coal. Reproduced by permission of P. Raymant (1991)

7.5.1.3   *Neutron log*

Neutron logs respond primarily to the hydrogen content of saturated rocks. The neutron log consists of a source which provides a continuous spectrum of high energy neutrons and a detector sensitive only to low energy (thermal) neutrons. Hydrogen is the most effective element in the slowing down or moderation of neutrons. Once slowed down, the neutrons diffuse away from the source and are gradually captured. Therefore as the log moves away from the source, the thermal neutron population first increases as more fast neutrons are moderated and then decreases as they are absorbed.

Hydrogen is found in the rock matrix itself, in water chemically bound to the rock molecules, and also in the fluid in the pore spaces of the rock. The last of these is a measure of the porosity of the rock and the amount of fluid it contains.

In sandstone, the neutron response is logarithmic with porosity, such that at low porosities it is sensitive but at high porosities it is less so. Coal gives a response of around 60% effective porosity due to its structure of hydrogen and carbon; any change in count rate can reflect changes in calorific values, which on an ash-free basis can be considered as a coal rank parameter. Where moisture is relatively constant, the neutron log can give an approximate guide to the amount of volatile matter present.

The response of a neutron log over a formation boundary is not as simple as a density log response, and cannot be used for such an accurate interpretation of thickness. The same approach as used with density logs must be taken to arrive at average formation log values for use in quantitative work. From experience, bed boundary location can be approximately interpreted at about one-fifth from the high count rate value of the curve for a coal-sandstone interface as shown in Figure 7.15.

Neutron logs have been used to synthesise rock quality indices which can be directly related to mining problems. The hydrogen held in micro- and macro-fractures in the borehole and bound to rock molecules is measured (known as the hydrogen index), and empirical relationships are established between it and the observed fracture density for those rock types most commonly encountered in coal-bearing sequences. This technique has been applied particularly in Europe and North America for geotechnical studies.

7.5.2   Caliper log

The caliper log measures the borehole diameter, and its main use is for correcting long and short spaced density readings. The caliper measuring system can either be part of the density logging tool, where it is a single arm used to force the logging tool against the side of the borehole, or as an individual tool with three arms at equal spacing. It is calibrated by measuring

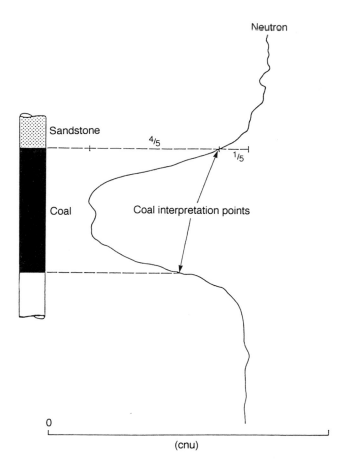

Neutron

Sandstone

4/5

1/5

Coal

Coal interpretation points

0

(cnu)

Figure 7.15 Response of neutron log over a coal seam. Reproduced by permission of P. Raymant (1991)

the log output at arm extensions fixed in place using a calibration plate marked out in borehole diameters.

The three arm caliper gives an average borehole diameter measured at three points. Difficulties arise when using the single arm tool where the hole size is enlarged due to caving in front of the density logging face, but not on the side of the borehole where the caliper is travelling.

The caliper log in association with the density log can be used to indicate rock strength. Figure 7.16 shows the response of caliper and density logs across a coal seam which has a good sound floor, but has a soft roof. Such coal seam profiles are of importance to the mining engineer in estimating the mining conditions likely to be encountered in underground workings.

7.5.3 Electric logs

In the examination of coal-bearing sequences electric logs may be used to support radioactive logs, but are rarely used alone.

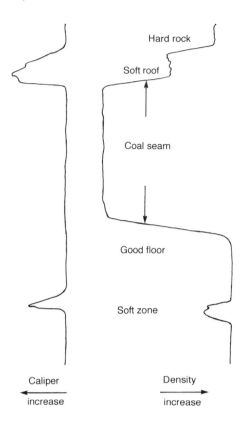

Figure 7.16   Use of the combination of caliper and density logs to determine coal seam roof and floor characteristics. Reproduced by permission of BPB Instruments Ltd (1981)

This can be illustrated by the fact that coal possesses high resistivity, but in boreholes coal is difficult to distinguish from many other rock types.

Single point resistance log and self potential logs have been superseded by the gamma ray log due to the latter's reliability in a variety of borehole conditions. Focused electric (FE) logs are designed to direct most of their energy through the borehole wall and as far into the surrounding rocks as possible. They give a more accurate representation of the resistivity of the strata than the conventional resistivity techniques. They are capable of a relatively high degree of resolution, and are used in conjunction with other logs to identify the lithological units in the borehole.

In coal, FE logs are frequently capable of picking out thin beds unresolved by the short spaced density log. To interpret bed thickness, boundary curves should be identified and located at the half-way point in resistivity between the two ends of the curve. A sequence containing three coals and showing the FE log response is given in Figure 7.17.

Coals in the form of lignite and anthracite give very low resistivity readings, whereas subbituminous and bituminous

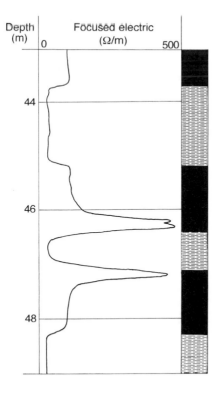

Figure 7.17   Response of focused electric log over a series of coal seams. Reproduced by permission of P. Raymant (1991)

coal can vary from low to high. A typical response of the resistivity log in a coal-bearing sequence is shown in Figure 7.18.

Resistivity logs can distinguish coal that is burnt close to an intrusion, or is oxidised due to weathering. Burning has the effect of reducing resistivity close to an intrusion, and Figure

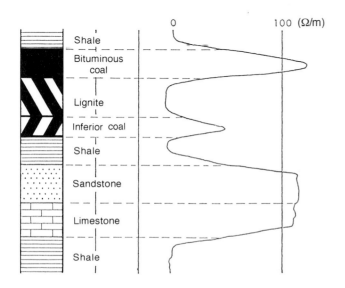

Figure 7.18   Response of resistivity log to coal-bearing lithotypes. Reproduced by permission of BPB Instruments Ltd (1981)

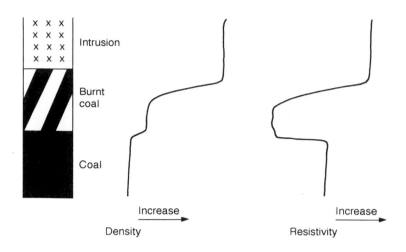

Figure 7.19 Response of density and resistivity logs over a burnt coal zone. Reproduced by permission of BPB Instruments Ltd (1981)

7.19 shows such a resistivity response across a burnt coal section.

7.5.4   Sonic log

The sonic log has a similar response to the density log as a result of the close relationship between compaction and density. In lithological interpretations it is not better than a density log, and is rarely run as a simple lithology log. The response of a sonic log in a typical coal-bearing sequence is shown in Figure 7.20.

The operational disadvantage of the sonic log is that it requires an open, fluid filled hole; in addition, it is adversely

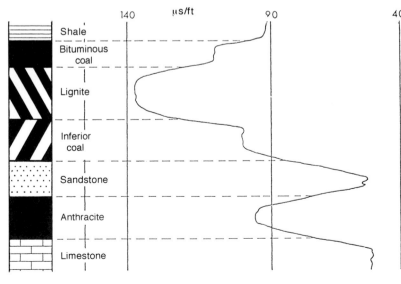

Figure 7.20 Response of sonic log to coal-bearing lithotypes. Reproduced by permission of BPB Instruments Ltd (1981)

affected by caving. Nevertheless, the sonic log is a useful indicator of rock strength. The log interprets the velocity of sound waves in different lithotypes, which is of great value in the processing and interpretation of seismic data. As the velocity is related to the geomechanical properties of the rocks, the sonic log may also be used to predict the engineering characteristics of the strata for mine planning purposes.

7.5.5 Temperature log

The standard bottom hole temperature is important in planning underground mining operations and, in particular, ventilation systems. Changes in the temperature log can also indicate the levels in the borehole at which significant groundwater inflow occurs.

7.5.6 Advanced interpretation

Further information on the lithology of the strata and the characteristics of the coal can be obtained by combining data from several different types of logs. For example, sonic and density logs can be combined for the interpretation of coal rank, as illustrated in Figure 7.21.

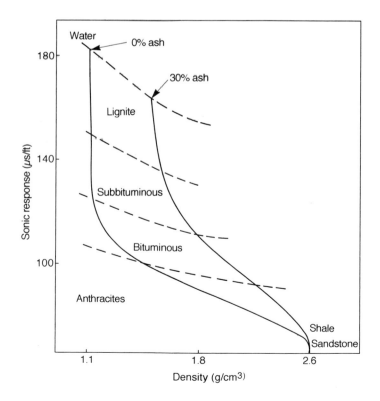

Figure 7.21 Interpretation of coal rank from sonic and density logs. Reproduced by permission of BPB Instruments Ltd (1981)

Figure 7.22 Display showing graphic interpretation of coal-bearing sequence together with density log response. Reproduced by permission of BP Coal Ltd (1984)

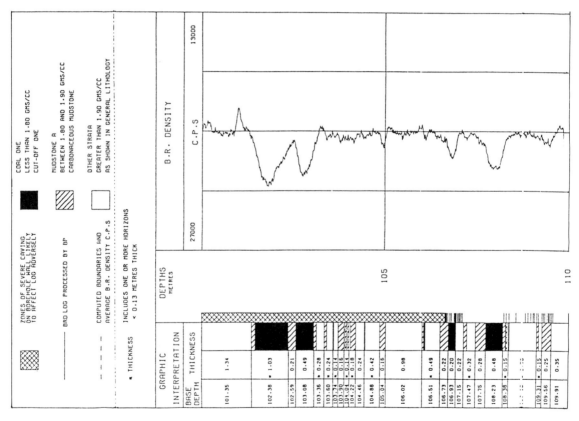

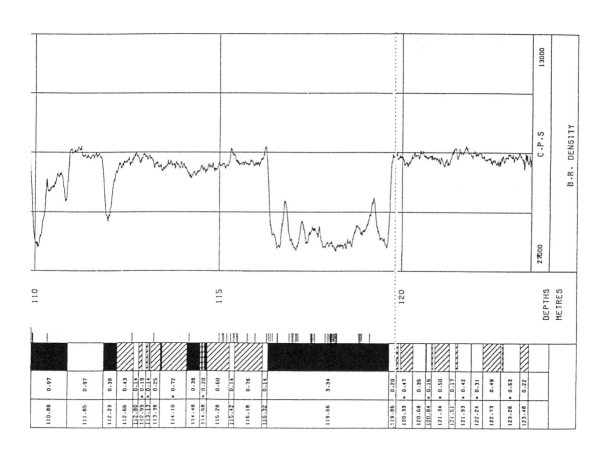

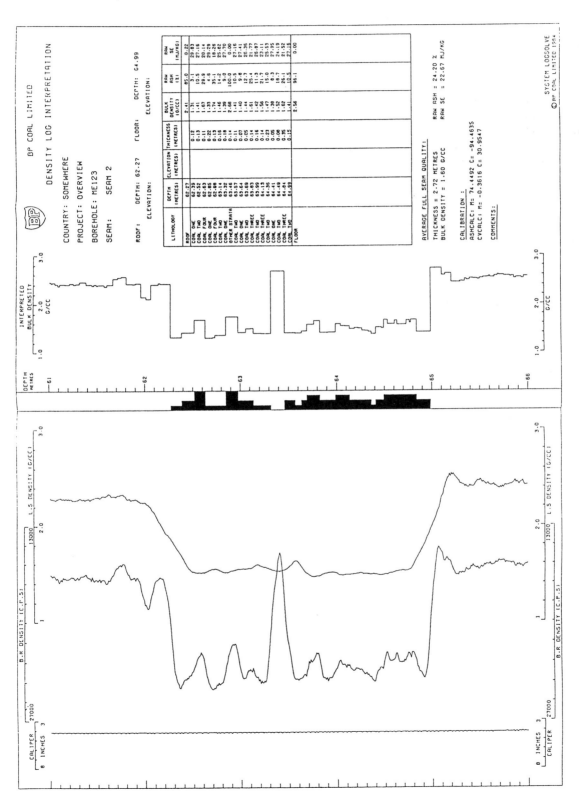

Figure 7.23 Density log interpretation together with interpreted coal seam bulk densities and raw ash content. Reproduced by permission of BP Coal Ltd (1984)

Attempts have been made to develop a simple method of measuring the *in situ* moisture content in coal, but moisture levels in coal deposits are usually too high and render conventional neutron tools insensitive.

The combination of gamma ray and density logs with lithological logs from boreholes is used for correlation within coal deposits. Figure 7.22 shows a typical lithological and density log combination, and Figure 7.23 shows a density analysis for a coal seam with bulk density, raw ash and raw calorific value calculations together with density and caliper logs. A series of such printouts for each seam in a lease area can be used for correlation and for estimations of likely raw coal quality across the area. Also, where horizons with high gamma readings are present they will readily show up on gamma ray logs, as will coal seams and clean sandstones which have low gamma radiation, all of which facilitates correlation.

The coal geologist will become familiar in carrying out this style of correlation during the exploration drilling phase of any project, together with ensuring the reconciliation of coal seam roof and floor depths on the geophysical logs with those on the lithological logs, the latter based on the open and cored borehole records made by the geologist.

The use of geophysical logs in coal exploration is now established practice, essential for any reserve assessment of a coal deposit. Using the various logs described, the required information can be summarised as follows: (a) correlation of coal seams and other horizons across a deposit; (b) accurate seam depths and thicknesses; (c) coal seam structure details; (d) control of drill core sampling; (e) assessment of core recovery percentages; (f) indication of coal quality and quality variation across the deposit.

More sophisticated geophysical logging techniques can provide the following additional information: (g) lithology interpretation; (h) assessment of geotechnical properties of formations, principally rock strength; (i) orientation (verticality and direction of deviation) of boreholes; and (j) measurement of stratigraphic dip of formations for use in the determination of geological structures.

Chapter 8
Hydrogeology of coal

8.1 INTRODUCTION

The influence that water has on the mining of coal is significant, both in terms of surface water and groundwater movement. Water poses some of the greatest problems in mining in opencast and underground coal operations.

The geologist needs to be aware of the presence of water, or sometimes the lack of it, in planning exploration and development programmes.

Field operations are strongly influenced in this way; for example, high and low water levels in stream and river sections will decrease or increase exposure. An abundant supply of water is required for water and mud flush drilling, but is not necessary for air flush drilling which is inhibited by a large head of water. Fundamental logistics such as transport are affected; dirt roads within the field area can become waterlogged and impassable, while very dry roads can create dust problems.

Of greater significance is how surface and groundwater will affect mine operations. The coal geologist can usually expect to be involved at some stage in either the collection of hydrogeological data or in assisting personnel who carry out such duties. To accomplish this, he or she should be aware of the basic hydrogeological properties of coals and coal-bearing sequences. The coal geologist will need to acquaint him- or herself with the theory of the retention and movement of groundwater, together with the movement of surface waters. There are numerous books which cover this subject in detail, but a summary of the basic properties of groundwater and those aspects of hydrogeology directly related to coal-bearing sequences and coal mining are described in this chapter.

8.1.1 Nature of groundwater and surface flow

The hydrological cycle begins and ends with the oceans. Water is evaporated from the ocean which then vaporises to form clouds. Water is precipitated from clouds, some of which falls on to the land surface and collects to form streams, rivers and lakes, and eventually flows overland back to the oceans. A portion of the rainfall passes through the soil to reach the water-table and so becomes groundwater.

8.1.1.1   *Groundwater*

The following brief summary of the principal terms used in hydrogeology is intended to provide a background for the coal geologist.

The upper part through which percolation occurs is known as the vadose zone, or zone of aeration, and water movement is primarily under the influence of gravity. The phreatic zone, or zone of saturation, is below the water-table in which pore spaces within the rock are filled with water. Water movement is primarily under the influence of hydrostatic and hydrodynamic pressures. These two zones are separated by the groundwater table which will vary in position as changes in the groundwater level occur. These changes can be negative resulting from groundwater movement and discharge, or positive resulting from groundwater recharge by percolating water from the vadose zone.

Rocks which contain groundwater and allow it to flow through them in significant amounts are called aquifers. Under normal circumstances water flows to natural discharge points such as springs and seepages. This process can be interrupted if wells are sunk into the aquifer and water is abstracted.

This ability to allow water to flow through the aquifer is termed permeability, and is controlled largely by geological factors. When the properties of the fluid are considered, the permeability or the ease at which the water can move through the rock is referred to as the hydraulic conductivity, expressed in metres per day. The changes in height or head that the water can attain naturally are known as the hydraulic gradient; the steeper the gradient, the faster the flow of water.

Groundwater may be contained in, and move through, pore spaces between individual grains in sedimentary rocks. Where rocks are fractured, this can significantly increase the hydraulic conductivity of the rock. The ratio of the volume of voids in the rock to the total volume of the rock is called the porosity. Some lithotypes do not allow the passage of fluids through them at significant rates or may allow only small amounts to pass through. These are termed aquicludes and aquitards, respectively, but are more commonly referred to as confining or impermeable horizons.

Groundwater usually flows under a hydraulic gradient, i.e.

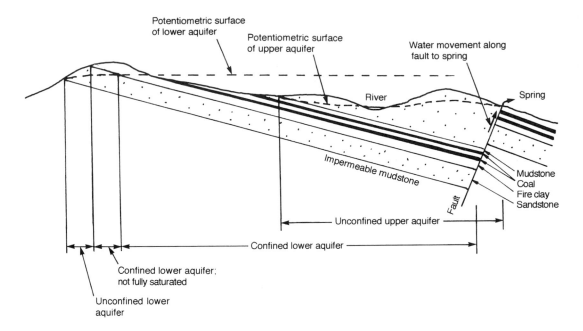

Figure 8.1 Groundwater conditions in a coal-bearing sequence, showing an upper unconfined aquifer and a lower confined aquifer with an intervening coal/mudstone sequence

the water-table. Where an aquifer is overlain by impermeable rocks, the pressure of groundwater may be such that the rest level of water would normally be well above the base of the impermeable layer. In such circumstances the aquifer is said to be confined, and the surface is known as the potentiometric or piezometric surface. The relationship of permeable and impermeable strata in confined and unconfined conditions in a coal-bearing sequence is illustrated in Figure 8.1.

In studying coal-bearing sequences, it is essential to identify the horizons which will act as aquifers and those which will remain impermeable. In the case of aquifers, it will be necessary to calculate how much water passes through in a given time. To study this phenomenon, Darcy's law is used. This states that a fluid will flow through a porous medium at a rate (Q) which is proportional to the product of the cross sectional area through which flow can occur (A), the hydraulic gradient (i) and hydraulic conductivity (K): $Q = KiA$. An aquifer's effectiveness to transmit water as calculated by Darcy's law is known as its transmissivity, usually expressed in square metres per day.

For an unconfined aquifer, the slope of the water-table is a measure of the hydraulic gradient; in this instance the transmissivity is the product of the hydraulic conductivity and the saturated bed thickness, the latter not being a constant feature. As the water-table is sloping, water flow is not purely horizontal, which means that the hydraulic gradient has a vertical as well as a horizontal component.

For a confined aquifer, the aquifer remains fully saturated. When water is removed from the pore spaces, the water pressure is lowered, and downward pressure on the pore spaces within the aquifer causes slight compression. This reduction in pressure also causes a slight expansion of the water. The volume of water released from or taken into storage per unit surface area of the aquifer for each unit change of head is known as the storage coefficient.

In practical terms, changes in water levels within the designated area of interest must be monitored and recorded. This is accomplished by installing piezometers and observation and pumping wells (boreholes). Boreholes which are sealed throughout much of their depth, so that they can measure the head at a particular depth in the aquifer, are known as piezometers. The information they supply forms an essential part of the geotechnical investigations carried out before the mine feasibility study.

Boreholes which pass through the sequence to be mined act as monitoring holes from which the water-table levels within the area can be measured on a regular basis.

The action of pumping water from a borehole causes a reduction in pressure around the pump. This creates a head difference between water in the borehole and that in the aquifer. Water then flows from the aquifer towards the borehole to replace the water pumped out. Gradually water flows towards the borehole from further and further out in the aquifer; this has the effect of lowering the hydraulic gradient so that around the borehole the hydraulic gradient becomes steeper, forming a characteristic lowering of the water-table. This is known as the cone of depression. The reduction in the head or lowering of the water-table at the borehole itself is called the drawdown. These features are illustrated in Figure 8.2.

8.1.1.2 Surface water

The area of land that drains to a river is called the catchment area. These areas are separated by high ground called a watershed or divide. Streams that flow throughout the year are termed perennial streams, those that flow only occasionally are termed ephemeral streams and those that flow only after the wet season are known as intermittent streams.

The discharge of a river or stream is the volume of water flowing past a given point in a unit of time. i.e. it equals the cross sectional area of the flow section times the speed at which the water is flowing. Most useful is the record of flow plotted against time, which is shown on a discharge hydrograph. Two components contribute to river flow: a baseflow component

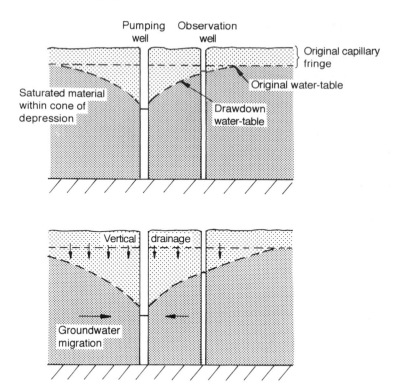

Figure 8.2 Drawdown of the water-table due to pumping in an unconfined aquifer. From Price (1985), by permission of the author and Chapman & Hall

consisting of groundwater flow and slow interflow, and a quickflow component, derived from rapid interflow, surface run-off and any rain that falls directly on to the river or stream.

Surface water flow measurements are usually made during the geotechnical studies stage following the geological exploration stage, particularly where it is likely that watercourses will need to be re-routed during the construction and working life of the mine.

8.1.2 Hydrogeological characteristics of coals and coal-bearing sequences

Most coal-bearing sequences contain sandstones, siltstones, mudstones, fireclays and coals. Of these, sandstones have the greatest potential for storing and transmitting groundwater; the other lithotypes have characteristically low permeabilities.

In older coal-bearing sequences, such as Carboniferous–Permian strata, the sediments are well indurated with low permeabilities. Sandstones are often well cemented, so reducing their porosity and permeability. In younger formations, such as those in the Tertiary, sandstones may still be only partially cemented or totally uncemented, and therefore have the potential to hold and transmit large amounts of groundwater by connected intergranular flow, i.e. they have primary permeability.

This is not to say that coals and coal-bearing strata do not allow the passage of groundwater. Most sequences are tectonically disturbed and contain numerous discontinuities such as joints and faults which, if open, will hold and allow groundwater flow, i.e. they have secondary permeability. In addition, it is a common feature for groundwater to flow along inclined bedding surfaces and appear in workings as a series of seepages, often staining the underlying strata with mineral precipitates.

The permeability of coal in general can be regarded as highly stress dependent, decreasing as the level of stress is increased. Coals react differently to stress due to their composition and rank. Coals with a high degree of elasticity and no apparent fractures are usually relatively unaffected by fluctuations in stresses exerted upon them. On the other hand, highly fissured or low mechanical strength friable coals tend to microfracture under stress. In the case of the latter, the subsequent release of stress will leave the coal permanently microfractured and this then creates an increase in the overall permeability of the coal. There is also a relationship between the compressibility of coal and the amount of volatile matter present. There seems to be an increase in compressibility with increasing volatile content up to around 36%, and then a decrease towards the lower rank coals.

Coals can hold significant amounts of water, which on being breached by mine workings is released and can cause mining difficulties, chiefly in underground workings as opencast operations tend to be dewatered before mining begins.

Fireclays or seat earths and other clay-rich sediments have the ability to hold water, both in those clay minerals which have expanding lattice structures and as adsorbed water on the individual clay particles. This relatively high porosity does not, however, result in high permeability as the water is retained around the clay particles, held by surface tension; this phenomenon is known as specific retention. Although such sediments have low permeability, their water content is important as they have geotechnical significance as horizons of weakness when subjected to increased stress or sudden depressurisation.

Table 8.1 gives the indicative porosities and hydraulic conductivities for selected unconsolidated and consolidated sediments found in coal-bearing sequences. For peats and brown and black coals it is difficult to give such indicative values. Porosity values for peat will be high, whereas brown and more particularly black coal will have low porosity values due to the increasing effects of compaction and coalification. Permeability values are difficult to quantify due to the fact that coals are dominated by discontinuities which may or may not allow the passage of

Table 8.1 Indicative porosities and hydraulic conductivities for unconsolidated and consolidated sediments which characterise coal-bearing sequences. From Brassington (1988) by permission of the Open University Press

Lithotype	Grain size (mm)	Porosity (%)	Hydraulic conductivity (m/day)
Unconsolidated sediments			
Clay	0.0005–0.002	45–60	$<10^{-2}$
Silt	0.002–0.06	40–50	10^{-2}–1
Sand	0.06–2.0	30–40	1–500
Gravel	2.0–64.0	25–35	500–10 000
Consolidated sediments			
Shale/mudstone	<0.002	5–15	5×10^{-8}–5×10^{-6}
Siltstone	0.002–0.06	5–15	5×10^{-8}–5×10^{-4}
Sandstone	0.06–2.0	5–30	10^{-4}–10†
Limestone	Variable	0.1–30*	10^{-5}–10†

*Secondary porosity.
†Secondary permeability.

water. High ash coals are known to have porosities of around 20%, with permeability values of less than one metre per day.

Studies of the hydraulic conductivity of peats have indicated that estimates showed time dependence, but that highly humified peat does not appear to transmit water strictly in accordance with Darcy's law, possibly due to air entrapment, whereas low humified peats tend to conform to Darcy's law.

In low rank coals all the water does not reside in pores alone; some water must actually be included in the organic structure. Experimentally, the pore size distribution can be determined by forcing mercury into coals at increasing pressures and measuring the volume of mercury intrusion (mercury porosimetry). However, corrections have to be made for the compressibility of coals; also, the high pressure may open or close pore space, which can be determined by measuring the helium density of the coal samples before and after mercury intrusion.

The experimental work of Gan *et al.* (1972) can be used to illustrate this. Twelve coals were tested by mercury porosimetry and the results are shown in Table 8.2. The pore volume distributions are given for the following pore ranges:

(i)   Total pore volume VT accessible to helium as estimated from helium and mercury densities
(ii) Pore volume V1 contained in pores >300 Å in diameter
(iii) Pore volume V2 contained in pores 300–12 Å in diameter
(iv) Pore volume V3 contained in pores <12 Å, V3 = VT − (V1 + V2)

Table 8.2 Gross open pore distributions in coals. See text for definitions of distributions. From Gan *et al.* (1972), by permission of the author and the publishers. Copyright © 1992 Butterworth–Heinemann Ltd

Sample	Rank*	Carbon (% daf)	VT (cm³/g)	V1 (cm³/g)	V2 (cm³/g)	V3 (cm³/g)	V3 (%)	V2 (%)	V1 (%)
PSOC-80	Anthracite	90.8	0.076	0.009	0.010	0.057	75.0	13.1	11.9
PSOC-127	lv	89.5	0.052	0.014	0.000	0.038	73.0	0	27.0
PSOC-135	mv	88.3	0.042	0.016	0.000	0.026	61.9	0	38.1
PSOC-4	hvA	83.8	0.033	0.017	0.000	0.016	48.5	0	51.5
PSOC-105A	hvB	81.3	0.144	0.036	0.065	0.043	29.9	45.1	25.0
Rand	hvC	79.9	0.083	0.017	0.027	0.039	47.0	32.5	20.5
PSOC-26	hvC	77.2	0.158	0.031	0.061	0.066	41.8	38.6	19.6
PSOC-197	hvB	76.5	0.105	0.022	0.013	0.070	66.7	12.4	20.9
PSOC-190	hvC	75.5	0.232	0.040	0.122	0.070	30.2	52.6	17.2
PSOC-141	Lignite	71.7	0.114	0.088	0.004	0.022	19.3	3.5	77.2
PSOC-87	Lignite	71.2	0.105	0.062	0.000	0.043	40.9	0	59.1
PSOC-89	Lignite	63.3	0.073	0.064	0.000	0.009	12.3	0	87.7

*Bituminous coals: lv = low volatile, mv = medium volatile, hv = high volatile.

The proportion of V3 is significant for all coals. Its value is a maximum for the anthracite sample (PSOC-80) and a minimum for the lignite sample (PSOC-89). From Table 8.2 it can be concluded that:

(i)   porosity in coals with carbon contents of <75% is predominantly due to macropores;

(ii) porosity in coals with carbon contents of 85–91% is predominantly due to micropores; and

(iii) porosity in coals with carbon contents of 75–84% is associated with significant proportions of macro-, meso- and micro-porosity.

8.2 COLLECTION AND HANDLING OF HYDROGEOLOGICAL DATA

During any mining operation it is important to minimise any disturbance of the surface hydrology or groundwater regimes. These regimes consist of the dynamic equilibrium relationships between precipitation, run-off, evaporation and changes in the groundwater and surface water store. They can also be extended to include erosion, sedimentation and water quality variations. It is therefore necessary to know the pre-mining conditions that exist in the area of interest. The intensity of investigations will be influenced by the particular circumstances existing in the area of interest, e.g. the rainfall characteristics, drainage characteristics, presence or absence of aquifers, and the geological and structural character of the area.

The collection of data relating firstly to surface water flow and secondly to groundwater flow, together with water quality analysis, will enable a hydrogeological model to be constructed which will form an integral part of the development studies before mine design.

The actual field techniques required to measure both surface and groundwater are outlined in detail in Brassington (1988).

8.2.1 Surface water

In most countries in which coal is mined, the bulk of precipitation is in the form of rainfall. To measure rainfall over the designated area, a network of rain gauges is sited and monitored on a regular basis to build up a detailed record of rainfall for the area; such rainfall is expressed in millilitres.

The flow of most springs is measured by filling a calibrated vessel in a given period of time. This can be a difficult operation in tropical terrain where the area around the spring may need to be cleared of vegetation before any measurement is taken.

The flow of rivers and streams is calculated by measuring the water velocity and the river cross sectional area, or by installing a weir. The former is more suitable for rivers, and the latter for streams. This flow is measured in litres per second.

8.2.2 Groundwater

To determine the potential groundwater problems that may be encountered during mining (particularly opencast operations), it will be necessary to determine the groundwater characteristics of the area, in particular the groundwater flow patterns, flow rates and depth to the water-table.

Flow patterns will be affected by lithotypes, their disposition, relative permeabilities, and the presence of faults, joints and open bedding planes. For a full understanding of the groundwater regime for a proposed mining area a site specific hydrogeological model needs to be developed.

To achieve this, a system of monitoring boreholes or wells will need to be constructed, their siting based on all the information gathered on the geology of the area plus all surface water occurrences. This information will be used to determine the expected direction and flow-rate of groundwater, and enable the monitoring boreholes to be favourably sited.

These boreholes will provide information on the position of the water-table, which in turn will define a baseline condition of any seasonal or climatic fluctuations against which the impact of mining can be assessed. In addition, samples taken from them will indicate the general water quality. This monitoring programme is particularly important if aquifers are present in the designated mining area.

Boreholes used as monitoring points may be of different types. Those boreholes that are sealed throughout much of their depth in such a way that they measure the head at a particular depth in the horizon selected are known as piezometers. Piezometers are installed in areas which have opencast mining potential. They monitor the groundwater conditions in both shallow formations such as superficial deposits, and formations likely to influence surface mining operations. Piezometers can also be drilled at an angle to intercept vertical fractures in less permeable strata. Piezometers are usually sited where they can function throughout the life of the mine. Figure 8.3 shows piezometers set to measure levels in two formations in an opencast site.

Boreholes that are used as observation wells will include those that have already been drilled in the area for stratigraphic purposes and have been kept open for such a use, plus new site specific boreholes. Of these, at least one observation borehole should be placed intersecting each aquifer both upstream and

Figure 8.3 Piezometer group measuring water levels in two formations in an opencast working. Photograph by LPT

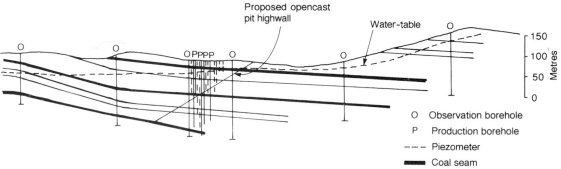

Figure 8.4 Section across proposed opencast pit showing position of observation boreholes, production boreholes and piezometers, placed to determine groundwater levels and pressurisation field around proposed position of highwall in opencast pit

downstream of the mine site; further boreholes should be placed around the periphery and within the mine site to ensure that a reliable estimation of the water level in each aquifer can be determined. Additional boreholes should be located at any geological discontinuities that may affect groundwater flow such as faults, folds, and abrupt changes in aquifer thickness.

Observation boreholes and piezometers are regularly placed to determine groundwater levels and the pressurisation field around the proposed position of a high wall in an opencast pit. Figure 8.4 shows the siting of such boreholes in a proposed opencast mine.

Water levels will be measured and recorded in all boreholes and piezometers on a regular basis. If any borehole is used to pump water then the drawdown and rest levels in the pumped borehole together with rest levels of water in surrounding observation boreholes will be recorded.

Once the network of piezometers and boreholes has been established in the designated area, regular monitoring and recording of field data will become an important routine operation.

Data obtained from piezometers and observation boreholes can be used to construct groundwater contour maps and flow nets. Groundwater contours are constructed from groundwater field levels related to a common datum plotted on a scale plan. Points of equal height are joined to form contours; flow lines are drawn at right angles from each contour. These give a plan view only, whereas in actual cross section flow paths curve towards a discharge point such as a spring, stream or a pumping well.

The groundwater contour map may represent a water-table surface or a potentiometric surface, which will be derived from the geological and well information. The spacing of contours gives an indication of aquifer permeability values; when they are close together it is indicative of low permeabilities as a steep hydraulic gradient is needed to impel the water through the aquifer, whereas widely spaced contours indicate a more permeable aquifer. Flow lines indicate the overall direction of groundwater flow and where such a flow is concentrating.

Current investigations utilise these hydrogeological data to produce computer models of the groundwater movement patterns likely to exist in a proposed mining site. This has the advantage that the model can be modified as more geological and hydrogeological data can be input into the system.

8.3 EFFECTS OF GROUNDWATER ON MINING

8.3.1 Opencast mining

8.3.1.1 Dewatering

The major problem that groundwater presents to opencast or surface mining is that if operations are to extend below the potentiometric surface, groundwater flow, either through permeable aquifers or by secondary permeability along faults and joints, is likely to result in the flooding of the workings or pit. In addition, confined aquifers immediately underlying the workings may, if the hydraulic pressures are sufficient, cause fracturing of the overlying impermeable layer and allow water into the pit.

Dewatering of opencast workings entails the production and maintenance of a cone of depression in and around the workings to reduce hydraulic pressure in aquifers and so prevent flooding and increase pit stability. This also reduces the inflow of groundwater from prolific recharge zones such as rivers or lakes. Vertical wells are used extensively for dewatering, the exact pattern of wells being dependent on the site specific hydrogeological characteristics. Water can be removed from an aquifer by gravity or by pumping. Gravity wells drain water from an upper aquifer into a lower aquifer below the level of the pit bottom. Pumping wells raise water from the aquifer to the ground surface to be disposed of. In Germany this method is used extensively to dewater large opencast operations in brown coal deposits; the shape of the resultant cone(s) of depression is constantly monitored by piezometers. Figure 8.5 shows a system of wells dewatering an opencast site in brown coals, together with a series of observation piezometers. The potentiometric surface of the groundwater is kept below the level of benching within the pit. The wells are installed through the overburden, coals and footwall sequence; when the coal is worked the well is sealed and reopened once the bench is cut.

A series of interconnected well points may be used to lower the water-table to a level below the proposed base of the excavations. In Figure 8.6 a two-stage dewatering scheme is depicted which is designed to lower the water-table below the two levels of excavation in the site.

In Saskatchewan, Canada, dewatering is required to opencast mine brown coals overlain by 15–35 m of overburden. Here the coal itself, plus sands occurring both above and below the coal, are the principal aquifers, with the coal acting as the major aquifer conducting water from the overburden sediments by joint and fissure flow. Dewatering tests included pumping from

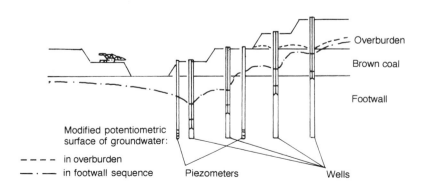

Figure 8.5   Position of production boreholes and piezometers in a brown coal opencast pit

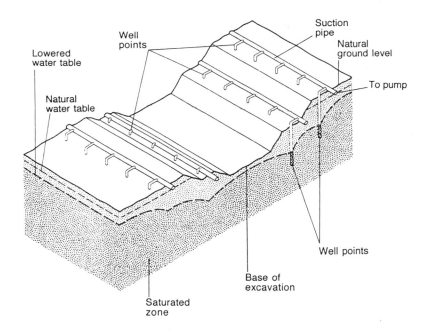

Figure 8.6 Site dewatering. A two-stage dewatering scheme using well points to lower the water-table below the base of an excavation. From Price (1985), by permission of the author and Chapman & Hall

the coal and measuring the response in the overburden, and the measurement of the response of potentiometric levels in the overburden during excavation of the test pits. The water levels in the coal were rapidly drawn down by pumping from structural lows in the coal seam. Figure 8.7 shows the migration of the 5.0 m drawdown contour from the pumping centres within the mine area. Pumping and test pit excavations caused relatively rapid reductions in potentiometric levels in the overburden. These tests showed that the overburden could be dewatered by directly pumping from the coal, the secondary permeability

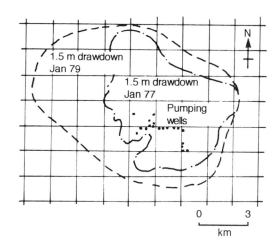

Figure 8.7 Migration of the cone of depression due to pumping. From Clifton (1987), *International Journal of Surface Mining and Reclamation* 1, 27–34, by permission of A.A. Balkema, Rotterdam, The Netherlands

being sufficient to provide drainage from the overburden if enough lead time was provided before mining. A lowering of potentiometric pressure by further dewatering would be required in the sands below the coal to eliminate floor heave in the pit.

In areas where the geology is more complex, wells may be concentrated in areas with potential water problems, e.g. in close proximity to a large fault. This will result in a local depression of the potentiometric surface, whereas the rest of the site may be served by a more general drawdown achieved by a grid of pump wells.

Wells can also be used as depressurisation wells to reduce hydraulic pressure in an aquifer, or perhaps to improve slope stability or prevent floor heaving.

A more specialised technique is the use of sealing walls. This involves the construction of an impermeable barrier between a prolific source of groundwater and the pit. They are designed to intercept groundwater and prevent it discharging into the pit or cone of depression. Sealing walls do not actively remove groundwater but can reduce the pumping requirements needed to maintain the cone of depression.

The dewatering of opencast sites which results in the draw-down of the groundwater level can disrupt water supplies to shallow wells, springs and even small surface streams. Under certain conditions deeper aquifers and regional groundwater regimes can be disturbed. This is of special significance in those countries which have water supply shortages, as dewatering can affect local agriculture, such as irrigation programmes and stock rearing. In such cases, water supplies have to be provided by the mining company to maintain such activities.

8.3.1.2 Stability

Large scale dewatering projects can produce land subsidence as unconsolidated or partially unconsolidated aquifers, or parts of aquifers that have been dewatered, are subject to lower pressures which can cause an increase in the effective stress within the sediments. This allows greater consolidation and so produces subsidence, particularly in the floor of the opencast pit.

Conversely, dewatering will be required to depressurise the pit floor, the high wall and end wall of an opencast pit. This is carried out to not only reduce inflows of groundwater, but to relieve pressure on the pit walls which may otherwise be subject to failure, particularly when shear zones and other discontinuities have been identified.

8.3.2   Underground mining

Water entering underground coal operations can be from several sources, e.g. groundwater flow, natural precipitation at the surface and abstractions from rivers and wells. The latter two occurrences are from infiltration of the workings via shafts and adits. Water may also enter from old abandoned workings situated in close proximity to the current mine.

It is an ongoing operation and expense to drain water from underground workings to facilitate working conditions and also to minimise potential hazards that water build-up can create.

During the mining operation it is necessary to monitor the amount and quality of the water flowing into the workings. Water pumped out of the mine should be utilised to the greatest practicable extent, but it may be necessary to improve the quality by treatment.

The planning and design of effective mine drainage systems requires the best possible knowledge of underground water flow patterns and reliable forecasts of future yields. It is important that comprehensive records of mining are maintained and co-ordinated. All mine areas to be abandoned must be sealed off and clearly recorded on the mine plans; the locations of all mine interconnections, boreholes, shafts and adits must also be plotted. In addition to this information the multiplicity of seams, faults and interseam connections must be recorded. The effective use of all of these data will allow long term planning of underground water control to be implemented. For example, in the UK up to 1000 million litres per day have been pumped from active underground mines and adjacent abandoned workings.

8.3.3   Groundwater quality and its effect on coal

8.3.3.1   *Groundwater quality*

In opencast workings, surface waters and shallow groundwaters do not have the concentration of elements found in deep groundwaters. This is not to say that water quality can be taken for granted; quality measurements are just as important an exercise as for deep mines, it is just that the problems of water quality are usually more acute in underground workings.

The groundwater that flows into mine workings is normally free from suspended particles, but always contains dissolved substances in concentrations related to the depth and hydrogeological conditions. However, such waters can become contaminated with fine grained particles of coal and other lithotypes through contact with underground working operations.

Table 8.3   Changes in groundwater quality with depth

Depth from surface (m)	Concentration of dissolved compounds (mg/l)									
	Na^+	Ca^{2+}	Mg^{2+}	Ba^{2+}	Sr^{2+}	Nh_4^+	Mn^{2+}	Cl^-	SO_4^{2-}	HCO_3^-
30	40	60	40	<2	<1	<0.1	<0.1	50	200	200
300	10 000	800	260	60	25	12	0.3	18 000	<5	200
900	41 500	11 700	2000	550	400	70	3.0	90 000	<5	80

In terms of chemical composition, the bulk of mine drainage waters are usually of reasonable quality; some may be moderately saline and a small percentage can be ferruginous or highly saline, or both, to such an extent that they would be precluded from utilisation and could lead to disposal problems.

Table 8.3 shows an example of the relationship between depth from the surface and the concentration of selected dissolved compounds found in underground mines. From this it can be seen that components such as sodium, calcium and chloride rapidly increase in concentration with increasing depth, whereas sulphate and hydrogen carbonate compounds decrease with depth.

Waters from shallow workings contain sulphates, chlorides, hydrogen carbonates, calcium, magnesium and sodium salts. Waters from slightly deeper workings become more heavily mineralised with calcium and magnesium salts, and at great depths concentrations of barium, strontium and ammonium chlorides are characteristic.

The minerals iron pyrite and marcasite (both FeS_2) are commonly present in coals and coal-bearing sequences, and these are reactive to atmospheric oxygen. The initial products of oxidation are iron(II) and iron(III) sulphates, sulphuric acid and hydrated iron(III) oxide. With the exception of iron(III) oxide, these products are soluble in water, and in turn react with clays and carbonate minerals to form aluminium, calcium, magnesium and other sulphates. Ferruginous waters that flow in the presence of air in mine workings precipitate iron(III) oxide; this produces the extensive red/orange staining of walls and equipment that characterises many underground workings.

8.3.3.2   *Effects of groundwater on coal*

Oxygenated groundwater in contact with coal results in the oxidation of the organic and inorganic constituents of the coal. Water is adsorbed on to the cleat faces and if it is held there for a period of time it will oxidise that coal immediately in contact with it. This has the effect of reducing the coal quality (see Section 2.3.4).

It is important to determine the extent of coal oxidation in both opencast and underground mines as this can seriously affect the reserve potential and possibly the life of the mine. An intensive coal sampling programme will identify those areas badly affected by oxidation. The mine plan can then be adjusted accordingly to avoid taking coal of an inferior quality which could contaminate the fresh coal and lower its commercial value.

8.4 ENVIRONMENTAL CONCERNS

8.4.1 Watercourse diversions

During surface mining operations, it is possible that certain drainage divisions may be required, particularly for the larger scale operations. All surface water originating upstream of a mining site should be diverted around the excavation and spoil areas to avoid contamination of the water and to reduce other problems within the pit. Diversions should be hydraulically efficient, and designed and constructed to control erosion and sediment load. Many countries have published regulations to establish design and performance standards for such diversions.

It is necessary to determine the design of the channel section which will carry the diverted flow, and also to ensure that the flow velocities will remain below that which can be tolerated by the chosen channel design. In the case of perennial streams, increased flow velocities and sediment loads in channel diversions may not be conducive to freshwater fauna and flora. The diversion should ideally include shallows and deeps and some meander pattern to suit the local ecological regime.

8.4.2 Run-off, erosion and sedimentation

Run-off results from precipitation and is the major cause of erosion in mining areas, particularly in regions of concentrated heavy rainfall as in tropical countries. Attempts to combat soil erosion are aimed at controlling run-off, reducing the erodibility of the soil itself and removing any sediment from the run-off that does occur.

Deforestation and the stripping of vegetation cover need to be kept to a minimum, and exposure of the required area of land should be for as short a time as possible. This requires effective mine planning and scheduling the sequential stages of vegetation removal, overburden stripping, mining and reclamation. Seasonal climatic variations may play an important part in this scheduling. Such planning should include the siting of haul roads and any banking, as these are the sites of much of the run-off and erosion. Diversion structures such as terraces and ditches can be sited to intercept run-off on long steep slopes, together with keeping the top soil loose to aid infiltration, and by using new vegetation types to stabilise slopes.

Concave slopes are the least affected by erosion, yield the least sediment, and change shape slower than other profiles. Convex slopes erode most rapidly, yield the most sediment and change shape quickly. Uniform and complex slopes are affected to an intermediate degree, but can still be severely eroded in a single storm. It is therefore recommended that slopes should be produced with as low a gradient as possible and be concave where feasible.

The loss of soil and land due to erosion can result in the degradation of streams and lakes as a result of increased sediment loads. As most run-off and erosion prevention measures are not 100% successful, all run-off originating within the mined area should be routed through a sedimentation pond, the primary purpose of which is to trap sediment movement from the mined area. Suspended sediment concentrations in waters draining from surface mining areas can be very high, with concentrations of 10 000–100 000 mg/l.

Such a sedimentation pond should be of sufficient size to store the sediment load without having the need for frequent removal of settled material, and to be of a size so that inflowing water has a sufficiently long detention period and low velocity to allow suspended sediment to settle out.

8.4.3 Mine water pollution

Current awareness and stronger legislation is restricting the pollution of surface water courses in mining areas. In the recent past, pollution from mine drainage was enormous; in the UK in the 1960s about 9000 km of streams were polluted by acid mine drainage. In the USA the total acid load from mine drainages was estimated to be 3.1 million tonnes, which had an overwhelming effect on particular rivers and streams within mining areas.

The principal causes of pollution are acidity and iron content, and centres around the oxidation of iron pyrite (see Section 8.3.3.1). Increased temperature leads to an increased rate of oxidation, and it has been suggested that the rate doubles for every 10 °C rise in temperature; the rate of oxidation of pyrite is also related to the reactive surface area of the pyrite.

In mine workings, the obvious effect of acidic and ferruginous mine waters is the corrosion of equipment such as conveyors, roof supports, chains and steel ropes, and they also attack concrete; fortunately, such mine waters are not toxic.

Acidic and ferruginous mine waters pollute rivers, streams and lakes firstly by discoloration (waters with iron contents of >0.5 mg/l will produce discoloration) and secondly by lowering the natural pH value which may be detrimental to industries abstracting water and to agriculture. Thirdly it can have noticeable effects on the fauna and flora present in the affected water courses if the pH drops below 5.5.

In addition, mine drainages from deep mines are extremely saline and if released into surface drainage will have a severe effect on the fauna and flora. For example, chloride concentrations of 70–500 mg/l are harmful to certain crops, and 100–200 mg/l of chloride will produce metallic corrosion. Sulphate concentrations of 300–3000 mg/l are also harmful to many crops. Such pollution is combated by chemical treatment or by draining the waters away from water courses into lagoons and allowing natural filtration.

8.4.4   Other forms of water pollution

Pollution of surface waters can occur from the use of drilling muds and additives. In both greenfield and developed areas, drilling programmes must avoid the pollution of streams and rivers by drilling fluids being allowed to flow into them. Discoloration of the water, while not necessarily toxic, is not desired by urban and rural populations alike. The building of a sealed circulation pit and the monitoring of flow-rates into and out of a borehole should avoid this situation. Similarly, in wells used for the abstraction of drinking water, as well as surrounding streams, the leakage of diesel, kerosene and other industrial fluids must be avoided.

The coal geologist in the capacity of supervising the drilling programme should liaise with the drilling manager and both should be alert to possible pollution, and should ensure that the project management is aware of any situation where this could occur.

Chapter 9
Coal sampling and analysis

9.1 INTRODUCTION

One of the most important duties of a coal geologist is the sampling of coal seams. Coal samples may be required as part of a greenfield exploration programme to determine whether the coal is suitable for further investigation, or as part of a mine development programme, or as routine samples in opencast and underground mines to ensure that the quality of the coal to be mined will provide the specified run of mine product.

In situ coal samples are taken from surface exposures, exposed coal seams in opencast and underground workings, and from drill cores and cuttings. Samples are also taken from run of mine coal streams, coal transport containers and coal stockpiles; these are referred to here as 'non *in situ*' samples.

Such coal samples may have to be taken under widely differing conditions, particularly those of climate and topography. It is essential that the sample taken is truly representative as it will provide the basic quality data on which decisions to carry out further investigations, development, or to make changes to the mine output will be made.

It is important to avoid weathered coal sections, coals contaminated by extraneous clay or other such materials, coals containing a bias of mineralisation, and coals in close contact with major faults and igneous intrusions.

9.2 *IN SITU* COAL SAMPLING

Several types of *in situ* samples can be taken depending on the analysis required.

9.2.1   Grab sampling

This is generally a most unsatisfactory method of obtaining coal for analysis as there are no controls on whether the coal is representative, and it can easily lead to a bias in selection, e.g. the bright coal sections attract attention. However, grab samples can be used to determine vitrinite reflectance measurements as an indicator of coal rank.

9.2.2   Channel sampling

This is the recommended technique for coal geologists to use. If the coal to be sampled is a surface exposure, the outcrop must be cleaned and cut back to expose as fresh a section as possible. Ideally the full seam section should be exposed, but for thick coals (especially in stream sections), sections of the roof and coal or coal and floor only may be seen. To obtain a full seam section under these circumstances, two or more channels will need to be cut and the overlap carefully recorded.

In opencast workings, the complete seam section should be exposed and is less likely to be weathered than natural surface exposures. In underground workings, the seam will be unweathered, but the whole seam section may not always be seen, due to the workings only exposing the selected mining section of the seam.

To carry out a channel sample, the coal is normally sampled perpendicular to the bedding. A channel of uniform cross section is cut manually into the coal seam, and all the coal within the cut section is collected on a plastic sheet placed at the base of the channel (Figure 9.1A). Most channels are around 1.0 m across and samples should not be less than 15 kg per metre of

Figure 9.1 Channel sampling procedure. (A) Whole coal seam channel sampling. From Robertson Research (Australia) Pty Ltd (1987), by permission. (B) Coal seam ply channel sampling

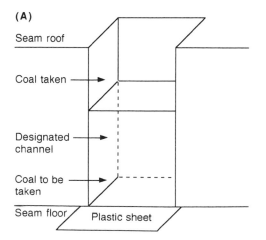

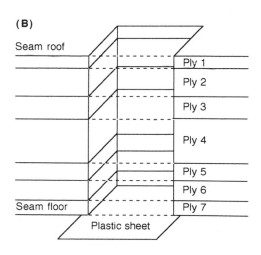

coal thickness. Such channel samples will provide a composite quality analysis for the seam, i.e. an analysis of all the coal and mineral matter present in the seam as a whole.

Although this is suitable for general seam quality assessment, more detailed analysis of the seam from top to bottom may be required. To achieve this, a channel ply sample is taken. This entails a similar procedure as for the whole seam channel sample except that the seam is divided into plies or subsections, as shown in Figure 9.1B.

Coal seams are rarely homogeneous throughout their thickness; most are divisible into distinct lithological sections. Plies are lithological subdivisions of the seam, each of which has a uniform character. When the lithology changes, such as at a clay parting in the seam, a separate ply is designated.

Where the roof and floor of a seam are exposed, ply samples of at least 0.25 m of roof material immediately above the seam and 0.25 m of floor underlying the seam should be included in the samples. This will allow the effects of dilution on coal quality to be assessed. In general, the thickness of coal plies should be a minimum of 0.1 m and a maximum of 1.0 m. For banded coals containing alternating thin (<0.1 m) layers of bright coal/dull coal/clay, the seams may be sampled as a series of composite plies, with the details of the individual layers shown on the record sheet. An interbedded non-coal ply greater than 0.25 m in thickness may be regarded as a seam split and recorded as such. Ply samples should be at least 2.0 kg where possible; it may be that the sample will be split into two fractions and one stored for later use.

Once the outcrop or face is cleaned, a shallow box cut is made for the total thickness of exposed coal seam. Once this is completed, the seam is divided into plies, each of which is measured and recorded on a record sheet similar to that shown in Figure 9.2.

The channel sample record sheet should show the following information: record card number; map or aerial photograph number on which the locality is located; location of sample point, grid reference or reference number; description of the locality, stream section, working face, including dip, strike, coal seam roof and floor contacts; extent of weathering, fracturing, mineralisation; lithological description of each ply interval; thickness of each ply interval; and designated sample number of each ply interval. Space can also be allocated on the record card for analytical details, i.e. proximate analysis, to be added later to complete the record.

The fresh surface is then sampled as a channel cut from top to bottom (Figure 9.1B), cutting and collecting all material from each ply section in turn. Each ply sample should be sealed in a

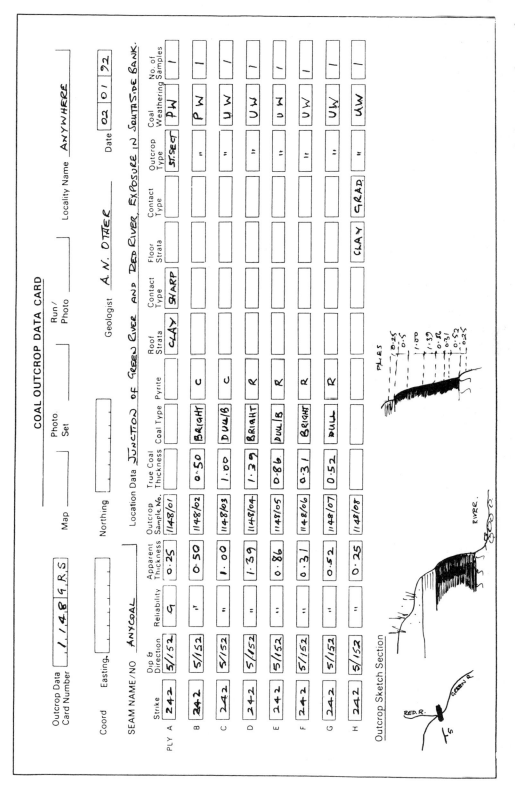

Figure 9.2 Coal outcrop data card. Reproduced by permission of BP Coal Ltd

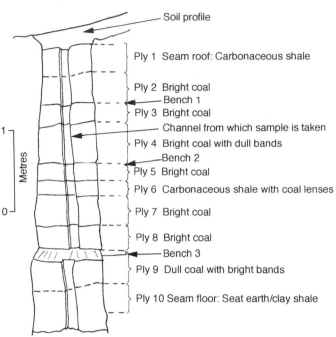

strong plastic bag immediately after collection to prevent moisture loss and oxidation. All sample bags must be clearly labelled
with a designated number, a copy of which should be placed in
a small plastic bag inside the sample bag, and another attached
to the outside of the sample bag. This number must be recorded
on the channel sample record sheet.

As this task is invariably a dirty one, labels get wet, blackened
and unreadable very easily and it is essential that care is taken to
ensure that the sample numbers do not get lost or obliterated
during transit to the laboratory as unidentifiable samples are
useless and an expensive waste of time.

The advantage of channel ply sampling is that not only can
the analysis of the individual plies be obtained, but that by
combining a fraction of each ply sample, a whole seam composite analysis can also be made. An example of a channel ply
sample from a surface exposure is illustrated in Figure 9.3,
which shows a channel cut to expose fresh coal, and then a
thinner channel (about 0.25 m wide) cut from the fresh coal from
which ply samples are collected for analysis.

Figure 9.3 Surface coal seam ply channel sample taken in shallow dipping
seam. Central narrow channel taken for
ply sample analysis, including coal seam
roof and floor. Photograph by LPT

9.2.3 Pillar sampling

In underground coal mining, samples of large blocks of undisturbed coal are taken to provide technical information on the

strength and quality of the coal. These pillar samples are taken when a specific problem may have arisen or is anticipated. Such samples are taken in much the same way as whole seam channel samples except that extra care is required not to disturb the cut-out section of the coal during removal. Samples are then boxed and taken to the laboratory. Pillar sampling is a long and arduous business and is only undertaken in special circumstances, such as when mining becomes difficult or when new roadways or faces are planned.

9.2.4   Core sampling

Core sampling is an integral part of coal exploration and mine development. It has the advantage of producing non-weathered coal including the coal seam floor and roof.

First, the borehole core has to be cleaned if drilling fluids have been used, and then lithologically logged. Following this, the lithological log should be compared with the geophysical log of the borehole to select ply intervals and to check for core losses and any other length discrepancies.

Once the core has been reconciled to the geophysical logs and the ply intervals have been selected, sampling can commence. Core ply samples are taken in the same way as for surface channel ply samples (as shown in Figure 9.4); again a ply sample of the coal seam roof and floor (up to 0.25 m) is taken to determine dilution effects. The individual plies are then sampled, making sure no core is discarded. As for surface samples, bright coal tends to fragment and make up the finer particles that may easily be left in the core tray.

The samples are bagged and labelled as for surface ply samples, and the sample numbers recorded on the core logging sheet in the manner shown in Figure 6.20.

Figure 9.4   Ply sampling of borehole core; run of samples to include all the coal seam and roof and floor. Core may be split in this fashion and one-half kept for future examination and analysis

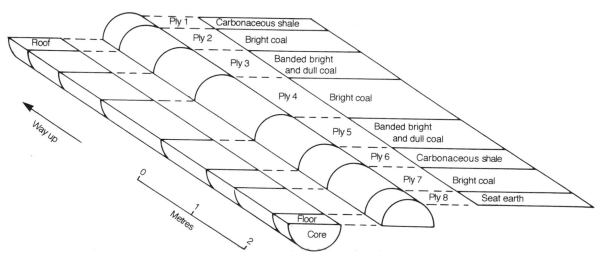

Large diameter cores may be split lengthways with a bolster chisel and then one half-ply sampled, the other being retained for future analysis.

9.2.5   Cuttings sampling

This method of sampling is considerably less accurate than that of core sampling. As with core samples, cuttings are un-weathered and are a useful indicator of the general nature of the seam. Air flush and mud flush non-core drilling is a quicker operation than core drilling and will produce cuttings for each horizon encountered in drilling. Mud flush cuttings will need to be washed to remove any drilling fluid before sampling.

Cuttings are usually produced for every metre drilled. The cuttings returns which are all coal may be collected, bagged and numbered in the same way as channel samples. The depth to the top and bottom of the seam sampled should be determined from the geophysical log. The drawback with using cuttings samples is that only a general analysis of the seam can be made, and even this is unlikely to be truly representative; also, contamination from strata above the coal may be included. A close study of the geolog will determine whether this is so.

9.2.6   Bulk sampling

Bulk samples are taken from outcrops, small pits or minishafts (i.e. 2 m diameter shaft excavations). A bulk sample is normally 5–25 tonnes and is taken as a whole seam channel sample on a large scale. Such a bulk sample is taken to carry out test work on a larger scale; this is designed to indicate the coal's likely performance under actual conditions of use.

Steam coals are taken for small combustion tests in a pulverised fuel rig to simulate conditions in a pulverised fuel boiler. Pulverised coal firing is the combustion of powdered coal suspended as a cloud of small particles in the combustion air. Substantially more heat is released per unit volume in pulverised fuel boilers than in stoker type boilers.

Coking coals are taken to carry out moving wall oven tests, i.e. to determine how much the coal swells when combusted and thus how much pressure is put on the oven walls, which are constructed of uncemented brickwork. High pressure coals are undesirable and are normally blended with low pressure coals to reduce the problem. In the USA, low volatile coking coals (volatile matter = 20–25%, swelling index = 9) are high pressure coals, whereas, in general, high volatile coals do not have such high pressures. It is significant that Gondwana coking coals are low pressure coals, an important factor in the export of coking coals from Australia.

Bulk samples are collected from a site already channel sampled, loaded into drums, numbered and shipped to the selected test centre.

9.2.7   Sample storage

In most instances the channel and core samples will be required immediately for laboratory analysis. However, there are circumstances where duplicate coal samples for future reference are taken. Usually the channel plies are divided into two or the cores are split and one-half retained.

If the duplicate samples are to be put into storage, this presents a problem; the exposure of the coal to air will allow oxidation to take place during storage and will result in anomalous quality results when analysed at a later date. The usual procedure to prevent the oxidation of samples is to store them under nitrogen or in water.

To store in nitrogen, a tube connected to a pressurised cylinder containing nitrogen is placed in a plastic sample bag, then the coal sample is added and the sample is flushed with nitrogen, regulating the flow with a flow meter. The nitrogen has to fill the spaces between the coal fragments, so flushing is required for several minutes. One difficulty with this method is that nitrogen is lighter than air so inevitably some is lost in the process. Once the bag has been thoroughly flushed, it should be heat sealed; no other form of sealing is anywhere near as effective. The coal samples can be as received or air dried and can be in the form of lump or crushed coal.

A cheaper method of storage is to immerse the channel or core sample in the form of lump coal in water. This method has the advantage over storing in nitrogen in that it preserves the fluidity of the coal, but it does present handling problems when the sample is required. The sample will have to be air dried before analysis can begin.

Samples can be stored for one to two years before analysis using these methods.

9.3   NON *IN SITU* SAMPLING

The object of collecting coal samples after mining is to determine the quality of coal actually being produced. This coal may differ significantly from the *in situ* seam analysis in that not all of the seam may be included in the mining section, or that more than one seam may be worked and fed to the mine mouth and mixed with coal from other seams. In addition, there may be dilution from the seam roof or floor, or both, which becomes part of the mined coal product.

The mined coal is broken up and therefore contains fragments which vary a great deal in size and shape. Representative samples are collected by taking a definite number of portions known as increments distributed throughout the total amount of coal being sampled. Such increments represent a sample or portion of coal obtained by using a specified sampling procedure, either manually or using some sampling apparatus.

Increments are taken by three methods: (i) systematic sampling, where increments are spaced evenly in time or in position over the unit; (ii) random sampling, where increments are spaced at random but a prerequisite number are taken; or (iii) stratified random sampling, where the unit is divided by time or amount into a number of equal strata and one or more increments are taken at random from each.

It is good practice that, whatever the method used, duplicate sampling should be employed to verify that the required precision has been attained.

Non *in situ* coal sampling is carried out on moving streams of coal, from rail wagons, trucks, barges, grabs or conveyors unloading ships, from the holds of ships and from coal stockpiles.

BS 1017 (see Appendix 1) stipulates the minimum number of increments required for gross samples of single load consignment up to 1000 tonnes, as indicated in Table 9.1.

Most of this kind of sampling is not carried out by the coal geologist; however, in certain circumstances he or she may be called upon to obtain samples from run of mine conveyor streams and from coal stockpiles.

Hand sampling from streams is carried out using ladles or scoops. The width of the sampler should be 2.5 times the size of the largest lump likely to be encountered; however, this type of sampling is not suitable for coal larger than 80 mm. For larger samples mechanical sampling equipment is used, consisting of a bucket the width of which equals the full width of the conveyor. The bucket should travel either at right angles or parallel to the conveyor and pass through the coal stream at uniform speed. Another method is the stop belt method whereby the conveyor is stopped and all coal occurring within a selected interval, usually a couple of metres, is collected.

To sample from stockpiles, the stockpile should be divided into a number of portions, each 1000 tonnes or less, from which a separate sample with a specified number of increments is taken. This normally takes a long time to accomplish, but can be

Table 9.1 Minimum number of increments required for gross samples of a single coal consignment up to 1000 tonnes. From Osborne (1988), by permission of Graham & Trotman

Sampling situation	Common sample for total moisture and general analysis			Total moisture sample		General analysis sample		Size analysis sample
	Sized coals, dry cleaned or washed	Washed smalls (50 mm)	Blended part treated, untreated, run of mine and 'unknown' coals	Sized coals: dry cleaned or washed; unwashed dry coals	Washed smalls (50 mm), blended, part treated, untreated, run of mine and 'unknown' coals	Sized coals: dry cleaned, or washed or unwashed dry coals	Blended, part treated, untreated, run of mine and 'unknown' coals	All coals
Moving streams	20	35	35	20	35	20	35	40
Wagons and trucks, barges, grabs or conveyors unloading ships	25	35	50	20	35	25	50	40
Holds of ships, stockpiles	35	35	65	20	35	35	65	40

speeded up if automated auger units are used. It is important that all levels in the stockpile are sampled.

9.4   COAL ANALYSIS

The marketability of coals depends on their quality. This will determine whether they are to be sold as steam or coking coals, prime or lower grade coals. Customer requirements vary considerably from those who will accept a broad spectrum of coal qualities to those who require coal for a specialised purpose and have set restricted specifications for the coal.

The coal producer, i.e. the mining company, will have assessed the potential market before developing any coal deposit, deciding, for example, whether to mine coal for export or local use. The mining company will also need to know the quality limitations of the coal that can be produced from the deposit.

The quality of the coal has to be determined at an early stage of exploration and monitored during all later phases of development.

All coals should be sampled using the procedures outlined in Sections 9.2.2, 9.2.4 and 9.2.6, and sent to the laboratory where they are weighed, crushed and split for analysis.

9.4.1   Outcrop/core samples

The procedure for weighing, crushing and splitting outcrop/core samples are shown in Figure 9.5 for steam (thermal) coals and Figure 9.6 for coking (metallurgical) coals. However, there is no universal set procedure and differences do occur.

In Australia, a standard similar to that shown in Figures 9.6 and 9.7 is set, with the difference that the samples are crushed to 11.2 mm. Large diameter core samples are preferred when sampling Gondwana coals to be more confident of yield values obtained during analysis. There should be a correlation in properties between outcrop/small diameter core, large diameter core and bulk samples.

The analysis undertaken for each float/sink fraction is proximate analysis plus total sulphur and calorific value. This is intended to produce a simulated product by combining several float/sink fractions. This product is then analysed for ultimate analysis, ash analysis, ash fusion temperatures, Hardgrove grindability index, swelling index and Geiseler plastometer test, the latter only if the coal has coking properties.

In South Africa, the coal is generally crushed to only 25 mm. It is then analysed for proximate analysis, total sulphur and

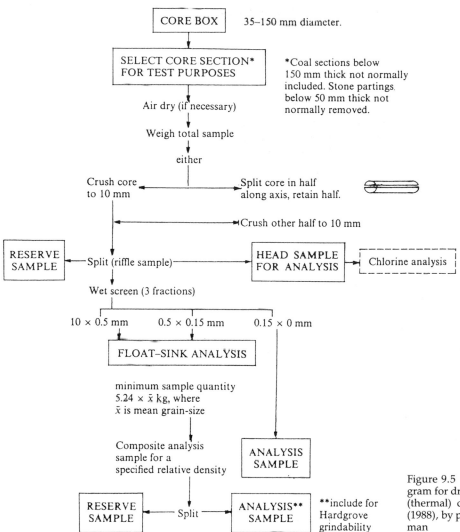

CORE BOX   35–150 mm diameter.

SELECT CORE SECTION*
FOR TEST PURPOSES

*Coal sections below
150 mm thick not normally
included. Stone partings
below 50 mm thick not
normally removed.

Air dry (if necessary)

Weigh total sample

either

Crush core
to 10 mm

Split core in half
along axis, retain half.

Crush other half to 10 mm

RESERVE
SAMPLE

Split (riffle sample)

HEAD SAMPLE
FOR ANALYSIS

Chlorine analysis

Wet screen (3 fractions)

10 × 0.5 mm   0.5 × 0.15 mm   0.15 × 0 mm

FLOAT–SINK ANALYSIS

minimum sample quantity
$5.24 \times \bar{x}$ kg, where
$\bar{x}$ is mean grain-size

Composite analysis
sample for a
specified relative density

ANALYSIS
SAMPLE

RESERVE
SAMPLE

Split

ANALYSIS**
SAMPLE

**include for
Hardgrove
grindability

Figure 9.5 Sample preparation diagram for drill core samples from a steam (thermal) coal deposit. From Osborne (1988), by permission of Graham & Trotman

calorific value. Float/sink tests are carried out but no simulated product is made.

In Australia and South Africa, the fine fraction (0.5 or 0.1 mm) is screened out before analysis, depending on the expectations for coal preparation. In the United Kingdom, a similar procedure is used except that for outcrop/core samples no float/sink analysis is carried out, only proximate analysis, total sulphur and calorific value.

In the USA, there are no defined crushed parameters; proximate analysis, total sulphur and calorific value are determined. Float/sink analysis is performed with the results reported to

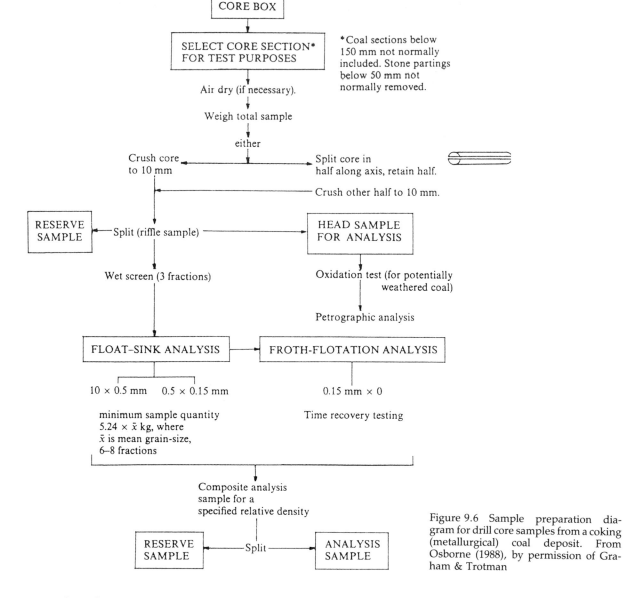

Figure 9.6 Sample preparation diagram for drill core samples from a coking (metallurgical) coal deposit. From Osborne (1988), by permission of Graham & Trotman

zero; this often means that the fines have to be screened out. As there is no hard and fast procedure for outcrop/core analysis in the USA, the individual procedures have to be verified to correctly assess the reliability of the analytical results.

9.4.2   Bulk samples

Procedures for the preparation of bulk samples are shown in Figure 9.7 for steam (thermal) coals and Figure 9.8 for coking

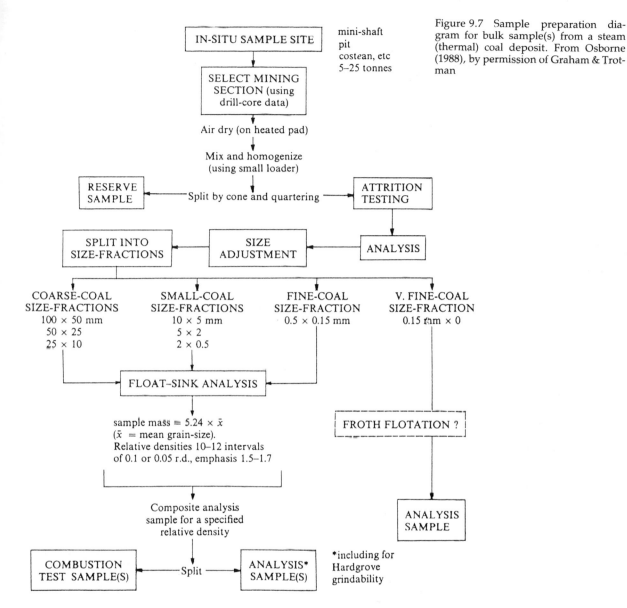

Figure 9.7 Sample preparation diagram for bulk sample(s) from a steam (thermal) coal deposit. From Osborne (1988), by permission of Graham & Trotman

(metallurgical) coals. The coals are analysed as for outcrop/core samples with additional tests for combustion and coking properties.

9.4.3 Non *in situ* samples

The analysis of non *in situ* coal samples is undertaken to determine the quality of the coal leaving the mine, leaving the coal preparation plant (if one is installed) and in stockpiles before

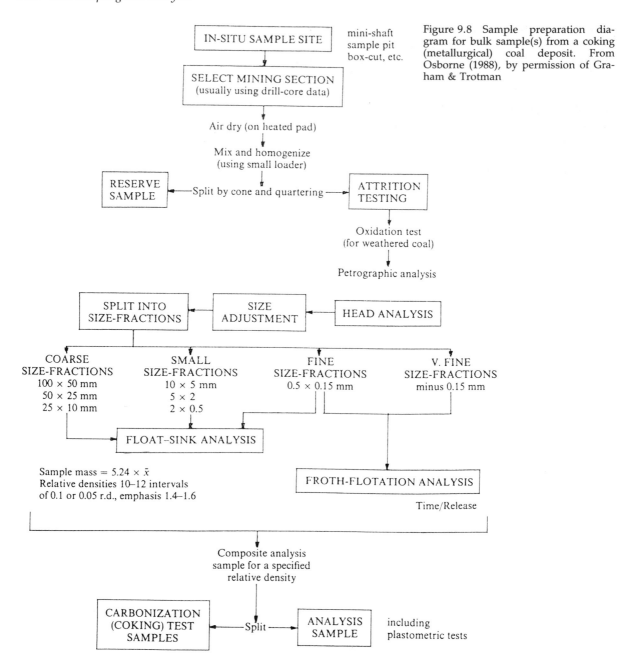

Figure 9.8 Sample preparation diagram for bulk sample(s) from a coking (metallurgical) coal deposit. From Osborne (1988), by permission of Graham & Trotman

shipment to ensure that the agreed specification of the coal is maintained.

Stream samples will be crushed and analysed for proximate analysis, total sulphur and calorific value, plus other properties if requested; usually no float–sink analysis is performed. In addition, other stream samples such as stop belt samples will be used for size analysis and float–sink analysis. Stockpile samples are rarely taken; for small stockpiles it is not worth it. For large stockpiles, although augured samples may be taken, it is difficult to obtain a truly representative sample.

Note: it should be noted that for all *in situ* and non *in situ* samples the top size to which any sample is crushed is important in determining the weight of the sample required. The size of the sample is calculated as:

$$5.24 \times \text{mean particle size } (\bar{x}) = n \text{ kg}$$

where the mean particle size is the top size × bottom size. The value 5.24 is an empirically determined number as quoted in BS 1017 and Australian Standard 2646 (see Appendix 1).

Chapter 10
Gas in coal

10.1 INTRODUCTION

The association of gases with coal has been a constant problem in mine workings since undergound coal mining first began.

Bituminous coals contain a number of gases including methane, carbon dioxide, carbon monoxide, nitrogen and ethane. The amount of gas retained and held by a coal depends on various factors, such as pressure, temperature, pyrite content and the structure of the coal. Fresh coal contains more gas than coal which has been subject to oxidation. Large volumes of gas can be accommodated on the internal surfaces of the coal as a result of adsorption. It is released by the removal of pressure, usually by mining or drilling. The gas may migrate into associated strata such as porous sandstones, which release the gas into openings such as boreholes and mine excavations.

Methane gas is developed by the decomposition of organic material. It is also known as 'firedamp', which is a methane-rich (80–95%) gas naturally occurring in coal seams. Methane consists of carbon and hydrogen and when mixed with air it forms a highly combustible gas. Therefore its presence in underground workings makes conditions extremely hazardous. The methane content of coal is seen to increase both with increasing depth and with increasing rank of the coal. This can be illustrated by Figure 10.1, which shows a typical methane content against depth curve, and Figure 10.2, which shows the variation of coal methane content with rank based on coals from the East Midlands Coalfield, UK.

The specific weight of methane is less than that of air so that it rises into the upper parts of the mine or upward in boreholes. The discharge of methane from coal can be from the voids and fissures in the coal, or by 'blowing' from fissures, or, more dangerously, a sudden burst out in great amounts in mine workings.

In underground workings, methane is released from coal exposed at the coal face, plus the broken coal being transported

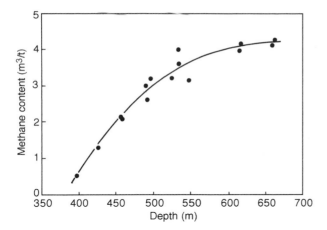

Figure 10.1 Typical methane content versus depth curve. Reproduced by permission of the Geological Society of London from Creedy (1991) 'An introduction to geological aspects of methane occurrence and control in British deep coal mines.' *Q. J. Engin. Geol.* **24**, 209–220

through the mine. The faster the coal is mined, the larger the amount of methane released into the workings, so that it is essential that an adequate ventilation system is in operation. When a geologist is working in disused parts of a mine, he or she should be alert to methane collecting in roof pockets and in the upper parts of 'manholes' or cuts in the roadway sidewalls where the rock sequence may still be exposed.

Carbon dioxide is more common in brown coal than in bituminous coal workings. However, bituminous coals which have a high pyrite content contain higher amounts of carbon dioxide, due to the fact that coals rich in pyrite absorb more oxygen when moist, and this absorbed oxygen produces not only water by combination with hydrogen, but also carbon dioxide by combination with carbon. Carbon dioxide, also known as 'black-

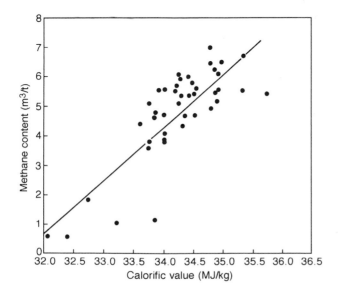

Figure 10.2 Variation of coal methane content with rank in the East Midlands Coalfield, UK. Reproduced by permission of the Geological Society of London from Creedy (1991) 'An introduction to geological aspects of methane occurrence and control in British deep coal mines.' *Q. J. Engin. Geol.* **24**, 209–220

damp', is a colourless gas and is heavier than air. It therefore tends to accumulate in the lower parts of mine workings.

Carbon monoxide originates from the incomplete oxidation of coal, especially after methane explosions. The gas is combustible and poisonous.

Only a small proportion of the nitrogen found in coal gases has its origin in the nitrogen present in the coal material; the bulk of the nitrogen originates from the surrounding air.

Free hydrogen occurs in small amounts associated with methane, but is not usually found in any great amounts.

Ethane is more prominent in gases derived from oxidised coals; cannel coal contains ethane in its pore structure.

10.2   GAS DETECTION

The following factors affect the rate at which gas is emitted from free surfaces into the mine atmosphere: the gas content of the coal seam and adjacent strata; the permeability of the coal seam and adjacent strata; the depth of the coal seam and the gas pressures in the undisturbed ground; natural fracturing of the coal; the presence of faults and igneous intrusions; the geometry of the workings; the method, pattern and rate of extraction; and the effects of extraction on stress distributions in the surrounding strata.

In underground workings, gas emanating from the coal face can be monitored by keeping a methanometer in close proximity to working personnel, as shown in Figure 10.3.

Figure 10.3   Methanometer being used to monitor gas levels in underground workings. Photo courtesy of MSA (Britain) Ltd

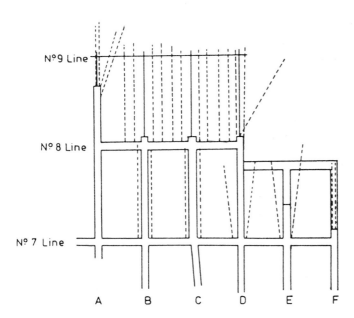

Figure 10.4 Pattern of drainage holes ahead of a panel front, Metropolitan Colliery, Sydney Basin, Australia. From Hargreaves and Lunarzewski (1985), by permission of *Bulletin and Proceedings of the Australian Institute of Mining and Metallurgy*

To reduce the amount of gas at the operating face, a system of methane drainage is applied to gassy coal seams. In the Sydney Basin in Australia, bituminous coals, both steaming and coking, contain methane, carbon dioxide and a mixture of nitrogen, carbon dioxide and hydrogen sulphide. Methane drainage is achieved by drilling a series of boreholes both vertically from the surface into the coal, and by drilling horizontal boreholes into the seam ahead of the working panels.

In Figure 10.4 a pattern of horizontal boreholes has been drilled in the panels ahead of heading B, each borehole ranging from 50 to 100 mm in diameter. Figure 10.5 shows a comparison of the resultant gas emissions in headings A and B; the gas emissions in heading B are reduced to less than half those of the undrained heading A, demonstrating the effectiveness of this method.

The geologist needs to be aware of the possibility of the presence of any of these gases, not only in mine workings but also in boreholes. Methane rising in boreholes has caused a number of accidents on drill rig platforms. One way to detect methane and other inflammable gases is by using a methanometer which can be held over the mouth of the borehole while the bit is being changed, or when the core barrel has been brought to the surface, or when drilling has ceased and before geophysical logging commences (Figure 10.6). Gas emanating from the borehole will register on the instrument and, if significant amounts of methane are detected, safety precautions should be taken, e.g. the use of water sprays on the drill bit in

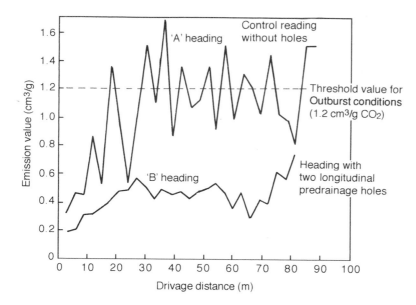

Figure 10.5 Reduction of gassiness resulting from pre-drainage. From Hargreaves and Lunarzewski (1985), by permission of *Bulletin and Proceedings of the Australian Institute of Mining and Metallurgy*

Figure 10.6 Field testing for methane and other gases at the borehole mouth before geophysical logging. Photograph by LPT

air flush operations to avoid sparks. The presence of gas in any borehole must be recorded on the drilling record; this is particularly important if another borehole is sited nearby at a later date.

10.3 METHANE GAS EXTRACTION

Although not strictly coal geology, the coal geologist may have to give input to projects involving the extraction of methane gas.

During the last ten years, coal bed methane gas has been exploited as a viable natural gas power source, principally in the USA.

To extract coal bed methane, a good geological knowledge of the area is essential, as is a good knowledge of the coal characteristics. Coal suitable for commercial methane production will generally exhibit some or all of the following: coal lying at depths greater than 250 m; coal lying below the water-table; coal with high vitrinite reflectance (0.7–2.0); and areas of structurally enhanced permeability.

The two extremes in coal rank, lignite and anthracite, have no value for methane extraction, although in the case of the latter, methane driven off during coalification may be trapped in formations higher in the sequence. For bituminous coals it is estimated that around 15 m^3 of methane can be generated for each tonne of coal. Considerably more methane can be extracted by drilling coal bed methane wells in advance of underground mining than will be obtained from underground sources. Vertical wells drilled ahead of mining will normally be cased, but the section of hole through the coal itself will be left open so that when mining eventually follows there will be no casing in the coal to interfere with mining equipment. Coal bed methane wells need to be artificially stimulated to achieve commercial gas flow rates, except in areas of high natural permeability. Foamed stimulation fluids (a mixture of water, nitrogen and a foaming agent) are used to hydraulically fracture the test wells; sand is added to assist in keeping the fractures open.

In the USA, about 2600 coal bed methane wells were in operation in 1990, which at full production could provide 5% of US domestic gas supplies. These wells are sited in the Warrior Basin, Alabama, and the San Juan Basin, north-west New Mexico/South Colorado. Of these, the Piceance Basin, Colorado, contains the largest concentrations of coal bed methane in the USA. The methane is present in coals of Upper Cretaceous age, and the total estimated coal bed methane in place is 250×10^{10} m^3 and underlies an area of 17 000 km^2.

In Australia, methane drainage is practised in the Sydney Basin, as described in Section 10.2. In addition, the Queensland Coalbed Methane Project is exploring for natural methane gasfields in Queensland to determine the potential for methanol production. In Africa, the Sabi Valley coalfield in Zimbabwe is under investigation for methane gas extraction.

The collection of commercial amounts of methane by horizontal drilling underground is more complex. However, such horizontal wells can achieve higher and quicker gas recoveries than vertical wells.

Methane drainage is being investigated in underground coal

mines in the eastern USA. In the UK, commercially exploited methane extraction has been practised at British Coal's Point of Ayr mine for 30 years. This mine contains gassy seams worked under the Irish Sea. Methane drainage is achieved by roof holes inclined at 45° and 60° in the return roadway of the coal face. The gas is then delivered to a large gas holder at the surface.

Coal bed methane extraction differs from natural gas in that it is less expensive, less risky, but of course is less remunerative. For coal deposits which may prove difficult to mine and which contain suitable coals, methane gas extraction may be a viable alternative to provide a source of energy to local commercial needs.

10.4   RADON

Radon is a naturally occurring radioactive gas, and as such is distinguished from the other gases present in coal.

Radon is produced in the decay series of both uranium and thorium. Initially, radon was regarded as a fairly harmless or even benign component of gases from geological sources; more recently its importance as the major contributor to the radiation dose received by the human body has been recognised.

Alpha particles are massive and relatively highly charged, but are not penetrative, being blocked by clothing and epidermal tissue. When ingested, however, they can give rise to tissue damage; the main intake of radon into the body is by inhalation. Consequently, the major health hazard from radon is thought to be an increased risk of lung cancer.

Various parameters of rocks and soils influence the migration of radon into the biosphere. These include uranium and thorium concentration, mineralogy, the permeability of the host rocks, and the nature and extent of carrier fluid transport systems. The degree of water retention in rocks can be critical in the generation of soil gas radon anomalies. Mudstones retain water more efficiently than limestones, so the mobility of radon is restricted in mudstones. The presence of open faults with their increased frequency of fluid flow can result in high radon concentrations in soil gases.

In coal-bearing sequences, radon can be encountered either by accumulation after upward permeation from underlying rocks containing uranium, as may be so for Gondwana coals overlying basement rocks, or from within the coal-bearing sequence itself, e.g. from uranium or thorium concentrations in marine shales.

Radon hazards in underground mines have not been monitored in the past, but levels are now currently being investigated. The principal preventative measure to combat radon build up is an adequate and efficient ventilation system. Several instances of the presence of radon have been recorded in UK mines, and the possibility must exist for mines elsewhere.

Chapter 11
Coal resources and reserves

11.1 INTRODUCTION

The investigation of any coal deposit is carried out to determine whether coal can be mined economically, and that a coal product can be obtained that will be marketable. An essential requirement of any coal investigation is that an assessment is made of the coal resources within the area of interest. Such an assessment will influence the decision of whether to develop the deposit, to extend existing mine operations, or conversely to curtail mining activity or even to cease development or operations altogether. In the case of the sale of a lease or mine prospect, the coal resource assessment will play an important part in determining the success or failure of the transaction.

Resources can be divided on the basis of two points of view, namely according to: (i) their degree of geological assurance; and (ii) their degree of economic feasibility. There is a third subdivision which distinguishes between the coal in place and the amounts that can be technically recovered. Unavoidable losses during exploitation represent the difference between the two amounts: those in place and those recoverable.

The reliability of a coal tonnage estimate is based on the definition and expression of geological assurance and the methods of its estimation. Geological uncertainties pertaining to coal arise from topographical and tectonic variations in the environment at the time when peat was being deposited, and from post-depositional erosion and structural alteration. As described in Chapter 3, the geometry and morphology of coals vary according to the depositional setting in which they were formed. For example, lenticular coals with great variations in thickness will need more data points than relatively undisturbed areally extensive coals of constant thickness. Data point spacing criteria should take into account such differences in the depositional settings and geological features specific to each coal deposit.

Coal resource categories range from the general evaluation of a coal basin to the calculation of specific reserves located within mine workings. The geologist is expected to calculate all categories of coal resources using the codes of practice adopted by the project management for the lease area under consideration.

It should be borne in mind that for providing information related to coal supply in the short term, reserve estimates have limitations; reserve estimates are more concerned with capacity and deliverability, whereas resource analysis is valid for longer term assessment, i.e. for ten years hence and longer.

11.2 COAL RESOURCES AND RESERVES ASSESSMENT

There is no one internationally recognised and uniform method for the recording, categorisation and designation of coal reserves. This has resulted in the development of a number of different definitions and methods.

The principal coal producing countries have devised codes for the assessment of coal resources to meet their particular requirements; these vary in complexity and degrees of scale.

11.2.1 United States of America

In the USA, a coal resource classification system was published by the United States Geological Survey (USGS) in 1983 (Wood *et al.*, 1983). The system is based on the concept by which coal is classified into resource; reserve base; reserve categories on the basis of the geological certainty of the existence of those categories and on the economic feasibility of their recovery. Categories are also provided that take into account legal, environmental and technological constraints.

Geological certainty is related to the distance from points where coal is measured or sampled, the thickness of coal and overburden, a knowledge of rank, quality, depositional history, areal extent, correlations of coal seams and associated strata, and structural history. The economic feasibility of coal recovery is affected not only by geological factors but also by economic variables such as the price of coal against mining costs, coal preparation costs, transport costs and taxes, environmental constraints and changes in the demand for coal.

The term resource is defined as naturally occurring deposits of coal in the earth's crust in such forms and amounts that economic extraction is currently or potentially feasible.

The hierarchy of coal resources/reserves categories outlined by the USGS in 1983 is given in Figure 11.1 and the application of the reliability categories based on distance from points of measurement, i.e. coal outcrops and boreholes, by the USGS is demonstrated in Figure 11.2.

Original resources are the amount of coal in place before production. The total of original resources is the sum of the identified and undiscovered resources plus the coal produced and coal lost in mining.

Remaining resources include all coal after coal produced and coal lost in mining is deducted.

Identified resources are those resources whose locations, rank, quality and quantity are known or estimated from specific geological evidence. The levels of control or reliability can be subdivided into inferred, indicated and measured resources. These subdivisions are determined by projecting the thickness of coal, rank and quality data from points of measurement and sampling on the basis of geological knowledge.

Inferred resources are assigned to individual points of measurement which are bounded by measured and indicated coal for 1.2 km, succeeded by 4.8 km of inferred coal. Inferred resources include anthracite and bituminous coal 0.35 m or more in thickness and subbituminous coal and lignite 0.75 m or more in thickness to depths of not more than 1800 m. Coal resources outside these limits are deemed hypothetical in nature.

Indicated resources are assigned to individual points of measurement bounded by measured coal for 0.4 km succeeded by 0.8 km of indicated coal. Indicated resources have the same thickness and depth limits as inferred resources.

Measured resources are determined by the projection of the thickness of coal, rank and quality data for a radius of 0.4 km from a point of measurement. Measured resources also have the same thickness and depth limits as indicated and inferred resources.

The reserve base is identified coal defined only by physical and chemical criteria as determined by the geologist. The concept of the reserve base is to define an amount of in place coal, any part of which is, or may become, economic. This will depend on the method of mining and the economic assumptions that will be used.

The reserve base includes coal categories based on the same distance parameters given for coal resources but further defining the coal thickness and depth criteria: anthracite and bituminous coal to be 0.7 m or more, subbituminous coal to be

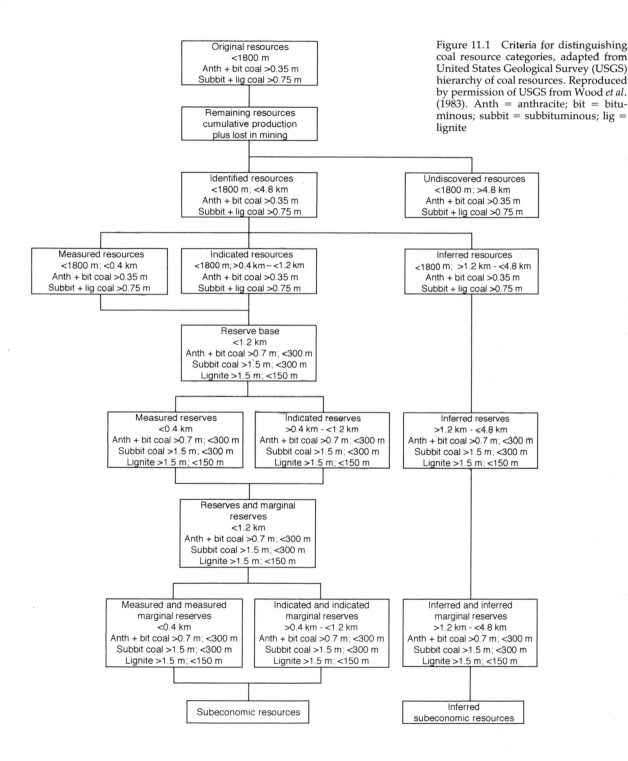

Figure 11.1 Criteria for distinguishing coal resource categories, adapted from United States Geological Survey (USGS) hierarchy of coal resources. Reproduced by permission of USGS from Wood *et al.* (1983). Anth = anthracite; bit = bituminous; subbit = subbituminous; lig = lignite

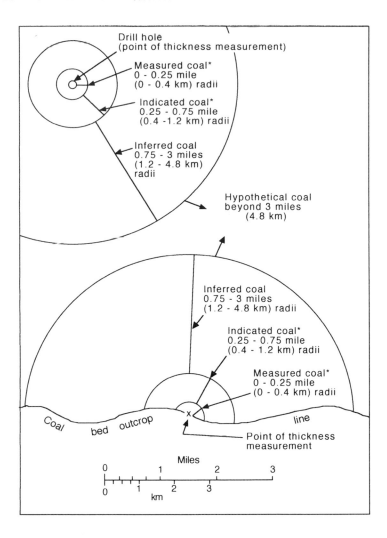

Figure 11.2 Diagram showing reliability categories based solely on distance from points of measurement. Reproduced by permission of USGS from Wood *et al.* (1983). *Measured and indicated coal can be summed to demonstrated coal.

1.5 m or more, all to occur at depths not more than 300 m, lignite to be 1.5 m or more at depths not greater than 150 m.

Inferred reserves include all coal conforming to the thickness and depth limits defined in the reserve base, and bounded by the same distance limits as given for inferred resources.

Indicated reserves include all coal conforming to the thickness and depth limits defined in the reserve base, and bounded by the same distance limits as given for indicated resources.

Measured reserves include all coal conforming to the thickness and depth limits defined in the reserve base, and bounded by the same distance limits as given for measured resources.

Marginal reserves are those reserves that border on being economic, i.e. they have potential if there is a favourable change in circumstances, mining restrictions are lifted, quality requirements are changed, lease areas become available, or there is a newly created demand for the type of coal held in this reserve category.

Subeconomic resources are those in which the coal has been lost in mining, is too deeply buried, or the seam thickness becomes too thin, or the coal quality deteriorates to unacceptable limits.

11.2.2   Australia

The Australian code for calculating the reporting coal reserves is more simplistic and is easier for the geologist to apply. Figure 11.3 outlines the framework on which the classification is based. Reserves should be estimated and allotted to one of the following categories, which are determined by an objective appraisal of the information available for the coal under consideration.

Inferred resources are those for which the points of measurement are widely spaced, so that only an uncertain estimate of the resource can be made. Points of measurement generally should not be more than 4.0 km apart, extrapolation of trends should extend not more than 2.0 km from points of measurement. Inferred resources can be subdivided into the following categories.

Inferred resources class 1 are those resources for which the points of measurement allow an estimate of the coal thickness and general coal quality to be made, and for which the geological conditions indicate continuity of seams between the points of measurement.

Inferred resources class 2 are those resources for which there is limited information and, as a result, the assessment of this

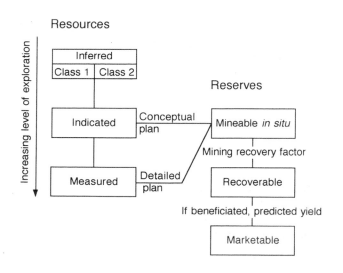

Figure 11.3   Australian code for reporting coal resources/reserves. Reproduced by permission of Department of Resource Industries, Queensland Government from Galligan and Mengel (1986)

type of resource may be unreliable. Provided the coal thickness can be determined, the order of magnitude of inferred resources class 2 may be expressed in the following ranges: 1–10; 10–100; 100–500; 500–1000; and >1000 Mt.

Indicated resources are those for which the density and quality of the points of measurement are sufficient to allow a realistic estimate of the coal thickness, quality, depth and *in situ* tonnage, and for which there is a reasonable expectation that the estimate of resources will not change significantly with more detailed exploration. Points of measurement should not be more than 2.0 km apart. Where geological conditions are favourable, it may be possible to extend trends up to 1.0 km from the points of measurement.

Measured resources are those for which the density and quality of points of measurement are sufficient to allow a reliable estimate of the coal thickness, quality, depth and *in situ* tonnage. Points of measurement should not be more than 1.0 km apart. Where geological conditions are favourable, it may be possible to extrapolate trends up to a maximum distance of 0.5 km from the points of measurement. The points of measurement should provide a level of confidence sufficient to allow detailed planning, costing of extraction and specification of a marketable product.

Mineable *in situ* reserves are the tonnages of *in situ* coal contained in seams or sections of seams for which sufficient information is available to enable detailed or conceptual mine planning. Mineable *in situ* reserves exclude coal which is prohibited from mining. Mineable *in situ* reserves are calculated only from measured and indicated resources; measured resources are required for detailed mine planning and are the preferred basis for mineable *in situ* reserves. Indicated resources may be used for conceptual mine planning. In general, further exploration will be required before beginning mining operations.

Mineable *in situ* reserves should be quoted separately for opencast and underground mines together with an outline of the proposed mining method.

Recoverable reserves (also called 'extractable reserves') are the proportion of mineable *in situ* reserves that are expected to be recovered, i.e. the amount of coal which will be extracted. If dilution is added to the recoverable reserves tonnage, the total equates to the run of mine tonnages. In calculating recoverable reserves, a mining recovery factor must be applied to the mineable *in situ* reserves. This factor depends on the mining method to be used. As a guide, a mining factor of 50% for underground reserves and 90% for opencast reserves may be applied.

Marketable reserves (also called 'saleable reserves') are the tonnages of coal that will be available for sale. If the coal is to be marketed raw, the marketable reserves will be the same as recoverable reserves (i.e. the run of mine tonnage). If the coal is beneficiated, e.g. by washing, the marketable reserves are calculated by applying the predicted yield to the recoverable reserves. The basis on which the predicted yield is calculated should be given.

11.2.3 United Kingdom

In the UK, the code used by the publicly owned sector of the coal industry, i.e. that used by the British Coal Corporation, applies to black coal mined underground, and is oriented towards mining and the reliability of achieving planned outputs. British Coal only include those reserves which are judged to be economically viable and likely to allow production within the maximum acceptable degree of risk. Classified reserves must be of suitable quality and thickness, and the effect of any mining hazards must be minimised. Reserves are defined as classes 1, 2 and 3.

Class 1 reserves are workable reserves of suitable quality which are sufficiently well proved in regard to thickness, depth, and tectonic and stratigraphic setting to warrant economic planning in accordance with a mine's future objectives. The effects and location of mining hazards can be predicted with sufficient accuracy that any significant annual production change can be avoided.

Class 2 reserves are those reserves to which hazards are sufficiently great as to preclude an assurance that a forecast production can be achieved when they are developed. Constant revision will be required to review hazards inherent in this class of reserves.

Class 3 reserves lack the degree of knowledge required to detect hazards that will stop or seriously hinder mining. Precipitant hazards are unpredictable in this class of reserves, and the mine will require spare capacity to insure against them. The mine's standby production potential is liable to be brought into operation because of the risks attached to class 3 reserves. These classes of reserves are roughly comparable with recoverable reserves (class 1), mineable *in situ* reserves (class 2) and measured reserves (class 3).

In opencast mining in the UK, British Coal use the terms proved and unproved reserves within the mining lease area.

Proved reserves are those areas of coal that have points of measurement with a spacing of 50 m or less.

Unproved reserves are those areas of coal that have points of measurement with a spacing of greater than 50 m. In practice, these reserves will regularly be at least of mineable *in situ* reserve status.

Unlike the resource/reserve classifications of the USA and Australia, the system in the UK is based on resources/reserves pertaining to lease areas. This is very localised and is not applicable to those large areas which may contain coal but are not mined. The UK system is centred on a geographically concentrated mining industry with a long history, a rather different scenario from the developing countries.

In practice, the geologist will work to the codes of reserve assessment used in the country where exploration is taking place. The USGS system is comprehensive in that it covers a wide range of coal types and classes of reserves. The Australian system is a simplified version which is easy for the geologist to implement during exploration and development programmes, and still retains the advantage in that it allows coal reserve assessments to be made for all levels of coal deposit. The UK system, while excellent for mining operations, makes little allowance for general exploration categories of coal reserves.

11.2.4   Germany

The definition of geological assurance in terms of the measured-indicated-inferred system is considered to be sound. To further identify the geological assurance limits Germany has attempted to define all their geological assurance categories in terms of statistical confidence criteria, as shown in Table 11.1, rather than relying just on point of measurement spacing criteria. For each category, both a confidence level and a confidence interval are specified. It is considered that this defining of the assurance categories in terms of statistical confidence criteria gives a clearer expression of the geological uncertainties.

Table 11.1 Degrees of geological assurance of coal resources according to the guidelines of Germany. Adapted from Steenblik (1986) by permission of IEA Coal Research

Assurance category	Confidence level (%)	Confidence interval (%)
In sight	>90	+10
Probable	70–90	+20
Indicated	50–70	+30
Inferred	30–50	+30
Prognostic	>10–30	No limit

11.2.5 United Nations

The classification system recommended by the United Nations Economic and Social Council (ECOSOC) in 1979 (Fettweis, 1985) is shown in Figure 11.4. As can be seen, the amounts in place (R) and the recoverable amounts (r) correspond to one another. The assessment starts with the resources in place and is divided into three categories (1, 2 and 3) according to the level of geological assurance that can be assigned to each category. New terms have been chosen to allow agreement with different national systems. Each of these categories can be further subdivided according to the viewpoint of economics.

'E' represents those resources exploitable in a particular country or region under the prevailing socio-economic conditions with currently available technology. 'S' represents the balance of resources that was not considered to be of current interest but

Figure 11.4 International classification system of mineral resources. E: Exploitable resources in a country or region under prevailing socio-economic conditions with available technology. S: Balance of resources not of current interest due to foreseen economic or technological changes. (United Nations, 1979). From Fettweis (1985), by permission of the author and publisher

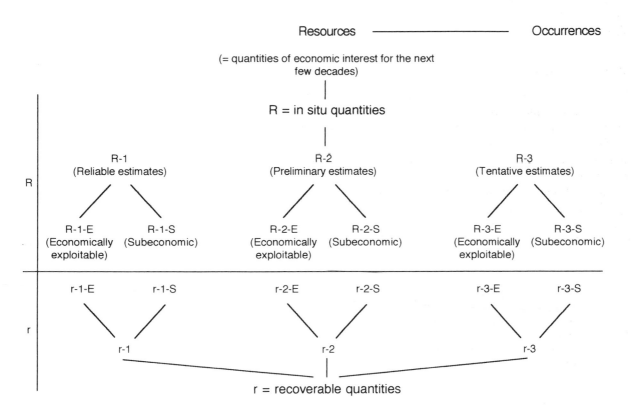

1 = reliable ~ demonstrated; reasonable assured; established; explored
2 = preliminary ~ inferred; estimated additional; possible
3 = tentative ~ undiscovered (hypothetical and speculative); potential; prognastic

might become of interest as a result of foreseeable economical or technological changes.

In practice, the resources group, r − 1 − E, is of prime interest as it represents the reliable estimated economically exploitable and recoverable tonnages. They are often referred to as reserves following the recommendations of the USGS given in Section 11.2.1.

The World Energy Council (1978) Conference Survey refers to this resources group as 'proved recoverable reserves' and the total estimated resources in place is put together in a single category called 'additional resources'.

The United Nations classification introduces a main group termed 'occurrences' in addition to that of 'resources'. 'Occurrences' cover any additional material with a lower economic potential, estimates of which would fall outside the boundaries of 'resources' and should be reported separately with some clarification as to the derivation and meaning of the estimates.

11.3   REPORTING OF RESOURCES/RESERVES

All factors used to limit resources and reserves that are necessary to verify the calculations must be stated explicitly. These will include the points of measurement, e.g. openhole, cored boreholes and outcrops. The relative density value that is selected for the calculation of the coal tonnage should be stated, together with the reasons for its selection.

11.3.1   Coal resources and reserves

To report resources and reserves, the required data will be based on the following. (1) Details on each coal seam within the lease area. (2) On a depth basis, in regular depth increments, if sufficient information is available. (3) On a seam thickness basis, the minimum coal thickness used and the maximum thickness of included non-coal bands should also be stated. Normally where a seam contains a non-coal band thicker than 0.25 m the two coal splits can be regarded as separate seams, and tonnages should be reported for each. The limits for non-coal bands in brown coal sequences may be greater, e.g. 1.0 m. Finally, (4) on a quality basis, maximum raw coal ash should be stated, and for marketable reserves, only that coal that can be used or beneficiated at an acceptable yield (which should be stated) should be included in the estimate. Other raw coal parameters, particularly those which affect utilisation, should be given, e.g. total sulphur and calorific value. Subdivisions of the resources may be made for areas of oxidised coal and heat affected coal.

11.3.2 Mineable *in situ* reserves

To report mineable *in situ* reserves, the following information is required.

(1) An outline of the proposed mining method

(2) The physical criteria limiting mining such as maximum and minimum working section thickness, minimum separation of seams, the maximum dip at which the coal can be mined by the stated method, geological structure, and areas where coal may not be mined, e.g. beneath motorways

(3) Quality restrictions, maximum and minimum levels for ash, sulphur, volatile matter, etc. For coals that have quality problems and need to be beneficiated, the predicted yield needs to be given

(4) Overburden or stripping ratios. For opencast operations, overburden removal costs are often quoted on a volumetric basis, the ratio is quoted in bank (*in situ*) cubic metres (bcm) of overburden per tonne of coal *in situ*, i.e.

$$\text{Stripping ratio (bcm)} = \frac{\text{overburden (m}^3)}{\text{coal (m}^3) \times \text{coal (SG)}}.$$

For coal deposits where the specific gravity (SG) of the coal is essentially constant, the stripping ratio is expressed simply as the ratio of thickness of overburden to the total workable coal section; however, the basis of the ratio must always be stated clearly. The most realistic results are achieved when the overburden thickness is calculated from the difference between the topographic surface and the structure contours of a seam at the selected data points within the area of interest. Where numerous data points exist, the stripping ratios are most conveniently calculated by computer and this data can later be plotted as stripping ratio contour plans.

In the UK, overburden and stripping ratios are calculated differently:

Overburden ratio (without batters) = *in situ* vertical ratio

Actual stripping ratio (including batters) = working ratio

The overburden ratio is calculated as follows:

In an area which has been drilled extensively, detailed contouring of the coal seams can enable reserve estimates to be made as a further definition of the estimated reserve figure. This method is also useful to highlight areas of geological hazards such as washouts or faulting.

An extension of the previous reserve calculation technique is to input geological data into a geologically significant computer model of the deposit. In this way coal deposits can be subdivided into major block units, each equating to the proposed working district of a coal mine. Within these units, smaller structurally delineated blocks provide the basic geological data which is transformed into computer data. Within each of these smaller units the coal seams provide the basic data for the whole assessment, i.e. depth, thickness, dip and size of the area. For example, the minimum coal thickness to be evaluated could be taken as 0.30 m while the minimum fault displacement to delimit a block could be 10.0 m. Such blocks consist of a series of vertically neighbouring coal seams and the projected stratigraphic column represents the series of coal seams within the block (Figure 11.11).

From these data, the spatial position, form and area of all intermediate coal seams are calculated using a mathematical

Figure 11.11 Schematic diagram of the calculation of sectional areas using the block model for coal resource/reserve calculations. From Juch *et al.* (1983), by permission of the author and publisher

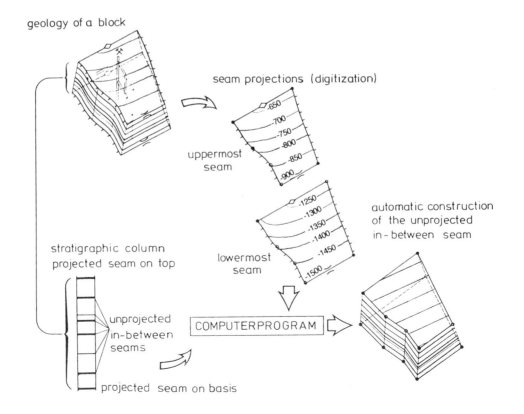

geology of a block

seam projections (digitization)

uppermost seam

automatic construction of the unprojected in-between seam

stratigraphic column projected seam on top

lowermost seam

unprojected in-between seams

COMPUTERPROGRAM

projected seam on basis

model. The top and bottom of a block are digitised to include regularly distributed depth values. On all the intermediate planes, sectional areas are defined by closed polygons. Data input of these sectional areas is performed by digitising seam projections at a 1:10 000 scale. Straight lines joining corresponding points on the top and bottom planes define the lateral delineation of the block on all intermediate planes and also all inbetween sectional areas, as shown in Figure 11.11.

In areas previously worked, the percentage of the worked areas is estimated for each sectional area, and has to be subtracted in the calculation process. Other coal seam data can be built into the computer model, such as seam thickness and coal quality data.

In Germany, where this method has been developed, experience has shown that for a reliable experimental variogram it is necessary to have at least 100 data points per coal seam in a major block unit, and at least 25 data points per coal seam for the estimation of one sectional area. Such data points need to be less than 1.0 km apart to assure a level of reliability acceptable to implement the computed reserve calculation.

It can be seen that computers now provide a means whereby statistical confidence criteria can be provided on a regular basis. The main limitation to these methods is the amount and quality of data required; most methods require data points relatively close together and evenly spaced and such conditions are only likely to occur in fairly well defined coal deposits.

11.4.2 Geological losses

The calculation of recoverable or extractable reserves requires the identification of those geological constraints that are likely to inhibit mining. Such constraints include the identification and positioning of fault zones, changes in dip, washouts, seam splitting and thinning, losses in quality, and igneous intrusions. In opencast workings, reserves will be affected by deleterious changes in the stripping ratio. All these factors contribute to a reduction in the mineable *in situ* reserve figure and are known collectively as geological losses.

In underground workings, the method of mining will influence those geological losses deducted from the mineable *in situ* reserve figure. If the method to be used is longwall mining, a larger geological loss will occur due to the fact that longwall operations need hazard free runs in a designated panel of coal. All faulted areas will need to be discounted if their amounts of throw displace the coal seam to be mined out of line with the preset coal shearer. If the coal panels between faults are too small, then the whole block may be discounted. If the bord and

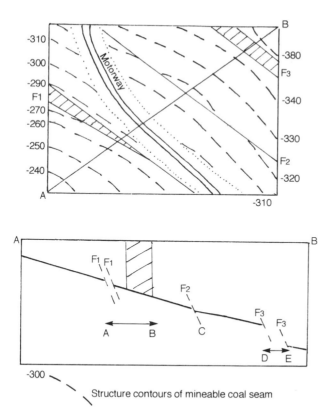

Figure 11.12 Example of geological losses and losses due to sterilisation of coal reserves beneath line of motorway. Geological hazards (faulting): F_1, downthrow 15 m to NW; F_2, downthrow 5 m to NW; F_3, downthrow 30 m to NW. Environmental hazards: motorway above proposed mine area. Therefore: area A–B in mineable coal seam to be discontinued; area D–E in mineable coal seam to be discontinued; area in coal seam at C may be discontinued if longwall mining method is used

pillar (room and pillar) method is adopted, small faults can often be worked through, and in some instances igneous intrusions can be worked around, as is seen in some South African coal mines. This method also allows for small blocks of coal to still be taken. All methods of mining are affected when coal is lost through washouts and changes in seam thickness or seam quality.

Geological losses will vary considerably from mine to mine but, in general, in opencast operations a 10% geological loss can be expected, whereas in underground operations geological losses of 25–50% may occur.

In addition, losses other than geological may need to be accounted for at this stage. Areas close to lease boundaries may be discounted, as well as reserve areas which run beneath railways, motorways and critical buildings and installations, as illustrated in Figure 11.12. Here coal reserves are sterilised both by faulting and by the presence of a motorway above the planned workings.

Those reserves deemed recoverable may under certain circumstances have a minimum depth limit imposed. This is often the case where reserves are accessed by drivages in from the base of the highwall in opencast workings. Such limits will be determined according to the nature of the particular surface area, and are intended to reduce the effects of subsidence, particularly close to areas of urban population.

Chapter 12
Report preparation

12.1 INTRODUCTION

Geological reports are the collation of all geological data acquired during all reconnaissance exploration and development programmes. The resultant layout and content of such reports are dependent on the level of investigation carried out, and the contractual requirements, if any, that may be specified in the original terms of reference.

Geological reports include technical briefs on a regional level, such as reviews of coal deposits covering hundreds of square kilometres, but more usually are the results of a particular survey or investigation.

Geological reports of reconnaissance surveys usually include existing geological map evaluation and/or aerial photographic interpretation in the form of maps and text, together with all ground survey data, traverse results, geological and structural interpretation of the area plus details of all coal occurrences and coal sample sites.

Geological reports of exploration and development programmes are much larger and more detailed documents. They include all geographical and surveying details, all geological maps, cross sections and correlation charts, all drilling details, coal seam sections and sample sites, resource and reserve calculations, coal quality results, structure contours, coal seam thickness, overburden/interburden, and coal quality plans.

In addition, there may be a requirement for smaller and concise monthly or quarterly geological reports to give the current progress on mapping, sampling, drilling and surveying as part of the exploration programme.

12.2 THE GEOLOGICAL REPORT

The compilation of the geological report is an important part of the coal geologist's duties, and his or her ability to produce concise accounts with good maps, plans and diagrams will enhance his or her professional standing.

All such reports should be self explanatory, and in the case of final or completion reports, all data must be included and concisely presented using internationally recognised units and standards. Maps and diagrams should be used where possible to facilitate understanding.

All reports should contain a summary and conclusion emphasising all points of significance. The conclusion may be accompanied by a list of recommendations depending on the terms of reference under which the geological programme was carried out. The summary is a synopsis of the findings of the

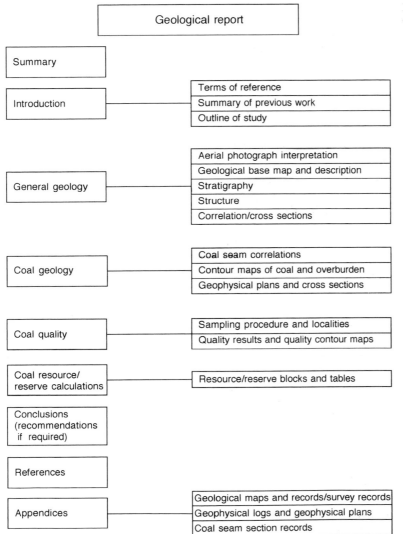

Figure 12.1   Basic elements required for compilation of the geological report

report; it is situated at the beginning of the report and may, along with the conclusions and recommendations, be the only part of the report actually read by non-geological and non-technical management. Therefore they are of prime importance in emphasising the major features of the coal geology in the report.

Any previous work in the area should be acknowledged, as this will have provided the first geological information even if modified or even disproved at a later date.

The stages required in the compilation of the geological report, as distinct from the geotechnical and hydrogeological reports are shown in Figure 12.1. This layout can be used for geological reports for both opencast and underground mine proposals. Some parts are more relevant to opencast operations, e.g. stripping ratio plans, oxidation or burning limits of coals, whereas the roof and floor characteristics of coal seams can have more bearing in underground mine planning.

12.2.1 Geology

The text of the report will describe the geology in terms of stratigraphy, structure, coal seam characteristics and geophysics. The principal structures present in the area should be described, including their history and effect, if any, on the mineable sequence, such as significant changes in dip, throws of faults and faults that die out both in a vertical and a horizontal sense.

Under general geology, the final geological map will be included and must show the location of all coals, coal sample sites, lithological boundaries, structural details and all borehole sites. Maps are usually on 1:50 000, 1:20 000 and 1:10 000 scales and are depicted as described in Section 6.2.1.

If an aerial photographic survey has been carried out, particularly in the absence of any published base maps, the photogeological interpretation maps showing all geological features as outlined in Section 6.2.2 will be included. In addition, all ground traverse plans (as shown in Figure 6.5) will be included; most of these will usually be at a 1:10 000 scale.

The stratigraphy of the area can best be shown in a general stratigraphic column showing the principal formations, their thicknesses, plus a broad description, similar to that illustrated in Figure 12.2. This can be given in more detailed form to incorporate coal seam characteristics and sedimentological analysis as shown in Figure 12.3. For more detailed stratigraphic correlation, based on outcrop and borehole data, the layout of laterally connecting vertical sections is most effective. Such figures can highlight local thickening and thinning of strata together with coal seam splitting characteristics. Figure 12.4

	Age	Formation	Thickness (m)	Details
Tertiary	Miocene–Pliocene	Coastal Plains Sands	?	Unconsolidated yellow–white cross bedded sands
Tertiary	Miocene	Lignite Formation	?	Coarse sandstones, shales, lignites
Tertiary	Miocene	Bende–Ameki	1460	Coarse sandstones, shales, thin limestones
Tertiary	Lower Eocene	Imo Clay Shales	1220	Dark grey–blue shale, ironstone, thin sandstone
Tertiary	Palaeocene			
Cretaceous	Maestrictian Campanian and ? Santonian	Upper Coal Measures	335	White–grey sandstone, carbonaceous shale coals thin limestone
Cretaceous	Maestrictian Campanian and ? Santonian	False-bedded Sandstones	335	Medium–coarse grained sandstone, sub. shales
Cretaceous	Maestrictian Campanian and ? Santonian	Lower Coal Measures	396	Fine–medium grained sandstone, shale, carbonaceous shale, coals
Cretaceous	Maestrictian Campanian and ? Santonian	Enugu Shales	762	Blue–grey mudstone & shale, white sandstone & thin limestone
Cretaceous	Maestrictian Campanian and ? Santonian	Awgu Sandstone	609	Fine–coarse grained sandstone, pebble beds, shale & limestone at base
Cretaceous	Maestrictian Campanian and ? Santonian	Nkporo Shales	457	Dark shale & mudstone, thick lenses sandstone carbonaceous shale
Cretaceous	Coniacian	Awgu–Ndeaboh Shales	914	Blue–grey shale with sub. sandstone & limestone
Cretaceous	Turonian	Eze-Aku Shales	609	Calcareous shale, mudstone, shelly limestone
Cretaceous	Albian–Cenomanian	Asu River Group	1828	Shale, sandstone & blue dense limestone

Figure 12.2 General stratigraphy of strata present in an area of coal exploration. From Swardt & Casey (1963)

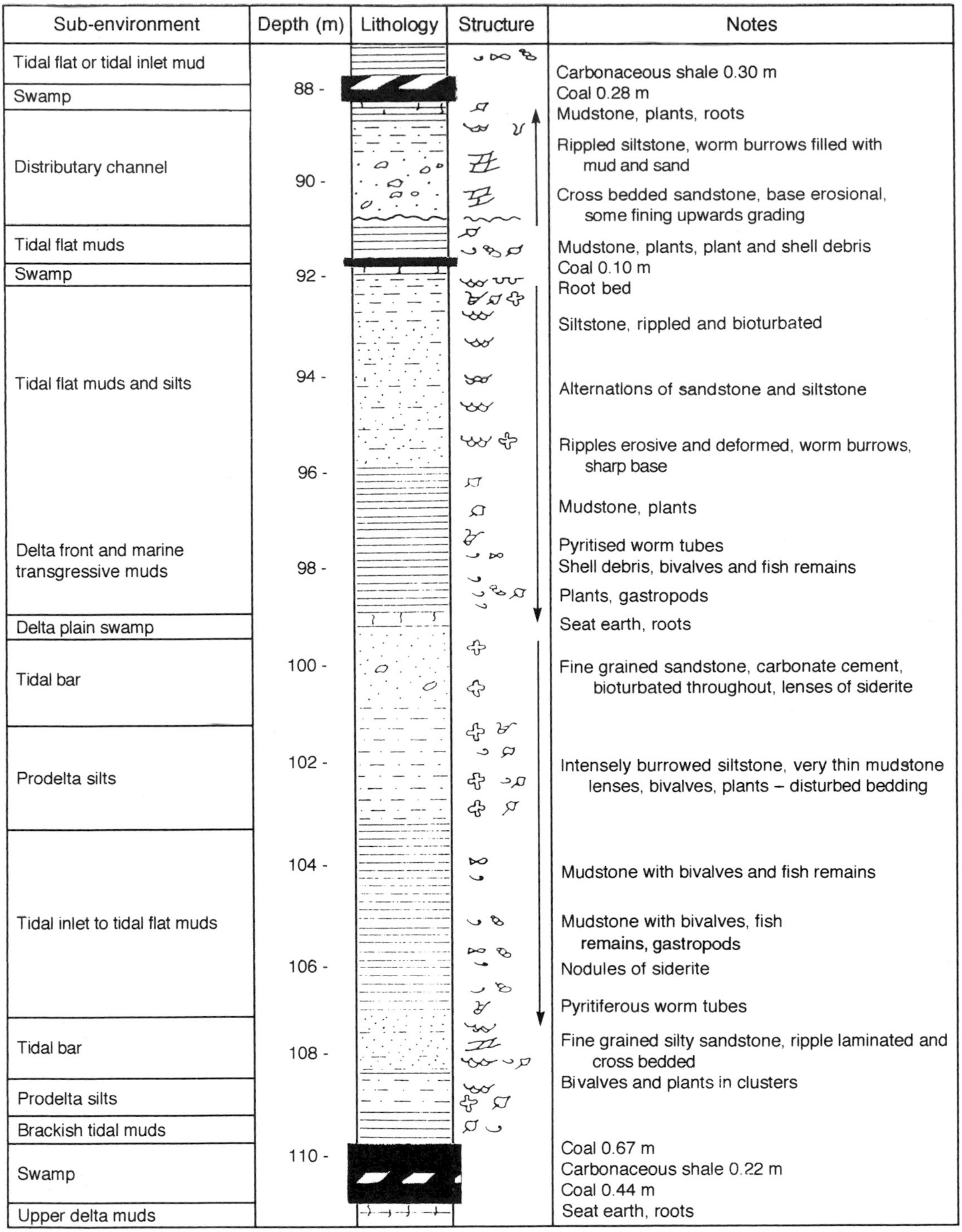

Sub-environment	Depth (m)	Lithology	Structure	Notes
Tidal flat or tidal inlet mud				Carbonaceous shale 0.30 m
Swamp	88 -			Coal 0.28 m
				Mudstone, plants, roots
Distributary channel	90 -			Rippled siltstone, worm burrows filled with mud and sand
				Cross bedded sandstone, base erosional, some fining upwards grading
Tidal flat muds				Mudstone, plants, plant and shell debris
Swamp	92 -			Coal 0.10 m
				Root bed
				Siltstone, rippled and bioturbated
Tidal flat muds and silts	94 -			Alternations of sandstone and siltstone
	96 -			Ripples erosive and deformed, worm burrows, sharp base
				Mudstone, plants
Delta front and marine transgressive muds	98 -			Pyritised worm tubes
				Shell debris, bivalves and fish remains
				Plants, gastropods
Delta plain swamp				Seat earth, roots
Tidal bar	100 -			Fine grained sandstone, carbonate cement, bioturbated throughout, lenses of siderite
Prodelta silts	102 -			Intensely burrowed siltstone, very thin mudstone lenses, bivalves, plants – disturbed bedding
	104 -			Mudstone with bivalves and fish remains
Tidal inlet to tidal flat muds				Mudstone with bivalves, fish remains, gastropods
	106 -			Nodules of siderite
				Pyritiferous worm tubes
Tidal bar	108 -			Fine grained silty sandstone, ripple laminated and cross bedded
				Bivalves and plants in clusters
Prodelta silts				
Brackish tidal muds				
Swamp	110 -			Coal 0.67 m / Carbonaceous shale 0.22 m / Coal 0.44 m
Upper delta muds				Seat earth, roots

Figure 12.3 Example of vertical representation of a coal-bearing sequence incorporating coal seam characteristics and sedimentological interpretation

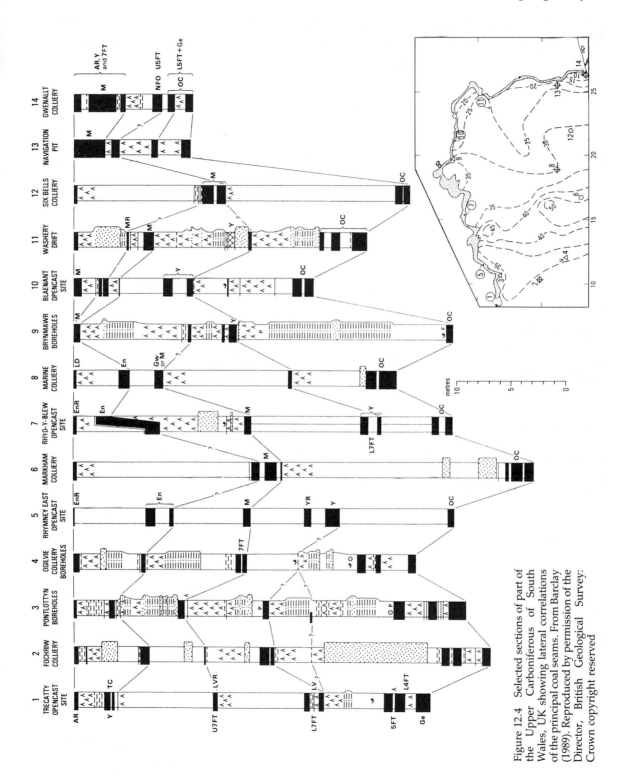

Figure 12.4 Selected sections of part of the Upper Carboniferous of South Wales, UK showing lateral correlations of the principal coal seams. From Barclay (1989). Reproduced by permission of the Director, British Geological Survey: Crown copyright reserved

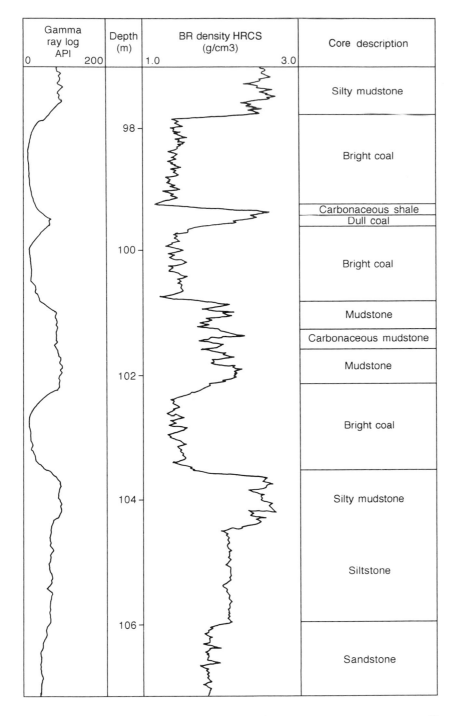

Figure 12.5 Vertical section of litho-types together with gamma ray and density geophysical log printouts and borehole depths

shows vertical sections correlated in this manner for part of the productive coal sequence in the South Wales Coalfield, UK. Any special stratigraphical features such as faunal or floral content should also be listed together with its significance.

Geological maps or plans showing the geological structure of the area, particularly faulting and folding likely to influence the future mining of the deposit should be described in detail in this section.

The use of vertical sections can be further enhanced by showing the geophysical log alongside the lithological log as seen in Figures 12.5 and 7.22. A modification of this can be seen in Figure 7.23 where the detailed interpreted density characteristics of a coal seam are shown alongside the geophysical logs, together with a table of actual density and ash values for each coal ply. Using such correlations, cross sections of the area of interest can be constructed showing the main stratigraphic horizons, with all significant coal seams highlighted, with their thicknesses given at each data point on the section (Figure 12.6).

In addition to the geological map which will show coal outcrops and all major structural features, a series of plans will

Figure 12.6   Cross sections across a coal prospect highlighting all principal coal seams. Reproduced by permission of P.T. Tambang, Batubara Bukit Asam, Indonesia

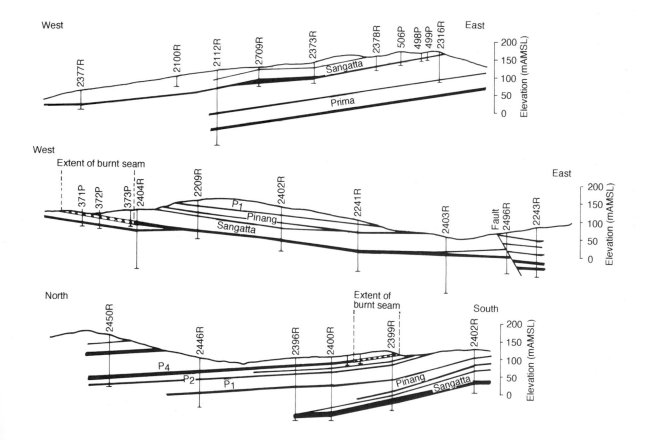

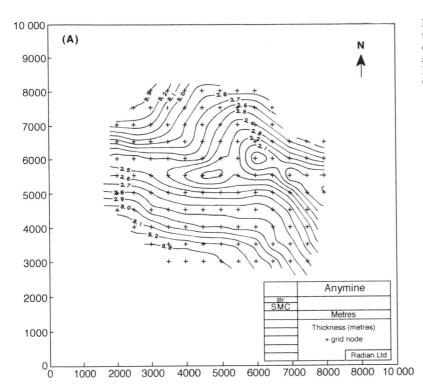

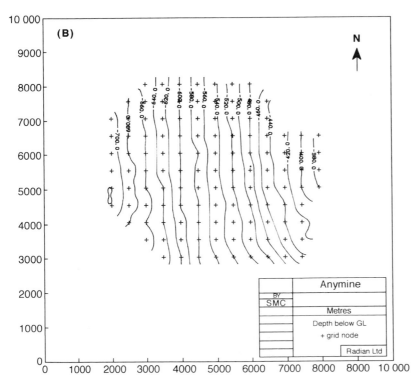

Figure 12.7   Computer generated contour plans of (A) coal seam thickness, (B) depth to top of coal seam and (C) (*opposite*) a plot of tonnage in the ground. Reproduced by permission of Radian Corporation

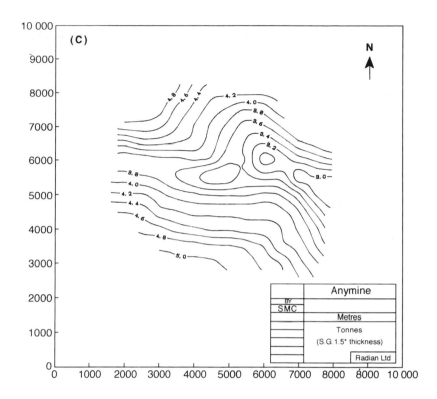

need to be produced. These will include the following: structure contours of all principal coal seams; thickness contours for all principal coal seams; thickness contours for the overburden; and stripping ratio plans for selected areas within the area of interest.

Usually such plans are drawn at 1:10000 and 1:5000 scales, depending on the size of the area and the intensity of the geological data points. All of these plans are readily constructed from the pattern of data points and the values at each data point, i.e. the depth to each seam from the surface, each seam thickness and the thickness of the interburden between seams. These plans can be produced manually, but are now usually computer generated. This means that plans showing all permutations of the main parameters can be produced rapidly and has the added advantage that extra data can be incorporated as regular updates. As an illustration, Figure 12.7 shows computer generated contour plans of (A) thickness, (B) depth to the top of the seam and (C) a plot of tonnage in the ground, i.e. seam thickness × specific gravity (S.G.) (in this instance S.G. = 1.5) for a hypothetical coal seam in a designated area.

Other plans which may be required are the limits of coal seam outcrop burning determined by geophysics (magnetic surveys) and shallow drilling, together with the results of all other

Ply thickness (m)	Depth from surface (m)	Seam thickness (m)	Ply description	Sample number	Ash fusion (reducing atmos) / Calc % ash analysis cumulative from floor DT (°C)	ST (°C)	HT (°C)	FT (°C)	Vol rec (%)	RD	Air dried moist (%)	Ash (%)	VM (%)	FC (%)	Total sulph (%)	Phos (%)	Crucible swelling no.	Gray-king coke type	Dry basis	Dry ash free
	162.810	3.490	Roof: sandstone/mudstone (50/50)																	
1.350			Coal: banded bright with 0.140 m cindered coal at base	12298	1210	1250	1310	1400	89.9	1.45	2.8	23.6	27.8	48.6	0.43	-	½	-	25.44	33.30
0.570	164.160	2.140	Igneous rock (white with 0.06 m core loss)	12304					92.3	1.92	0.9	55.4	-	-	-	-	-	-	-	-
1.570	164.730	1.570	Coal: dull with cindered coal at top; banded bright at base	12310	1170	1210	1290	1330	9.6	1.34	1.7	13.6	36.3	50.1	0.72	-	1	-	28.90	33.45
	166.180	0.000	Floor: siltstone, grey																	
			Composite 162.810 m–164.160 m F1.60	12303	1300	1340	1360	1410	HGI 52	1.30	2.3	6.7	14.5	58.8	0.49	0.061	1	-	31.18	33.42
			Composite 164.730 m—166.180 m F1.60	12315	1280	1300	1330	1400	HGI 39	1.32	1.4	7.4	40.9	51.7	0.60	0.019	1½	-	31.12	33.87

Specific energy (MJ/kg): Dry basis / Dry ash free

Individual ply analysis — Analysis ~ dry basis

Core diameter = 0.045 m

Seam		Depth to base of seam	Depth
Location	Sampled by	Analysed at	Drn. by
Date drilled	Field data		Appv'd
Date rec'd at lab	Sheet		File no.
Date analysis completed			Title
			Date
			Date

Figure 12.8 Coal seam data sheet showing plies, thicknesses, coal ply and coal composite quality analyses. From Australian Standard 2519-1982, by permission of Standards Association of Australia

geophysical surveys, both regional and site specific, in the form of maps, plans or sections.

Coal seam section sheets for each surface site and borehole showing individual plies, depths and thicknesses, plus a brief description, should be included in an Appendix; Figure 9.2 and Table 12.1 illustrate this type of data display.

Detailed coal seam sections for the principal coal seams may be given to indicate the preferred mining section(s) for each coal. This should include details of the coal seam roof and floor and individual ply analyses where available. Figure 12.8 shows a typical data sheet recording a coal seam section and known quality information.

12.2.2 Coal quality

The section on coal quality should describe the qualities for all the principal coal seams in the area of interest. Contour plans showing coal quality for the most important coal seams should be included, in particular, ash, volatile matter, sulphur and calorific value, produced on similar scales to the geological plans, i.e. $1:10\,000$ and $1:5\,000$. Figure 12.9 shows computer generated contour plans for sulphur (wt%) and ash (wt%) values for the same model as shown in Figure 12.7.

Coal quality data should also be included with the detailed seam sections to highlight any special features such as the top ply in the coal being high in sulphur when underlying a marine mudstone, or whether a thick sandstone directly overlies a seam and therefore may be liable to erode into it, or whether there is a split in the coal seam close to the roof which may produce unstable roof conditions in underground mining operations.

Data sheets showing all coal seam ply and seam composite analyses, as illustrated in Table 12.2, should be included in an Appendix.

12.2.3 Resource/reserve calculations

The area of interest will be divided into blocks for which resource or reserve calculations will have been made, each category of resources or reserves being determined in accordance with the system of calculation selected by the project management and as outlined in Chapter 11.

The reserves are usually listed for each seam, indicating the stripping ratio, and as *in situ* reserves, recoverable reserves and theoretically saleable coal (also called marketable coal) for each designated block area, as shown in Table 12.3.

Table 12.1   Coal seam section description sheets showing individual plies, depths and thicknesses, plus brief lithological description. Reproduced by permission of Antrim Coal Company Ltd

Depth to base (m)	Thickness (m)	Recovered (%)	Lithology (%)	Description	Formation/seam split
67.700	0.950	—	Lignite	Irregularly laminated, sparse clayey laminations, 10° bedding. Dark brown, red–brown, slightly weathered, weak rock. Common woody lignite lenses, medium spaced 200–600 mm, vertical joints	Lower lignite—zone three
68.720	1.020	—	Lignite (68) Clayey lignite (32)	Lignite: dark brown, red–brown, slightly weathered, weak rock. Clayey lignite (towards top of unit) dark brown, black, slightly weathered, weak rock, medium spaced 200–600 mm, low angle 0–30° fractures, 5° bedding	Lower lignite—zone three
69.800	1.080	—	Lignite (81) Lignite (19)	Lignite: dark brown, red–brown, slightly weathered, weak rock. Lignite (very thin interbeds 20–60 mm) dark brown, black, woody, slightly weathered, moderately weak rock, medium spaced 200–600 mm, low angle 0–30° fractures, 5° bedding	Lower lignite—zone three

Depth			Material (%)	Description	Zone
70.900	1.100	81	Lignite (69)	Lignite: dark brown, red–brown, slightly weathered, weak rock	Lower lignite—zone three
			Clayey lignite (31)	Clayey lignite (towards base of unit) dark brown, medium brown, slightly weathered, weak rock, closely spaced 60–200 mm, low angle 0–30° fractures, 5° bedding	
73.190	2.290	—	Lignite (91)	Lignite: dark brown, red–brown, slightly weathered, weak rock	Lower lignite—zone three
			Clayey lignite (9)	Clayey lignite (very thin interbeds 20–60 mm) dark grey–brown, medium brown, slightly weathered, weak rock, irregularly laminated, medium spaced 200–600 mm, low and medium angle fractures, 5° bedding	
74.520	1.330	—	Lignite (88)	Lignite: dark brown, red–brown, slightly weathered, weak rock	Lower lignite—zone three
			Clayey lignite (12)	Clayey lignite (towards middle of unit) dark brown, slightly weathered, weak rock, closely spaced 60–200 mm, low and medium angle fractures, 5° bedding	
76.000	1.480	—	Lignite (89)	Lignite: dark brown, red–brown, slightly weathered, weak rock	Lower lignite—zone two
			Lignite (11)	Lignite: (thin interbeds 60–200 mm) dark orange brown, finely comminuted, porous, slightly weathered, very weak rock, medium spaced 200–600 mm, low and medium angle fractures	

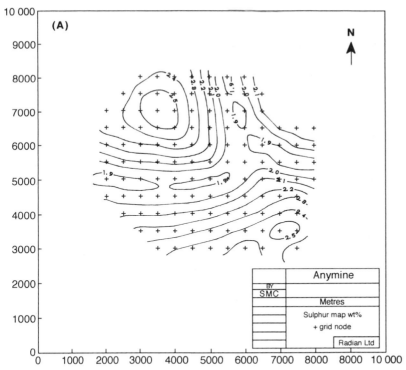

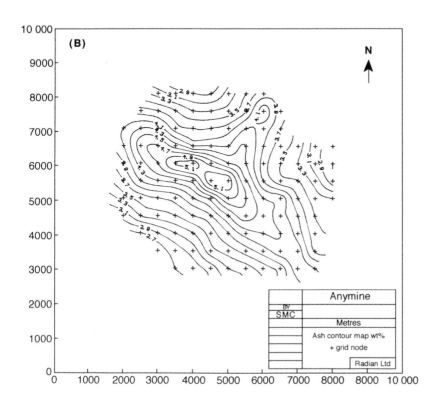

Figure 12.9   Computer generated contour plans showing coal quality. (A) Sulphur (wt%) and (B) ash (wt%). Reproduced by permission of Radian Corporation

Table 12.2 Example of one style of layout showing coal plies, samples and analytical data. Reproduced by permission of Antrim Coal Company Ltd

Borehole	Depth from (m)	Depth to (m)	Sample number	Float type	Analysis basis*	Moisture (%)	Ash (%)	Calorific value MJ/kg	Total sulphur (%)
CCL-50	67.70	68.72	CCL50/LL8	Raw	AR	49.10	15.10	9.76	0.15
CCL-50	68.72	69.80	CCL50/LL9	Raw	AR	50.90	8.10	11.32	0.14
CCL-50	69.80	70.90	CCL50/LL10	Raw	AR	49.50	12.20	10.48	0.17
CCL-50	70.90	73.19	CCL50/LL11	Raw	AR	51.20	6.40	11.89	0.10
CCL-50	73.19	74.52	CCL50/LL12	Raw	AR	51.30	6.20	11.78	0.08
CCL-50	74.52	76.00	CCL50/LL13	Raw	AR	51.80	2.20	13.58	0.05
CCL-50	76.00	82.00	CCL50/LL14	Raw	AR	50.80	1.80	13.93	0.02

*AR = as received.

Table 12.3 Display of coal reserves within individual blocks, giving both total reserves as *in situ*, recoverable and theoretically saleable, and reserves to the same bases to a selected maximum stripping ratio of 10:1

Coal reserves within individual blocks

Seam name	Block A*			Block B*			Block C*			Block D*			All blocks*		
	Ins.	Rec.	Sal.	Ins.	Rec.	Sal.	Ins.	Rec.	Sal.	Ins.	Rec.	Sal.	Ins.	Rec.	Sal.
A (total)	4.223	2.870	2.124	3.904	2.579	1.908	3.068	1.979	1.464	5.051	3.671	2.717	16.247	11.099	8.213
A (to 10:1 ratio)†	1.239	0.916	0.678	0.000	0.000	0.000	0.397	0.294	0.218	1.053	0.811	0.600	2.689	2.021	1.496
B (total)	3.348	2.323	1.719	7.058	4.437	3.283	2.749	1.993	1.475	4.728	3.281	2.428	17.882	12.034	8.905
B (to 10:1 ratio)†	1.572	1.131	0.837	1.029	0.627	0.464	0.881	0.668	0.494	1.249	0.978	0.724	4.731	3.404	2.519
C (total)	0.292	0.212	0.157	5.200	3.666	2.713	1.043	0.806	0.596	2.877	2.057	1.522	9.412	6.741	4.988
C (to 10:1 ratio)†	0.292	0.212	0.157	1.858	1.448	1.072	0.846	0.644	0.477	1.113	0.869	0.643	4.109	3.173	2.348
D (total)	0.000	0.000	0.000	1.958	1.464	1.083	0.267	0.214	0.518	2.011	1.458	1.079	4.236	3.136	2.321
D (to 10:1 ratio)†	0.000	0.000	0.000	1.003	0.773	0.572	0.264	0.212	0.157	0.428	0.310	0.229	1.696	1.259	0.958
E (total)	0.000	0.000	0.000	5.082	3.632	2.688	0.000	0.000	0.000	6.178	4.672	3.457	11.260	8.304	6.145
E (to 10:1 ratio)†	0.000	0.000	0.000	4.577	3.350	2.479	0.000	0.000	0.000	4.701	3.564	2.637	9.278	6.914	5.116
All seams total	7.863	5.405	4.000	23.202	15.778	11.676	6.860	4.992	3.694	20.844	15.139	11.203	58.770	41.314	30.572
All seams to 10:1 ratio†	3.103	2.259	1.672	8.467	6.198	4.587	2.388	1.818	1.345	8.544	6.532	4.834	22.502	16.807	12.437

*Ins. = *In situ* coal; Rec. = recoverable clean coal; Sal. = theoretically saleable coal.
† Volume to volume basis.

12.3   REPORT FINALISATION

The conclusions of the report should then be given and must include all the main findings of the report. A full reference list should be given together with all Appendices, which should include all original maps and stratigraphic, lithological and coal quality record sheets. The breakdown of each block area for reserve calculations can also be given if desired. All detailed plans and maps should be clearly labelled including geographical co-ordinates, and a title box, usually in the bottom right hand corner, should include the geologist's name, scale, dates when the work was carried out and produced, plus the name (if applicable) of the person who checked the work.

Chapter 13
Geological practice

13.1 INTRODUCTION

The term geological practice is interpreted as encompassing the accepted code of behaviour of the geologist, the adherence to working to required international standards, the relationship(s) of the geologist with other technical disciplines, and the consideration and recognition of environmental requirements and constraints.

In general, the geologist is already working within a framework in which most of these practices are pre-determined. However, his or her own code of behaviour and his or her relationship to other technical disciplines can still be regarded as variables. For the reputation of the company and for the geologist's professional standing, a high level of geological practice must be maintained.

13.2 GEOLOGICAL CONDUCT AND STANDARDS

The activities that the coal geologist is likely to be involved in and to be responsible for are outlined in Chapters 6–12. To accomplish these to the standards acceptable to both management and to recognised international standards, levels of quality have been determined. These may be in the form of a standard definition, as for coal reserve assessments and coal quality determinations; such standards can vary from country to country as shown in earlier chapters. In addition to the technical requirements defined in this way, the personal professional conduct of the geologist is important to the success of any project. The geologist first and foremost must be methodical in the collection and recording of geological data, and be competent in the interpretation of the data, so that if for any reason he or she was taken from the project, another geologist could carry on and be able to make both sense and use of the data.

The geologist will also need to be able to organise and supervise geological assistants, field labourers and drilling crews, as well as assisting in geophysical, geotechnical and hydrogeological investigations, and may, in the case of remote field activities, be responsible for the running of the project.

Obviously the performance of the geologist will be improved by experience, but in the early stages of any project, whether exploration or development, the geologist is an important player who is in touch with the basic data on which later decisions involving large capital outlays will be made.

With the development of computing facilities, the role of the geologist is becoming broader based and more integrated with other technical disciplines. This can only serve to benefit the better co-ordination of projects, and enable a higher level of data input and manipulation to take place.

The establishment of quality assurance practices, as outlined in BS 5750 or ISO 9000 (see Appendix 1), will now ensure that companies can establish, document and maintain an effective management system, and compliance with it will help to provide the necessary consistency of both working practice and product quality (Hall, 1992). The standards enable companies to demonstrate to their customers that they are committed to quality and are able to supply their quality needs; in coal trading this is of paramount importance. The standards allow the company to monitor all stages of production, which in turn facilitates the control of the rate of production and product quality.

Overall monitoring by management is carried out through the assessment of the results of internal technical and quality audits, performed in accordance with a documented procedure. The coal geologist will be required to report to management on the activities and performance of his or her part of the programme, and how it measures up in terms of the budget and timing in the agreed project schedule.

13.3   TECHNICAL RELATIONSHIPS

During the reconnaissance and then the exploration phases of a project, the geologist is the focal point of data acquisition. As the project progresses, the geologist becomes the point of contact for other technical disciplines involved in the project, but which are dependent on the basic information provided by the geologist. Figure 13.1 shows the generalised relationship of the coal geologist to the other technical disciplines and to project management.

This information will be supplied to the mining engineers and coal preparation engineers, who in turn feed back their require-

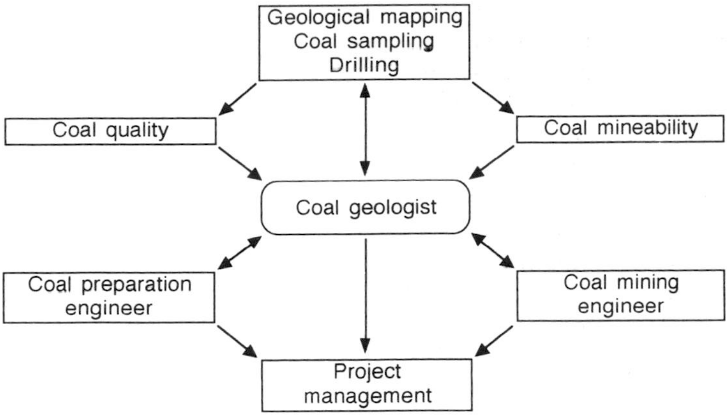

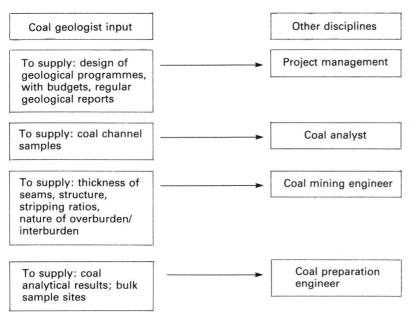

Figure 13.1   Technical interfaces of the coal geologist

ments to the geologist. For example, if a group of seams becomes thinner or the overburden thickness increases, or both, the stripping ratios may become uneconomic and the mining engineers will prefer the geologist to concentrate on more favourable areas; similarly, the coal quality results may suggest to the coal preparation engineer that a coal seam is unsuitable for inclusion in the mine plan because of unfavourable chemical or physical properties such as high sulphur values, low calorific value, or unfavourable Hardgrove index.

The technical input of the coal geologist is illustrated in Figure 13.2, which summarises the role of the coal geologist in

Figure 13.2   Input of the coal geologist into management and other technical disciplines

supplying information to management and other technical disciplines.

It is essential that coal geologists bear in mind that for a project to reach a successful conclusion, close collaboration with mining engineers and coal preparation engineers is essential. This will also serve to avoid confusion and misunderstandings emerging during the course of a project. It has been a fact that for many years such relationships have been tenuous, but it is clear that in the modern economic climate, a more enlightened attitude is required and will now become the current practice.

The geotechnical and hydrogeological studies are usually conducted in co-operation with the geologist and the mining engineers, and any large or bulk sampling programmes are carried out in co-operation with the geologist and the coal preparation engineers.

Once the likely coal product can be determined, and a production cost per tonne estimated, the sales and marketing department (SMD) will take this information and see, in the case of a targeted export coal, where in the marketplace it will fit, or, if targeted for domestic use, which industries will be interested, and in both instances how the product will stand up against the competition. If the SMD would like any modifications, or need to know reserves tonnages, the geologist may be called in to discuss the possibilities of product modification and to provide any necessary data.

13.4   THE COAL GEOLOGIST AND THE ENVIRONMENT

Although this book is not directly concerned with the environmental effects of coal mining and coal utilisation, it is important that the coal geologist is aware of the consequences of his or her actions with respect to the surroundings. The history of coal mining, both underground and opencast, has shown the damage that can be caused to the environment. The modern coal geologist has to bear in mind the potential threat to the environment that irresponsible exploration and development of coal can have.

The factors defining the physical environment need to be constantly appraised during the exploration and then development phases of the project to enable the most suitable mine plan to be formulated; during the course of the project an environmental impact statement (EIS) will be produced. On a local level, the geologist needs to be conscious of environmental considerations right from the beginning of the programme, and may be required to provide a preliminary environmental report to support the EIS.

If the area is a 'greenfield' site, i.e. not previously mined and relatively unspoilt by development, care should be taken during the field programme to ensure that a minimum of unnecessary disturbance is caused which could upset the local fauna and flora, ground stability and surface water patterns.

If the area has an established infrastructure, and has undergone a degree of development, care has to be taken to protect the water supply, keep roadways clear and to keep dust and noise levels to a minimum, particularly in areas of human settlement.

Where the development of a surface coal mining operation is planned, the diversion of surface water, building of access roads to drill sites and mining areas, designation of stockpile areas plus increased levels of dust and noise are all environmentally sensitive activities and all need careful planning and supervision.

Table 13.1 Factors that the geologist needs to consider during the exploration and mining of coal

Factor	Effects
Landform	Changing natural topography; threatening unique areas, national parks, etc
Water	Surface water, diversion for opencast mining; groundwater, contamination from drilling fluids or diesel Ocean—harbour drilling and dredging
Vegetation	Cutting and burning of natural vegetation; preservation of rare species
Fauna	Rare and endangered species disturbed by noise, vibration and loss of habitat
Erosion	Indiscriminate removal of vegetation cover, alteration of gradients, road building, oversteepened run-off areas, alteration of water courses
Sedimentation	Unwanted deposition of materials through changed water courses and rates of flow, dumping of topsoil
Subsidence	Collapse of drill holes and sample sites, effects of underground workings
Contamination	Input of oils, drilling fluids, other chemicals into surface and groundwater; exhaust, smoke and dust emissions
Waste disposal	Ocean dumping; industrial waste, tailings ponds, non-coal fraction disposal; domestic waste, effects on health and general cleanliness
Noise	Levels of disturbance produced by drilling, transportation and earth-moving on local fauna and human populations

In the case of underground mining, the geologist will require advice on the degree and pattern of possible subsidence, particularly when underlying residential areas, waterways and environmentally protected areas. To understand the implications of actions taken during the various phases of a project, the coal geologist will need to consult experts brought in to advise in a specialist capacity; these will include hydrogeologists, botanists, zoologists, foresters, geotechnical engineers, acoustic engineers and, in certain circumstances, archaeologists, if the area has a known history of human habitation.

The coal geologist, in carrying out his or her normal duties, should ensure that at drill sites there is no leakage of diesel or other substances into the surface or groundwater system, that there are no materials discarded and left at sites and that such sites are restored on completion of drilling, logging and surveying.

The project management team will, as a matter of course, liaise with the national and local authorities and work within the framework of their environmental legislation. Such legislation varies throughout the world, from little consideration for the environment, to extremely strict guidelines which can severely limit the mining operations in sensitive areas.

The coal geologist must have a grasp of the relevant legislation, and should remember that he or she is in the front line for the initial part of any project, and must realise his or her obligation in this respect. Table 13.1 summarises some of the factors that the coal geologist will need to consider during the exploration for, and the development and mining of, coal.

Bibliography

Abdullah, Z.B. (1986) Plans for coal use in Malaysia. *Energy* **11**, 1097–1102

Alexander, J. & Hattersley, R. (1980) Coal. In: *Australian Mining, Minerals, and Oil*, David Ell Press, Sydney, 14–24

American Society for Testing & Materials (1977) Classification of coals by rank, D 388–77

American Society for Testing & Materials (1978) Megascopic description of coal and coal seams and microscopical description and analysis of coal, D 2796–78

Barclay, W.J. (1989) *Geology of the South Wales Coalfield. Part II. The Country Around Abergavenny, Mem. Br. Geol. Surv, Sheet 232 (England and Wales)*, 3rd edn, 147pp

Barnes, J.W. (1981) *Basic Geological Mapping. Geological Society of London Handbook*, Open University Press, Buckingham, 112pp

Barnett, J.A.M., Mortimer, J., Rippon, J.H., Walsh, J.J. & Watterson, J. (1987) Displacement geometry in the volume containing a single normal fault. *Am. Assoc. Petrol. Geol. Bull.* **71**, 925–937

Berbano, M.C. (1986) Status of the Philippine Coal Development Programme. *Energy* **11**, 1113–1121

Berkowitz, N. (1979) *An Introduction to Coal Technology*, Academic Press, New York, 345pp

Berkman, D.A. & Ryall, W.R. (1987) *Field Geologists Manual*, 2nd edn, The Australasian Institute of Mining and Metallurgy, Parkville, Victoria, Australia, 301pp

Black, P. (1986) New Zealand's coalfields. Their geology, petrology and inorganic chemistry. In: *Advances in the Study of the Sydney Basin: Proceedings of 20th Symposium, 15–18 May 1986*, Newcastle, New South Wales, Australia, 7–12

Bless, M.J.M. & de Voogd, N. (1980) Exploration for coal in The Netherlands. *Meded. Rijks Geol. Dienst* **33–3**, 17–32

BPB Instruments Ltd (1981) *Coal Interpretation Manual*, BPB Instruments, East Leake, Loughborough, 100pp

Brassington, R. (1988) *Field Hydrogeology, Geol. Soc. London Prof. Handbook Ser.*, Open University Press, Buckingham, 175pp

Brawner, C.O. (1986) Groundwater and coal mining. *Min. Sci. Technol.* **3**, 187–198

British Coal (1964) *Coal Classification System* (revision of 1964 system), National Coal Board, London, 9pp

British Petroleum (1990) *BP Statistical Review of World Energy 1990*, British Petroleum, London, pp. 26–29

British Petroleum (1991) *Statistical Review of World Energy 1991*, British Petroleum, London, pp. 26–29

British Standards Institution (1989) BS 1016, Part 12 (1980) 1989, *Cake and Swelling Properties of Coal*, BSI, London

Broadhurst, F.M. & Simpson, I.M. (1983) Syntectonic sedimentation, rigs and fault re-activation in the Coal Measures of Britain. *J. Geol.* **91**, 330–337

Brugmans, P.J. (1987) Spitzbergen—mining coal within the Arctic Circle. *Min. Mag.* **156** (June), 479–481

Busby, J.P. & Evans, R.B. (1988) *Depth to Magnetic Basement in North-west Bangladesh from Digital Aeromagnetic Data. Br. Geol. Surv. Tech. Rep. No. WK/88/3*, 11pp

Bustin, R.M., Cameron, A.R., Grieve, D.A. & Kalkreuth, W.D. (1983) *Coal Petrology, Its Principles, Methods and Applications, Short Course Notes, Geol. Assoc. Can. No. 3*, 273pp

Casshyap, S.M. & Tewari, R.C. (1984) Fluvial models of the Lower Permian coal measures of Son-Mahanadi and Koel-Damodar Valley Basins, India. In: *Sedimentology of Coal and Coal-bearing Sequences* (Eds R. A. Rahmani & R. M. Flores), *Spec. Publ. Int. Assoc. Sedimentol. No. 7*, Blackwell Scientific Publications, Oxford

Chadwick, J. (1991) Coalbed methane potential. *Min. Mag.*, **165**(1), July, 27–30

Clifton, A.W. (1987) Pre-mining geotechnical investigations for a Saskatchewan coal mine. *Int. J. Surf. Min.* **1**, 27–34

Clymo, R.S. (1987) Rainwater-fed peat as a precursor to coal. In: *Coal and Coal-bearing Strata: Recent Advances* (Ed. A. C. Scott), *Spec. Publ. Geol. Soc. London No. 32*, pp. 17–23

Cohen, A.D. & Spackman, W. (1972) Methods of peat petrology and their application to reconstruction of paleoenvironments. *Geol. Soc. Am. Bull.* **83**, 129–142

Cohen, A.D. & Spackman, W. (1980) Phytogenic organic sediments and sedimentary environments in the Everglades mangrove complex of Florida. Part III. The alteration of plant material in peat, and origin of coal macerals. *Paleontogr. B* **162**, 144

Creedy, D.P. (1991) An introduction to geological aspects of methane occurrence and control in British deep coal mines. *Q. J. Engin. Geol.* **24**, 209–220

Daly, T.E. & Hagemann, R.F. (1976) Seismic methods for the delineation of coal deposits. *Coal Expl.* **1**, 192–226

Duff, P.McL.D. (1987) Mesozoic and Tertiary coals—a major world energy resource. *Mod. Geol.* **11**, 29–50

Durucan, S. & Edwards, J.S. (1986) The effects of stress and fracturing on permeability of coal. *Min. Sci. Technol.* **3**, 205–216

Elliott, R.E. (1973) Coal mining risks and reserves classification. In: *Septieme Congres Internationale de Strat. et de Carbonifere. Congres Internationale Stratigr. Geol. Carbonifere, Krefeld. C.R.* Vol. 7, No. 2, pp. 467–477, Ed. K.-H. Josten, Geologisches Landesamt Nordrhein-Westfalen, Krefeld

Elliott, T. & Lapido, K.O. (1981) Syn-sedimentary gravity slides (growth faults) in the coal measures of South Wales. *Nature* **291**, 220–222

Evans, R.B. & Greenwood, P.G. (1988) Outcrop magnetic susceptibility measurements as a means of differentiating rock types and their mineralisation. In: *Asia Mining '88*, Kuala Lumpur, Institute of Mining and Metallurgy, London, pp. 45–57

Ferm, J.C. (1979) Allegheny deltaic deposits: a model for the coal-bearing strata. In: *Carboniferous Depositional Environments in the Appalachian Region* (Eds J. C. Ferm and J. C. Horne), Carolina Coal Group, Dept of Geology, University of South Carolina, Columbia, USA, pp. 291–294

Ferm, J.C. & Staub, J.R. (1984) Depositional controls of mineable coal bodies. In: *Sedimentology of Coal and Coal-bearing Sequences* (Eds R. A. Rahmani & R. M. Flores), *Spec. Publ. Int. Assoc. Sedimentol. No. 7*, p. 275, Blackwell Scientific Publications, Oxford

Ferm, J.C., Staub, J.R., Baganz, B.P., Clark, W.J., Galloway, M.C.C., Hohos, E.F., Jones, T.L., Mathew, D., Pedlow, G.W. & Robinson, M.J. (1979) The shape of coal bodies. In: *Carboniferous Depositional Environments in the Appalachian Region* (Eds J. C. Ferm & J. C. Horne), Carolina Coal Group, Dept of Geology, University of South Carolina, Columbia, USA, pp. 605–619

Ferm, J.C. & Weisenfluh, G.A. (1991) *Cored Rocks of the Southern Appalachian Coalfields*. University of Kentucky, 93pp

Fielding, C.R. (1984) 'S' or 'Z' shaped coal seam splits in the coal measures of County Durham, UK. *Proc. Yorks. Geol. Soc.* **45**, 85–89

Fettweis, G.B. (1979) *World Coal Resources, Methods of Assessment and Results, Dev. Econ. Geol. Ser. No. 10*, Elsevier, Amsterdam, 415pp

Fettweis, G.B. (1985) Considerations on coal deposits on basis of coal production. In: *Xth Congress on Carboniferous Stratigraphy and Geology, Madrid, Spain, 1983, Symposium 5: Economic Geology: Coal Resources and Coal Exploration, Compte Rendu*, Instituto Geologico y Minero de Espana, Madrid, pp. 93–110

Findlay, M.J., Goulty, N.R. & Kragh, J.E. (1991) The crosshole seismic reflection method in opencast coal exploration. *First Break* **9**, 509–514

Fuels Research Institute (1978) Classification standards for South African coals. In: *Coal, Gold, Base Metals, Southern Africa*, pp. 67–87

Galligan, A.G. & Mengel, D.C. (1986) Code for reporting of identified coal resources and reserves. *Queensland Govt Min. J.* **87**, May, 201–203

Gan, H., Nandi, S.P. & Walker, P.L. Jr (1972) Nature of the porosity in American coals. *Fuel* **51**, 272–277

Gayer, R., Cole, J., Frodsham, K., Hartley, A.J., Hillier, B., Miliorizos, M. & White, S.C. (1991) The role of fluids in the evolution of the South Wales Coalfield foreland basin. *Proc. Ussher Soc.* **7**, 380–384

Geological Society Engineering Group Working Party (1970) The logging of rock cores for engineering purposes. *Q. J. Engin. Geol.* **3**, 1–24

Ghosh, P.K. (1976) Coal exploration in India. In: *Coal Exploration: Proceedings of the 1st International Exploration Symposium, 18–21 May, London, UK* (Ed. L. G. Muir), Miller Freeman Publications Inc., San Francisco, USA, pp. 648–659

Glover, H.G. (1975) Acidic & Ferruginous Mine Drainages: In: *The ecology of resource degradation and renewal. 15th Symposium of the British Ecological Society, 10–12 July 1973*, Blackwell Scientific Publications, Oxford, pp. 173–195

Gochioco, L. (1991) Advances in seismic reflection profiling for US coal exploration. *Geophysics* **10**(12), December, 24–29.

Goscinski, J.S. & Robinson, J.W. (1978) Megascopic description of coal drill cores. In: *Field Description of Coal: Symposium of the ASTM Committee D-5 on Coal & Coke, Ottawa, Canada, 22–23 September 1976*, ASTM Technical Publication 661 (Ed. R. R. Dutcher), 1916 Race Street, Philadelphia, Pennsylvania, USA, pp. 50–57

Goulty, N.R. & Brabham, P.J. (1984) Seismic refraction profiling in opencast coal exploration. *First Break* **2**, 26–34

Goulty, N.R., Daley, T.E., Walters, K.G. & Emsley, D.B. (1984) Location of dykes in coalfield exploration. *First Break* **2**, 15–21

Goulty, N.R., Thatcher, J.S., Findlay, M.J., Krach, J.E. & Jackson, P.D. (1990) Experimental investigation of crosshole seismic techniques for shallow coal exploration. *Q. J. Engin. Geol.* **23**, 217–228

Grayson, R.L., Wang, Y.J. & Sandford, R.L. (Eds) (1990) *Use of Computers in the Coal Industry: Proceedings of the 4th Conference on the Use of Computers in the Coal Industry, West Virginia University, Morgantown, WV, USA, 20–22 June 1990*, A. A. Balkema, Rotterdam, 275pp

Greaves, R.J. (1985) Coal prospect evaluation using high-resolution reflection seismology: a case study. *Min. Engin.* **37**, 1061–1064

Hagemann, H.W. (1978) Macropetrographic classification of brown coal. *Unpublished Proposal Presented to Members of the International Committee for Coal Petrology (ICCP), Essen, Germany, April 1978*

Hagemann, H.W. (1980) *Part 1. Identification of Lithotypes in Lignites of Southern Saskatchewan. Part 2. Macropetrographic Examination and Collecting Samples from Cores Stored at the Hat Creek Mine Site, British Columbia. Geol. Surv. Can. Open File Rep.*, 67pp

Hall, T.J. (1992) *The Quality Manual. The application of BS 5750 ISO 9001 EN 29001*. John Wiley & Sons, Chichester

Hargreaves, A.J. & Lunarzewski, L. (1985) Review of gas seam drainage in Australia. *Bull. Proc. Aust. Inst. Min. Metall.* **290**(1), 55–70

Haughton, S.H. (1969) Karroo System. In: *Geological History of Southern Africa*, Geological Society of South Africa, Ch. 13, pp. 349–415

Hill, I.A., Mansbridge, S. & Morris, D. (1990) A shallow reflection survey over a lignite deposit in Northern Ireland, UK. In: *Proceedings of the 6th Extractive Industry Geological Conference, Birmingham, UK, April 1989* (Eds J. W. Gaskarth and A. C. Lumsden), Institute of Geologists, London, pp. 238–250

Hilt, C. (1873) Die Beiziehungen zwischen der Zusammensetzung und den technischen Eigenschaften der Steinkohle. Bezirksvereinigung Ver. Deutsch. Ingenieure Zeitschrift, **17**(4), 194–202

Hooper, R.L. (1987) Factors affecting the magnetic susceptibility of baked rocks above a burned coal seam. *Int. J. Coal Geol.* **9**, 157–169

Horne, J.C. (1979) Sedimentary responses to contemporaneous tectonism. In: *Carboniferous Depositional Environments in the Appalachian Region* (Eds J. C. Ferm and J. C.

Horne), Carolina Coal Group, Dept of Geology, University of South Carolina, Columbia, USA, pp. 259–265

Horne, J.C., Howell, D.J. Baganz, B.P. & Ferm, J.C. (1978) *Splay Deposits as an Economic Factor in Coal Mining, Colorado Geol. Surv. Resour. Ser. No. 4*, pp. 89–100

Horne, J.C., Ferm, J.C., Caruccio, F.T. & Baganz, B.P. (1979) Depositional models in coal exploration and mine planning in Appalachian Region. In: *Carboniferous Depositional Environments in the Appalachian Region* (Eds J. C. Ferm and J. C. Horne), Carolina Coal Group, Dept of Geology, University of South Carolina, Columbia, USA, pp. 544–575

Huck, G. & Patteisky, K. (1964) Inkohlungsreaktionen unter Druck. *Fortschr. Geol. Rheinld. U. Wesf.* **12**, 551–558.

Hughes, V.J. & Kennett, B.L.N. (1983) The nature of seismic reflections from coal seams. *First Break* **1**, 9–18.

IEA Coal Research (1983) *Concise Guide to World Coalfields, World Coal Resources and Reserves Data Bank Service*, IEA Coal Research, London, 380pp

Ingram, H.A.P., Rycroft, D.W. & Williams, D.J.A. (1974) Anomalous transmission of water through certain peats. *J. Hydrol.* **22**, 213–218

International Coal Report (1991) *Coal Year 1991*. Ed. G. McCloskey, F.T. Business Information Ltd, London, 53pp

Jackson, L.J. (1981) *Geophysical Examination of Coal Deposits. IEA Coal Research Rep. No. ICTIS/TR13*, 116pp

Jerzykiewicz, T. & McLean, J.R. (1980) Lithostratigraphical and Sedimentological framework of Coal-bearing Upper Cretaceous and Lower Tertiary strata Coal Valley, Central Alberta Foothills. *Geol. Surv. Canada, Paper 79-12*, 47pp

Jones, T.A., Hamilton, D.E. & Johnson, C.R. (1986) *Contouring Geologic Surfaces with the Computer. Computer Methods in the Geosciences*, Van Nostrand Rheinhold, New York, 314pp

Jongmans, W.J., Koopmans, R.G. & Roos, G. (1936) Nomenclature of coal petrography. *Fuel* **15**, 14–15

Juch, D. & Working Group (1983) New methods of coal resources calculation. In: *Xth Congress on Carboniferous Stratigraphy and Geology, Madrid, Spain, 12–17 September. Symposium 5: Economic Geology: Coal Resources and Coal Exploration, Compte Rendu, Instituto Geologico y Minero de Espana, Madrid*, pp. 117–124

Karr, C. Jr (Ed.) (1978) *Analytical Methods for Coal and Coal Products*, Vols 1 & 2, Academic Press, New York

Knutson, H.A. (1983) Planning and implementation of coal exploration programs in reconnaissance geology for coal exploration. In: *Proceedings of the 4th International Coal Exploration Symposium, 15–20 May, Sydney, NSW, Australia*, 24pp

Komphasouk, B., Douang, S., Many, Aphay, Saman, Aneka & Thac, Nguyen Huu (1986) Main structural features and distribution of coal in Laos. In: *1st Cong. Geol. Indoch. Ho Chi Minh City, Vietnam 5–7 December 1986*, General Dept of Geology, Hanoi, Vietnam, pp. 579–589

Kragh, J.E., Goulty, N.R. & Findlay, M.J. (1991) Hole-to-surface reflection surveys for shallow coal exploration. *First Break* **9**, 335–344

Land, D.H. & Jones, C.M. (1987) Coal geology and exploration of part of the Tertiary Kutei Basin in East Kalimantan, Indonesia. In: *Coal and Coal-bearing Strata: Recent Advances* (Ed. A. C. Scott), *Spec. Publ. Geol. Soc. London No. 32*, pp. 235–255

Lindqvist, J.K., Hatherton, T. & Mumme, T.C. (1985) Magnetic anomalies resulting from baked sediments over burnt coal seams in southern New Zealand. *N.Z. J. Geol. Geophys.* **28**, 405–412

McCabe, P.J. (1984) Depositional environments of coal and coal-bearing strata. In: *Sedimentology of Coal and Coal-bearing Sequences* (Eds R. A. Rahmani and R. M. Flores), *Spec. Publ. Int. Assoc. Sedimentol. No. 7*, Blackwell Scientific Publications, Oxford, pp. 13–42

McCabe, P.J. (1987) Facies studies of coal and coal-bearing strata. In: *Coal and Coal-bearing Strata: Recent Advances* (Ed. A. C. Scott), *Spec. Publ. Geol. Soc. London No. 32*, pp. 51–66

McCabe, P.J. (1991) Geology of coal: environments of deposition. In: *Economic Geology of the USA* (Eds H. J. Gluskoter, D. D. Rice and R. B. Taylor), *DNAG: The Geology of North America*, Vol. P2, Geological Society of America, Boulder, CO, pp. 469–482

McFaull, K.S., Wicks, D.E., Sedwick, K. & Brandenburg, C. (1987) An analysis of the coal and coalbed methane resources of the Piceance Basin, Colorado US. In: *SPE/DOE 16418 Low Permeability Reservoir Symposium, Denver, CO, USA, 18–19 May 1987*, Society of Petroleum Engineers, pp. 283–295

Mahajan, O.P. (1982) Coal porosity. In: *Coal Structure* (Ed. R. A. Meyers), Academic Press, New York, pp. 51–86

Martinson, M.J. (1986) The dust explosion hazard in South African coal mines. *S.A. Min. World* **5**(1), 99–116

Mason, I.M., Buchanan, D.J. & Booer, A.K. (1980) Fault location by underground seismic survey. *IEE Proc. Part F127*, pp. 322–336

Milligan, E.N. (1976) Coal; status of coal exploration and mine development in Australia. In: *Circum Pacific Energy and Mineral Resources* (Eds M. T. Halbouty, J. C. Maher and H. M. Liam), *Am. Assoc. Petrol. Geol. Mem. No. 25*, 80–83

Milsom, J. (1989) *Field Geophysics. Geological Society of London Handbook*, Open University Press, Buckingham, 182pp

Ministry of Commerce and Industry, Korea (1974) *Geologic Atlas of the Chungnam Coalfield*, MCIK, Seoul, Korea, 30 plates

Montgomery, W.J. (1978) Standard laboratory test methods for coal and coke. In: *Analytical Methods for Coal and Coal Products* (Ed. C. Karr Jr), Vol. 1, Academic Press, New York

Moore, P.D. (1987) Ecological and hydrological aspects of peat formation. In: *Coal and Coal-bearing Strata: Recent Advances* (Ed. A. C. Scott), *Spec. Publ. Geol. Soc. London No. 32*, pp. 7–15.

National Coal Board (1982) *Technical Management of Water in the Coal Mining Industry*, National Coal Board Mining Department, London, 129pp

Nelson, W.J. (1987) Coal deposits of the United States. *Int. J. Coal Geol.* **8**, 355–365

Newman, J. & Newman, N.A. (1982) Reflectance anomalies in Pike River coals: evidence of variability in vitrinite type, with implications for maturation studies and 'Suggate' rank. *N.Z. J. Geol. Geophys.* **25**, 233–243

Osborne, D. (1988) *Coal Preparation Technology*, 2 vols, Graham & Trotman, London

Parasnis, D.S. (1966) *Mining Geophysics. Methods Geochem. Geophy. No. 3*, Elsevier, Amsterdam, 356pp

Parasnis, D.S. (1986) *Principles of Applied Geophysics*, 4th edn,

Chapman & Hall, London, 402pp

Patzen, Wu. (1974) *Coal Resources of Taiwan—Summary.* Circum-Pacific Energy and Mineral Resources Meeting, 26–30 August, Honolulu. *Am. Assoc. Petrol. Geol. Mem. No. 25*, pp. 89–93

Peace, D.G. (1979) Surface reflection seismic—looking underground from the surface. In: *Coal Exploration: Proceedings of the International Coal Symposium, Denver, CO, USA, Vol. 2* (Ed. G. O. Argall), Miller Freeman Publications Inc., San Francisco, USA, pp. 230–266

Pinchin, J., Baquiran, G.B., Coleby, B.R. & Ryan, D. (1982) MINI-SOSIE. In: *Seismic Techniques for Coal Exploration in Australia and the Philippines. Proc. 4th International Coal Explor. Symposium, Sydney, Australia, 15–20 May*, pp. 1–14

Price, M. (1985) *Introducing Groundwater*, Allen & Unwin, London, 195pp

Rahmani, R.A. & Flores, R.M. (1984) Sedimentology of coal and coal-bearing sequences of North America: a historical review. In: *Sedimentology of Coal and Coal-bearing Sequences* (Eds R. A. Rahmani and R. M. Flores), *Spec. Publ. Int. Assoc. Sedimentol. No. 7*, Blackwell Scientific Publications, Oxford, pp. 3–10

Raymant, P. (1991) *Unpublished Notes on Interpretation of Geophysical Logs in Coal Exploration*, 38pp

Ricketts, B.D. & Embry, A.F. (1986) Coal in the Canadian Arctic archipelago. A potential resource. *GEOS (Ottawa)*, **15**(1), 16–18

Robertson Research (Australia) Pty Ltd (1987) *Coal Geologist's Manual*, (Ed. P. G. Strauss & C. M. Atkinson), 172pp

Robinson, P.L. (1967) The Indian Gondwana formations—a review: *1st Symposium on Gondwanaland Stratigraphy*, Mar del Plata, Argentina, 1–4 October, IUGS (September 1967), pp. 201–268

Ruter, H. & Schepers, R. (1979) In-seam seismic methods for the detection of discontinuities applied to West German coal deposits. In: *Coal Exploration: Proceedings of the 2nd International Coal Exploration Symposium, October 1978, Denver, CO, USA* (Ed. G. O. Argall), Vol. 2, Miller Freeman Publications Inc, San Francisco, USA, pp. 267–293

Schiller, E.A. (1982) Coal in Canada. *Min. Mag.* **147**(1), July, pp. 40–47

Schiller, E.A. (1983) Coal in Western Australia. *Min. Mag.* **148**(2), February, pp. 110–115

Schiller, E.A. & Grieve, D. (1983) The coalfields of SE British Columbia. *Min. Mag.* **149**(2), August, pp. 81–87

Schopf, J.M. (1960) Field description and sampling of coal beds. *US Geol. Surv. Bull.* **1111-B**, 70pp (Plates 6–27)

Seyler, C.A. (1899) The chemical classification of coal. *Proc. South Wales Inst. Eng.* **21**, 483–526; *Inst. Eng.* **47**(3), 1–17

Seyler, C.A. (1931) I. Petrology and the classification of coal. II. Fuel technology and the classification of coal. *Proc. South Wales Inst. Eng.* **47**, 557–592

Seyler, C.A. (1938) Petrology and the classification of coal. *Proc. S. Wales Inst. Eng.* **53**, 254–327

Shabad, T. (1986) Review of the Soviet coal industry. *Int. Geol. Rev.* **28**(3), 372–376

Sherborn Hills, E. (1975) *Elements of Structural Geology*, 2nd edn, Chapman & Hall, London, 502pp

Shimoyama, T. & Iijima, A. (1976) Influence of temperature on coalification of Tertiary coal in Japan—summary. *Circum Pacific Energy and Mineral Resources* (Eds M. T. Halbouty, J. C. Maher and H. M. Liam), 26–30 August

1974, *Am. Assoc. Petrol. Geol. Mem. No. 25*, pp. 98–103

Smith, A.H.V. (1968) Seam profiles and seam characteristics. In: *Coal and Coal-bearing Strata* (Eds D. G. Murchison and T. S. Westoll), Oliver & Boyd, London, pp. 31–40

Stach, E. (1982) *Textbook of Coal Petrology*, 3rd Edn. Gebrüder Borntraeger, Berlin, 535pp

Stach, E., Mackowski, M.Th., Teichmuller, M., Taylor, G.H., Chandra, D. & Teichmuller, R. (1975) *Textbook of Coal Petrology*, 2nd edn, Gebrüder Borntraeger, Berlin, 428pp

Standards Association of Australia (1970) *Symbols for the Graphical Representation of Coal Seams, AS K183–1970.* Sydney, Australia, 8pp

Standards Association of Australia (1982) *Guide for the taking of samples from hard coals in situ, AS 2519–1982.* Sydney, Australia

Standards Association of Australia (1987) *Classification and coding systems for Australian coals, AS 2096–1987.* Sydney, Australia

Staplin, F.L. (1969) Sedimentary organic matter, organic metamorphism, and oil and gas occurrences. *Can. Soc. Petrol. Geol. Bull.* **17**, 47–56

Staub, J.R. & Cohen, A.D. (1979) The Snuggedy Swamp of South Carolina. A back-barrier estuarine coal-forming environment. In: *Carboniferous Depositional Environments in the Appalachian Region* (Ed. J. C. Ferm & J. C. Horne), Carolina Coal Group, Dept of Geology, University of South Carolina, Columbia, USA, pp. 499–508

Steenblik, R.R. (1986) *International Coal Resource Assessment: Working Paper No. 73*, IEA Coal Research, London, 79pp

Stopes, M.C. (1919) On the four visible ingredients in banded bituminous coals. *Proc. Royal Soc.* **90B**, 470–487

Stopes, M.C. (1935) On the petrology of banded bituminous coals. *Fuel* **14**, 4–13

Stutzer, O. & Noe, A.C. (1940) *Geology of Coal*, University of Chicago Press, Chicago, 461pp

Styan, W.B. & Bustin, R.M. (1983) Sedimentology of Frazer River delta peat: a modern analogue for some ancient deltaic coals. *Int. J. Coal Geol.* **3**, 101–143

Suggate, R.P. (1982) Low rank sequences and scales of organic metamorphism. *J. Petrol. Geol.* **4**, 377–392

Suggate, R.P. & Lowery, J.H. (1982) The influences of moisture content on vitrinite reflectance and the assessment of maturation of coal. *N.Z. J. Geol. Geophys.* **25**, 227–231

Swardt, A.M.J. & Casey, C.P. (1963) The coal resources of Nigeria. *Geol. Surv. Nigeria Bull.* **28**, 110pp

Tasker, B.S. (1985) Technical note on polygonal blocks of influence in triangular grids. *Bull. Proc. Aust. Inst. Min. Metall.* **290**(3), 71–72

Teichmuller, M. (1987) Coalification studies and their application to geology. In: *Coal and Coal-bearing Strata: Recent Advances* (Ed. A. C. Scott), *Spec. Publ. Geol. Soc. London, No. 32*, pp. 127–169

Teichmuller, M. & Teichmuller, R. (1968) Geological aspects of coal metamorphism. In: *Coal and Coal-bearing Strata* (Eds D. G. Murchison and T. S. Westoll), Oliver & Boyd, Edinburgh, pp. 233–267

Teichmuller, M. & Teichmuller, R. (1982) The geological basis of coal formation. In: *Stach's Book of Coal Petrography*, 3rd edn (Eds E. Stach, M.-Th. Mackowski, M. Teichmuller, G. H. Taylor, D. Chandra & R. Teichmuller). Gebrüder Borntraeger, Berlin, pp. 5–86

Telford, W.M., Geldart, L.P. & Sheriff, R.E. (1990) *Applied Geophysics*, 2nd edn, Cambridge University Press, Cambridge. 770pp

Thomas, L.P. (1967) A sedimentary study of the sandstones between the horizons of the Four Feet Coal and the Gorllwyn Coal of the Middle Coal Measures of the South Wales Coalfield. *Unpublished Ph.D. Thesis*, University of Wales

Thomas, L.P., Evans, R.B. & Downing, R.A. (1983) The geothermal potential of the Devonian and Carboniferous rocks of South Wales. In: *Investigation of Geothermal Potential of UK: Br. Geol. Surv. Rep. Ser.*, 72pp

United Nations Economic Commission for Europe (1956) *International Classification of Hard Coals*. UN Pub. No. 1956 11. E.4. E/ECE/247, E/ECE/COAL110. UN, Geneva, Switzerland

United Nations Economic Commission for Europe (1957) *International Classification of Brown Coals*. UN Pub. No. 1957 11. E.Min 20. UN, Geneva, Switzerland

United Nations Economic and Social Council (1979) *The International Classification of Mineral Resources, Economic Report No. 1 (E/C.7/104), May 1979*. Annex to Natural Resources & Energy 4(1), Centre for Natural Resources, Energy & Transport, UN Secretariat, New York, USA

van Krevelen, D.W. (1961) *Coal*, Elsevier, Amsterdam, 514pp

Venter, R.H. (1976) A statistical approach to the calculation of coal reserves for the plains region of Alberta. *Can. Inst. Min. Bull.* **69**(771), July, 49–52

Verma, R.K. & Bandyopadhyay, T.K. (1983) Use of resistivity method in geological mapping—case histories from Raniganj Coalfield, India. *Geophys. Prospect.* **31**, 490–507

von Schwartzenberg, T. (1986) The Air Laya coal deposit, south Sumatra, Indonesia. *Braunkohle* **38**(11), 307–315

Ward, C.R. (1984) *Coal Geology and Coal Technology*, Blackwell Scientific Publications, Oxford, 345pp

Williams, E.G. & Keith, M.L. (1963) Relationship between sulphur in coals and the occurrence of marine roof beds. *Econ. Geol.* **58**, 720–729

Wood, G.H. Jr, Kehn, T.A., Devereux Carter, M. & Culbertson, W.C. (1983) *Coal Reserve Classification System of the US Geological Survey. USGS Circular No. 891*, 65pp

World Energy Council (1978) *An Appraisal of World Coal Resources and their Future Availability*. Full report on coal resources issued by WEC Conservation Commission at tenth WEC Conference, Istanbul, 1978. IPC Science and Technology Press, 139pp

Ziolkowski, A. & Lerwill, W.E. (1979) A simple approach to high resolution seismic profiling for coal. *Geophys. Prosp.* **27**, 360–393

Appendix 1
List of international and national standards used in coal analysis and evaluation

The following standards are given for coal and associated practices; specific tests for coke products which are separate from coal tests are not included.

BRITISH STANDARDS INSTITUTION (BSI)

Breckland, Linford Wood, Milton Keynes MK14 6LE, UK

Recent amendments to these standards are given after the title of the standard, together with the date of the amendment. Years in which the standard was reconfirmed are shown in parenthesis after the year of issue. Complete copies of BSI standards can be bought from BSI Sales at the above address.

BS 1016 Methods for the analysis and testing of coal and coke. Parts 1–21

BS 1016, Part 1, 1973 (1989) Total moisture of coal

BS 1016, Part 3, 1973 Proximate analysis of coal

BS 1016, Part 5, 1977 Gross calorific value of coal and coke

BS 1016, Part 6, 1977 Ultimate analysis of coal

BS 1016, Part 8, 1977 (1984) Chlorine in coal and coke

BS 1016, Part 9, 1977 (1989) Phosphorus in coal and coke

BS 1016, Part 10, 1977 (1989) Arsenic in coal and coke

BS 1016, Part 11, 1977 (1987) Forms of sulphur in coal

BS 1016, Part 12, 1980 (1989) Caking and swelling properties of coal

BS 1016, Part 14, 1963 (1979) Analysis of coal ash and coke ash

BS 1016, Part 15, 1970 (1979) Fusibility of coal ash and coke ash

BS 1016, Part 16, 1981 (1989) Methods for reporting results

BS 1016, Part 17, 1979 (1987) Size analysis of coal

BS 1016, Part 19, 1980 (1990) Determination of the index of abrasion of coal

BS 1016, Part 20, 1981 (1987)   Determination of the Hardgrove grinda-
bility index of coal
BS 1016, Part 21, 1981 (1987)   Determination of moisture hold-ing
capacity of hard coal
BS 1016, Part 107.3, 1990   Determination of swelling properties of coal
using a dilatometer
BS 1017, Part 1, 1977 (1989)   Methods for sampling of coal
BS 1293–2074, 1977   Methods for the size analysis of coal and coke
BS 3323, 1978 (1987)   Glossary of coal terms
BS 3552, 1962   Glossary of terms used in coal preparation
BS 5750, ISO 9000 1979 (1987)   A positive contribution to better busi-
ness
BS 5930, 1981   Code of practice for site investigations
BS 6068, Part 0, 1988   Introduction to water quality
BS 7022, 1989   Guide for geophysical logging of boreholes for hydrolo-
gical purposes
BS 7067, 1990   Guide to determination and presentation of float and
sink characteristics of raw coal and of products from coal preparation
plants

INTERNATIONAL ORGANISATION FOR STANDARDISATION (ISO)

Casa Postale 56, CH 1211, Geneve 20, Switzerland

ISO 157, 1975   Hard coal—determination of forms of sulphur
ISO 331, 1975   Coal—determination of moisture in the analysis
sample, direct gravimetric method
ISO 332, 1981   Coal—determination of nitrogen, macro Kjeldahl
method
ISO 333, 1979   Coal—determination of nitrogen, semi-micro Kjeldahl
method
ISO 334, 1975   Coal and coke—determination of total sulphur, Eschka
method
ISO 335, 1974   Hard coal—determination of caking power, Roga test
ISO 348, 1981   Hard coal—determination of moisture in the analysis
sample, direct volumetric method
ISO 349, 1975   Hard coal—Audibert–Arnu dilatometer test
ISO 351, 1984   Solid mineral fuels—determination of total sulphur,
high temperature combustion method
ISO 352, 1981   Solid mineral fuels—determination of chlorine, high
temperature combustion method
ISO 501, 1981   Coal—determination of the crucible swelling number
ISO 502, 1982   Coal—determination of caking power, Gray–King coke
test
ISO 540, 1981   Solid mineral fuels—determination of fusibility of ash,
high temperature tube method
ISO 562, 1981   Hard coal and coke—determination of volatile matter
content
ISO 587, 1981   Solid mineral fuels—determination of chlorine using
Eschka mixture
ISO 589, 1981   Hard coal—determination of total moisture

ISO 601, 1981 Solid mineral fuels—determination of arsenic content using the standard silver diethyldithiocarbamate photometric method of ISO 2590

ISO 602, 1983 Coal—determination of mineral matter

ISO 609, 1975 Coal and coke—determination of carbon and hydrogen, high temperature combustion method

ISO 622, 1981 Solid mineral fuels—determination of phosphorus content, reduced molybdophosphate photometric method

ISO 625, 1975 Coal and coke—determination of carbon and hydrogen, Leibig method

ISO 647, 1974 Brown coals and lignites—determination of the yields of tar, water, gas and coke residue by low temperature distillation

ISO 923, 1975 Coal cleaning test, expression and presentation of results

ISO 925, 1980 Solid mineral fuels—determination of carbon dioxide content, gravimetric method

ISO 975, 1985 Brown coals and lignites—determination of yield of toluene-soluble extract

ISO 1015, 1975 Brown coals and lignites—determination of moisture content, direct volumetric method

ISO 1017, 1985 Brown coals and lignites—determination of acetone-soluble material (resinous substances) in the toluene-soluble extract

ISO 1018, 1975 Hard coal—determination of moisture holding capacity

ISO 1170, 1976 Coal and coke—calculation of analyses to different bases

ISO 1171, 1981 Solid mineral fuels—determination of ash

ISO/R 1213/2, 1971 Vocabulary of terms relating to solid mineral fuels, part 2, terms relating to coal sampling and analysis

ISO 1928, 1976 Solid mineral fuels—determination of gross calorific value by the calorimeter bomb method and calculation of net calorific value

ISO 1952, 1976 Brown coals and lignites—method of extraction for the determination of sodium and potassium in dilute hydrochloric acid

ISO 1953, 1972 Hard coals—size analysis

ISO 1988, 1975 Hard coals—sampling

ISO 1994, 1976 Hard coals—determination of oxygen content

ISO 2950, 1974 Brown coals and lignites—classification by types on the basis of total moisture content and tar yield

ISO 5068, 1983 Brown coals and lignites—determination of moisture content, indirect gravimetric method

ISO 5069, 1983 Brown coals and lignites—principles of sampling
  Part 1, sampling for determination of moisture content and for general analysis
  Part 2, sample preparation for determination of moisture content and for general analysis

ISO 5073, 1985 Brown coal and lignite—determination of humic acids

ISO 5074, 1980 Hard coal—determination of Hardgrove grindability index

ISO 7404 Methods for the petrographic analysis of bituminous coal and anthracite
    1984 Part 1, glossary of terms
    1985 Part 2, method of preparation of coal samples
    1984 Part 3, method of determining maceral group composition

1988   Part 4, method of determining microlithotype, carbo-
minerite and minerite composition
1984   Part 5, method of determining microscopically the
reflectance of vitrinite
ISO 8264, 1989 Hard coal—determination of the swelling properties
using a dilatometer
ISO 9000   see BS 5750

STANDARDS ASSOCIATION OF AUSTRALIA

80–86 Arthur Street, North Sydney, New South Wales 2060, Australia

AS 2418   Glossary of terms relating to solid mineral fuels
   2418.1-1980   Terms relating to coal preparation
   2418.2-1982   Terms relating to coal mining and geology
   2418.3-1982   Terms relating to brown coal
   2418.4-1982   Terms relating to sampling, sample preparation, analysis, testing and statistics
   2418.5-1982   Terms relating to the petrographic analysis of bituminous coal and anthracite (hard coal)
   2418.6-1982   Terms relating to coal utilization and coke
   2418.7-1982   Terms relating to coal classification
AS 2519-1982   Guide to the evaluation of hard coal deposits using borehole techniques
AS 2617-1983   Guide for the taking of samples from hard coal seams *in situ*
AS 2646   Sampling of solid mineral fuels
   2616.2-1984   Hard coal—sampling from moving streams
   2616.4-1984   Hard coal—sampling from stationary situations
   2616.6-1984   Hard coal—preparation of samples
AS 1038   Coal and coke—analysis and testing
   1038.1-1980   Total moisture in hard coal
   1038.3-1989   Proximate analysis of higher rank coal
   1038.5   Gross specific energy of coal and coke
   1038.5.1-1988   Adiabatic calorimeters
   1038.5.2-1989   Automatic isothermal-type calorimeters
   1038.6   Ultimate analysis of higher rank coal
   1038.6.1-1986   Determination of carbon and hydrogen
   1038.6.2-1986   Determination of nitrogen
   1038.6.3.1-1986   Determination of total sulphur (Eschka method)
   1038.6.3.2-1986   Determination of total sulphur (high temperature combustion method)
   1038.6.3.3-1986   Determination of total sulphur (infrared method)
   1038.8-1980   Chlorine in coal and coke
   1038.9-1977   Phosphorus in coal and coke
   1038.9.3-1991   Coal and coke—phosphorus–ash digestion method
   1038.10-1980   Arsenic in coal and coke
   1038.10.1-1986   Determination of trace elements—determination of eleven trace elements in coal, coke and fly ash—flame absorption spectrometric method

1038.10.3-1988   Determination of trace elements—coal, coke and fly ash—determination of boron content—spectrophotometric method

1038.10.4-1989   Determination of trace elements—coal, coke and fly ash—determination of fluorine content—pyrohydrolysis method

1038.11-1982   Forms of sulphur in coal

1038.12.1-1984   Determination of crucible swelling number of coal

1038.12.2-1990   Carbonization properties of higher rank coal—determination of Gray–King coke type

1038.12.3-1984   Determination of the dilatometer characteristics of higher rank coal

1038.14.1-1981   Analysis of coal ash, coke ash and mineral matter (borate fusion–flame atomic absorption spectrometric method)

1038.14.2-1985   Analysis of higher rank coal ash and coke ash (acid digestion–flame atomic absorption spectrometric method)

1038.15-1987   Fusibility of higher rank coal ash and coke ash

1038.17-1989   Determination of moisture-holding capacity (equilibrium moisture) of higher rank coal

1038.19-1989   Determination of the abrasion index of higher rank coal

1038.20–1981   Hardgrove grindability index of hard coal

1038.21-1983   Determination of the relative density and apparent relative density of hard coal

1038.22-1983   Direct determination of mineral matter and water of hydration of minerals in hard coal

1038.23-1984   Determination of carbonate carbon in higher rank coal

AS 1661-1979   Method for float and sink testing of hard coal and presentation of results

As 2137-1981   Hard coal—determination of plastic properties by the Gieseler plastometer

AS 2434   Methods for the analysis and testing of lower rank coal and its chars

2434.1-1991   Determination of the total moisture content of lower rank coal

2434.2-1983   Determination of the volatile matter in low rank coal

2434.3-1984   Determination of the moisture-holding capacity of lower rank coals

2434.4-1985   Determination of the apparent density of dried lower rank coal and its chars (mercury displacement method)

2434.5-1984   Determination of moisture in bulk samples and in analysis samples of char from lower rank coal

2434.6.1-1986   Ultimate analysis of lower rank coal

2434.7-1986   Determination of moisture in the analysis sample of lower rank coal

2434.9-1991   Determination of four acid-extractable inorganic ions in lower rank coal

AS 2486-1989   Methods for microscopical determination of the reflectance of coal macerals

AS 2579   Hard coal—froth flotation testing

2579.1-1983   Laboratory procedure

AS 2856-1986   Coal—maceral analysis

AS 3881-1991   Higher rank coal—size analysis

AS 3899-1991   Higher rank coal and coke—bulk density

AS 3980-1991   Guide to the determination of desorbable gas content of coal seams—direct method

AS 2061-1989   Preparation of coal samples for incident light microscopy
AS 2096-1987   Classification and coding systems for Australian coals
AS 2916-1986   Symbols for graphical representation of coal seams and
associated strata

AMERICAN SOCIETY FOR TESTING AND MATERIALS (ASTM)

1916 Race Street, Philadelphia, PA 19103-1187 USA

Figures after standard number give the year of most recent re-approval.

D 121-91   Definitions of terms relating to coal and coke
D 197-87   Sampling and fineness test of pulverised coal
D 291-86   Cubic foot weight of crushed bituminous coal
D 310-80   Test for size of anthracite
D 311-76   Sieve analysis of crushed bituminous coal
D 388-91   Classification of coals by rank
D 410-76   Sieve analysis of coal
D 409-91   Grindability of coal by the Hardgrove–Machine method
D 431-76   Designating the size of coal from its sieve analysis
D 440-86   Drop shatter test for coal
D 441-86   Tumbler set for coal
D 547-80   Test for index of dustiness of coal and coke
D 720-83   Free swelling index of coal
D1412-89   Equilibrium moisture of coal at 96% to 97% relative humid-
ity and 30°C
D1756-89   Carbon dioxide in coal
D1757-86   Sulphur in ash from coal and coke
D1857-87   Fusibility of coal and coke ash
D2013-86   Samples, coal, preparing for analysis
D2014-90   Expansion or contraction of coal by the Sole heated oven
D2015-91   Gross calorific value of coal and coke by the Adiabatic bomb
calorimeter
D1989-91   Gross calorific value of coal and coke by microprocessor
controlled Isoperibol calorimeters
D2234-89   Collection of a gross sample of coal
D2361-91   Chlorine in coal
D2492-90   Forms of sulphur in coal
D2639-90   Plastic properties of coal by the constant-torque Gieseler
plastometer
D2795-86   Analysis of coal and coke ash
D2796-88   Megascopic description of coal and coal seams and micro-
scopical description and analysis of coal
D2797-90   Preparing coal samples for microscopical analysis by
reflected light
D2798-88   Microscopical determination of the reflectance of the or-
ganic components in a polished specimen of coal
D2799-86   Microscopical determination of volume percent of physical
components of coal
D2961-87   Moisture, total, in coal reduced to No. 8 (2.38 mm) top sieve
size (limited purpose method)

D3173-89   Proximate analysis of coal and coke
D3178-87   Moisture in the analysis sample of coal and coke
D3174-89   Ash in the analysis sample of coal and coke from coal
D3175-89   Volatile matter in the analysis sample of coal and coke
D3176-89   Ultimate analysis of coal and coke
D3177-89   Total sulphur in the analysis sample of coal and coke
D3178-89   Carbon and hydrogen in the analysis sample of coal and coke
D3179-89   Nitrogen in the analysis sample of coal and coke
D3180-89   Calculating coal and coke analyses from as-determined to different bases
D3286-91   Gross calorific value of coal and coke by the Isoperibol bomb calorimeter
D3302-89   Total moisture in coal
D3682-87   Major and minor elements in coal and coke ash by atomic absorption
D3683-89   Trace elements in coal and coke ash by atomic absorption
D3684-88   Total mercury in coal by the oxygen bomb combustion/atomic absorption method
D3761-91   Total fluorine in coal by the oxygen bomb combustion/ion selective electrode method
D4182-91   Evaluation of laboratories using ASTM procedures in the sampling and analysis of coal and coke
D4208-88   Total chlorine in coal by the oxygen bomb combustion/ion selective electrode method
D4239-83   Sulphur in the analysis sample of coal and coke using high temperature tube furnace combustion methods
D4371-91   Washability characteristics of coal
D4596-86   Collection of channel samples of coal in the mine
D4621-86   Accountability and quality control in the coal analysis laboratory
D4749-87   Sieve analysis for coal, performing and designating coal size
D5016-89   Sulphur in ash from coal and coke using high temperature tube furnace combustion method with infrared absorption
D5142-90   Proximate analysis of the analysis sample of coal and coke by instrumental procedures

Appendix 2
Tables of true and apparent dip; slope angles, gradients and percentage slope

The following table gives values of apparent dip calculated from true dip and angle between strike and direction of section. All values are in degrees. Values of true dip can be calculated from: tan (apparent dip) = tan (true dip) × sin (angle between strike and direction of section).

True dip	Angle between strike and direction of section															
	80	75	70	65	60	55	50	45	40	35	30	25	20	15	10	5
10	10	10	9	9	9	8	8	7	6	6	5	4	3	3	2	1
15	15	14	14	14	13	12	12	10	10	9	8	6	5	4	3	1
20	20	19	19	18	18	17	16	14	13	12	10	9	7	5	4	2
25	25	24	24	23	22	21	20	18	17	15	13	11	9	7	5	2
30	30	29	28	28	27	25	24	22	20	18	16	14	11	9	6	3
35	35	34	33	32	31	30	28	26	24	22	19	16	13	10	7	4
40	40	39	38	37	36	35	33	31	28	26	23	20	16	12	8	4
45	45	44	43	42	41	39	37	35	33	30	27	23	19	15	10	5
50	50	49	48	47	46	44	42	40	37	34	31	27	22	17	12	6
55	55	54	53	52	51	49	48	45	43	39	36	31	26	20	14	7
60	60	59	58	58	56	55	53	51	48	45	41	36	30	24	17	9
65	65	64	64	63	62	60	59	57	54	51	46	42	36	29	20	11
70	70	69	69	69	68	67	65	63	60	58	54	49	43	35	25	13
75	75	74	74	74	73	72	71	69	67	65	62	58	52	44	33	18
80	80	80	79	79	78	78	77	76	75	73	71	67	63	56	45	26
85	85	85	85	84	84	84	83	83	82	81	80	78	76	71	63	45

Dips of strata and land surfaces can be expressed in either angles, gradients or percentage slope. The values most commonly encountered are included in this table.

Angle of slope (degrees)	Gradient	Percentage slope
1	1:57	1.7
2	1:29	3.5
3	1:19	5.2
4	1:14	7.0
5	1:11.4	8.7
6	1:9.5	10.5
7	1:8.1	12.3
8	1:7.1	14.1
9	1:6.3	15.8
10	1:5.7	17.6
11	1:5.1	19.4
12	1:4.7	21.3
13	1:4.3	23.1
14	1:4.0	24.9
15	1:3.7	26.8
16	1:3.5	28.7
17	1:3.3	30.6
18	1:3.1	32.5
19	1:2.9	34.4
20	1:2.7	36.4
25	1:2.1	46.5
30	1:1.7	57.7
35	1:1.4	70.0
40	1:1.2	83.9
45	1:1.0	100.0
50	1:0.8	119.2
55	1:0.7	142.8
60	1:0.6	173.2
65	1:0.5	214.5
70	1:0.4	274.7
75	1:0.3	373.2
80	1:0.2	567.1
85	1:0.1	1143.0
90	1:0	—

Appendix 3
Calorific values expressed in different units

MJ/kg	Btu/lb (MJ/kg × 429.923)	kcal/kg (MJ/kg × 239.006)	lb/lb (MJ/kg × 0.442763)	MJ/kg	Btu/lb (MJ/kg × 429.923)	kcal/kg (MJ/kg × 239.006)	lb/lb (MJ/kg × 0.442763)
4.5	1935	1076	1.99	7.6	3267	1816	3.36
4.6	1978	1099	2.04	7.7	3310	1840	3.41
4.7	2021	1123	2.08	7.8	3353	1864	3.45
4.8	2064	1147	2.13	7.9	3396	1888	3.50
4.9	2107	1171	2.17				
				8.0	3439	1912	3.54
5.0	2150	1195	2.21	8.1	3482	1936	3.59
5.1	2193	1219	2.26	8.2	3525	1960	3.63
5.2	2236	1243	2.30	8.3	3568	1984	3.67
5.3	2279	1267	2.35	8.4	3611	2008	3.72
5.4	2322	1291	2.39	8.5	3654	2032	3.76
5.5	2365	1315	2.44	8.6	3697	2055	3.81
5.6	2408	1338	2.48	8.7	3740	2079	3.85
5.7	2451	1362	2.52	8.8	3783	2103	3.90
5.8	2494	1386	2.57	8.9	3826	2127	3.94
5.9	2537	1410	2.61				
				9.0	3869	2151	3.98
6.0	2580	1434	2.66	9.1	3912	2175	4.03
6.1	2623	1458	2.70	9.2	3955	2199	4.07
6.2	2666	1482	2.75	9.3	3998	2223	4.12
6.3	2709	1506	2.79	9.4	4041	2247	4.16
6.4	2752	1530	2.83	9.5	4084	2271	4.21
6.5	2794	1554	2.88	9.6	4127	2294	4.25
6.6	2837	1577	2.92	9.7	4170	2318	4.29
6.7	2880	1601	2.97	9.8	4213	2342	4.34
6.8	2923	1625	3.01	9.9	4256	2366	4.38
6.9	2966	1649	3.06				
				10.0	4299	2390	4.43
7.0	3009	1673	3.10	10.1	4342	2414	4.47
7.1	3052	1697	3.14	10.2	4385	2438	4.52
7.2	3095	1721	3.19	10.3	4428	2462	4.56
7.3	3138	1745	3.23	10.4	4471	2486	4.60
7.4	3181	1769	3.28	10.5	4514	2510	4.65
7.5	3224	1793	3.32	10.6	4557	2533	4.69

MJ/kg	Btu/lb (MJ/kg × 429.923)	kcal/kg (MJ/kg × 239.006)	lb/lb (MJ/kg × 0.442763)	MJ/kg	Btu/lb (MJ/kg × 429.923)	kcal/kg (MJ/kg × 239.006)	lb/lb (MJ/kg × 0.442763)
10.7	4600	2557	4.74	15.4	6621	3681	6.82
10.8	4643	2581	4.78	15.5	6664	3705	6.86
10.9	4686	2605	4.83	15.6	6707	3728	6.91
				15.7	6750	3752	6.95
11.0	4729	2629	4.87	15.8	6793	3776	7.00
11.1	4772	2653	4.91	15.9	6836	3800	7.04
11.2	4815	2677	4.96				
11.3	4858	2701	5.00	16.0	6879	3824	7.08
11.4	4901	2725	5.05	16.1	6922	3848	7.13
11.5	4944	2749	5.09	16.2	6965	3872	7.17
11.6	4987	2772	5.14	16.3	7008	3896	7.22
11.7	5030	2796	5.18	16.4	7051	3920	7.26
11.8	5073	2820	5.22	16.5	7094	3944	7.31
11.9	5116	2844	5.27	16.6	7137	3967	7.35
				16.7	7180	3991	7.39
12.0	5159	2868	5.31	16.8	7223	4015	7.44
12.1	5202	2892	5.36	16.9	7266	4039	7.48
12.2	5245	2916	5.40				
12.3	5288	2940	5.45				
12.4	5331	2964	5.49	17.0	7309	4063	7.53
12.5	5374	2988	5.53	17.1	7352	4087	7.57
12.6	5417	3011	5.58	17.2	7395	4111	7.62
12.7	5460	3035	5.62	17.3	7438	4135	7.66
12.8	5503	3059	5.67	17.4	7481	4159	7.70
12.9	5546	3083	5.71	17.5	7524	4183	7.75
				17.6	7567	4207	7.79
13.0	5589	3107	5.76	17.7	7610	4230	7.84
13.1	5632	3131	5.80	17.8	7653	4254	7.88
13.2	5675	3155	5.84	17.9	7696	4278	7.93
13.3	5718	3179	5.89				
13.4	5761	3203	5.93				
13.5	5804	3227	5.98	18.0	7739	4302	7.97
13.6	5847	3250	6.02	18.1	7782	4326	8.01
13.7	5890	3274	6.07	18.2	7825	4350	8.06
13.8	5933	3298	6.11	18.3	7868	4374	8.10
13.9	5976	3322	6.15	18.4	7911	4398	8.15
				18.5	7954	4422	8.19
14.0	6019	3346	6.20	18.6	7997	4446	8.24
14.1	6062	3370	6.24	18.7	8040	4469	8.28
14.2	6105	3394	6.29	18.8	8083	4493	8.32
14.3	6148	3418	6.33	18.9	8126	4517	8.37
14.4	6191	3442	6.38				
14.5	6234	3466	6.42	19.0	8169	4541	8.41
14.6	6277	3489	6.46	19.1	8212	4565	8.46
14.7	6320	3513	6.51	19.2	8255	4589	8.50
14.8	6363	3537	6.55	19.3	8298	4613	8.55
14.9	6406	3561	6.60	19.4	8341	4637	8.59
				19.5	8383	4661	8.63
15.0	6449	3585	6.64	19.6	8426	4685	8.68
15.1	6492	3609	6.69	19.7	8469	4708	8.72
15.2	6535	3633	6.73	19.8	8512	4732	8.77
15.3	6578	3657	6.77	19.9	8555	4756	8.81

MJ/kg	Btu/lb (MJ/kg × 429.923)	kcal/kg (MJ/kg × 239.006)	lb/lb (MJ/kg × 0.442763)	MJ/kg	Btu/lb (MJ/kg × 429.923)	kcal/kg (MJ/kg × 239.006)	lb/lb (MJ/kg × 0.442763)
20.0	8598	4780	8.86	24.8	10 662	5927	10.98
20.1	8641	4804	8.90	24.9	10 705	5951	11.02
20.2	8684	4828	8.94				
20.3	8727	4852	8.99	25.0	10 748	5975	11.07
20.4	8770	4876	9.03	25.1	10 791	5999	11.11
20.5	8813	4900	9.08	25.2	10 834	6023	11.16
20.6	8856	4924	9.12	25.3	10 877	6047	11.20
20.7	8899	4947	9.17	25.4	10 920	6071	11.25
20.8	8942	4971	9.21	25.5	10 963	6095	11.29
20.9	8985	4995	9.25	25.6	11 006	6119	11.33
				25.7	11 049	6142	11.38
21.0	9028	5019	9.30	25.8	11 092	6166	11.42
21.1	9071	5043	9.34	25.9	11 135	6190	11.47
21.2	9114	5067	9.39				
21.3	9157	5091	9.43	26.0	11 178	6214	11.51
21.4	9200	5115	9.48	26.1	11 221	6238	11.56
21.5	9243	5139	9.52	26.2	11 264	6262	11.60
21.6	9286	5163	9.56	26.3	11 307	6286	11.64
21.7	9329	5186	9.61	26.4	11 350	6310	11.69
21.8	9372	5210	9.65	26.5	11 393	6334	11.73
21.9	9415	5234	9.70	26.6	11 436	6358	11.78
				26.7	11 479	6381	11.82
22.0	9458	5258	9.74	26.8	11 522	6405	11.87
22.1	9501	5282	9.79	26.9	11 565	6429	11.91
22.2	9544	5306	9.83				
22.3	9587	5330	9.87	27.0	11 608	6453	11.95
22.4	9630	5354	9.92	27.1	11 651	6477	12.00
22.5	9673	5378	9.96	27.2	11 694	6501	12.04
22.6	9716	5402	10.01	27.3	11 737	6525	12.09
22.7	9759	5425	10.05	27.4	11 780	6549	12.13
22.8	9802	5449	10.09	27.5	11 823	6573	12.18
22.9	9845	5473	10.14	27.6	11 866	6597	12.22
				27.7	11 909	6620	12.26
23.0	9888	5497	10.18	27.8	11 952	6644	12.31
23.1	9931	5521	10.23	27.9	11 995	6668	12.35
23.2	9974	5545	10.27				
23.3	10 017	5569	10.32	28.0	12 038	6692	12.40
23.4	10 060	5593	10.36	28.1	12 081	6716	12.44
23.5	10 103	5617	10.40	28.2	12 124	6740	12.49
23.6	10 146	5641	10.45	28.3	12 167	6764	12.53
23.7	10 189	5664	10.49	28.4	12 210	6788	12.57
23.8	10 232	5688	10.54	28.5	12 253	6812	12.62
23.9	10 275	5712	10.58	28.6	12 296	6836	12.66
				28.7	12 339	6859	12.71
24.0	10 318	5736	10.63	28.8	12 382	6883	12.75
24.1	10 361	5760	10.67	28.9	12 425	6907	12.80
24.2	10 404	5784	10.71				
24.3	10 447	5808	10.76	29.0	12 468	6931	12.84
24.4	10 490	5832	10.80	29.1	12 511	6955	12.88
24.5	10 533	5856	10.85	29.2	12 554	6979	12.93
24.6	10 576	5880	10.89	29.3	12 597	7003	12.97
24.7	10 619	5903	10.94	29.4	12 640	7027	13.02

MJ/kg	Btu/lb (MJ/kg × 429.923)	kcal/kg (MJ/kg × 239.006)	lb/lb (MJ/kg × 0.442763)	MJ/kg	Btu/lb (MJ/kg × 429.923)	kcal/kg (MJ/kg × 239.006)	lb/lb (MJ/kg × 0.442763)
29.5	12 683	7051	13.06	33.5	14 402	8007	14.83
29.6	12 726	7075	13.11	33.6	14 445	8031	14.88
29.7	12 769	7098	13.15	33.7	14 488	8055	14.92
29.8	12 812	7122	13.19	33.8	14 531	8078	14.97
29.9	12 855	7146	13.24	33.9	14 574	8102	15.01
30.0	12 898	7170	13.28	34.0	14 617	8126	15.05
30.1	12 941	7194	13.33	34.1	14 660	8150	15.10
30.2	12 984	7218	13.37	34.2	14 703	8174	15.14
30.3	13 027	7242	13.42	34.3	14 746	8198	15.19
30.4	13 070	7266	13.46	34.4	14 789	8222	15.23
30.5	13 113	7290	13.50	34.5	14 832	8246	15.28
30.6	13 156	7314	13.55	34.6	14 875	8270	15.32
30.7	13 199	7337	13.59	34.7	14 918	8294	15.36
30.8	13 242	7361	13.64	34.8	14 961	8317	15.41
30.9	13 285	7385	13.68	34.9	15 004	8341	15.45
31.0	13 328	7409	13.73	35.0	15 047	8365	15.50
31.1	13 371	7433	13.77	35.1	15 090	8389	15.54
31.2	13 414	7457	13.81	35.2	15 133	8413	15.59
31.3	13 457	7481	13.86	35.3	15 176	8437	15.63
31.4	13 500	7505	13.90	35.4	15 219	8461	15.67
31.5	13 543	7529	13.95	35.5	15 262	8485	15.72
31.6	13 586	7553	13.99	35.6	15 305	8509	15.76
31.7	13 629	7576	14.04	35.7	15 348	8533	15.81
31.8	13 672	7600	14.08	35.8	15 391	8556	15.85
31.9	13 715	7624	14.12	35.9	15 434	8580	15.90
32.0	13 758	7648	14.17	36.0	15 477	8604	15.94
32.1	13 801	7672	14.21	36.1	15 520	8628	15.98
32.2	13 844	7696	14.26	36.2	15 563	8652	16.03
32.3	13 887	7720	14.30	36.3	15 606	8676	16.07
32.4	13 930	7744	14.35	36.4	15 649	8700	16.12
32.5	13 972	7768	14.39	36.5	15 692	8724	16.16
32.6	14 015	7792	14.43	36.6	15 735	8748	16.21
32.7	14 058	7815	14.48	36.7	15 778	8772	16.25
32.8	14 101	7839	14.52	36.8	15 821	8795	16.29
32.9	14 144	7863	14.57	36.9	15 864	8819	16.34
33.0	14 187	7887	14.61	37.0	15 907	8843	16.38
33.1	14 230	7911	14.66	37.1	15 950	8867	16.43
33.2	14 273	7935	14.70	37.2	15 993	8891	16.47
33.3	14 316	7959	14.74	37.3	16 036	8915	16.52
33.4	14 359	7983	14.79	37.4	16 079	8939	16.56

Appendix 4
Useful information

1 million tonnes coal equivalent = 1 million tonnes of coal at 28.0 MJ/kg
or 6692 kcal/kg gross calorific value

1 million tonnes oil equivalent = 1.5 million tonnes of coal
(approximately)
= 3.0 million tonnes of lignite
(approximately)

1 tonne of coal at 25.1 MJ/kg or 6000 kcal/kg will produce approximately 7.5–9.0 tonnes of cement

1 tonne of coal at 25.1 MJ/kg or 6000 kcal/kg will produce approximately 2400 kW h of electricity

A 1000 MW power station requires 3 million tonnes of coal, at 25.1 MJ/kg, per annum

1 tonne of coal at 28.0% volatile matter, after coking, will produce approximately 1.5 tonnes of iron

Index

Abandoned workings 231
Abrasion index 38
Absorption 202, 206
Abstraction 217, 231
Acid mine drainage 234
Acidic 234, 235
Acid rain 2
Acoustic impedance 185, 187
Acoustic signal 183
Adsorbed 232
Adsorption 252
Aerial photographs 141, 143, 147, 153, 154, 282, 284
Aeromagnetic survey 194
Afghanistan 114, 138
Africa 96, 108, 109, 110, 111, 112, 113, 135, 136, 137, 185, 257
Aggradation 65
Air-dried basis 25, 27, 243
Air quality 2
Albania 100
  Tirene 101
  Tepelene 101
  Korce 101
Algae 8
Alginite 6, 9, 10
Alluvial 6, 9, 10
Alluvial plain 82
Alpha particles 258
Aluminium 232
Amazon Basin 120
Amelioration 91, 99, 104, 112, 119, 120, 130
American Petroleum Institute (API) Units 202
American Society for Testing and Materials (ASTM) 20, 23, 44, 46, 47, 153, 315, 316
Ammonium 232
Analysis 166, 201, 238, 243, 246
  composite 238, 293
  outcrop/core 246

proximate 24, 26, 246, 247, 250
  ultimate 24, 30, 246
Andean Cordillera 116, 120
Angola 108
  Lungue-Bungo 108
  Luanda 108
Ankerite 5, 13
Antarctica 96, 134
  James Ross Island 134
  Transantarctic Mountains 134
Anthracitisation 21
Anticline see Folds
Angularity 171
Apatite 15, 31
Apparent density 37
Aquicludes 217
Aquifers 217, 218, 219, 224, 225, 227, 228, 230
Aquitards 217
Area-of-influence technique 275
Argillaceous shale 15
Argentina 116, 117, 138
  Austral-Patagonia 116, 117
  La Rioja 117
  Mendoza 117
  Neuquen 117
  Pico Quemada 117, 118
  Rio Turbio 118
  San Juan 117
As received basis 25, 243
As sampled basis 25
Ash 4, 24, 28, 29, 34, 39, 51, 65, 77, 151, 201, 202, 214, 215, 222, 246, 270, 271, 275, 289, 293, 296
Ash analysis 32, 246
Ash content 15, 80, 81
Ash free basis 25, 27, 206
Ash fusion temperatures 32, 33, 246
Attenuation 186
Attrinite 12

Audibert-Arnu dilatometer 37
Australasia 96, 132, 133, 134, 137, 138
Australia 47, 132, 133, 135, 137, 138, 139, 151, 185, 188, 192, 193, 197, 198, 243, 246, 247, 255, 257
  Bowen Basin 132, 133
  Brisbane 133
  Burragorang Valley 133
  Cardiff 132
  Collie coalfield 132, 192, 193
  Cooper Basin 133
  Fitzroy basin 132
  Galilee Basin 132, 133
  Gippsland Basin 133
  Hunter Valley 133
  Latrobe Valley 133
  Muja 132
  New South Wales 132, 133
  Queensland 132, 133, 257
  South Australia 132
  Southern District 133
  Sydney Basin 132, 133, 255, 257
  Tasmania 132
  Victoria 132, 133
  Western Australia 132, 192, 193
  Western District 133
Austria 101
  West Styria 101
Avulsion 66
Axial plane 89

Background 182
Background radiation 198
Backwall 87
Baked sediments 197
Baked zones 195
Bangladesh 114, 115, 136, 194
  Barapukuria 115
  Jamalganj 115

Bangladesh (*cont.*)
  Khalaspir 115
  Sylhet 115
Banking 234
Barium 232
Barnsley seam 107
Barrier 56, 58
  back 56, 57, 58, 59
  coastal 57
Basalt 186, 187
Base flow 219
Bases calculation 27
Batters 271
BCURA formula 26
Bedding 153, 165, 166, 172, 173
  boundaries 201
  contorted 78
  deformed 78, 79
  disturbed 166
  folded 78
  open 225
  spacing 170
Belgium 101, 136, 137
  Kempen 101
Benches 228
Beneficiation 270, 271
Biosphere 258
Bioturbation 57, 59, 166
Bitumen 19
Bituminite 9
Blackdamp 253, 254
Blade bit 158
Block diagram 177
Block model 278
Blowing 252
Bolivia 118
  Copacabana Peninsula 118
  Isla del Sol 118
  Tarija Basin 118
Bord 88
Bord and pillar *see* Room and pillar
Boreholes 156, 160, 175, 182, 188, 189, 190, 191, 200, 201, 204, 206, 207, 211, 215, 219, 225, 226, 227, 231, 255, 256, 262, 276, 284, 288, 293
  casing 156, 160, 202
  diameter 156, 204, 206, 207
  logging *see* Logging
  Number 160
Borehole grid 162
Botswana 108, 136, 137, 168
  Mmamabula 108
  Morupule 108

Bouguer gravity anomaly 192, 193
Boundary zone 276, 277
Brazil 116, 117, 118, 138, 192
  Candiota 118
  Parana 118
  Rio Fresco 118
  Rio Grande do Sul 118
  Santa Caterina 118, 119
  Sao Paulo 119
  Tocantins-Araguaia 118
  Upper Amazon 118
  Western Piaui 118
Breccia 171
Britain *see* United Kingdom
British Coal 47, 48, 151, 153
British Standards 26, 27, 35, 36, 168, 242, 300, 310, 311
British Thermal Units (BTU) 33, 46, 319, 320, 321, 322
Broken strata 158, 173
Brunei 123
  Bandar Seri Begawan 123
  Belait River 123
Bulgaria 102, 136, 137
  Dobrudza 102
  Maritsa 102
Burma 123, 124
  Henzada 124
  Kalewa 123
  Pakokku 123
  Panluang 124
Burnt coal 158, 194, 196, 197, 209, 210, 271
Burning limits 284, 291
Burning zones 163, 195, 197, 210, 274

Cainozoic 100, 114, 115, 116, 122, 123, 127, 128, 132
Caking properties 32, 35, 42, 44
Caking tests 34
Calcite 5, 13, 173
Calcium 232
Calibration graph 204
Caliper log *see* Geologs
Calories per gram 33
Calorific value 17, 19, 20, 22, 28, 29, 32, 33, 42, 44, 206, 215, 246, 247, 250, 271, 293, 301, 319, 320, 321, 322
  net calorific value 33
  gross calorific value 33, 51
Cameroun 108
  Bamenda 108
Campsites 144

Canada 21, 96, 99, 100, 136, 137, 228, 229
  Alberta 70, 71, 99
  British Columbia 99
  Canadian Arctic Islands 100
  Minto coalfield 99, 100
  Northwest Territories 100
  Remus Basin 21
  Saskatchewan 99, 228, 229
  Sydney coalfield 99, 100
  Yukon Territory 100
Carbargillite 15
Carbon 17, 30, 31, 206, 223, 224, 252
Carbon dioxide 17, 31, 252, 253, 255
Carbon monoxide 252, 254
Carbonaceous mudstone (shale) 65, 153
Carbonate minerals 31, 95, 232
Carboniferous 23, 58, 59, 88, 90, 96, 97, 100, 101, 102, 103, 104, 105, 106, 107, 108, 109, 111, 113, 117, 118, 121, 122, 220, 286
Casing *see* Boreholes
Catchment area 219
Caving 203, 204, 211
Cavities 197, 198
Cells 10
Cellular structure 10
Cement industry 2, 30, 31, 126
Cementation 165, 220
Central and South America 96, 116, 117, 118, 119, 120, 121, 135, 136, 138
Channel 188, 189, 233 *see also* Sand, Sandstone
Channel-fill deposits 59, 75
Channel sample (see sample)
Channel sample record sheet 238, 239
Channel waves 198, 199
Chile 119, 136, 138
  Arauco 119
  Copiapo 119
  Magallenes 119
  Valdivia 119
China 123, 124, 125, 126, 135, 136, 138, 139
  Anhwei 125
  Heilungkiang 125
  Honan 125
  Hopeh 125
  Hupeh 125

Inner Mongolia 125
Kirin 125
Kweichow 125
Liaoning 125
Shansi 125
Shantung 125
Shensi 125
Sinkiang-Uighur 125
Yunnan 125
Chippings 166, 168
Chlorides 182, 232, 235
Chlorine 31
Chlorite 15
        Cindering 91
Circulation loss 168
Circulation pit 235
CIS (formerly USSR) 22, 96,
    121, 122, 123, 135, 136, 138
  Dnepr 122, 123
  Donetsk 122
  Ekibastuz 122, 123
  Kansk-Achinsk 122, 123
  Karaganda 122
  Kuznetsk 122
  Moscow 22, 122, 123
  Neryungri 123
  Pechora 122
  South Yakutsk 122
Clarain 5, 6, 7
Clarite 10, 11
Clarodurite 11
Clastic 65, 74, 75, 86
Clay 173, 186, 200, 232, 236,
    238
Clay minerals 14, 115, 202,
    221
Claystone 171
Cleat 82, 87, 89, 95, 153, 232
Coal
  age 96
  anthracite 4, 17, 18, 20, 35,
      47, 89, 90, 91, 96, 97,
      101, 102, 103, 104, 105,
      106, 107, 111, 112, 117,
      118, 119, 120, 121, 125,
      127, 128, 131, 135, 136,
      137, 138, 151, 208, 223,
      224, 257, 262, 263
  attrital 5, 7, 8
    bands 73, 238
  bituminous 4, 17, 18, 20,
      28, 33, 47, 97, 98, 99,
      101, 104, 105, 106, 107,
      108, 112, 113, 114, 116,
      118, 120, 121, 122, 123,
      124, 125, 126, 127, 129,
      130, 135, 136, 137, 138,

150, 151, 194, 208, 223,
      252, 253, 255, 257, 262,
      263
  bituminous high volatile
      18, 20, 97, 100, 102, 103,
      104, 107, 110, 112, 113,
      115, 117, 118, 119, 121,
      122, 123, 126, 128, 130,
      131, 132, 133, 134, 223
  bituminous low volatile 18,
      20, 97, 100, 102, 103,
      105, 106, 107, 111, 113,
      115, 117, 118, 120, 121,
      122, 125, 126, 129, 130,
      131, 134, 223
  bituminous medium
      volatile 18, 20, 97, 100,
      104, 110, 113, 115, 117,
      223
  black 4, 87, 96, 100, 102,
      103, 104, 105, 106, 107,
      108, 110, 111, 113, 116,
      122, 123, 135, 136, 137,
      138, 139, 221
  boghead 6, 7, 8, 19
  bone 6, 7, 151
  boghead-cannel 8
  bright 5, 7, 150, 151, 238,
      151
  brown 4, 6, 8, 17, 20, 47, 52,
      54, 100, 102, 103, 104,
      105, 106, 107, 108, 110,
      113, 115, 122, 123, 125,
      135, 136, 137, 138, 139,
      221, 253, 270
  cannel 6, 7, 8, 19, 151, 254
  cannel-boghead 8
  chemical properties 24
  coking 29, 30, 31, 32, 37,
      100, 102, 103, 105, 106,
      107, 113, 117, 120, 122,
      125, 126, 127, 129, 130,
      131, 133, 139, 242, 246,
      248, 250, 255
  dirty 151
  dull 5, 7, 151, 238
  geographic distribution 97
  hard 4, 5
  humic 4, 5, 6, 7, 19, 20, 44
  impure 5, 7
  lenticular 59
  lignite 4, 6, 7, 12, 16, 20, 47,
      52, 54, 96, 98, 99, 100,
      101, 102, 103, 104, 105,
      106, 107, 109, 110, 111,
      112, 115, 116, 118, 119,
      120, 121, 123, 126, 127,

128, 129, 131, 133, 134,
      135, 136, 137, 138, 165,
      186, 187, 188, 208, 223,
      224, 257, 262, 263
  meta-anthracite 17, 18, 120
  minerals 13, 14
  mineralised 7, 8
  per-hydrous 44
  rank *see* Rank
  sapropelic 4, 5, 6, 7, 8, 19
  semi-anthracite 4, 17, 18,
      47, 98, 118, 130, 131
  semi-graphite 18
  steam 29, 31, 32, 47, 97,
      113, 120, 126, 133, 139,
      242, 246, 247, 249, 255
  subbituminous 4, 6, 12, 16,
      20, 23, 47, 91, 98, 99,
      100, 101, 102, 104, 105,
      107, 109, 110, 112, 115,
      118, 119, 120, 121, 122,
      123, 126, 127, 128, 129,
      130, 131, 132, 133, 134,
      135, 136, 137, 138, 208,
      262, 263
  subhydrous 55
  thermally altered 47
  type 4
Coal basins 178
Coal bed methane 257, 258
Coal bed methane wells 257
Coal blocks 280, 293
Coal classification 8, 43, 44,
    45, 46, 48, 50, 51, 52, 53,
    54
Coal excavation area 273
Coal gasification 187
Coal mine development 143
Coal occurrences 282
Coal panel 200, 255, 279
Coal pillars 198
Coal preparation 177, 247
Coal preparation engineer 41,
    300, 301
Coal product value 273
Coal recovery 261, 274
Coal reserves see Reserves
Coal resource/reserve
    classification 261, 262,
    263, 264, 265, 266, 267,
    268, 269, 270
Coal seam
  area 275
  characteristics 286
  depth 157, 162, 164, 166,
      201, 215, 270, 278, 290,
      291

Coal seam (*cont.*)
  floor 153, 162, 163, 164, 165,
    201, 207, 215, 237, 238,
    241, 244, 284, 293
  Roof 153, 162, 163, 164, 165,
    200, 201, 207, 215, 237,
    238, 241, 244, 284, 293
  Thickness 157, 162, 164,
    175, 185, 186, 200, 201,
    215, 238, 270, 274, 275,
    278, 279, 280, 282, 289,
    290, 291
Coal sampling *see* Sampling
Coal splitting *see* Splitting
Coal quality *see* Quality
Coal seam data sheet 292,
  293, 294, 295, 297
Coal streams 236, 244, 250
Coal stockpiles 236, 244, 246,
  249, 251
Coal transport containers 236
Coalfields 84
Coalification 9, 16, 17, 19, 20,
  22, 23, 65, 87, 188, 221, 257
Coarsening upwards
  sequences 59, 60
Code of behaviour 299
Coke 120, 125
Coking properties 32, 44, 130
Coking tests 35
Collaboration 302
Collinite 9, 10, 12
Colloidal 8
Colombia 119, 120, 136, 138,
  139
  Bogota 120
  Cordoba 120
  Cundinamarca-Santander
    120
  Valle del Cauca 120
Colour 165, 171
Combustable 252, 254
Combustion 32, 33
  tests 242
Compaction 23, 74, 87, 210,
  221
Components 232
Compression 83, 87
Compressibility 221
Computer 165, 173, 177, 201,
  227, 278, 290, 296, 300
  applications 173
  coding sheets 165
  graphics 175
Concave slope 234
Conchoidal 6, 8
Concretions 153

Conductivity 21
Conductors 182
Cone-in-cone structure 87
Cone of depression 219, 228,
  229, 230
Confidence level 274
Confined 218, 219, 227
Conglomerate 171
Consolidated 221, 222, 230
Contamination 231, 233, 303
Contouring 175, 290, 293, 296
Contour interval 176
Contour programme 176, 177
Contour plans 177
Convex slope 234
Core 156, 158, 160, 162, 168,
  236, 247
Core barrel 156, 158, 159, 160,
  161, 168, 179, 215, 255
Core box 160, 162, 164
Core logging 160, 162, 163,
  164
Core logging shed 164, 168,
  173
Core logging sheet 165, 166,
  167, 241
Core losses 162, 164, 165, 168,
  172, 241
Core recovery 160, 172
Core run 164, 172
Cored boreholes 162, 166,
  201, 215, 270
Corpocollinite 9, 12
Corpohumite 12
Correlation 66, 67, 68, 69, 70,
  71, 147, 148, 171, 177, 179,
  189, 202, 215, 246, 282,
  284, 286, 289
Corrosion 234
Cosmic radiation 182
Costa Rica 119
  Talamanca Cordillera 119
  Uatsi 119
  Venado 119
  Zent 119
Costs 261
Cretaceous 71, 96, 98, 99, 106,
  108, 110, 111, 119, 122,
  129, 133, 134, 257
Crevasse-splay 59, 60, 63, 64,
  73
Cross beds 57
Cross borehole seismic *see*
  Seismic
Cross section 176, 196, 282,
  289
Crucible swelling number

(CSN) *see* Free swelling
  index
Crystalline basement 192, 194
Cumulative floats curve 39
Cumulative sinks curve 39
Cuticles 7, 9, 10
Cutinite 9, 10
Cycle 57
Cyclothem 57
Czechoslovakia 102, 136, 137
  North Bohemia 102
  Ostrava-Karvina 103
  Sokolov 102

Darcy's Law 218
Data collection 141, 173, 300
Data points 175, 260, 261, 271,
  291
Data recording 144, 173
Data storage 173
Deforestation 233
Degradation 234
Deltaic 55, 57
Denmark 102
  Herning 102
Densimetric curve 39, 42
Densinite 12
Density 37, 39, 178, 179, 180,
  181, 192, 202, 203, 204, 215
Density contrast 187
Densospore 11
Deposition 55, 59, 62, 64, 65,
  76, 260
Depositional models 56, 57,
  63, 64
Depressurisation 221, 230
Depth 201, 232, 252, 254, 293
Depth of burial 20, 22
Desmocollinite 9, 12
Detector 204, 205
Detritus 82
Development 201, 216, 224,
  246, 260, 282
Devolatilisation 195
Devonian 96, 100
Dewatering 221, 227, 228,
  229, 230
Diagenesis 17, 78, 82, 87
Diapiric intrusion 82
Differential compaction 187
Digitising 279
Dilution 75, 238, 244
Dips 8, 9, 89, 147, 153, 154,
  156, 157, 185, 188, 215,
  271, 278, 279
Discharge 217, 219

Discharge hydrograph 219
Discharge point 217
Discoloration 235
Discontinuities 168, 169, 172,
   173, 198, 200, 221, 226, 230
Disposal 232
Dissolved compounds 232
Distance of separation 277
Distributary mouth bar
   deposits 59
Ditches 234
Dolerite 91, 119, 194, 195
Double tube core barrel 159
Drawdown 219, 220, 227, 230
Drift mine 99
Drill holes *see* Boreholes
Drill sites 156
Drilling 144, 154, 156, 157,
   162, 163, 168, 178, 188,
   194, 215, 216, 242, 255,
   256, 257, 274, 282, 291
Drilling fluid 157, 158, 163,
   235, 241
Drilling procedure 156
Drilling programme 156, 193
Drilling rigs
   diamond drill 158, 160, 161
   rotary 157, 158, 160, 161
      air flush 157, 158, 160,
         161, 216, 242, 256
      mud flush 157, 158, 160,
         161, 216, 242
Drinking water 235
Drivages 280
Dry ash free basis 25, 27
Dry basis 25, 27
Dry mineral matter free basis
   25, 27
Dummy value *see* Nul value
Durain 5, 6
Durite 10, 11
Duroclarite 11
Dyke 91, 94, 119, 195, 197
Dynamite energy source 187,
   188

Ecological 233
Economic assumption 262
Economic feasibility 250,
   261
Ecuador 120
   Malacatus Basin 120
   Loja Basin 120
   Canar-Azuay Basin 120
Egypt 108, 109
   Al Maghara 109

Sinai Peninsula 109
Elasticity 221
Electric current 181
Electrical 178, 182
Electrical conductivity 181,
   182
Electrical conductor 200
Electrical mapping 197
Electrical resistivity 178, 179,
   180, 182, 197
Electricity 1, 2, 29, 99, 100,
   103, 105, 106, 107, 108,
   112, 113, 115, 116, 118,
   120, 128, 130, 131, 133
Elementary ash-curve 39
Elements 31, 231
End cleat 89
End wall 230
Energy 1
Engineering studies 166
Environment 188
Environment of deposition 55
Environmental 185, 205, 302,
   303, 304
Environmental constraints
   261, 299
Environmental factors 303
Environmental impact
   statement (EIS) 302, 303
Environmental legislation 304
Ephemeral streams 219
Erosion 224, 233, 234, 260, 303
Ethane 252, 254
Ethiopia 110
   Chelga 110
   Wuchalle 110
   Dobre-Brehan 110
Evaporation 224
Excavation 228, 229, 233
Exinite 6, 9, 10, 17
Exploration 2, 67, 141, 154,
   156, 157, 166, 178, 192,
   200, 201, 215, 216, 220,
   241, 246, 274, 282, 300
   greenfields 2, 303
   budget 178
   geological input 142
Explosive 191
Export 246, 302
Extraction 254
Exudatinite 9

Facies 59, 66, 148
Facies correlation 66
Facies maps 71
Failure 230

Falling weight 191
Far East 96, 123, 124, 125, 126,
   127, 128, 129, 130, 131,
   135, 136, 138
Faults 144, 147, 148, 153, 154,
   170, 173, 185, 186, 187,
   189, 193, 197, 199, 200,
   201, 221, 225, 226, 227,
   230, 231, 236, 254, 258,
   274, 278, 279, 280, 289
   patterns 83
   growth 74, 80
   contemporaneous 74
   bedding plane 81
   activation 81
   reverse 82, 84, 85
   normal 83
   drag 84
   zones 172
   lag 84, 85
   thrust 85, 86, 87, 91, 148
   strike-slip 86
Fauna 148, 233, 235, 289, 303
'Fence' diagram 67, 69
Ferruginous 232, 234, 235
Field equipment 144, 145
Field operations 216
Field survey 178
Field traverses 143, 145, 147,
   148, 154, 156, 197, 282, 284
Fieldwork 143, 144, 145, 147,
   154
Filtration 235
Fining upwards sequences 59
Fireclays *see* Seatearth
Firedamp 252
Fischer assay 35
Fissure flow 228
Fixed carbon 29, 44
Flame structures 78
Flint clays 13
Float sink tests 39, 246, 247,
   250, 251
Flooding 227, 228
Flood-tide delta 59
Floor *see* Coal
Floor heave 230
Floor rolls 71, 75
Flora 148, 233, 235, 289, 303
Flow nets 227
Flow rates 225, 233, 235, 258
Fluid content 201
Fluid temperature (FT) 34
Fluidity 37, 243
Fluids 203, 204, 217, 235
Fluorinite 9
Fluvial 57

Fluviatile 55
Foamed stimulation fluids
    257
Focused electric log *see*
    Geologs
Folds 144, 147, 148, 153, 154,
    185, 193, 201, 226, 289
  monoclinal 83
  growth 82
  anticlines 82, 187
  synclines 82
  zig zag 91, 92
  asymmetrical 91, 92
  overturned 92
Footwall 87, 228
Form 171
Formation boundary 206
Formation density 205
Fossil content 166
Fracture logging 172
Fracture spacing index 172
Fracture zone 172
Fractures 197, 206, 217, 221,
    225
Fracturing 166, 168, 170, 172,
    221, 228, 254
France 102, 136, 137
    Lorraine 102
    Nord et Pas de Calais 102
    Provence 103
Free swelling index (FSI) 34,
    35, 47, 50, 51, 246
Fresh 187, 238, 240, 252
Friable 221
Frost action 187
Fully cored boreholes 162, 166
Fusain 5, 6, 7
Fusinite 6, 9, 10
Fusite 10

Gas 94, 95, 252, 253, 254, 255,
    256
Gas content 254
Gas drainage 255, 257, 258
Gas emissions 255
Gelification 6, 7
Gelinite 12
Gelocollinite 9, 12
Geological assurance 260, 268
Geological certainty 261, 274
Geological conduct 299
Geological database 201
Geological framework 179
Geological hazards *see* Hazards
Geological losses 201, 279,
    280

Geological mapping 141, 144,
    148, 192
Geological maps 141, 143,
    149, 154, 282, 284, 289
Geological organisation 299
Geological practice 299
Geological standards 299
Geological supervision 300
Geological symbols 146
Geological uncertainties 261,
    268
Geophysical logs (geologs)
    67, 70, 71, 162, 164, 177,
    200, 201, 215, 241, 242,
    255, 256, 288, 289
  analysis 201
  calibration 201
  caliper 201, 205, 206, 207
  density 177, 178, 201, 204,
    205, 206, 207, 208, 210,
    212, 213, 214, 215, 288,
    289
  electrical 178, 207
  electromagnetic 178
  focused electric (FE) 208,
    209
  gamma ray 177, 201, 203,
    215, 288
  neutron 201, 205, 206, 207
  radioactive 207
  radiometric 178
  resistivity 201, 208, 209, 210
  self potential (SP) 208
  single point resistance 208
  sonic 201, 210, 211
  temperature 211
Geophysical logging limit
    200, 201, 204
Geophysical maps 154
Geophysical measuring
    instruments *see* Sondes
Geophysical surveys 175, 274,
    293
Geophysical technique 198
Geophysics 141, 177, 178
Geomechanical Properties
    211
Geophone 183, 185, 189
Geotechnical 201, 215, 219,
    220, 221, 273
Geotechnical logging sheet
    173, 174
Geotechnical studies 141, 153,
    162, 206, 302
Geothermal gradient 21, 22,
    118
Germany 21, 84, 103, 136,

    137, 139
    Aachen Basin 103
    Halle-Leipzig Borna Basin
        103
    Lower Lausitz Basin 103
    Lower Saxony 103
    Rhenish Basin 103
    Ruhr Basin 103
    Saar Basin 103
    Upper Rhinegraben 21
    Wurm Basin 91, 92
Gieseler plastometer 35, 37,
    246
Glacial deposits 187, 192
Global warming 2
Gondwana 19, 43, 108, 114,
    115, 116, 118, 121, 192,
    193, 194, 242, 246, 258
Graben 84, 115, 194
Gradients 175, 176, 234, 317
Grainsize 165, 168, 223
Granite 193
Graphic display 177
Graphic portrayal 147, 151,
    152, 153
Gravimeter 191
Gravity 83, 188, 192, 194, 217,
    228
Gravity sliding 80, 82
Gravity survey 182, 192, 193
Gray-King coke type 35, 36,
    47, 48, 50, 51
Greece 103, 136, 137
    Florina Amyndaeon 103
    Megalopolis 103
    Ptolemais 103
    Serrae 103
Greenland 103, 104
    Disko 104
    Nugssuaq 104
Grids 175, 176, 177
Gridding 176, 177
Grindability 38
Ground magnetic 178
Groundwater 63, 158, 169,
    211, 216, 217, 218, 220,
    221, 225, 228, 230, 232, 304
    Contour maps 227
    flow 224, 225, 226, 227, 231
    levels 226
    movement 216
    quality 231, 232
    retention 216
'Gun' energy source 185, 186

Haematite 181

Hardgrove grindability index (HGI) 38, 246, 247, 301
Hardness 38
Hazard 185, 200, 231, 252, 274, 278, 279
Head 219
Health and hygiene 143, 144
Helium 222
Hemisphere temperature (HT) 34
High resolution seismic *see* Seismic
High wall 226, 230, 281
High wall depth 273
Higher heating value 33
Hilt's Law 20, 21
Hole to surface seismic *see* Seismic
Humified peat 222
Huminite 10, 12, 17
Hungary 104, 136, 137
  Mecsek 104
Hydrated iron (III) 232
Hydraulic conductivity 217, 218, 221, 222
Hydraulic gradient 217, 218, 219, 227
Hydraulic pressure 228, 230
Hydrocarbon entrapment 182
Hydrodynamic pressure 217
Hydrogen 17, 30, 33, 205, 206, 252, 253, 254
Hydrogen carbonate 232
Hydrogen index 206
Hydrogen sulphide 255
Hydrogen characteristics 216
Hydrogeological cycle 216
Hydrogeological data 216, 224, 227
Hydrogeological model 224
Hydrogeological properties 216, 220
Hydrogeological studies 302
Hydrogeology 201, 216
Hydrophones 190
Hydrostatic pressure 217
Hydroxide 195

Igneous 20, 71, 78, 85, 119, 126, 129, 130, 145, 179, 181, 182, 192, 194, 201, 203, 236, 254, 274, 279, 280
Illite 14, 15
Impermeable 64, 217, 218, 228, 230
Impulse source 183

In Situ tonnage calculation 274–9
Incompetent 86
Increments 244, 245
India 69, 114, 115, 136, 138, 192, 194, 197
  Bihar 115
  Bisrampur 115
  Borako 115
  Godavari 115
  Jharia 115
  Karanpura 115
  Makum 115
  Neyveli 115
  Orissa 115
  Pench-Kanhan-Tawa 115
  Ramgarh 115
  Raniganj 115, 197
  Singrauli 115
  Talchir 115
Indian Subcontinent 96, 114, 115, 116, 135, 136, 138
Indonesia 79, 80, 83, 91, 92, 93, 126, 127, 136, 138, 139, 150, 151, 163, 195, 196
  Borneo 126
  East Kalimantan 79, 80, 91, 92, 93, 126, 150, 151, 163, 195, 196
    Berau 126
    Sangatta 126
    Tarakan 126
  Java 126
  South Kalimantan 126
    Senakin-Tanah Grogot 126
    Tanjung 126
  Sulawesi 126
  Sumatra 83, 126
    Bengkulu 126
    Bukit Asam 126
    Ombilin 126
  West Irian 126
    Bintuni 126
    West Kalimantan 127
Indurated 220
Inertinite 6, 9, 10, 12, 17, 19, 43
Inertite 10, 11
Inertodetrinite 9, 10
Infiltration 231, 234
Inflammable 255
Inhomogeneities 197
Initial deformation temperature (IT) 34
In-seam Seismic *see* Seismic
Interburden 71, 76, 175, 273, 282, 291

Inter-channel areas 64, 65
Interdistributary Bay 59
Interface 181, 187, 191
Interflow 220
Intergranular flow 221
Intermittent streams 219
International Coal Classification 50
Internationl Organisation for Standardisation (ISO) 23, 52, 54, 300, 311, 312, 313
International standards 299
Interpretation 201, 282
Interseam connections 231
Iran 114, 116, 138
  Elburz 116
  Kerman 116
  Korasan 116
Ireland 104
  Connaught 104
  Kanturk 104
  Leinster 104
  Slieveardagh 104
Iron 232
Iron enrichment 195
Irrigation programmes 230
Isometric 177
Isopachyte maps 76
Italy 104
  Apennines 104
  Sardinia 104
  Sulcis 104

Japan 127, 136, 138
  Chikuho 127
  Hokkaido 127
  Honshu 127
  Ishikari 127
  Joban 127
  Kushiro 127
  Kyushy 127
  Miike 127
  Miyagi 127
  Mogami 127
  Nishitagawa 127
  Omine 127
Joints 82, 83, 87, 153, 165, 172, 173, 201, 221, 225, 227, 228
Joules 33
Jurassic 89, 92, 94, 96, 99, 113, 114, 116, 122, 125, 128, 133

Kalahari group 111
Kaolinite 15
Karroo 108, 110, 111, 112, 113, 195

Kilocalories per kilogram (kcal/ kg) 33, 319, 320, 321, 322
Korea (North) 127, 128, 137, 138, 139
  Anju 128
  Kilchu-Hyongchon 128
  Kowon-Muchon 127
  Kyongsang 128
  North Pyongyang 127
  Pyongyang 127
  Tumangang 128
Korea (South) 89, 90, 91, 92, 94, 128, 137, 138
  Boeun 128
  Chungnam 128
  Danyang 128
  Honam 128
  Jeongseon 128
  Kangnung 128
  Kimpo 128
  Mungyeong 128
  Samcheog 128
  Yeongcheon 128
KMC formula 26

Laboratory test 169
Lag deposits 59
Lagoonal 57
Lagoons 235
Lakes 228, 235
Land access 143
Land subsidence 230
Landform 303
Landsat imagery 153, 154
Laos 128, 129
  Bam O 128
  Hua Xieng 128
  Khang Phanieng 128
  Muongphan 128, 129
  Phongsaly 128
  Saravan 128
  Ventiane 128
Laterite 193
Leaf 72, 74, 76
Liptite 10, 11
Liptinite 9, 10, 19
Liptodetrinite 9, 10
Limestone 66, 148, 181, 258
Liquefaction 78, 153
Lithofacies 57, 68
Lithofacies maps 71, 72
Lithological logging 165, 215, 241, 289
Lithological variations 165
Lithology 165, 166, 183, 185, 208, 210, 215

Lithotype 6, 8, 57, 66, 67, 74, 76, 89, 147, 162, 165, 201, 202, 203, 209, 210, 211, 217, 220, 225, 231, 288
  graphic portrayal 147, 151, 152, 153, 212, 213
Litres per second 225
Loading 78
Logging 158
Logging tool *see* Sonde
Logging unit *see* Geophysical logging unit
Long spaced density log *see* Geologs
Longwall mining 89, 200, 279, 280
Losses *see* geological
Loss of production 200
Low wall depth 273
Lower delta plain 56, 59, 60, 63
Lower heating value 33
Lung cancer 258
Lustre 5, 6
Lycospore 11

'M' curve 41, 42
Macerals 4, 9, 10, 12, 23, 42
  maceral group 9, 10, 17
  submacerals 9, 10, 17
Macrinite 9, 10
Macrostructure 80
Madagascar 110
  Antanifotsy 110
  Ianapera 110
  Imaloto 110
  Sakamena 110
  Sakoa 110
  Vohibory 110
Maghaematite 195
Magnesium 232
Magnetic
  anomaly 194, 195, 197
  disc 201
  profile 196, 197
  survey 182, 194, 291
  susceptibility 179, 180, 181, 194, 195
  tape 201
Magnetite 181, 195
Malawi 110, 136
  Lengwe 110
  Livingstonia 110
  Mwabvi 110
  Ngana 110
  North Rukuru 110

Malaysia 129
  Balingian 129
  Batu Arang 129
  Bintulu 129
  Bukit Arang 129
  Silantek 129
  Silimpopon 129
Mali 110, 111
  Bourem 111
  Mali-Niger Basin 110
Manholes 253
Map scales 143, 284, 291, 293
Marcasite 253
Marker beds 147, 148
Market requirements 166
Marketing 302
Mass movement 89
Mass strength *see* Rock strength
Material strength *see* Rock strength
Megajoules per kilogram (MJ/ kg) 33, 51, 319, 320, 321, 322
Melange 79, 80
Mercury 222
Mercury porosimetry 222
Mesozoic 99, 100, 104, 107, 108, 114, 116, 119, 122, 123, 125, 127, 128, 129, 131, 132, 133
Metal oxides 32
Metallurgical industry 2, 16, 31, 32, 115, 116, 118, 125, 127
Metamorphic 179, 181, 182, 192
Metamorphism 17
Methane 17, 20, 94, 198, 252, 253, 255, 256, 257, 258
Methane gas extraction 256
Methanometer 254, 255
Method of mining 262, 279, 280
Mexico 120, 136, 138
  Coahuila 120
  Sonora 120
Micrinite 9, 10
Microfracturing 88
Microgravity 178
Microlithotypes 9, 10, 11, 12, 15
Middlings 41, 42
Migration interval 189, 190, 191
Millilitres 224
Mine
  design 166, 168, 185, 224

development 173, 188, 241
drainage 231, 235
feasibility 219
operation 260
planning 179, 185, 190, 201, 211, 233, 273
plans 231, 233
scheduling 177
site 226, 227, 233
Mineability 77
Mined coal product 244
Mineral matter 4, 23, 24, 28, 32, 42
Mineral precipitation 82, 88, 94, 221
Mineralisation 153, 162, 166, 236
Mineralogy 165
Minerals 13, 15
Minimum depth limit 280
Mining 153, 198, 206, 225, 227, 230, 233, 234, 246, 275, 289
Mining engineers 300, 301
Minishaft 242
MINI-SOSIE 185, 188
Miospore 9
Mire 63, 64, 65, 73, 77, 82
Moisture 24, 26, 28, 30, 33, 47, 160, 215
  adventitious 28
  air-dried 28
  as delivered 28
  as received 28
  capacity 28
  equilibrium 28
  inbed 28, 47
  inherent 26, 30
  insitu 20, 22, 28
  surface 28
  total 28
Moisture content 17, 18, 23, 30, 52, 54
Moisture holding capacity 28
Moisture loss 240
Mongolia 129
  Achit Nuur 129
  Baganur 129
  Khartarbagat 129
  Nalayh 129
  Sharin Gol 129
  Taban Tologoy 129
Monitoring 300
Morocco 108, 111, 137
  Ezzhiliga 111
  Jerada 111
  Meknes-Fez 111

Tindouf-Draa 111
Moving wall oven test 242
Mozambique 111, 136, 137
  Chiomo 111
  Itule 111
  Mmambansavu 111
  Motaize 111
Mud volcanoes 82
Mudstone 65, 66, 74, 78, 80, 82, 85, 86, 149, 168, 171, 182, 189, 197, 198, 202, 203, 204, 218, 220, 258, 293
  marine 66, 182, 198, 202, 258, 293
  non-marine 182, 202

Namibia 111
Natural gas 258
Natural radioactivity 182–202
Negative anomaly 192
Neutrons 206
  thermal 206
Neutron log *see* Geologs
Netherlands, The 104
New Zealand 133, 137, 138, 197
  North Island 133
    Waikato 133
    Northland 133
    Taranaki 133
  South Island 133, 134
    Buller 134
    Charleston 134
    Collingwood 134
    Greymouth 134
    Kaitangata 133
    Ohai 133
    Otago 133
    Pike River 134
    Reefton 134
    Southland 133
    Westland 134
Niger 111
Nigeria 111, 112, 136
  Asaba 112
  Enugu 112
  Ezimo 112
  Lafia 112
  Ogboyoga 112
  Okaba 112
  Orukpa 112
Nitrogen 30, 243, 252, 254, 255
Nodules 153
Noise 303
Non-saline wetlands 63

North America *see* USA
NO_x emissions 30
Nuclear radioactivity 202
Nuclear well logging instruments 182
Nul values 175

Observation well 219, 225, 226, 227
Occurrences 270
Offshore mining 100, 127
Oil 1
Old mine workings 190, 192, 198, 231
Ombrotrophic peat 63
Opencast 75, 76, 83, 84, 97, 98, 99, 103, 104, 125, 126, 128, 130, 133, 178, 188, 189, 190, 191, 192, 195, 198, 216, 221, 225, 226, 227, 228, 230, 233, 236, 237, 271, 274, 275, 279, 280, 281, 284, 302, 303
Openhole drilling 156, 157, 158, 162, 201, 270
Openhole logging 166, 215
Outcrops 143, 144, 145, 146, 147, 175, 179, 237, 238, 239, 242, 247, 248, 249, 262, 270, 276, 289, 291
Overburden 71, 228, 229, 230, 233, 271, 272, 273, 282, 291, 301
  thickness 76
  in situ volume 271, 272
  in situ vertical ratio 271, 272
  in situ thickness 271
Oxidation 9, 42, 160, 170, 181, 209, 232, 233, 240, 243, 252, 254, 271, 274, 284
Oxygen 17, 20, 30, 31, 195, 253
Oxygenated 232

Pacific Coast 120
Pakistan 114, 116, 136, 138
  Duki-Chamalang 116
  Hyderabad 116
  Indus Basin 116
  Khost Sharig-Harnai 116
  Lakhra 116
  Meting-Shimpir 116
  Quetta Kalat 116
  Salt Range-Makerwal 116
  Sonda-Thatta 116
  Sor Range-Daghari 116

Palaeoenvironment 77
Paleostrike 82
Palaeozoic 96, 100, 107, 114, 115, 116, 122, 123, 125, 127, 128, 129, 132
Panel *see* Coal panel
Paper chart 201
Parallel sided drill rod 205
Parr formula 25
Parting 65, 72, 73, 162, 165, 201, 205, 238
Peat 17, 20, 23, 55, 63, 64, 65, 75, 81, 119, 127, 221, 260
Peat/coal facies 63
Pepper pot structure 90, 91
Percentage coal recovery 171
Percentage slope 317
Percolation 217
Perennial streams 219, 233
Permeable 218, 225
Permeability 88, 217, 220, 222, 225, 227, 254, 257, 258
  primary 221
  secondary 221, 222, 227
Permian 69, 96, 108, 113, 118, 121, 122, 127, 220
Peru 120, 121, 138
  Alto Chicama 121
  Jatunhuasi 121
  Oyon 121
  Santa 121
pH value 14, 235
Philippines 91, 129, 130, 137, 138
  Bislig 130
  Cagayan 129
  Catanduanes 130
  Cebu 130
  Gigaquit 130
  Luzon 129
  Malangas 130
  Mindanao 130
  Mindoro 130
  Semirara 130
  Zamboanga 130
Phosphorite 15
Phosphorus 15
Photogeological symbols 154, 155
Photogrammetric maps 143
Phreatic zone 217
Physical properties 179, 180, 181, 182, 185, 200, 201
Piezometer 219, 225, 226, 227, 228
Piezometric surface 218
Pilot holes 162, 201

Pinchout 199
Pit 227, 228, 230, 233, 242
Planimeter 275
Plant material 9, 10
Pleistocene 193
Ply 149, 164, 237, 238, 239, 293
Points of measurement 262, 264, 268, 270, 274, 275, 276, 277
Poisonous 254
Poland 102, 104, 136, 137
  Belchatow 105
  Konin 105
  Lower Lausitz 105
  Lower Silesia 105
  Lublin 105
  Turoscow 105
  Upper Silesia 105
Pollution 234, 235
Polygon 275, 276, 279
  construction 276, 277
Pore spaces 206, 217, 219, 222, 223
Pore structure 254
Porosity 23, 88, 179, 201, 206, 217, 220, 221, 222, 224
Porous 182
Porous medium 218
Portable drilling 162, 163
Portugal 105, 137
  Cabo Mondego 105
  Rio Maior 105
Positive anomaly 192
Post depositional 82, 260
Post sedimentary 55
Potassium 182
Potentiometric surface 218, 227, 228, 229, 230
Powered winch 200
Precambrian 110, 111, 112, 113, 193
Precipitation 217, 224, 231, 233
Preferred mining section 293
Pressure 17, 23, 78, 252, 254
Pressurisation field 226
Print out 177
Production boreholes 226
Professional standing 299
Progressive easy-slip thrusting 86, 87
Project management 300, 301, 304
Prospecting 182
Proximate analysis *see* Analysis
Pulse radar 198

Pulverised fuel 29, 34
Pulverised fuel boiler 242
Pulverised fuel rig 242
Pumping 228, 229, 231
Pumping centres 229
Pumping well 219, 227, 230
Pyrite 5, 13, 43, 95, 153, 181, 232, 234, 252, 253
Pyrrhotite 181

Quality 23, 71, 76, 77, 78, 141, 156, 157, 195, 215, 231, 232, 236, 241, 246, 271, 273, 279, 280, 282, 293, 301
Quality assurance 300
Quartz 13, 15, 95
Quaternary 96, 187
Queue anticline 90
Quick flow 220

Radiation 202, 258
  nuclear 202
  natural 202
Radioactive gas 258
Radioactive isotopes 202
Radioactive methods 198
Radioactive source 204, 205
Radioactive surveys 198
Radioactivity 23, 179, 182, 198
Radiometric *see* Geologs
Radon 258, 259
Rainfall 233, 234
Rain gauges 224
Rank 4, 9, 12, 16, 17, 19, 20, 21, 22, 23, 28, 31, 38, 43, 44, 48, 49, 55, 82, 87, 91, 96, 102, 123, 165, 179, 195, 206, 207, 221, 222, 223, 237, 253, 257
Rank gradient 21
Reactive 232
Receiver 200
Recent 193
Recharge 217, 288
Reclamation 233
Reconnaissance 143, 282, 300
Recording instrument 200
Recrystallisation 179
Reflected ray 83
Reflected wave 191
Reflection 179, 185, 187, 189
Reflection coefficient 183, 185, 187, 189
Reflection point 185
Reflection seismic *see* Seismic

Refracted ray 183
Refraction 192
Refraction seismic *see* Seismic
Regional gravity 178
Regional trends 175
Rehandling 273
Relative density 38, 270, 275
Remote sensing 153, 154
Report preparation 282–298
  compilation 283, 284
  finalisation 298
  monthly 282
  quarterly 282
Reserve base 282
Reserves 67, 78, 141, 166, 260,
    243
  assessment 215, 261, 268,
    273
  calculations 141, 277, 279,
    282
  class 1 267
  class 2 267
  class 3 267
  extractable 279
  indicated 263, 264
  inferred 263, 264
  marginal 263, 264
  marketable 265, 266, 267,
    270, 293
  measured 263, 264
  mineable *in situ* 265, 266,
    268, 271, 273, 279
  potential 233
  proved 267
  proved recoverable 270
  proven 67
  recoverable 265, 266, 268,
    271, 273, 279
  unproved 267, 268
  zone 276
Resin 7, 9
Resinite 9, 10
Resistivity *see* Electrical
    resistivity
Resolution 208
Resources 260
  additional 270
  assessment 260, 261, 273
  calculation of 274–281, 282
  categories 261, 273
  exploitable 269
  identified 262, 263
  indicated 262, 263, 265, 266
  inferred 262, 263, 265
  original 262, 263
  measured 262, 263, 265, 266
  R1 (reliable estimates) 269

R2 (preliminary estimates)
    269
R3 (tentative estimates) 269
  remaining 262, 263
  subeconomic 263, 265, 269
Resource/reserve
  block 275, 276, 277
  block units 278
  maps 274
  reporting 270, 293, 297
Rest levels 227
Rhaetic 119
Ripples 56, 78
River cross-section 224
Rivers 224, 228, 231, 235
Rock colour charts 171
Rock head 185
Rock molecules 206
Rock name 168
Rock quality designation
    (RQD) 172
Rock strength 165, 166, 168,
    169, 170, 171, 207, 211, 215
Rock type 201
Rock volume 217
Roga Index test 35, 47, 50
Roller bits 158, 162
Romania 150, 136, 137
  Almas 105
  Banat 105
  Comanesti 105
  Jiu 105
  Oltenia 105
Room and pillar 280
Roof *see* Coal
Rosary structure 90
Ruhr dilatometers 37
Run of mine 236
Run off 224, 233, 234

Saddle reefs 91
Safety 143
Sales *see* Marketing
Saline 232, 235
Sample bags 240
Sample locations 147, 282, 284
Sample storage 243
Sampling 143, 144, 145, 165, 233
  in situ 236, 237, 238, 239,
    240, 241, 242, 243
  bulk 242, 243, 246, 248,
    249
  channel ply 238, 239, 240,
    241, 242
  channel wholeseam 237,
    238, 241, 242, 243

  core 241, 243, 247, 248,
    249
  cuttings 242
  grab 237
  pillar 240, 241
  non *in situ* 236, 243, 244,
    249
  augured 251
  hand 244
  mechanical 244
  stockpile 251
  stop belt 250
  stratified random 244
  systematic 244
Sampling apparatus 244
Sand channel 199
Sandstones 57, 59, 66, 71, 74,
    75, 78, 80, 82, 94, 149, 153,
    164, 168, 171, 181, 182,
    189, 201, 202, 206, 215,
    220, 293
  barrier 57
  channel-fill 57, 91
  erosive 66, 78, 164
  lithic 59, 82
  plane-bedded 57
  porous 94
  stacked-channel 66, 75
Saturated 186, 205, 219
Saturated bed thickness 218
Saturated density 179
Saturation zone 217
Satellite imagery 141
Sclerotinite 9, 10
Sealing walls 230
Seam *see* Coal
Seam depth contours 274
Seam isopachs 274
Seam quality contours 274
Seam section 275
Seatearth 85, 86, 220
Sediment load 232
Sedimentary basins 182, 192,
    194
Sedimentary character 166
Sedimentary dykes 78
Sedimentation 55, 76, 80, 224,
    233, 234, 303
Sedimentological
    interpretation 286
Sediments 179, 182
Seismic 178
  cross borehole 183, 189,
    190, 191
  deep 178
  depth section 189, 190
  high resolution 183

Seismic (*cont.*)
  hole to surface 190, 191
  in-seam 198, 199, 200
  recorder 198
  reflection 182, 183, 189,
    185, 186
  reflection profile 186, 187,
    188, 189
  refraction 182, 183, 191
  sections 181
  shallow 178
  velocity 179, 180, 181, 183,
    185, 186, 192
  vertical profiling 189, 190
  wave 183, 185, 186, 188
Seismic data 184, 186
Seismic ray 189
Selected mining section 237
Semifusinite 9, 10
Seylers classification 45
Seylers coal chart 44
Shales 57, 62, 149, 171, 181,
    182, 195, 200 *see also*
    Mudstone
Shear 170, 172, 173
  zones 230
Shearing 86
Shipment 250
Short spaced density logs *see*
    Geologs
Shot hole 200
Shot point 185
SI units 180, 181
Side looking radar 153, 154
Siderite 5, 13, 57, 59, 94
Sills 91, 94, 195
Siltstone 57, 59, 62, 80, 149,
    153, 171, 182, 195, 202, 220
Single arm caliper 206, 207
Size distribution 39, 251
Slickensides 87, 153, 173
Slope angles 317
Slope stability 230
Slumping 78, 153
Smectite 14, 15
Sodium 232
Sodium chloride 182
Softening (sphere)
    temperature (ST) 34
Soil erosion 233
Soil gas radon anomalies 258
Solid core recovery 171, 172
Sonde 200, 204
  density 204, 206
  output 204
  neutron 215
Sorting 165

Source 204
South Africa 47, 91, 94, 112,
    136, 138, 139, 151, 192,
    195, 246, 247, 280
  Eastern Transvaal 112
  Highveld 112
  Lebombo 112
  Limpopo 112
  South Rand 112
  Springbok Flats 112
  Springs Witbanks 112
  Utrecht 112
  Vereeniging 112
  Vierfontein 112
  Waterberg 112
South America see Central and
    South America
South-East Asia 96
Spain 105, 136, 137
  Arenas Del Rey 106
  Calaf 106
  Garcia Rodriquez 106
  Leon 105
  Mequinenza 106
  Teruel 106
Specific energy *see* calorific
    value
Specific gravity 38, 271
Specific retention 221
Spitzbergen 106
  Longyearbyen 106
  Svea 106
Spontaneous combustion 43
Spores 8, 9
Sporinite 6, 9, 10
Spring 217, 224, 227, 230
Springloaded caliper 204
Stability 230, 234
Staining 232
Standards Association of
    Australia 26, 51, 151, 292,
    313, 314, 315
Statistical confidence criteria
    268
Steel production 2
Sterilisation 280
Stoker-fired boilers 29, 34
Storage coefficient 219
Storm washover sands 57
Strain see rock strength
Stratigraphic 147, 153, 215,
    225, 278, 289
Stratigraphy 189, 190, 191,
    200, 284, 285
Streams 224, 227, 230, 235
Stress *see* rock strength
Strike 153, 154, 197

Stripping ratio 89, 271, 272,
    273, 279, 284, 291, 301
Strontium 232
Structural elevation 175
Structural framework 156, 194
Structure 77, 18, 156, 162,
    168, 170, 179, 215, 260,
    273, 282, 284, 289
Structure contours 271, 282,
    291
Suberinite 9
Subsidence 74, 77, 80, 281,
    303
Sulphates 30, 31, 43, 182, 232,
    235
Sulphur 30, 77, 81, 246, 247,
    271, 293, 296, 301
  inorganic 13, 30, 31, 95
  organic 13, 30, 31, 95
  pyritic 30
Sulphuric acid 232
Superficial deposits 185, 186,
    225
Surface
  geophysical methods 182
  hydrology 224
  run-off 220
  site 293
  tension 221
  water 216, 219, 225, 234
  water flow 224
Swamp 63, 64
Swaziland 112, 138
  Maloma 112
  Mhlume 112
Swelling index *see* Free
    swelling index
Syn depositional 78
Synsedimentary 55

Taiwan 130, 137
  Chilung 130
  Hsinchu 130
  Mushan 130
  Nanchuang 130
  Shuangchi 130
Tanzania 112, 113, 136
  Galula 113
  Ketewaka-Mchuchma 113
  Ngaka 113
  Njuga 113
  Ruhuhu 113
  Songwe-Kiwiri 113
  Ufipa 113
Tar yield 52, 54
Taxes 261

Technical brief 282
Technical interfaces 301
Technological constraints 261
Tectonic deformation 91
Telinite 9, 10, 12
Telocollinite 9, 12
Temperature 20, 22, 34, 43, 252
Terrace 234
Tertiary 71, 79, 80, 83, 96, 98, 99, 102, 103, 104, 105, 106, 107, 108, 110, 111, 112, 114, 115, 116, 117, 118, 119, 120, 121, 123, 127, 128, 129, 130, 131, 133, 186, 194, 220
Textinite 12
Texture 168, 170
Thailand 131, 137, 138
  Krabi 131
  Li 131
  Mae Moh 131
  Mae Tip 131
  Mae Tun 131
  Na Duang 131
  Nong Ya Plong 131
  Vaeng Haeng 131
Thermal metamorphism 195
Thickness 201, 205, 208, 226, 293 *see also* Coal thickness
Thickness ratio 76
Thorium 23, 182, 202, 258
Three arm caliper 206, 207
Tidal channel deposits 57
Titano-magnetite 181
Tonstein 13, 66, 82, 182
Topographic surface 271
Topography 143, 147, 175, 272, 273
Toxic 234
Trace elements 16, 32
Transitional lower delta plain 56, 61
Transmission properties 185
Transmissivity 218
Transport 216
Traverses *see* Field traverses
Triassic 88, 96, 122, 128, 131
Trimacerite 10
Triple tube core barrel 159
Trough 193
True bulk density 179
True density 37
Turkey 106, 136, 137
  Ankara 106
  Bingol 106
  Bursa 106
  Cankiri 106
  Elbistan 106
  Mugla 106
  Zonguldak 106
Two dimensional surfaces 175
Two-way travel time (TWT) 183, 185

Ulminite 12
Ultimate analysis *see* Analysis
Unconfined 218, 220
Unconsolidated 221, 22, 230
Underground geophysical methods 198
Underground mining 73, 75, 76, 83, 102, 125, 126, 127, 128, 130, 133, 157, 178, 190, 195, 200, 207, 211, 216, 221, 231, 232, 233, 236, 237, 240, 252, 254, 257, 259, 274, 275, 279, 280, 293, 302, 303, 304
United Kingdom (UK) 47, 106, 107, 136, 137, 149, 150, 151, 186, 188, 190, 191, 195, 198, 200, 231, 234, 247, 252, 253, 258, 259, 271, 273, 287, 289
  East and West Midlands 106, 107, 253
  Kent 106, 107
  Lancashire and North Wales 106, 107, 258
  Leicestershire 107
  North and South Staffordshire 107
  North-east England 106
  Northern Ireland 107
  Nottinghamshire 106, 107
  Scotland 106
  Selby 107
  South Wales 21, 67, 84, 86, 106, 107, 287, 289
  Vale of Belvoir 107
  Warwickshire 107
  Yorkshire 88, 106, 107
United Nations (UN) 47, 50, 52
United States of America (USA) 96, 97, 98, 99, 135, 136, 137, 139, 148, 149, 151, 185, 186, 187, 188, 189, 197, 198, 200, 206, 234, 242, 247, 248, 257, 258, 261
  Alaska 99
  Arkoma Basin 98
  California 99
  Eastern Province 97
  Gulf Coastal Plain Province 98
  Interior Province 97
  Kentucky 58, 60, 61, 62
  Montana 98
  North and South Dakota 98
  Northern Great Plains Province 98
  Pacific Coast Province 98
  Pennsylvania 197
  Powder River Basin 98
  Rocky Mountains 99
  Rocky Mountains Province 98
  San Juan Basin 257
  Warrior Basin 257
  Washington 99
  West Virginia 61, 63, 68, 72
  Williston Basin 98
  Wyoming 98, 197
Unweathered 241, 242
Upper delta plain 56, 82
Upper Palaeozoic 55
Upwarping 82
Uranium 23, 182, 202, 258
Uruguay 116, 121

Variance 277
Variogram 277, 279
Vegetation removal 233
Velocity 181, 185, 189, 233
Venezuela 121, 136, 138, 139
  Caracas-Barcelona Basin 121
  Fila Maestra 121
  Lara 121
  Lobatera 121
  Naricual 121
  Orinoco Basin 121
  Zulia 121
Ventilation 211, 253, 259
Vertical sections 286, 287, 288
Vertical seismic profile *see* Seismic
Vietnam 88, 89, 131, 137, 138
  Bo Ha 131
  Hong Gai 131
  Huong Khe 131
  Nan Meo 131
  Nong Son 131
  Phan Me 131
  Quang Yen 131
Vitrain 5, 6, 7

Vitrinertite 10, 11
Vitrinertoliptite 10
Vitrinite 6, 9, 10, 11, 12, 17, 42
Vitrinite reflectance 18, 19,
    21, 237, 257
Vitrite 10, 11, 20
Voids 217
Volatile matter 19, 20, 44, 47,
    48, 49, 51, 77, 91, 206, 221,
    293
Volcanics 66, 148, 179
Volumetric 271, 272

'Want' 72
Washability 15
Washability curves 39, 41, 42
Washability data 41
Washouts 71, 74, 185, 186,
    188, 200, 201, 274, 278,
    279, 280
Waste disposal 303
Water 206, 216, 217, 219, 221,
    231, 232, 234, 235, 243, 303
  conductivity 182
  flow 231
  level 226, 227, 229
  movement 217
  quality 224, 225, 231
  retention 258

supply 143, 230
  table 64, 158, 189, 190, 217,
      218, 220, 225, 227, 229
  velocity 224
Watercourses 220, 233
Watershed 219
Wave *see* Seismic
Wave motion 180
Weathering 42, 47, 153, 162,
    165, 166, 168, 169, 170,
    171, 179, 185, 186, 187,
    188, 197, 198, 209, 236, 237
Weighted mean seam
    thickness 276
Weir 225
Wells 225, 228, 229, 230, 231
Wet bottom boilers 34
Wireline drilling 160, 161
Workable coal section 271
Worked out coal 190
Working ratio 271
Workings 227, 231
World coal consumption 139
World coal production 135,
    137, 138, 139
World coal reserves 135, 136, 137
World coal reserves/
    production ratio 140

Xylitic 6, 7, 8

Yield 15, 41, 42, 231, 246, 270,
    271, 273
Yugoslavia 107, 136, 137
  Dobra 107
  Istra 107
  Kolubara 108
  Kosovo 108
  Sarajevo-Zenica 107
  Trans-Sava 107

Zaire 113, 138
  Luena 113
  Lukuga 113
Zambia 113, 136, 138
  Kahare 113
  Laungwa 113
  Luano 113
  Maamba 113
Zimbabwe 113, 136, 138, 257
  Bubye 113
  Limpopo 113
  Lumimbi 113
  Sabi valley 257
  Sessami-Kaonga 113
  Tuli 113
  Wankie 113
  Zambezi Basin 113